MW00716821

Critical Thinking and the Bible in the Age of New Media

Edited by
Charles M. Ess

University Press of America,® Inc.
Dallas · Lanham · Boulder · New York · Oxford

Copyright © 2004 by
University Press of America,® Inc.
4501 Forbes Boulevard
Suite 200
Lanham, Maryland 20706
UPA Acquisitions Department (301) 459-3366

PO Box 317
Oxford
OX2 9RU, UK

Library of Congress Control Number: 2004104607
ISBN 0-7618-2862-1 (hardcover: alk. ppr.)
ISBN 0-7618-2863-X (paperback: alk. ppr.)

Acknowledgments

"Lay Women's Feminist Critical Thinking about the Bible" is copyrighted by Dr. Elizabeth Dodson Gray, who reserves all rights to the essay and has permitted its reproduction in this volume.

"Critical Thinking: Keynote Address" is copyrighted by Peter Facione, who reserves all rights to the essay and has permitted its reproduction in this volume.

The remaining essays in this collection are proprietary to the American Bible Society and reproduced by permission. We also gratefully acknowledge kind permission from the Sunday School Publishing Board (Nashville, TN) to reproduce selections from Ottie L. West's Townsend Press Sunday School Commentary: International Bible Lessons for Christian Teaching; 1999-2000 as part of the essay by Isaac Mwase.

Table of Contents

Introduction

Critical Thinking and the Bible in the Age of New Media

Charles Ess

How great are your works, O Lord,
how profound your thoughts!
— Psalm 93.5

What is a man
If his chief good and market of his time
Be but to sleep and feed?—a beast, no more.
Sure, he that made us with such large discourse,
Looking before and after, gave us not
That capability and god-like reason
To fust in us unused.
—*Hamlet*, 4.4[1]

I was privileged to serve as the convener and co-organizer of the conference "New Voices, New Views: Thinking about Bible Study in the Twenty-First Century," sponsored by the Research Center for Scripture and Media of the American Bible Society.[2] The conference, second in a series of three and held on February 11, 2000, brought together scholars from a wide range of religious tradition, belief, and experience, in order to explore together what critical thinking in the age of new media might mean as focused on the Bible. The essays collected here represent often extensive revisions of what began as conference

3

presentations—revisions reflecting the highly productive exchanges that followed formal presentations. These essays thus speak to one another in more complete and coherent ways than their ancestors did, as collected in the conference proceedings (Ess et al, 2000).

While these chapters refer to one another in multiple ways, they are organized here as follows. We begin with Peter Facione's *Keynote Address*, as Facione provides us with central understandings of critical thinking skills, dispositions, and developmental stages: together, these constitute an extensive framework for understanding diverse postures or views on critical thinking vis-à-vis the Bible in particular and faith claims more generally. We then turn to two explorations of *Critical Thinking Within Biblical Texts*— Christof Hardmeier's account of "fear-critical thinking" in Deuteronomy and and Byron Eubanks' analysis of passages in the Christian Scriptures that encourage— indeed, *require*— critical thinking of both *listeners* and *readers*. Following these are *Three Contemporary Perspectives on Critical Thinking and the Bible*, beginning with Jim and Susan Bachman's application of logician Jaakko Hintikka's interrogative model to critical reading of the Christian Scriptures. Isaac Mwase analyzes how critical thinking is both fostered and hindered in a widely used Sunday School commentary, with a focus on how the evolution-creationism debate is treated. Finally, Elizabeth Dodson Gray helps us understand forms of feminist critical thinking as these occur *outside* the more familiar domains of academic teaching and discourse. In these two specific examples, both Mwase and Dodson Gray thus make the point established by Hardmeier's and Eubanks' analysis of biblical texts: critical thinking is not simply for scholars and academics, but for all believers, especially as we seek a liberation from oppression that fulfills God's call to Moses and the message of the Gospel.

Postmodernism, as characterized especially by a suspicion of reason and thus of traditional conceptions of logic and critical thinking, further emphasizes the revolutionary dimensions of the new media. Three of our contributors powerfully represent *Postmodern Perspectives*, beginning with James Voelz who develops a postmodern hermeneutic. More particularly, Donald Colhour reviews for us especially Marshall McLuhan's contribution to the postmodern conception of communication technologies. More broadly, responding to the seminal work of Leonard Sweet (1999), Ben Witherington argues that the church must "get with it"—in Witherington's terms, to take up the new media and all their revolutionary implications, or otherwise run the risk of becoming roadkill on the Information Superhighway.

By contrast, as *Voices of Caution*, Terry Lindvall and Michael Palmer articulate important reservations about jumping on the postmodern bandwagon too quickly. Drawing on an extensive literature— from the 2nd commandment to contemporary psychological research— concerning the promise and dangers of the *image*, Lindvall worries that the predominance of the visual in the age of new media will override our ability to approach the Bible as *text*, and in ways that will render us not *free* but simply *superficial*. Palmer explores the role of the (embodied, offline) *community* as shaping habits of reading and interpretation distinctive for each religious tradition. Lindvall and Palmer, as more cautious than Voelz and Witherington, thus make clear the *contestability* of postmodernist views *within* a shared context of Evangelical religious beliefs and traditions. Again, such contestability and the concomitant open- mindedness are crucial for sustaining critical thought on these issues.

We close with *Middle Grounds*, approaches to the new media that represent neither reactionary insistence that there is indeed nothing new under the sun nor postmodern enthusiasm for revolutionary rejection of all that has preceded it. Phil Mullins develops an account of "post-critical thinking," one that recognizes salient postmodern critiques of modern and pre-modern conceptions of logic while also building on the work of Polanyi and Pierce in order to shape our thought and knowledge in ways that overcome the *epistemological relativism* frequently associated with radical postmodernism. Eep Talstra gives us a careful historical overview of the roles of the Scribe, the Librarian, the Scholar, and the Reader as a way of understanding the age of new media vis-à-vis the age of the book and the age of the manuscript. From this perspective, there is more continuity than radical diremption between these earlier ages and the age of new media than radical postmodernists recognize. Finally, Kate Lindemann gives a concrete example of such continuity with her suggestions for web page design, based on Medieval models in illuminated manuscripts, that encourage *lectio divina*, the "divine reading" of contemplative prayer. Such an application of the new media is thus a concrete example of a middle ground between postmodern revolution and reactionary stodginess.

In my *Preliminary/Contestable Conclusions*, I explore especially the larger themes evoked and implicated as a whole by these contributions. Drawing first on the literatures of Computer-Mediated Communication (CMC) and philosophy of technology, I review the shared assumptions of especially postmodern understandings of the new media, especially as these assumptions support a *revolutionary* view, i.e., the claim that the new media and what Walter Ong (1988) has called "the secondary orality of electronic culture" will *force* a radical overturning of modernity and earlier ages—including a rejection of earlier understandings of logic and critical thinking. These assumptions include a sharp dichotomy between the eras of orality, literacy, print, and secondary orality; a *technological determinism* asserting the power of technology to *force* radical changes; and a Gnostic/Cartesian dualism and contempt for the body that fuels much of the 1980s and 1990s postmodern enthusiasm for "liberation in cyberspace." We will see, however, that more recent CMC theory and research—including studies of what happens in *praxis* as Western CMC technologies are implemented in diverse cultural settings—have called these assumptions into question, issuing in a turn towards more moderate stances, including a (re)new(ed) emphasis on the central significance of *embodiment* and offline *communities* in our knowing and being.

Second, I explore the debates at work here between creation and evolution, faith and reason, as implicated by our shared discussion of the Bible and critical thinking. Drawing on the literatures in the history and philosophy of science and the philosophy of religion, I first argue that the sense of *opposition* between faith and reason that marks especially North American discussion is both a relatively recent phenomenon (i.e., sparked primarily and precisely by Darwin) and a minority position in the history of Western science and philosophy. Rather than such opposition, we find much more often in the Ancient, Medieval, and early Modern worlds an emphasis on the *complementarity* between science and religion as distinct but related modes of knowing. Second, the outcomes of the epistemological debates in philosophy of science between *realism* and *anti-realism* and the larger correlative debates in the "Science Wars" between the views of **modern positivism** and **postmodern** *relativism* point precisely to middle grounds between these two poles—middle grounds that further issue in a (re)new(ed) sense of the *complementarity* of science and religion.

These larger frameworks thus support Lindemann's model of web pages based on illuminated manuscripts as instantiating a *continuity* between old and new as well as their difference—a continuity we further see in Mullins' and Talstra's positions that the age of new media represents new opportunities for *extending* older forms of thought and belief in ways that take advantage of the distinctive potentials of the new technologies, while not abandoning the skills and insights developed in earlier phases of hearing and responding to the Word. These frameworks likewise resonate with the more moderate forms of postmodernism we see in Voelz and Witherington. Most broadly, these larger frameworks suggest that critical thinking in the age of new media might well resemble the models developed here especially by Facione, the Bachmans, Mwase, Dodson Gray, and Mullins—i.e., critical approaches to the biblical texts that both exploit the potentials of the new media in the service of new forms of critical thinking while remaining connected with understandings of critical thought developed from Aristotle through Pierce and Polanyi. In other words, our contributors and these recent turns in computer-mediated communication and philosophy of science suggest that we learn to use the new media not simply for the sake of *information*: rather, despite the fact that—indeed, precisely because—we live in an *Information Age*, our contributors provide us with much-needed lessons in how we, as embodied members of communities of interpreters, may use critical thinking in the age of new media in the quest for *wisdom*.

Keynote Address: Peter Facione on Critical Thinking: Skills, Dispositions, Development

Peter Facione locates our thematic interest in Bible, new media, and critical thinking within the larger discussion of the relationship between reason and religion. Beginning with the mythic story of Icarus, Facione briefly explores our "fear of thinking" as one locus on a continuum characterizing the relationship between faith and reason. One of his central contributions to our volume is his development of this continuum—i.e., a range of possible postures or understandings of the relationship between reason and faith, from outright hostility towards reason and an emphasis on faith alone (known as *fideism* in the philosophy of religion) to its opposite, i.e., the demand that all faith claims pass muster before the tribunal of reason (a position we will refer to, following common usage, as *strong rationalism*).[3] Of course, there are multiple middle grounds between these two extremes: Facione expands the continuum of possible postures towards faith and reason with most helpful examples from myth, biblical narrative, and historical figures.

Before developing his own account of what he suggests are the most characteristic postures towards faith and reason in Christian tradition, Facione provides a comprehensive overview of critical thinking as defined through a process involving scholars from diverse disciplines and nations (the Delphi Report: Facione 1990). Facione emphasizes that the several cognitive skills and sub-skills of critical thinking— including the primary skills of interpretation, analysis, evaluation, inference, explanation, and self-regulation—are not all we need to know about critical thinking. In addition, critical thinking requires a number of *dispositions*: truth-seeking, open-mindedness, analyticity, systematicity, self-confidence as a critical thinker, inquisitiveness, and cognitive maturity.

The last disposition helps make a crucial point: critical thinking is thus dependent upon *cognitive development*—the stages of which begin with "naïve observers" who believe that "knowledge is absolute, concrete, and available," i.e., as proven by "direct personal experience." This position, in epistemological terms, rests on a naïve *empiricism*— one that assumes that "Things are as they appear to be." A further stage of particular interest for us is that of the "committed skeptics." As certain that "external validation of any knowledge is impossible," this skeptical stage is affiliated with what we can call *epistemological relativism*, i.e., precisely the view that, in the face of uncertainty and the role of subjectivity and culture in shaping belief, there is no possibility of anything resembling "objective knowledge," knowledge that somehow would hold true for more than a given individual and/or culture. By contrast, the final stage—that of "the sage"—recognizes that knowledge entails both uncertainty and interpretation dependent upon context. Unlike the skeptic and epistemological relativist, however, the sage further recognizes that "justifiable claims about the relative merits of alternative arguments and claims can be made." That is, "We (not just I) can assert with justifiable confidence, that some judgments are more reasonable, warranted, justifiable, sensible, or wiser than others." In other terms, we can identify this last stage as committed to an *epistemological pluralism*—i.e., to the recognition that a plurality of viewpoints can be argued for and held as plausible, justified, etc. As we will explore more fully in the conclusion, this pluralism, as a middle ground between the dogmatism of the naïve observer and the relativism of the skeptic, thus coheres with contemporary epistemologies in the philosophy of science that hew a middle ground between modernist/positivist insistence that (only) science provides absolute objectivity and postmodernist arguments that all "objectivities" are reducible to the relativities of individuals and cultures.

For his part, Facione identifies three basic postures regarding the relationship between critical thinking vis-à-vis religious belief and the Bible as religious authority. Again, these run a continuum from "Faithful servant" through "External Agent" to "Hostile Antagonist."

As examples of the first, Facione names Anselm and Augustine, as well as the sort of critical study of the Biblical narrative that moves beyond literalism and can read, say, the first and second creation stories in Genesis on symbolic and metaphorical levels as well. A central exemplar here, in fact, is Jesus' parable about the Good Samaritan: from a critical standpoint, the moral point of the story is not whether it is literally and thus absolutely true—it is rather what the story teaches us in specific, concrete terms regarding the meaning of the highly general commandment "Love your neighbor."

Reason acquires greater independence from religious claims in the posture of "critical thinking as an external agent." This posture is exemplified in the use of Ockham's razor, or the principle of parsimony—i.e., do not multiply explanatory principles beyond what is necessary. As Facione's examples make clear, when two otherwise equally adequate explanations for a given phenomenon conflict, applying Ockham's razor to choose between them means choosing the simpler. But this further means: frequently, the more complex explanation is complex precisely because it *includes* religious and/or supernatural elements of explanation, while the simpler explanation *excludes* these in favor of strictly material causes and conditions. Hence Ockham's razor characteristically forces us to eliminate an explanation—and the worldview undergirding it—that involves faith claims in favor of the material or naturalistic explanation. While such a critical thinking posture isn't essentially hostile to religious claims—it often must suspend those claims, at least when they are employed to explain specific events in the ordinary world.

In the third posture in Facione's schema, critical thinking becomes the "hostile antagonist" to religious belief—a posture reflected especially in modern critiques of religion from Voltaire through Marx to Sartre. Facione sees this posture at work in the debate between creationism and evolution, especially as portrayed in the film *Inherit the Wind*, a (somewhat misleading) dramatization of the Scopes "monkey trial."[4] Other examples of such hostile antagonism include contemporary debates regarding abortion, homosexuality, and stem cell research.

In the face of these various possibilities, Facione closes by arguing for a fourth posture—that of reflective or reasoned judgment. Facione's example here is a (fictional) rabbi—one counseling the President of the TV series *West Wing* on the question of capital punishment. While the Torah and the Talmud sanction capital punishment in specific cases—the rabbi also points out that these cases include death as punishment for a rebellious son. As well, the Torah and the Talmud sanction slavery.[5] In developing his recommendation that the President commute a condemned man's sentence, as Facione puts it, the rabbi's advice is not a rejection of his tradition and its most important texts. Rather, the rabbi is using reason "as a tool to reflectively reinterpret the core meanings of the sacred text in a situation where knowledge includes uncertainty and yet justifiable claims can and, in this example, should be made." This is, in Facione's schema, the level of the sage—a level that merges all three postures of critical thinking.

Facione concludes with two observations. The first consists in a series of suggestions for nurturing reasoned judgment in particular and teaching critical thinking skills more generally; these round out his earlier outlines of critical thinking skills and dispositions. Second, he points out that the Bible itself—precisely because it is a rich, complex, and ambiguous text, one reflecting a diversity of often conflicting historical, cultural, philosophical, and religious sources—provides us with exceptional material on which to focus and hone our critical thinking skills.[6]

Critical Thinking Within Biblical Texts

In fact, for Christof Hardmeier and Byron Eubanks, the Bible exemplifies critical thinking in several ways.

Christof Hardmeier: "Fear-Critical Thinking" in Deuteronomy

Hardmeier first argues that Moses' speech in Deut. 1-30 is a narrated speech, a kind of performance like Readers Theatre such that the text seeks to retain the character of the Torah as an artifact of *oral* tradition. In doing so, both the details of context and the description of how this text is to be read, both contained in the text itself, shape the Torah text as a performative process of teaching—one that is consciously intended to be reproduced in a contemporary setting (e.g., by public reading every seven years, according to Deut. 31.11). In this way, the Torah text is not simply a recorded memory that traps it in a past history. Indeed, the goal of the Torah text, both in its construction and the process of communal remembering through its public reading, is to shape the right relationship with God in both present and future. To do so, the text and its performance contribute to the proper respect for and sense of dependence on God by recalling God's saving acts in Israel's history and reminding us from this history of the dangers of falling victim to *hybris*, to an excessive (because empirically false) belief in the power of one's own abilities.

This proper relationship is specifically required in the face of the daunting task of crossing the Jordan and going into Canaan. More broadly, however, Hardmeier makes the crucial *theological* claim that the Torah text *as a specific mode of communication*—as a literate-oral performative recollection, designed for public reading and remembering— thus teaches humility and reliance on God *not* as a *dogmatic* claim, i.e., as the *logical* conclusion following with deductive validity from abstract premises. Hardmeier argues that this performative recollection—also at work, in his view, in the Scriptures recalling the parables of Jesus—is not an accident or simply determined by available communication media. On the contrary, avoiding dogmatism regarding the nature of God in this way means that the Torah text thereby fulfills the first and second commandments: the second commandment (see Exodus 20.4-6), as it prohibits against graven images in particular, Hardmeier argues, forbids "any dogmatic concepts or theoretical descriptions of God's being or nature." In short, the Torah as performative text hews a precise middle ground between silence and (both prohibited and impossible) dogmatism regarding the Divine. If Hardmeier is correct about this, then, as he points out, any re-presentation of God—whether in text, image, and/or the various combinations of these with other forms of representation in the new media—will have to be done very carefully in order to avoid violating the Commandments! (We will see this same point argued forcefully by Terry Lindvall.)

Hardmeier's second thesis is that a specific form of *critical thinking* thus emerges here—one clearly distinct from either philosophical or scientific forms as bound up with objectivity, logical validity, etc. (Hardmeier's comments on these forms of thought as *objective*—i.e., as engaging with *objects* held at a distance [so far as this is true]—can be fruitfully compared to Lindemann's contrast between objectivity as connected with print exclusive of images and the more subjectively-engaged forms of prayer connected with *lectio divina* and the Medieval illuminated manuscript.) This distinctively biblical form of critical thinking, he argues, is centrally *practical*—it focuses on "a realistic perception of risks and opportunities" in the face of danger, and it does so in such a way as to avoid both paralysis through fear and disaster through *hubris*. It does this in part because the performative text works to establish a directly performative relationship with God—the relationship that grounds and makes possible precisely this distinctive form of critical thinking. In Paul's words, this is a "belief-thinking" that is to emerge from *hearing* with faith (Rom. 10.17, Gal. 3.2).

Hardmeier establishes this through careful exegesis of key texts in Deut. 2-3, issuing in his account of "fear-critical thinking" as the sort of critical thinking both preserved in the text and intended to be evoked through its reading and recollection. Rooted in the performative relationship with God, this form of critical thinking is open to new situations, in part as it recognizes the possibility of unexpected opportunities contained within dangerous, fearful, and uncertain situations. At the same time, this form of critical thinking is clearly *self-critical:* the narrative includes examples as arguments that warn *against hubris* on one's own part.

We will see that Hardmeier's account of Deuteronomy as "inscribed orality" thus blurs the line between the stages of communication as technology developed in the Innis/McLuhan/Eisenstein/Ong theory of communication, the view that the development of new technologies inevitably lead to irresistible changes, and one that rather insists on a sharp distinction between the oral and the textual. At the same time, Hardmeier brings to the foreground the *theological* significance—indeed, potential idolatry—of the image and thus of the visual as a mode of knowledge. As we will see, both in Terry Lindvall's more extensive analysis of the image (which also invokes the second commandment) and in my concluding discussion, blurring the otherwise sharp boundaries drawn by the Innis-Ong theory first of all undermines 1980s and 1990s postmodern enthusiasm for new media as making possible an ostensibly revolutionary new form of communication, the "secondary orality of electronic culture"—one that is to free us from the putative tyrannies of the book in particular and modernity in general, seen to be largely the artifact of the technology of print. We will also see that more recent theory and research in computer-mediated communication are consistent with Hardmeier's account of Deuteronomy as a conjunction of both the oral and the textual.

Byron Eubanks: Critical Thinking in the Christian Scriptures

Byron Eubanks urges a form of critical thinking and skepticism that is both needed to help faithful people protect themselves from deception and hoaxes, and, more importantly, is founded in the Scriptures. He does so by first reviewing the inventory of Scriptures often offered as justification for opposing critical thinking (itself a logical move!). Through attention to context, pertinent scholarship, and the glaring fact that Paul himself makes use of reason and argument in numerous places, Eubanks argues that the attack on reason in these passages is not so much on reason and critical thinking *per se*, but rather on an idolatrous use of human wisdom—i.e., one that would have human beings forget God and their own limits (what Hardmeier discusses in considerable depth in terms of *hubris* or excessive pride).

Turning to positive Biblical examples of critical thinking, Eubanks first expands on the instances of Paul's use of reason and argument. His extensive review allows him to conclude that, *contra* the fideists, "Based on a reading of Acts, there is no evidence that the early Christian leaders saw any intrinsic incompatibility between using human critical faculties and having a vibrant Christian faith."

Eubanks then turns to Jesus, noting that Jesus himself has recently been characterized as a logician *par excellence* (Willard 1999). In addition to the logic at work in Jesus' arguments and rationale offered for Jesus' interpretation of the Hebrew Scripture, Eubanks points out that Jesus further assumes basic logical skills in his hearers—in part, in order to practice a particular kind of persuasive rhetoric: "The incompleteness of Jesus' arguments allow the hearers to come to the truth on their own, to achieve an inner understanding that is far more effective than it would be had Jesus made the logic of the argument so explicit as to force the conclusion on his hearers." (Philosophers will recognize here as well that in doing so, Jesus thus imitates Socrates' rhetorical approach in the dialogues—i.e., one that works to teach his listeners how to thereby become adept at the art of dialogical reasoning.)

Indeed, Eubanks goes further: people of faith are not only allowed to think critically—at least if they are to follow the examples of Paul and Jesus: people of faith are further *required* to think critically, both directly and indirectly, as Eubanks' numerous examples suggest. Consistent with Facione's schema, then, critical thinking appears to be central to the life of faith, as portrayed in both the TANAKH (what Christians call, in rearranged order, the books of the Old Testament[7]) and Christian Scriptures ("New Testament").

Three Contemporary Perspectives on Critical Thinking and the Bible

Susan and James Bachman: the Interrogative Model

The Bachmans begin by reminding us that in Lutheran tradition (echoing Hamlet, we can note), Reason is emphatically understood to be God's gift and a useful tool in understanding Scripture. *Contra* the Lockean notion that somehow reasoning does not require a logic teacher such as Aristotle, the Bachmans assert that "structured models of reasoning"—specifically, Jaakko Hintikka's "interrogative model" of reason—are helpful in developing an approach to Scripture that conjoins critical thinking with a form of "biblically disciplined thought."

The Bachmans demonstrate their model first in *praxis*, by taking up a famous passage in Mark 13:14 which includes the parenthetical phrase "let the reader understand." Their interrogative model consists of two elements—the first is just the "interrogative steps," articulated as a series of questions, that help us gather and select information pertinent to the possible interpretations of the passage. (These questions can be helpfully compared to those articulated by Elizabeth Dodson Gray as fostering a specifically feminist approach to critical thinking.) The second element, "logical inference steps," then deduces through logically sound inference what is presupposed and implied by whatever information emerges out of the initial interrogation. The Bachmans then follow this initial example with a series of helpful observations and questions that will be of immediately practical use to anyone attempting to incorporate the interrogative model into their own reading, teaching, and research.

In the second part of their essay, the Bachmans evaluate the promise and perils of the new media for critical thinking as developed in the interrogative model. On the one hand, they see the new media as opening up new and more efficient ways of raising the sorts of questions at work in the interrogative model, including the development of online "virtual" communities that can make it easier to raise questions simultaneously with others. On the other hand, they recognize several threats to critical thinking in the new media, beginning with the problem of an information overload that can lead to "impatience and a search for too quick or shallow closure." They also worry that "the ill-defined, relatively anonymous, and individualistic nature" of virtual communities may run against the grain—both experientially and theologically—of the church as a community gathered together *in body* to invoke Christ's real, rather than virtual, presence.

The Bachmans' concerns on this last point are explored more fully in this volume by Ben Witherington's discussion of "incarnational learning" and especially in Michael Palmer's discussion of the role of *community* in shaping our habits of reading and interpretation. Together, the Bachmans and Palmer raise a crucial concern with *embodiment*— where embodiment figures crucially, we will see by way of conclusion, in contemporary discussion of computer-mediated communication, especially with regard to online communities. By way of anticipation:

the debate here is between a largely postmodern enthusiasm for a "liberation in cyberspace" as achieved through escape from and overcoming of the body, seen to be radically divorced from the person/identity/mind that could exist in various ways online, on the one hand— and, on the other hand, an emerging body of research and theory that make clear that embodiment is inescapable in computer-mediated interactions. We will see that this more recent turn towards embodiment calls into question the very possibility, much less the *wisdom*, of seeking a postmodern escape into cyberspace. At the same time, of course, emphasizing the central importance of body in CMC research and theory brings us closer to the *prophetic* strands of Christian and Jewish traditions, as these emphasize the goodness of creation and thereby of body and human communities living out God's injunctions of justice and mercy.

Isaac Mwase: Critical Thinking in the Black Church

As a way of exploring critical thinking in *praxis*, Mwase takes up a specific publication commonly used in Sunday School teaching about the Bible in a predominantly African-American denomination. Mwase directly takes up several of Peter Facione's critical thinking dispositions as elements for analysis, including contestability as an expression of *open-mindedness*. While Mwase finds several instances in the materials he analyzes that demonstrate such open-mindedness—primarily, as these moments in the commentary recognize the validity of more than one interpretation of a given text—he further finds that the publication becomes dogmatic as it holds to a specific conservative doctrine, i.e., that of dispensational millenialism. In doing so, on his showing, the commentary commits itself not only to a theological viewpoint that is increasingly suspect among more reflective readers—but also forces the commentary into the position of requiring "a uniform commitment to one contestable eschatalogical perspective." This dogmatism—i.e., a way of short-circuiting the critical thinking requirement for contestability as a marker of open-mindedness—is also at work in the commentary's treatment of the role of Israel in human history and issues involving science and religion.

For Mwase, critical thinking should be encouraged in these and other areas—including questions of religious pluralism, the authority of Scripture, Black Christian identity, gender roles, and homosexuality. But here he closes most helpfully by developing an alternative version of the commentary's discussion of creationism and evolution—where his alternative version emphasizes precisely the contestability of the claims involved, in hopes of thereby encouraging open-mindedness in particular and critical thinking still more broadly understood.

Elizabeth Dodson Gray:
Feminist Critical Thinking Outside Academe

Elizabeth Dodson Gray, while recognizing the critical contributions to feminist critical thinking *within* the academy as marked by the works of Mary Daly, Elisabeth Schüssler Fiorenza, and many others, brings to the foreground feminist critical thinking as embodied in women who are not academics. Such women, in particular, encounter the shocking recognition that their religious traditions, including their Bible, are largely male-centered *without* the buffer of an academic "distancing" vocabulary—including the jargon of postmodernism, deconstruction, etc. To help us better understand this shock, Dodson Gray reviews the emergence of Judaism and Christianity within the larger framework of a patriarchy constructed as males— represented in Adam as the archetype—have enjoyed the power of *naming* and thereby the power of creating the larger symbolic frameworks taken to *be* "reality" within patriarchal cultures. But as Dorothy discovers that behind the curtain of the Wizard of Oz stands but a little man at the machinery projecting the impressive images of power and knowledge—so women are recognizing that, in Dodson Gray's terms, patriarchy represents a conceptual trap, beginning with its images of God as male in ways that exclude women and their experience. Dodson Gray helps focus this recognition through three questions that encourage a feminist critical thinking about the Bible:

> Is this passage really about me, or is it just about men?

> Can I get past all this male language, all this male imaging of God, so as to find some spiritual truth that illuminates my female life?

> What do I do with my anger when women are ignored, invisible or denigrated in these heretofore revered passages?

It is to be emphasized that these questions—like the fundamental shock of recognition that evokes them—are not simply "academic" but rather *existential* questions, what Dodson Gray calls "existential disturbers" of faith, i.e., questions of central and concrete relevance to how women and men must rethink their lives in light of this new understanding of their spiritual and Biblical traditions. Dodson Gray makes this point in characteristically feminist fashion—i.e., precisely by recounting the *experiences* of women *and* men who undergo this recognition in different ways. Perhaps the most striking is the experience occasioned by her husband, David Dodson Gray, by his insight prior to a communion service that in Christian tradition women's blood *defiles* but men's blood *saves*—a recognition that broke open the floodgates of recognition for an ordained woman minister. This articulation helped her understand her *experience* of pain and discomfort in standing at the sacred space of the altar in her female body—i.e., a body declared unclean in so many ways in the tradition she sought to represent and serve.

Postmodern Perspectives

James Voelz: Postmodern Hermeneutics

As his title suggests, Jim Voelz's "Reading Scripture as Critical-Thinking Christians in the Post-Modern Era" takes up seriously what many Biblical scholars in the 1980s and 1990s perceived as the "postmodern challenge" to then-prevailing hermeneutical approaches to Scripture. Voelz grounds postmodernism in the challenges to earlier thought as articulated by Freud, on the one hand, and the emergence of Quantum Mechanics and relativity theory, on the other hand. Voelz builds especially on the sharp contrasts he draws between a modern "Newtonian" science and "Einsteinian" science as postmodern in order to establish a postmodern hermeneutical approach to Scripture that rejects any modernist assumption of a single "objective" meaning as the goal of interpretation. Rather, Voelz's postmodern hermeneutics emphasizes the role of context and perspective in shaping our interpretation of texts—and, correlatively, the legitimacy of a wide range of possible meanings and interpretations. Voelz then articulates what he sees as analogous differences between Newtonian/phenomenological and Einsteinian perspectives in theological claims regarding God and God's actions, the state of humankind, personal salvation, and the Christian life. By doing so, he argues that *both* sets of claims are legitimate *from within the given perspective* of each. This hermeneutical and theological pluralism, he argues, thus leads to several distinctive advantages of his postmodern approach—first of all, as they teach exegetes "...to respect the 'logic' of the writings we interpret, which includes paradox and antinomy, and to respect the 'logic' of the Christian life, which includes paradox and antinomy, as well." In particular, recognizing both

perspectives, he argues, helps us re-interpret otherwise apparently contradictory statements within the biblical texts: that is, where we can
understand these statements as rooted in different perspectives, their
ostensible contradiction is erased. More broadly, he concludes, such a
postmodern hermeneutics may help believers present the Christian
Good News more effectively in the postmodern world that surrounds us.

Donald Colhour: McLuhan and Religion

Prior to the well-known McLuhan of "the medium is the message" is McLuhan's 1943 doctoral dissertation that concerned itself precisely with the decline of the church as the result of its failure to come
to grips with new technologies and new media. Donald Colhour's essay
takes us back to this lesser-known but critically important moment in
McLuhan's thinking, as he reviews and elaborates McLuhan's original
argument that the decline of the church is the result of its inability to
recognize and adapt to the new contexts created by new media.

Part of Colhour's contribution here consists in his rehearsal of the
perhaps now familiar arguments of the Innis/McLuhan/Eisenstein/Ong
axis of communication theory, one emphasizing the radical dichotomy
between orality, literacy, and the "secondary orality of electronic culture"—a theory that undergirds postmodern claims predominant in the
1980s and 1990s that the emergence of electronic culture amounted to
a revolution in cultural notions of literacy and self-understanding at
least as profound as the Gutenberg revolution of the 16th century.[8] In
this way, Colhour's essay makes clear that postmodern proponents—
represented in this volume especially by Witherington and Voelz—echo
McLuhan more than they know. That is: it is not just a matter of using
the later McLuhan and postmodernism as the bases for arguments
encouraging the contemporary church to "get with it" and recognize the
manifold changes wrought by new media, as Witherington (relying
especially on Leonard Sweet) and Voelz argue. In fact, on Colhour's
showing, this is McLuhan's original message—a message apparently
unnoticed and unremarked upon in mainstream communication literature, at least until now.

Colhour makes this case in part by connecting McLuhan's discussion of Kierkegaard with the historical conditions surrounding the
emergence, expansion, and subsequent decline of the Christian Church
(Disciples of Christ). This history, he argues, exemplifies McLuhan's
central claims regarding the ways in which the emergence of new communications technologies and media fundamentally change the condi-

tions under which churches will either prosper or decline, depending on their ability to adapt themselves to new contexts.

Ben Witherington: Adapting to the New Media

Echoing Colhour's insistence that the church take the new media seriously, Ben Witherington draws primarily on the seminal work of Leonard Sweet to urge the church, especially the Evangelical church, to "get with it"—i.e., to recognize the perhaps epochal changes in our culture and epistemology wrought by the emergence of new media, and to retool our education and evangelism accordingly.

Witherington further emphasizes that the Information Age is "about the convergence of all knowledge"—a convergence that requires us to overcome traditional boundaries, so as to become more interdisciplinary in general, and more conversant with new science in particular (as Voelz illustrates in this volume). At the same time, however, Witherington's enthusiasm is not itself uncritical. For example, he urges caution in our enthusiasm for the Internet and its various forms of disembodied communication: while such disembodiment may promise equality in an environment ostensibly blind to age, gender, etc., Witherington also recognizes the danger of falling into the characteristically postmodern, deconstructionist view that "there is only text." In philosophical terms, the point here is not to fall into various forms of *relativism*—where such relativism (e.g., in the assumption that there is no "meaning" apart from what the reader constructs) is clearly and directly at odds with the theological commitment to specific absolutes that defines Evangelical belief. Witherington makes this point in a different way, as he cites T.S. Eliot's lament that *wisdom* has been lost in knowledge, as knowledge has been lost in information. Part of Witherington's sense of urgency is just that wisdom—specifically Biblical wisdom—is both missing and desperately needed in the Information Age.[9]

Indeed, Witherington raises the critical question—occasioned precisely by his recalling the importance of "incarnational learning," one which "seems to require presence rather than virtual reality"—i.e., can such learning in fact happen online? "Or," he wonders, "is the Internet just one more rough beast lumbering its way toward Bethlehem, making false messianic claims to save us and deliver us from various educational woes and problems?" While this "either/or"— i.e., between utopian hopes and dystopian fears as wrapped up in new technologies—is itself a dualism we should avoid, Witherington again raises for us the importance of *embodiment* in learning. Again, we will explore more fully in the conclusion the debate between more recent emphases on *embodiment* in CMC theory and *praxis* vis-à-vis especially postmodernist claims made for the new media in the 1980s and 1990s, as these claims rested in part on the presumption of the possibility and desirability of *disembodiment*.

Voices of Caution

Terry Lindvall:
From Commandment to Psychology—the Power of the Image

In contrast with the representatives of a more postmodern enthusiasm for embracing the new media, Terry Lindvall raises a series of critical questions that proponents should consider before committing the Word to what Lindvall characterizes as "the postmodern cultural hegemony of visual imagery." Lindvall makes his argument first by reviewing 16 centuries of Christian response to and analysis of the visual vis-à-vis Bible study, religious piety, and the impact of image on memory and imitation. So he reminds us, for example, of the approved role of image—including three-dimensional sculpture and architecture, as well as two-dimensional painting, stained glass, manuscript illumination—in conveying Biblical narrative especially in the Medieval period. (Here, he points us towards Kate Lindemann's celebration of the medieval illuminated manuscript as a model for building contemporary web pages designed for contemplation.) As well, he points out that early on, motion pictures were lauded by believers as nothing less than "the best teachers and the best preachers in the history of the world" (Jump, cited in Lindvall)—an enthusiasm that should remind us of the initial enthusiasm for TV in the 1950s and the Internet in the 1990s.

Second, Lindvall explores the essential connection between the Word in tradition and the communication technologies of orality and literacy: the Word, he warns, as emerging from and defined by these technologies and cultural contexts, runs the risk of humiliation and extinction in an era of the visual. Lindvall reminds us here of the Second Commandment and draws on the analysis of Lionel Kochan, who makes clear the connection between "graven images" and idolatry. Here, Lindvall and Kochan remind us of the point that Christhof Hardmeier develops in much greater detail in his analysis of Deutronomy—i.e., that the primary form of communication between God and God's creatures is direct and oral, in contrast with the mediated forms of communication that take place through images and the material order more generally. Lindvall then expands upon the dangers of the image as argued by a number of scholars and studies—including to the specific task of conveying Biblical narrative and message. At the same time, however, he recognizes—along with those in the Christian tradition he cites—the *positive* role of imagery in helping one communication and pursue the Gospel.

In presenting us with both sides of this debate, Lindvall's chapter helps balance the more unequivocal optimism of 1980s and 1990s postmodernism. He thereby makes the point—to borrow from Peter Facione and Isaac Mwase—that claims about the power of image are contestable. Critical thinking on these issues requires us to recognize their contestability. In particular, as he calls into question an uncritical (indeed, potentially idolatrous!) endorsement of the visual over the textual—Lindvall thereby questions the ostensibly radical distinctions in the Innis/McLuhan/Ong schema undergirding especially radical postmodern rejections of modernity as an artifact of the technologies of print. In doing so, as we will see more fully in the conclusion, he thereby anticipates more recent scholarship in computer-mediated communication that likewise calls into question a sharp distinction between orality, literacy, etc.

Michael Palmer: the Embodied Community of Interpreters

Palmer begins with a careful account of his own experiences with Bible study as a member of a faith community. This account emphasizes the *oral* dimension of that study, and its embeddedness in interpersonal, face-to-face engagements with specific individuals—in contrast with a distanced text. Palmer then argues two central claims: (1) that electronic media, for all of their advantages and powers, blur the crucial distinction between gathering information and the careful, reflective acts of making sense and meaning out of information, and (2) that the Internet, especially as biased in favor of anonymity and use in isolation, thus threatens estrangement from the traditional faith community of the sort Palmer initially describes. (Eep Talstra will develop these points still more fully.)

To support these claims, Palmer especially draws on the analyses of Albert Borgmann and learning theory to uncover and powerfully critique a number of assumptions underlying the enthusiastic claims of new media proponents, e.g., that increased efficiency in the use of time or "user friendliness" lead to increased understanding of difficult texts.

In addition, Palmer argues that electronic Bible study materials fail to foster what learning theorists describe as problem-finding abilities and the sorts of reflective judgment needed for coping with ill-structured problems. Palmer further takes up Peter Facione's account of critical thinking to note that CT involves both skills and *dispositions*—including the willingness and ability to live with ambiguity and indeterminacy. These dispositions, however, seem to require the nurture of family, community, and faith communities: hence we cannot expect, Palmer argues, electronic Bible study resources and Internet-based databases *by themselves* to foster the CT dispositions needed to make sense and meaning of complex and ambiguous texts.

Given that communities of interpretation are thus needed to foster the kind of CT required for the reflection that leads to *wisdom*—Palmer asks what sorts of impacts the new media may have on these communities. Despite proponents' claims that the new media liberate and enhance community in general and biblical literacy in particular, Palmer notes first of all that biblical literacy continues to decline in the United States. As well, the (in)famous CMU and Stanford studies of Internet use suggest that the greater amount of time spent online means a proportional reduction in the amount of time spent on real-world relationships as well as a shift from the strong social ties predominant in the face-to-face world to the weak social ties predominant online. Appropriately enough, Palmer does not accept these studies uncritically— but even given their noted limits and weaknesses, they suggest that communication online can at best only augment real-world relationships, and this only under specific conditions. Palmer's emphasis on the importance of embodied communities in shaping how we learn to read the Bible echoes Witherington's concern that "incarnational learning" may be lost online. In fact, as we will explore more fully in the conclusion, this sense of online relationships as *complementing* rather than *replacing* offline ones is in keeping with recent turns from the more revolutionary postures of postmodern enthusiasm for "liberation in cyberspace" to more balanced efforts to conjoin the genuinely new possibilities of new media with those of earlier technologies and eras.

If we are interested in fostering critical approaches to the Bible, all this means, finally, that critical study needs to be revived—and in ways that make appropriate use of the new media. Palmer argues that this can be done, not through a Luddite-style rejection of new technologies, but through a clear understanding that the technologies must always serve as means to well-defined ends, rather than becoming ends-in- themselves that obscure or replace our most important goals—in this case, critical study of the biblical text that leads to greater understanding and *wisdom*. Eep Talstra (below) will make this last point still more fully in his analysis of the new media vis-à-vis the roles of Scholar, Scribe, Librarian, and Reader.

Middle Grounds: Post-Critical Thought, Tools for the Reader, and Lectio Divina

Phil Mullins: Post-Critical Thought

Both Facione's and the Bachmanns' analyses of critical thinking rely in large measure on what we might think of as classical notions of logic—i.e., the Western rationalist tradition of formalized reflection on what stands as valid and sound argument, a tradition rooted in Aristotle. But as Voelz helpfully reminds us, postmodernism begins with a "suspicion of reason,"—i.e., precisely of the rationalist tradition, especially in its modern form, one that would include the Bachmanns' primary logician, Jaakko Hintikka. And, as we have begun to see, postmodern enthusiasm for the possibilities of new media rests centrally upon the Innis/Eisenstein/McLuhan/Ong communication theory, one that begins with the view that communication in all its forms, including speech and listening, can be understood as technologies of communication. Briefly, each cultural phase is *determined*, in this view, by its technologies of communication—the technologies of orality, literacy, print, and "the secondary orality of electronic culture" (Ong 1988, 135-38). Postmodern enthusiasm for the new media, then, includes the hope that these media, as engaging us with new forms of communication *technologies*, will thus free us from the ostensible tyrannies of modernity as defined by the book and the communication technologies of literacy and print, including *logic* and *critical thinking* as understood from Aristotle through the moderns. The issue raised by new media, then, is not simply how the Bible, as a premier artifact of the eras of literacy and of print, may be altered in dramatic, if not revolutionary ways by its "transmediation" into electronic forms: even more fundamentally—will new media further mean a revolutionary *rejection* of those forms of logic and critical thinking ostensibly tied to the eras of literacy and print? In particular: must a postmodern "suspicion of reason" issue in a *rejection* of the forms of logic and critical thinking articulated here by Facione and the Bachmanns?

In this light, Phil Mullins' essay is especially helpful. Mullins takes the point of the Innis-Ong theory and its implications as developed in postmodernism—indeed, he has already written insightfully on the particular implications of these views for modernist, including fundamentalist, understandings of the Bible as religious authority (1996). Here, however, consistent with more recent "post-post-modern" thought, Mullins conjoins his recognition and appreciation for postmodern insights with an important effort to develop a "post-critical" notion of critical thinking that avoids the now well-known problem of *epistemological relativism* in postmodernism. His contribution can be understood as a *synthesis* that both recognizes the importance of postmodern critiques of earlier epistemologies and logics *and*, in parallel with earlier notions of logic, attempts to avoid postmodern *epistemological relativism* by developing a new "post-critical" epistemology and logic that affirms the possibility of knowledge as more than individual interpretation and social constructivism.

Using Michael Polanyi's epistemology as his primary framework, Mullins' essay frames and unites comments treating Bible study and critical thinking within the context of the history of ideas. Mullins begins by characterizing diverse approaches to Bible *qua* text in late modernity. Mullins first of all demonstrates that what we may take to be polar opposites—the historical-critical approaches of especially the 19th and 20th centuries, on the one hand, and literalist/fundamentalist approaches on the other—in fact share common ground in modernist assumptions regarding the availability and desirability of "objective" knowledge. Mullins then reminds us of the dramatic shift to postmodernism in the last third of the 20th century—a shift that thus radically calls into question the shared foundations of both literalist/fundamentalist approaches and historical-critical approaches. Mullins calls our attention to the epistemological difficulties of postmodernisms that emphasize the role of power and interest in shaping knowledge to the point that they become—whether they recognize it or not—self-contradictory (most obviously, by insisting that all truth is relative because all truths are merely the result of power and interest—thus undermining any validity of this claim itself as anything other than itself an expression of power and interest that is thus only relative in turn).

Mullins acknowledges the attraction—and difficulties—of any appeal to critical thinking in the face of such postmodern relativisms, where conceptions of critical thinking remain rooted in modernist assumptions that no longer appear to hold. He then develops a distinctive account of a "post-critical" form of critical thinking—one that relies on Polanyi and the semiotic theory of C.S. Peirce—that overcomes the relativism inherent in much of postmodern thought while at the same time preserving the greater pluralism characteristic of postmodernism in its rejection of narrowly modernist (indeed, positivist) insistence that only "objective" knowledge is valid or desirable. We have seen something of this pluralism as a feature emphasized by James Voelz in the hermenetical approach he argues in this volume. As well, this pluralism is consistent with the pluralism that marks Facione's final stage of cognitive development in critical thinking—i.e., that of "the sage" who fully acknowledges the role of subjectivity and context in shaping knowledge, but who further argues, *contra* epistemological relativism, that some views and positions are more defensible than others. And as we will explore more fully in the conclusion, this pluralistic understanding of truth, as a middle ground between dogmatism and relativism, coheres with contemporary epistemologies as developed in the philosophy of religion and philosophy of science.

Eep Talstra: New Electronic Tools for Connected Readers

To anticipate this point another way: we will see more contemporary views developing middle grounds that synthesize both object and subject, both old and new, in contrast with the 1980s and 1990s *either/or* between modernity and postmodernity. And: just as Mullins' notion of post-critical thought marks out such a middle ground, so Talstra establishes similar middle grounds as he develops an extensive historical survey and framework for helping us better understand the complex relationships between technologies of communication and our reading of the Bible.

Talstra begins by identifying the suite of interrelated skills involved in establishing texts and communities of interpreters—namely, those of the Scribe, the Librarian, the Scholar, and the Reader. His large claim is that while the new media have influenced these interactions, these interactions remain central to reading and communication. He then argues that the new media have successfully imitated the Scribe (who produces or copies texts) and the Librarian (who stores and retrieves texts)—but as yet there are no effective tools to support Scholarly analysis or Readers' hermeneutical tasks.

Along the way, Talstra raises a number of important points—beginning with the recognition that the new media will encourage a more private style of reading, in contrast with the more public style of reading associated with printed texts and especially manuscripts. (This thus reinforces the concern expressed in this volume by the Bachmans and Palmer that as electronic media remove the individual from the community of interpreters, so the individual is less likely to acquire the habits of reading that the Bachmans characterize as "biblically disciplined.") In this direction, he further highlights the role of commercialism, as it renames the reader as "the user" or the "web-surfer," by which is always meant "our potential customer."[10]

Talstra further bolsters his argument with a series of precise examples drawn from his own extensive experience as a bible scholar long engaged with projects to develop computer-based resources in support of careful reading. In his view, so far at least, much of existing Bible software amounts to an "echo" of traditional scholarship—i.e., ways of more quickly imitating especially the role of the Librarian, but not of the Scholar or Reader. Put humorously, "in the area of Bible and computing we tend to ride quicker horses instead of inventing better cars." What is needed, in addition, are readers' tools "that can analyze texts, compare texts and make readers aware of the historical interaction of texts and their readers." His examples of these functions are drawn from the *praxis* of reading and comparing texts such as the Massoretic text of the TANAKH with those from Qumran, the Septuagint, the Targum, and other versions. These illustrate first how texts are adapted through the interaction of the Scribe and the Librarian, i.e., such that later texts are "corrected" in order to match earlier ones—or, more dramatically, to interpret or appropriate a text from one cultural tradition, language, and theology to another. As well, Talstra provides examples of the interaction between Scholar and Reader that also demonstrate changes in texts as they are appropriated and applied in new contexts, so as to make an older text appear to predict a latter event.

Talstra thus argues for the development of new electronic tools that will provide readers with "the tools of critical reconstruction given to us by the era of the book"—ones that will help readers further apply "the hermeneutical processes of reading and appropriation from the era of manuscripts." Such tools would first of all help readers understand the complex interactions of texts and communities of readers through time. In this way, such new tools would represent a "creative continuation of the ancient communities of reading."

This emphasis on *continuity* with the past means, of course, that Talstra is somewhat critical of more postmodern enthusiasts who argue that the new media amount to a revolution and and radical rejection of the past. So he calls into question, for example, whether James Voelz's account of modern biblical scholarship in fact does justice to that scholarship. (In logical terms, he raises the possibility that Voelz's more revolutionary rejection of modern scholarship in favor of a postmodern hermeneutic in some measure rests on a straw man account of that scholarship.) Similarly, *contra* Ben Witherington's enthusiasm for appropriating new media in teaching and scholarship, Talstra wonders how much is gained through simply faster access to materials (the Librarian function) if we lack the analytical tools that, in giving us direct access to original texts, allow us to ask the sorts of questions needed to help us understand the reception and transformation of texts through diverse communities of readers, so as to sustain what Talstra calls a "creative continuation" with those communities?

By contrast, Talstra's position endorses Kate Lindemann's notion of "seeing contemplatively"in Medieval illuminated manuscripts (below) as another example of appropriation—suggesting that Lindemann's project of building web pages that replicate and enhance such contemplative seeing stands as an example of the sort of *continuity* with earlier communities of readers that Talstra endorses. Similarly, Talstra's position favors Phil Mullins' notion of "post-critical thought" as something less than a radical postmodern rejection of all that has gone before and more of an effort to both recognize the important lessons and insights of postmodernism, while we also seek "to re-root in human responsibility and human communities" (Mullins, 2000, cited in Talstra).

The point here is not to argue which of these views is correct— but rather to make clear again, in keeping with our opening emphasis on open-mindedness as a hallmark of critical thinking, that many of the fundamental claims represented in this volume are indeed contestable. Thus, additional critical thinking is required!

We close with an example of suggested *praxis*, one that would instantiate a middle ground coherent with those argued by Mullins and Talstra.

Kate Lindemann: Lectio Divina on the World Wide Web

Kate Lindemann provides numerous examples of how extant web texts incorporate the design style of Medieval illuminated manuscripts, specifically, examples of how illuminators use images "not to illustrate but to illuminate or shape the acceptable meaning for the text."

Taking up a phenomenological approach, she then distinguishes between observation as an objective, scientific way of seeing—one that

has dominated the West, she argues, for the past 300 years—and contemplative seeing. Rather than leading to objective data and theoretical
conclusions about objects at a distance, contemplative seeing on
Lindemann's account results in a sense of kinship and understanding of
objects, as they are allowed to enter one's soul or psyche through such
seeing. A few examples of religiously-based web pages currently exist
that exploit the conjunction of text and image to induce a contemplative
seeing that Lindemann associates with *lectio divina*, "divine reading."
But she argues that such design, one that imitates the Medieval patterns
of design in illuminated manuscripts, is both possible and desirable for
pages on the Web. Indeed, the further addition of audio files of diverse
communities *reading aloud* a Psalm or other religious text, she suggests, would help Christian communities replicate for the web visitor
the contemplative religious experiences associated with reading in the
ancient and medieval worlds—experiences overshadowed and lost with
the rise of a modern scientific sense of objective observation and an
exclusive emphasis on reading *texts* exclusive of image and sound.

Preliminary/Contestable Conclusions

Taken together, then, our contributors mark out a range of often
sharply divergent positions and viewpoints while they simultaneously
echo and reinforce shared themes. Their essays can be viewed through
a number of lenses—most obviously, those of biblical studies, media
studies, and logic. For my part, I begin by reviewing these essays in
light of the multiple disciplines of computer-mediated communication
(CMC)—including the philosophy of technology—as well as the perspectives of the history and philosophy of science and philosophy of
religion. I will discuss more recent views on the Innis/Eisenstein/
McLuhan/Ong theory of communication that underlies much of the
1980s and 1990s postmodern enthusiasm for a "liberation in cyberspace," as well as the underlying philosophical assumptions of technological determinism and technological instrumentalism. I then explore
the modern / postmodern debate in light of more recent theory and *praxis*-oriented research on the issues of *embodiment* and online communities. Here I will sketch out the recent turns from a variety of epistemological and ontological dualisms characterizing postmodern views,
including their theological expression in what I call "cyber-gnosticism."
In place of these dualisms, a range of philosophers, theorists, and
researchers increasingly focus on epistemological and ontological models that highlight a logic of complementarity and synthesis. In particu-

lar, this is a turn *from* a Gnostic and Augustinian *contempt* of the body, the feminine, and the material world more generally, *to* views that— consistent with the importance of *incarnation* in Christian traditions— validate the goodness and significance of our existence as embodied human beings intrinsically implicated in a vast web of relationships.

Second, I will take up the larger issues of faith and reason, creation and evolution—as implicated by the specific discussion of critical thinking vis-à-vis biblical texts—in light of (a) the history of the relationship between faith and reason in the Western tradition, (b) recent *epistemological* debates in philosophy of science between *realism* and *anti-realism*, and (c) the "Science Wars" of the 1980s and 1990s as particular expressions of modern, specifically *positivist* views of science vs. postmodern, specifically *relativist* views. Here we will see that rather than an *opposition* between faith and reason, the two are much more frequently understood to stand in *compatible* or *complementary* relationships: in this light, the sense of opposition and hostility that has marked especially the specific debate between evolution and creationist views indeed appears to be a relatively recent phenomenon—one that is challenged, moreover, by a number of recent (re)turns among both scientists and people of faith towards more compatibilist and complementary views. This (re)new(ed) sense of complementarity is then further supported and reinforced by the shifts in philosophy of science towards middle grounds between modernist positivism and postmodernist relativism. These large turns, finally, from a more fideistic sense of opposition between faith and reason—and its particular expression in the ostensible debates between religion and science, between creation and evolution—to a more compatibilist sense of these as complementary modes of knowing and being thus cohere with and reinforce the multiple middle grounds articulated by our contributors, especially those marked out by Mullins, Talstra, and Lindemann.

The Age of Print vs. the Information Age?

We have seen in a preliminary way that as especially the Bachmans' chapter suggests, critical thinking for many is closely tied to the systems of formal and informal logic that have developed since Aristotle's first codification of the basic rules of thought. By contrast, proponents of postmodernism argue, in part, on the basis of a communication theory developed by Innis, Eisenstein (1983), Mcluhan (1965), and Ong (1981, 1988), that our very conceptions of logic are dependent upon—indeed, in its strong form, *determined* by—the "technologies of communication" that define a given culture or society. Walter Ong has been especially influential in this direction as he has articulated these technologies in terms of orality, literacy (the invention of writing), print, and "the secondary orality of electronic culture" (1988, 135-38). On this view, the emergence of new media—as a new technology of communication—means precisely that we are in the midst of a *communication* and thus profound *cultural* revolution, one that represents a radical overturning of modernity (as dependent upon, if not caused by, the invention of the printing press) and all its notions of knowledge, including *logic*. From the standpoint of computer-mediated communication, however, this more radical version of the relationship between communication technologies, cultural epistemologies and notions of logic, and thus the revolutionary implications of new media and electronic culture has been called into serious question on both theoretical and empirical grounds.

To begin with, especially the categorical distinctions between *orality* and *literacy* are increasingly suspect—precisely in light of more recent analysis of computer-mediated communication.[11] In this way, Hardmeier's account of Deuteronomy, as already conjoining the oral and the literate, helps us see that the biblical text, far from standing solely as an artifact of literacy and especially print cultures in sharp contrast with oral cultures and thus the orality of electronic culture (so Ong), rather stands in striking *continuity* with the most contemporary understandings of how human beings use CMC technologies, i.e., as *conjoining* various aspects of orality *and* text (a point also made by Lindvall). Along these lines, as Hardmeier and Lindvall remind us specifically of the second commandment's prohibition *against* images, as well as (so Lindvall) of the positive role of imagery in Christian tradition—we are warned against the danger of a kind of imagistic idolatry, should we focus on the visual to the exclusion of the aural and the textual as we seek to "trans-mediate" the Bible into electronic forms. At the same time, however, as Kate Lindemann's suggestion of exploiting Medieval conjunctions of image and text in support of *lectio divina* suggests, it is precisely by holding together the visual, the aural, and the textual that we can extend older forms of literacy into our appropriations of new technologies—i.e., an extension that exploits the best possibilities of the new media without, however, letting the new media simply reshape older materials, frameworks, and approaches.[12] In turn, this emphasis on "both/and"—i.e., both the old and the new in conjunction and continuity with one another—in contrast with the more dualistic presumptions of modernity and post-modernism (i.e., one hews to either the old or the new—not both) can be seen in Phil Mullins' notion of a "post-critical" thought that sustains an older notion of critical thinking while also seeking to reshape critical thinking in ways appropriate to the new technologies.

Technological instrumentalism? Technological determinism?

This drive towards a logic of an *inclusive* "both/and" or *complementarity*, in contrast with the logic of an *exclusive* "either/or," is further reinforced when we review two of the critical philosophical assumptions underlying the Innis/Eisenstein/McLuhan/Ong schema— and thus much of the 1980s and 1990s postmodern enthusiasm for new media as a revolutionary overturning of the Age of Print. On the one hand, McLuhan assumes the position of *technological instrumentalism*—the view that technologies are themselves neutral in the sense that they embed no values or preferences, but are "just tools." This assumption is crucial, we must notice, for any vision of an "electronic global village" we may hope to emerge from "wiring the world." *Only by assuming that our technologies are neutral tools can we avoid seeing this "wiring of the world" as simply a form of computer-mediated colonialism*—i.e., precisely the imposition of specific cultural values, as embedded in the technologies of computer-mediated communication, upon the "target" cultures in which these technologies are deployed.

On the other hand, proponents of the electronic global village also assume the contrasting view of *technological determinism*, i.e., the assumption that once CMC technologies are deployed, *precisely as technologies that embed and foster democracy, individualism, freedom of expression, etc.—"target" cultures will be transformed as these values will automatically take root in the machines' users.*[13]

Beyond the logical problem of a contradiction between these underlying assumptions of the popular icon of an electronic global village—it is now apparent that *neither* assumption stands up to either theoretical analysis or the results of what happens in *praxis* when CMC technologies are deployed and diffused in diverse cultural settings. On the one hand, especially the *conflicts* that emerge as Western-designed CMC technologies are taken up in diverse cultural settings, including non-Western and indigenous cultures, demonstrate that CMC technologies are *not* free of culturally-specific values and preferences. On the contrary: much as postmodern proponents had hoped, these technologies *do* embed and foster specific values, including precisely the *democratic* values of egalitarian relationships, freedom of information and expression, etc. At the same time, however, those in "target" cultures that take up these technologies are not automatically reshaped to fit the cultural mold of Western democratic preferences. On the contrary: while there are examples of CMC technologies facilitating cultural moves in more open and democratic directions (e.g., Israel [Dahan 1999] and Kuwait [Wheeler 2001])—there are also examples of people in target cultures resisting the imposition of specific cultural values, in part as they redesign and reshape these technologies (e.g., in Japan [Heaton 2001], Malaysia [Rahmati 2000, Harris et al 2001], and Thailand [Hongladarom 2001]) . These results from theory and *praxis* hence point towards a middle ground between technological instrumentalism and technological determinism (and thus between related dichotomies, e.g., between McWorld vs. violent fragmentation, between a (modern) single homogenous world culture that threatens to erase all cultural distinctiveness and a (postmodern) decentering and fragmentation that threatens to only juxtapose diverse cultures in relationships of opposition and violence.[14] In this middle ground, as especially Thai *praxis* exemplifies, non-Western peoples can appropriate Western CMC technologies in ways that allow for *both* a global communication via these technologies *and* ways of preserving and enhancing their own cultural values and communication preferences (Hongladarom 2001; Ess 2001a; Ess & Sudweeks 2001).

In this light, the presumption of 1980s and 1990s postmodernism—i.e., that the technologies of the new media would inevitably overturn the technologies, and thus the values and logics ostensibly tied to modernity as solely the artifacts of print technology—as a form of technological determinism is refuted by more recent experience in *praxis* as well as theory. At the same time, the dualistic *either/or* underlying the postmodern vision of revolution through technology is likewise called into question by *praxis*—i.e., precisely the ability of diverse cultures and peoples to take an inclusive *both/and* process of hybridization, one that conjoins both the global and the local, both Western and non-Western. Such "glocalization" and hybridizing, finally, suggest that rather than an *either/or* between modernity and postmodernism, the results in *praxis* of the deployment of new media may be a range of middle grounds that conjoin elements of both. In this light, the middle grounds we have seen elucidated here on both theoretical and practical levels by Mullins, Talstra, and Lindemann are thus consistent with this more recent scholarship and experience.

Embodiment and community in "post-post-modernism": The "post-human" and the resurrection of the body

This shift from a more *exclusive* or *dualistic* logic to a more *complementary* or inclusive logic can also be seen in two further, tightly correlated arenas—first, in modern and postmodern conceptions of the relationship between *mind* and *body*, vis-à-vis a more recent emphasis on the *connection* between mind and body in an emerging literature on *embodiment*. Correlatively, as attention turns toward especially hermeneutical and phenomenological perspectives that emphasize embodiment as entailing an inextricable *connection* between mind-and-body—what Barbara Becker (2000, 2001) calls *LeibSubjekt*, "BodySubject"—so there is a turn *from* especially a postmodern *dualism* that emphasizes the revolutionary dichotomy between modernity and postmodernity, *towards* a more inclusive, *complementary* view that seeks to incorporate *both* modern and postmodern perspectives.

Especially the postmodern enthusiasm for a "liberation in cyberspace" is now clearly seen to rest on a Cartesian (i.e., characteristically *modern*) emphasis on the radical difference between body and mind. Perhaps most notably, Donna Haraway argued that especially women would find the equality and liberation as disembodied minds in cyberspace—ostensibly a communicative space in which gender was invisible—that they would not find in the offline world, where women's bodies are constantly subject to male objectification and manipulation (1990). This radical opposition between the oppression of the offline world vs. liberation in the online world is further thematic of John Perry Barlow's famous "Declaration of Independence in Cyberspace" (1996), in which he juxtaposed the new freedoms of the mind in cyberspace vs. oppression of the individual in what he called "meatspace"—a reference to the founding novel of cyberpunk fiction, William Gibson's *Neuromancer* (1986). As a last example, Hans Moravec (1988) clearly presumes this Cartesian dualism in his hope that human beings will be able to download their consciousness into computer systems, and thereby attain freedom from the body and immortality.[15]

Moreover, this presumed dualism and its project of achieving liberation in cyberspace is not simply Cartesian *philosophy*: it is explicitly Cartesian *theology*—a theology derivative of Augustine. Most notably, Gibson writes of a contempt for the body as meat, as a "prison" of flesh, in precisely the Augustinian terms of "the Fall"—complete with the Augustianian association between body, sexuality, and woman as encapsulated in the doctrine of Original Sin.[16] Just as the Augustinian reading of the 2nd Genesis creation story coheres with (indeed, in some measure derives from) a Gnostic dualism that emphasizes the conflict between soul and body—so the dualism and accompanying contempt for body and "meatspace" we see here coheres with what I have called a "cyber-gnosticism," as characterized precisely by a dualistic contempt for the body in favor of salvation in a disembodied cyberspace (Ess 2001b).

At least since the early 1990s, however, this dualism has been increasingly called into question, beginning with feminist critics who recognized that, presuming the Augustinian association between contempt for body and contempt for the female—a putative liberation in cyberspace thus runs the risk of simply *reiterating* the basic philosophical and theological assumptions that drive the oppression of women in the first place.[17] As a counterpoint to such Cartesian/Augustinian dualisms, Katherine Hayles develops a "post-post-modern" framework that that stresses instead a web of complimentary relationships, beginning at the *epistemological* level: "reflexive epistemology replaces objectivism; embodiment replaces a body seen as a support system for the mind; and a dynamic partnership between humans and intelligent machines replaces the liberal humanist subject's manifest destiny to dominate and control nature" (Hayles 1999, 288). That is: in place of an objectivist epistemology that radically divorces the knowing subject from the object of knowledge, thus issuing in the positivist insistence that only "objective" modes of knowledge are legitimate—Hayles turns to a reflexive or connectivist epistemology that echoes Kant as it emphasizes the dynamic relationship between subject and object in shaping our knowledge of the world. Consistent with this shift from a logic of dualism to a logic of complementarity, Hayles further emphasizes the significance of *embodiment* in our understanding of who we are as human beings *in the world* (cf. Hillis 1999, especially ch. 6). Among others, Barbara Becker (2000, 2001) recovers and develops non-dualistic understandings of identity through a phenomenological analysis: in doing so, she introduces the neologism "BodySubject" (*LeibSubjekt*) as a way of referring to the human being as a mind-*and*-body. Hubert Dreyfus, likewise drawing primarily on the phenomenology of Merleau-Ponty as well as the existential analyses of Kierkegaard, extends Becker's analysis to critique especially the limitations of distance education as a specific case of postmodern enthusiasm for disembodied existence online (2001). In this way, Dreyfus underscores Witherington's, Palmer's and Talstra's concerns with the loss of incarnational learning and those critical reading skills developed within the context of embodied faith communities. More broadly, this recovery of embodiment and community coheres with an increasing recognition in CMC research that the 1980s and 1990s enthusiasm for "virtual communities" as a *replacement* for offline community has largely failed in *praxis*. Instead, virtual communities work primarily as extensions and supplements to real-world communities—i.e., those made up of embodied persons engaged in a web of real-world relationships (see especially Baym 1995, 2002).

Admittedly, Hubert Dreyfus is known as a prominent critic of especially the more grandiose claims of "hard" Artificial Intelligence in the 1950s-1990s. But it is not simply the venerable critics who contribute to this turn from the dualism of post/modern enthusiasm for a mind divorced from body. On the contrary, it is especially telling that two of the foundational voices of 1980s and 1990s postmodern enthusiasm for disembodied liberation in cyberspace—Jay David Bolter (2000) and Harold Rheingold (2000)—have likewise turned in these most recent writings as well to more moderate and cautious positions. This is to say: Bolter and Rheingold—coherent with the *epistemological* shift of Hayles' "post-human"—thus move from the either/or of modernity vs. postmodernity to a complementarity that conjoins something of both perspectives. (As we will see when we turn to questions of religion and science, this same debate between modernity and postmodernity is played out in both the "realism/anti-realism" debates in philosophy of science and, more broadly, in the "Science Wars" of the 1980s and 1990s. In parallel with the turn we see here *from* the either/or between modernity and postmodernity *toward* their synthesis vis-à-vis communication, embodiment, and community—there is a crucial turn *from* the opposition between modernist realism/objectivism and postmodern critiques emphasizing the subjective in the construction of knowledge *toward* more synthetic views and middle grounds that hold together elements of both.)

In *theological* terms, the debate here is between more dualistic— at the extreme, *gnostic*—contempt for the body and views that elevate instead the goodness of body as part of God's creation. As especially Witherington reminds us in this volume, and I have argued elsewhere, as diverse Christian traditions take up *incarnation*—both as central to their Christologies and their understandings of the meaning of the central sacrament of *communion*—those traditions that foreground the affirmation of the body as God's expression, affirmation, and communication of the Word may want to pause at the edge of cyberspace and consider the possible contradictions between these theological commitments and the contempt for the body and the material dimension of the created order more generally that characterizes especially postmodern enthusiasm for liberation in cyberspace.[18]

Larger Questions:
Faith and reason, science and religion, evolution and creation

As Facione first points out, our discussion of critical thinking and its role in approaching biblical texts, especially as these may be transformed in fundamental ways by the new media, further implicates the larger debates regarding the proper relationship between faith and reason—a debate that in turn implicates such central controversies as the debates between evolution and creationism.

Of course, in the form of apparent conflict between evolution and creationism, this debate seems to presume still another dualistic logic—one that insists we must have either *faith* to the exclusion of reason (*fideism*) or reason to the exclusion of faith (*positivism*—what Facione identifies as a posture of critical thinking as "hostile antagonist" to faith). While fideism in the Christian tradition is as old as Tertullian's famous question, "What does Athens have to do with Jerusalem?"—this dualism in its modern form is grounded in Descartes' method of radical doubt and dualistic epistemology that allowed only for two modes of knowledge—i.e., the certain and the false, with whatever is subject to the smallest doubt to be counted along with the false (*Discourse on Method*, Part IV: [1637] 1972, 101; *Meditations on First Philosophy*, Meditation I [1641] 1972, 145). This epistemological *either/or* is subsequently manifest in *both* 19th century fundamentalism *and* positivism as these both insist that only *certain* knowledge, as established respectively either by faith or by natural science (but not both) stands as "real" knowledge: anything less counts along with the outright false.

It is arguable, however, that this dualism, while dominating Anglo-American discussion over the past 100 years or so, is in part an artifact precisely of the publication of Darwin's *Origins of the Species* (Wertheim 1998). More broadly, if we briefly review its history, we will see that such dualism is a minority position in the history of Western science and philosophy. Indeed, recent developments in philosophy of science— specifically, the realism/anti-realism debate and, more broadly, the "Science Wars" debates of the 1980s and 1990s—point as well *away* from the dualism characterizing postmodernism's attack on modern natural science towards more *complementary* positions that incorporate elements of both views. We will see, finally, that they cohere with a similar turn—one made possible precisely by the *epistemological* shifts demarcated in philosophy of science—in the most recent debates regarding faith and reason, including their specific form in the debate between evolution and creationism, from the more dualistic to the more complementary view.

Dualism as a minority position[19]

As especially Hardmeier, Eubanks, and the Bachmann's have argued, reason in the form of critical thinking appears to be squarely embedded in the TANAKH and the Christian Scriptures as integral to the life of faith. This sense of their complementarity, moreover, is apparent in the Talmud, as we have seen.[20]

In the Medieval world, a foundational complementary position is developed by Thomas Aquinas, in part, building on the "turn towards nature" at work in St. Francis and the Franciscans[21]—precisely in contrast with the Medieval version of dualism between faith and reason, i.e., the doctrine of the two-fold truth. Proponents of the two-fold truth (introduced from the Muslim world by Averroes) held that "Two incompatible assertions are held to be true at the same time"—that is, if we utterly divorce the truths of reason and the truths of faith, then the latter, in particular, can*not* be disproved by the former when they contradict one another (Alioto 1993, 129). This epistemological dualism further means: "Revealed truth, therefore, could not be the province of reason, only of faith. All else, [including] the science of the physical world, belonged to reason" (Alioto 1993, 130). This same doctrine is expressed in its modern form by Descartes (e.g. *Discourse on Method*, I [1637] 1972, 85). (And as we have seen, Descartes' *epistemological* dualism issues in an *ontological* correlate—most famously, the split between mind and body [echoing the orthodox Christian split between soul and body], with the former continuing to enjoy the traditional characteristics of the Christian soul as revealed by faith, while the latter becomes utterly subject to the reason of the emerging sciences. It is this dualism, to recall Hayles, that issues precisely in the modern liberal project to dominate nature—in Descartes' phrase, to "render ourselves masters and possessors of nature" (*Discourse*, Pt. VI [1637] 1973, 119).)

In the Medieval world, however, the doctrine of two-fold truth was soon overshadowed by other views, beginning with the effort to subordinate natural science/philosophy to theology—what Facione here calls the "faithful helper" posture. More important, however, is the turn, begun in part by St. Francis and then systematized by Thomas Aquinas, to develop an understanding of the *complementarity* between reason and faith, science and religion, nature and grace. As Thomas argues early on in the *Summa Theologiae* (in part by citing Paul in II Cor. 10:5 and Acts 17:28):

> Christian theology also uses human reasoning, not indeed to prove the faith, for that would take away from the merit of believing, but to make manifest some implications of its message. Since grace does not scrap nature but brings it to perfection, so also natural reason should assist faith as the natural loving bent of the will ministers to charity. (1A. 1, 8: 1969, 55)

As Alioto characterizes it, "For Aquinas there simply cannot be two separate or contradictory truths; all knowledge and hence all truth come from a single source" (1993, 132). This unity, however, is a *complementary* one—i.e., one that preserves the irreducible differences between faith and reason, divine and human alongside their complex connections, as can be seen in Thomas' doctrine of Being.[22]

Moreover, this understanding of a *complementary* relationship between faith and reason, science and religion, is characteristic not only of Thomas and much of the later Medieval world: it is further *presumed* by many of the leading figures of the Renaissance and the (so-called) Scientific Revolution, including Copernicus, Kepler, and Newton. As Margaret Wertheim stresses, not only were these founders of the new science deeply religious men "who wanted a science that would harmonize with their faith": at the same time, their belief in a sun-centered understanding of the universe was "an offshoot of their theology" (1998).[23]

Wertheim's view that there is great *continuity* between the Medievals and the Moderns, in contrast with a prevailing—at least, late 19th century—view emphasizing the radical *discontinuity* between modern natural science as a "Revolution," points to a last vehicle for the contrast between the logics of *complementarity* and of *dualism*. This is the "continuity debate" among historians of science—i.e., precisely as to whether modern natural science represents more of a continuity or connection with Medieval and Ancient practices, discoveries, insights, etc. (expressed in Newton's well-known phrase, "If I have seen further than others, it is because I stand on the shoulders of giants")—or whether modern natural science, as most moderns (beginning with Bacon and Descartes) urge, is indeed a revolutionary start *de novo*, with (more or less) entirely new and distinctive results that set us apart from those who came before. David Lindberg argues for an interesting middle ground between this either/or (!)—one that sees modern natural science as distinctive in light of its new methodologies and new (Cartesian) conception of nature, but yet dependent *within* specific disciplines for vocabulary, insights, and theories (1992, 355-68). In particular, he notes that "Copernican astronomy preserved the basic aims and principles of astronomy as it had been practiced since Ptolemy." (1992, 368).

Realism/anti-realism and the "Science Wars"

Lindberg's position, applied analogously to the debates between modernity and postmodernity, would likewise point towards a synthesis or middle ground that includes elements of both views. In fact, those familiar with the "realism/anti-realism" debate in the philosophy of science[25] and, more broadly, the "Science Wars" of the 1980s and 1990s, will recognize here precisely the debates between the social constructivists (including some feminists and postmodernists) who, at the extreme, argued the anti-realism view that *all* claims to objectivity were invalidated by the emergence of quantum mechanics, relativity theory, the role of subjectivity in the construction of knowledge, etc.—and those who defended at least modified (i.e., "post-positivist") realist views and conceptions of objectivity. In the minds of many, this debate was settled firmly on the side of the natural sciences by Alan Sokal's brilliant spoof on postmodernist abuse of the new sciences, accepted and published as a serious essay by the journal *Social Text* in 1996.[26]

Out of these debates, as a final version of an *either/or* between modernity and postmodernity, a number of prominent theorists have proposed middle ground *epistemologies* that synthesize elements of each. For example, Sandra Harding develops precisely an extensive middle ground between the poles of postmodernist relativism (a frequent—but not necessary—outcome of stressing the role of the subject in the construction of knowledge) and classical positivism: her position acknowledges both (post-Kuhnian) feminist and postcolonial perspectives *and* "some of the still immensely valuable elements of the European philosophic tradition" (1998, x). In somewhat the same direction, Philip Kitcher also argues for a modified version of realism—one that further includes a plea for a *democratic* process of establishing the ethics of science (2001).

Consistent with these turns in recent *epistemology*—we can also note, finally, a correlative turn in the larger discussion regarding the relationship between science and religion. While the relevant literature is rapidly expanding[27]—here we can note here, for example, Pope John Paul II's 1998 encyclical *Fides et ratio* (Faith and reason) as a recent articulation of Catholic teaching on the complementary relationship between science and religion. Barbara Brown Taylor (2000) provides a recent Protestant expression of this complementarity. Perhaps most ambitiously, Henry Rosemont, Jr., seeks to extend scientific naturalism beyond the Abrahamic religions (Judaism, Christianity, and Islam) to the non-Abrahamic traditions, most especially Confucianism (2001).[28]

In sum, *complementary* relationships between reason and faith have been the norm throughout much of the Ancient, Medieval, Renaissance, and early Modern worlds—with the notable exception of modern Cartesian dualism and the 19th century oppositions between an emerging North American fundamentalism vis-à-vis positivism in the sciences. In particular, the dualistic opposition between fideism and positivism in the last third of the 19th century can be tied specifically to Darwin and the reactions his *Origins of the Species* evoked between apologists for both science and religion (Wertheim 1998). But just as we've seen a more recent shift from dualistic oppositions between modernity and postmodernity in the realism/anti- realism debates and Science Wars—we can also note a (re)turn to the more *complementary* understandings of the relationship between science and religion with regard to the specific discussion of evolution, So, for example, Kenneth Miller (2000) stands as an important recent example to conjoin religious commitment with the claims and implications of evolutionary theory. His understanding of the faith-reason relationship, in particular, directly reflects that of the Medieval natural philosophers, for whom discovering the truth about nature, as the Creation of God, was to thereby better understand something of the Creator:

> Each of the great Western monotheistic traditions sees God as truth, love, and knowledge. This should mean that each and every increase in our understanding of the natural world is a step toward God and not, as many people assume, a step away. If faith and reason are both gifts from God, then they should play complementary, not conflicting, roles in our struggle to understand the world around us. As a scientist and as a Christian, that is exactly what I believe. True knowledge comes only from a combination of faith and reason. (267)

To sum up: just as the Medievals turned from the dualism of the doctrine of the two-fold truth to Thomas' understanding of the ways in which science and religion *complement* one another—so there are a range of recent turns from positivist and fundamentalist dualisms to more complementary views.

Past + Future?

Finally, we can return from these large frameworks developed especially in the history and philosophy of science to our contributors. In light of the large turns we have seen—what amount to *returns* to a complementarity between religion and science that predominates throughout Western traditions—Facione's final posture, as it likewise endorses a complementarity between science and religion, faith and reason, thus coheres with these important contemporary turns. By the same token, the integration of at least some forms critical thinking with the life of faith is established by Hardmeier, Eubanks, the Bachmanns, and Dodson Gray. Especially in light of views such as Miller's on faith and evolution—Mwase's example of bible study materials that encourage an openness to multiple views on debate between creation and evolution is timely indeed. And, *contra* the more extreme postmodern rejections of reason and critical thinking as understood in the Western tradition from Aristotle through Hintikka, Peirce, and Polanyi—we may likewise find ourselves on more secure middle grounds, such as those marked out here especially by Mullins, Talstra, and Lindemann.

In historical terms, we may find ourselves no longer living in a modern or even postmodern era. Rather, as these manifold turns from the dualisms at work in both modernity and postmodernity suggest, we may find ourselves enjoying a new Renaissance, i.e., a time of unprecedented cultural flows that encourage precisely the synthetic and complementary approaches apparent precisely in Erasmus' Christian humanism—the humanism that introduced critical approaches to the biblical text in important ways.[29] In this light, critical thinking and the Bible in the age of new media will not represent so much a radical departure from all that has gone before, but rather an extension of modes of critical reading and interpretation into the new opportunities made possible by the new technologies. Rather than an *either/or* between the ages of literacy and print vs. the secondary orality of electronic culture, we may expect to emerge instead a *both/and* that sustains and enhances the literacies and logics of manuscript and print while developing new forms reading and analysis suited to electronic media— i.e., a both/and presaged by our contributors in a number of ways. In particular, especially if we retain our sense of ourselves as *embodied* creatures who are inextricably interwoven with others as members of communities and communities of faith—we may heed the concerns expressed specifically by Lindvall and Palmer that we not be overwhelmed by the "hegemony of the visual" and the dissolution of the self in cyberspace. On this trajectory, rather, the ideal will be to exploit the possibilities of the new media, most enthusiastically represented here by Voelz and Witherington, while avoiding the Gnostic error of seeking liberation in *opposition* to the body in a cyberspace that offers *information*—but, in its isolation from embodiment and community, perhaps not *wisdom*.

Notes

1. My thanks to Peter Meidlinger (Literature Department, Drury University) for helping me identify the source of this quote.

2. I am delighted to acknowledge here the extraordinary contributions of "my" co-organizers, Naomi Lauture and Scott Elliott, to the conference. In addition, as overseeing the larger American Bible Society "New Paradigms Project," as including this conference and volume, Dr. Robert Hodgson provided invaluable direction and inspiration. By all accounts, the conference was an extraordinary event, in part because of the vision, energy, and skill of Ms. Lauture, Mr. Elliott, and Dr. Hodgson; in part because of the exceptional quality of the presentations offered by conference participants; and in part because of the generous support of the American Bible Society. I am profoundly grateful to all who were involved and came to New York City to engage in such an exceptional and productive discussion. I very much hope that these essays will convey to our readers much of the insight and energy we enjoyed that day.

Finally, my thanks also to Paul Soukup, S.J., who kindly provided most able assistance in the final formatting and indexing of this volume.

3. For a more extensive discussion of these positions and views, as placed within the context of the history of the faith-reason debate in the Western tradition and framed within traditional categories in philosophy of religion, see especially Helm (1999). In particular, Helm's account of the various postures possible regarding the relationship between faith and reason, as we shall see, is consistent with those developed here by Facione. We should notice especially that what Facione will here call the "Faithful Servant" posture of reason vis-^-vis faith more broadly stands as part of the Augustinian tradition of "faith seeking understanding" (Helm 1999, 10f.).

4. Stephen Jay Gould, as he argues for what he hopes will be a posture that will end the battles between especially creationists and evolutionists, points out that *Inherit the Wind* involved more than one distortion of history. In particular, relying on more recent scholarship, he endorses the view that William Jennings

Bryan's opposition to evolutionary theory had less to do with a commitment to fundamentalist literalism and more to do with Bryan's concern that evolutionary theory "...would weaken the cause of democracy and strengthen class pride and the power of wealth"—a fear more than justified by the rise of Social Darwinism, including its use among German intellectuals to justify war and domination (1999, 155).

Gould's own proposal for a solution to the creationism/evolution controversy—his so-called NOMA, or "non-overlapping magisteria"—appears to be a contemporary version of the Medieval doctrine of the two-fold truth, i.e., another expression of dualism, in contrast with both Medieval (Thomist) and contemporary views of more complementary relationships between faith and reason. We will discuss these views more fully in the conclusion.

5. Indeed, Dartmouth philosopher Bernhard Gert likes to ask people if they believe that society would be a more moral place if we all followed the Ten Commandments. Of course, many people agree. He then points out that the Ten Commandments presume the moral legitimacy of slavery—i.e., the fourth commandment on keeping the Sabbath includes male and female servants (along with the cattle) as those who are not to work on the Sabbath, and the tenth commandment includes male and female servants (again, along with the cattle as well as the neighbor's wife) among those "things" we are not to covet.

6. This sense of a critical reason that is capable of reinterpreting biblical commands in light of new circumstances and knowledge is powerfully captured in the famous Talmudic story of the debate between Rabbi Eliezer and Rabbi Joshua (Babylonian Talmud, Bava Metzia 59b). In his exasperation with his opponents, Rabbi Eliezer finally calls on the divine voice for support — i.e., the voice of God that last spoke at Sinai as God gave the Torah to Moses. The divine voice, indeed, is heard—and in support of Rabbi Eliezer's interpretation of the Law on all points. Nonetheless, Rabbi Joshua, quoting Deut. 30:12, argues that since "...the Torah had already been given at Mount Sinai; we pay no attention to a heavenly voice, because Thou has long since written in the Torah at Mount Sinai, After the majority must one incline (Exod. 23.2)." Far from being the occasion of angry rebuke by the Divine, the story continues to say that God then "laughed [with joy]...saying, "My sons have defeated Me, My sons have defeated Me." In short, our using reason to interpret and apply the Commandments in the new contexts of our own time is part of our "growing up" as children of God. ("A Heavenly Voice" 2000).

7. New Testament scholar Amy-Jill Levine emphasizes that what Christians call the Old Testament is not simply another name for the collection of books drawn from the TaNaKh (i.e., the Torah [the five books of Moses], the Nevi'im [the Prophets], and the Kethuvim [the Writings]). As this listing makes clear, the order of the books, first of all, is different from the order of the "Old Testament" in Christian Bibles (which in turn vary between Orthodox, Catholic, and Protestant traditions—see the HarperCollins Study Bible [1993], xxxvii-xl, for a handy comparison). Levine notes

> Jews use the TaNaK; Christians read the 'Old Testament.' Jews read from scrolls; Christians read from codices. Jews conjoin Torah and Haftarah; Christians pair OT with NT. (Levine, 2001)

While it may seem more neutral to refer to the TaNaKh as, for example, the Hebrew Bible - unless these differences are noted at the same time, "Hebrew Bible" may in fact simply refer to the Old Testament, i.e., the books and their ordering as found in Christian Bibles. Instead, Levine writes,

> I'd rather keep these as separate texts, with separate teleologies and separate hermeneutics. Having acknowledged the differences makes it easier, again at least for me, to see where church and synagogue can agree and can agree to disagree. (Levine, 2001)

8. We will explore this theory much more fully in the conclusion, beginning with reference to a representative overview in Chesebro and Bertelson (1996).

9. Stephen D. O'Leary and Brenda Brasher have taken up this thematic—primarily epistemological—distinction in their discussion of contemporary online versions of Gnosticism (what I have called 'cybergnosticism'), defined as "the mystical quest for the knowledge that saves" (1996, 262). They draw here on the physicist Heinz Pagels:

> Some intellectual prophets have declared the end of the age of knowledge and the beginning of the age of information. Information tends to drive out knowledge. Information is just signs and numbers, while knowledge has semantic value. What we want is knowledge, but what we often get is information. It is a sign of the times that many people cannot tell the difference between information and knowledge, not to mention wisdom, which even knowledge tends to drive out. (1988, 49, cited in O'Leary and Brasher 1996, 262).

We will return to the topic of cyber-gnosticism in the conclusion.

10. In the Anglo-American literature on computer-mediated communication, the role of commercialization in reshaping early, especially libertarian assumptions regarding the individual and his/her interactions on the Internet, is only starting to receive serious attention, e.g., Bolter's observation that in multiple ways, "the Web is reaffirming the construction of the individual as a consumer of popular culture" (2000). In this light, Talstra reflects a more characteristically European sensibility—e.g., the long-standing critiques of commercialization developed by the Frankfurt School of Critical Theory, etc. (cf. Ess 2002a).

11. See Chesebro and Bertelson (1996) for a very useful overview of this theory—one, however, that reiterates the technological determinism I call into

question here (cf. Ess 1999). For a helpful overview of more recent critiques of especially the notion that the stages of orality, literacy, and print are as sharply distinct and opposed to one another as especially postmodern proponents have assumed, see Sveningsson (2001), especially her discussion of research showing that CMC technologies—specifically chat rooms—issue in forms of communication that are hybrids between oral and written forms of communication (26-44). Mike Sandbothe, an otherwise thoroughly postmodernist media philosopher, expresses this same point with the phrases "scripturalization of [oral] language" and "[oral] verbalization of writing" as characterizing the use of language in chat rooms (1999, 429). For her part, Sveningsson wants to argue, however, that "Computer-mediated communication may instead be regarded as a completely different form that stands alone beside both speech and written text" (2001, 44).

12. Fred Craddock (2001) has provided a striking example of the latter—one that directly violates basic theological commitments. Referring to a major "mega-church" whose services are televised, he noted that there was no communion as part of worship. He asked: why the omission of communion? It was explained that the visual imagery of people passing communion plates and cups was "boring" and a waste of air time. Communion was available for those interested—but not as part of worship.

Whatever one's views on the importance of communion, this seems a clear example of how the requirements and priorities of a communications medium—in this case, the priority of the visual for television—reshaped worship practices. For those who share Craddock's Christian Church (Disciples of Christ) belief in the centrality of communion—so much so that it is the centerpiece of worship every Sunday—this is a striking example of the requirements of a communication technology inappropriately overriding a central doctrinal belief and worship practice.

13. Such technological determinism is apparent especially in one of the foundational documents of postmodernism, namely Lyotard's The Postmodern Condition (1984). It is echoed in the most significant proponents of hypertext and CMC technologies as facilitating such postmodern understandings as the fragmentation and decentering of identity—as well as the postmodern hope that, in contrast with the apparent tendency of modern regimes to self-destruct into authoritarianism, democracy would be realized and expanded precisely through the extension of shared computer networks and databases (e.g., Bolter 1984, 1991, and Landow 1992, 1994). Technological determinism, finally, can be seen in one of the most significant documents of computer ethics, Gorniak-Kocikowska (1996). For additional discussion, see Ess 2001a, 2002c.

Criticism of technological determinism in the literatures of philosophy of technology and CMC is extensive: see Ess 2001a, ftn. 14, 33f. Here it will suffice to mention the general discussions in Ihde (1993) and Shrader-Frechette and Westra (1997).

14. In philosophical terms, this middle ground is articulated by the soft determinism represented by Don Ihde (1975).

15. Indeed, it is arguable that the Cartesian dualism apparent in these shared hopes for liberation in cyberspace derives from the earliest work on Artificial Intelligence (AI). More precisely, the debate we are examining here between Cartesian dualism, on the one hand, and views that rather stress the connection between mind and body, on the other hand, closely echoes this debate among the foundational figures of AI—with Douglas Engelbart and Winograd and Flores (1987) emphasizing precisely the importance of embodied knowledge and a connectivist epistemology. See Bardini (2000) and Ess (2002b) for further discussion.

16. Early on, Gibson describes his main character, Case, after he had had his nervous system dramatically attacked so as to erase his virtuoso skills as a "cowboy," a hacker who worked by projecting his disembodied consciousness into cyberspace:

> For Case, who'd lived for the bodiless exultation of cyberspace, it was the Fall. In the bars he'd frequented as a cowboy hotshot, the elite stance involved a certain relaxed contempt for the flesh. The body was meat. Case fell into the prison of his own flesh. (6)

The theological language—and its reference to a later, Augustinian reading of the 2nd Genesis creation story that stresses precisely the contempt of sexuality and body—is perhaps not accidental. In a later episode, an Artificial Intelligence attempts to distract Case from his primary mission by constructing for him an alternative space, one inhabited by a former girlfriend. Echoing the role of Eve, as interpreted by Augustine, she becomes the temptress who occasions his fall:

> There was a strength that ran in her, something he'd known in Night City and held there, been held by it, held for a while away from time and death.... It belonged, he knew—he remembered— as she pulled him down, to the meat, the flesh the cowboys mocked. It was a vast thing, beyond knowing, a sea of information coded in spiral and pheromone, infinite intricacy that only the body, in its strong blind way, could ever read. (239)

For an historical overview of the emergence of diverse traditions of interpretation of the 2nd Genesis creation story, see Ess (1995).

17. Jay David Bolter—as part of his own shift from his earlier, more dualistic postmodern enthusiasm to a more moderate sense of the differences and connections between the Age of New Media and earlier eras—cites Allucquere Roseanne Stone's critique of Cartesian dualism at work in especially the hopes for online communities as radically divorced from embodied identity and the offline world (1991, 113, cited in Bolter, 2001). See also Sobchack (1995).

18. Somewhat more fully:

> Both Catholicism and some Protestant traditions emphasize pre-
> cisely the goodness of the body and Creation as they develop a
> Christology which argues that when God takes on human form
> (the specific meaning of in-carnation—"becoming flesh"), the
> human body is thus reaffirmed as sacred. These traditions, of
> course, fully endorse a notion of the soul as distinct from the body,
> and the correlative belief in an afterlife and salvation as entailing
> (but not exclusively so) the everlasting life of the soul as opposed
> to the mortal body. But by foregrounding such doctrines of incar-
> nation, they reassert something of an originally Jewish affirmation
> of the goodness of body, sexuality, and life "in this world."
> Moreover, as Catholicism and some strands of Protestantism stress
> incarnation, they further stress that God is known in important
> ways through the material world, not against it. That is, just as the
> disciples knew Jesus "in the breaking of the bread" (Luke 24.30-
> 35), so Catholics experience the real presence of the Divine in the
> bread and wine really consumed by embodied creatures in com-
> munion. While Protestants, of course, insist that the bread and
> wine are symbols, not really the body and blood of Christ, com-
> munion remains a central sacrament, one that brings the commu-
> nity of believers together through a ritualized common meal. Even
> for Protestants, communion is a sacrament of real bread and real
> wine (or grape juice) that represents an embodied Lord who brings
> the believers together as embodied creatures in a face-to-face
> community. (Ess 2001b)

(As a reminder: we have seen these issues raised in this volume by especially the Bachmans' questions regarding online communities, Witherington's
discussion of "incarnational learning," and in Palmer's and Talstra's discussion
of embodied communities of faith as crucial environments for acquiring the
skills and habits of critical Bible reading.) Still more broadly, this affirmation of
the material and the bodily is part of the larger prophetic tradition of Judaism
and Christianity, and Islam—

> the call to imitate a God who liberates human beings as embodied
> beings in history (the Exodus event), a God whose Presence
> among us is marked by the freeing of slaves and prisoners
> (Leviticus 25), and to form a community characterized by the
> elimination of all social distinctions (Galatians 3.28), a communi-
> ty of shared human prosperity that will not be bought at the cost of
> exploiting nature, but rather will arise precisely in a harmony with
> the natural order that ostensibly reflects the Creator's intentions at
> the beginning of the world (Isaiah 11.1-9). This prophetic vision

follows from an essentially optimistic vision of the world—one that affirms first of all the goodness of all Creation, including body, sexuality, and community among the human, natural, and divine domains. But as cybergnosticism replicates the Gnostic disdain of the material world—what Nietzsche calls "the metaphysics of the hangman" ([1888] 1988: 500)—it emphasizes a contempt for the created order that seeks escape from rather than fulfillment in the material world. If our basic ontology, by presuming a radical difference between body and soul, thereby locates salvation in flight from the world of body, community, and nature - then clearly we are not likely to endorse the prophetic insistence on doing justice (Micah 6.8) and making righteousness flow like an everlasting stream (Amos 5.24). (Ess 2001b)

Along these lines, theologian Tex Sample (1998) takes up incarnational theology as central to his discussion of the implications of postmodernism—as marked by the rising importance of participatory spectacle, performance, music and dance—for the church (see esp. pp. 105f., 108). Contra the 1990s rush to liberation in cyberspace, Sample instead argues for worship styles now familiar as "celebration" or "contemporary" worship that include live rock bands, images projected on screens, etc.,—i.e., worship and liturgy as practiced by embodied believers who come together in the real world rather than online. See also Brenda Brasher's recent work (2001) on these issues.

19. Here, of course, we can only barely sketch out the larger history of the relationship between science and religion. In addition to the sources we are about to review—Kristen (Buck) Strickland has developed an accessible and more detailed overview of this history, organized by whether a figure favors a more dualistic or more complementary view, as a webpage: <http://www.drury.edu/ess/philsci/Religion_and_science.html>.

20. See note 6, above.

21. See Sorrell (1988) for an extensive analysis of Francis' understanding of nature and its impact on subsequent art and more scientific approaches to nature. It is also a striking fact that many of the most significant figures in the continuation and development of natural science—including Bacon (ca. 1220-ca. 1292), Duns Scotus (ca. 1266-1308), and William of Ockham (ca. 1285-1347)—pursued their work as members of the Franciscan order. And, as Lindberg points out, while Grosseteste (ca. 1168-1253) was not himself a member of the Franciscan order, he was "...the first lecturer in the Franciscan school at Oxford, thereby exercising a formative influence on the intellectual life of the Order,"—including the incorporation of Platonic, Neoplatonic, and Aristotelian views (1992, 224). See Lindberg's discussion, however, of the historical debate as to how far these developments in the 12th —14th centuries worked for and/or against the development of experimental science (1992, 240-44).

22. A technical but important issue here is Thomas' use of analogical predication as part of his establishing an epistemology and metaphysics that replaces dualistic oppositions with complementary syntheses. See, to begin with, Summa Theologiae I, Part 1, Question 13. Here, Thomas builds on Aristotle's use of analogy (derived in turn from Plato)—thereby instantiating at the base of his systematic metaphysics and epistemology Greek reason in a complementary relationship with Christian faith.

23. We can also notice here that the theology of these astronomers included a Pythagorean emphasis on the nobility of the sun—which, transposed into the framework of Christianity, meant for Kepler that the sun, as an icon for God, must hence be at the center of things (Alioto 1993, 188f.). For more on these figures and their religious sensibilities, see their treatments in Ronald C. Pine, ch. 5 (online version) <http://www.hcc.hawaii.edu/~pine/Chapter5.htm> and Jones (1969, 91-98).

In these directions, we can also note that Wertheim likewise sees a strong continuity between Medieval conceptions of space and those at work in our discussions of cyberspace (1999).

24. This of course forces the question: does our new science—the sciences of Quantum Mechanics, Relativity Theory, Chaos theory, etc.—force quite the "revolution" in knowledge that especially postmodern proponents have argued? Or is there a greater continuity between these relatively recent branches of physics and mathematics? Briefly, the "revolutionary" implications are indeed enormous—especially as they turn us from an atomistic and mechanical conception of the universe (17th-19th centuries) to one that emphasizes complementarity and interconnectedness (see especially Peat, 1990) At the same time, however, it is simply mistaken to understand these "new" sciences as radically discontinuous with the scientific methods and insights of Newton et al. Rather, the "classical" universe of Newtonian mechanics and atomism represent a special case of the more encompassing laws of Quantum Mechanics and Relativity. Similarly, chaos theory does not defy classical mechanism and determinism—it rather limits, on deterministic grounds, how far one can predict the outcomes of nonlinear dynamic systems. Echoing Lindberg, then, it is at least arguable that we should see the relationship between modern Newtonian science and "postmodern" science as a relationship of complementarity—i.e., of both continuity and difference—rather than, as postmodernists often claim, a relationship of radical discontinuity.

25. For representative readings and discussion, see: Chapter 2, 9, Curd and Cover (1998, 83-253, 1049-1289); Chapter 10, Klee (1997, 206-239); Part V, Kourany (1998, 339- 440).

26. See Sokal and Bricmont (1998), including their specific analyses of such premier postmodernists as Lacan, Kristeva, Irigaray, Latour, Baudrillard, and others.

27. Beyond Helm's helpful introduction and anthology (1999), additional useful readings in the philosophy of religion are collected in Peterson et al

(1997). Schick has collected a series of essays on science and religion oriented towards issues in philosophy of science (chapter 8, 2000, 312-358).

28. For a more focused discussion of critical realism, scientific naturalism, complementarity, and other contemporary approaches, see Gregersen and Van Huyssteen (1998). Ursula Goodenough (1998, 2000) stands as one of the most significant contemporary proponents of scientific naturalism—a view that seeks to incorporate religious sensibilities of the world as sacred, coupled with the ethical implications of that sacredness (see also Goodenough and Woodruff 2001).

29. Stephen Toulmin (1990) develops the historical groundwork and important arguments for our reconnecting with the Renaissance in these ways. First of all, he emphasizes what I have called the complementary relationship between faith and reason—manifest here in Erasmus' Christian humanism as it conjoins critical thinking and the Bible (cf. Toulmin1990, 25)—in the figures of Newton, Boyle, and Leibniz, whose "revolutionary" discoveries in mathematics and the natural sciences were fueled in good measure by primary *theological* commitments (Toulmin 1990, 20f.).

Moreover, Toulmin argues for recovering a Renaissance appreciation for Aristotle's *practical* philosophy—one that includes reviving the Renaissance/ Aristotelian conjunction of logos, ethos, and pathos—in contrast with Cartesian dualism that opposes logos and pathos (20, 26-31, 186ff.). In this volume, the Bachman's model of interrogative thinking stands as a concrete example of just such a conjunction (see esp. pp. 123f.), and thereby can be seen to contribute to the Renaissance/Aristotelian revival envisioned by Toulmin.

For discussion of additional parallels with the Renaissance and their implications, see Ropolyi (2000), Mehl (2000), and Ess (2002b). As other expressions of continuities with earlier eras, see Pierre Levy's connections between cyberspace and the Medieval and Catholic worldviews (1997) and David Noble's comparisons with the Protestant Reformation (1999).

For discussion of additional parallels with the Renaissance and their implications, see Ropolyi (2000), Mehl (2000), and Ess (2002b). As other expressions of continuities with earlier eras, see Pierre Levy's connections between cyberspace and the Medieval and Catholic worldviews (1997) and David Noble's comparisons with the Protestant Reformation (1999).

References

A Heavenly Voice (Bava Metzia 59b, Babylonian Talmud). In *The Soul of the Text: An Anthology of Jewish Literature*, 93f. Chicago: Great Books Foundation, 2000.

Alioto, Anthony M. 1993. *A History of Western Science*, 2nd edition. Englewood Cliffs, NJ: Prentice-Hall.

Aquinas, Thomas. 1969. *Summa Theologiae: Volume 1: The Existence of God. Part One: Questions 1-13.* New York: Image Books.

Bardini, T. 2000. *Bootstrapping: Douglas Engelbart, Coevolution, and the Origins of Personal Computing.* Stanford: Stanford University Press.

Baym, Nancy K. 1995. The Emergence of Community in Computer-Mediated Communication. In Steven G. Jones (ed.), *CyberSociety: Computer-Mediated Communication and Community,* 138-63.. Thousand Oaks, CA: Sage.

_____. Interpersonal Life Online. 2002. In L. Lievrouw. & S. Livingstone (Eds.), *Handbook of New Media,* 62-76. Thousand Oaks: Sage.

Becker, Barbara. 2000. Cyborg, Agents and Transhumanists. *Leonardo* 33 (5): 361-65.

_____. 2001. Sinn und Sinnlichkeit: Anmerkungen zur Eigendynamik und Fremdheit des eigenen Leibes [Sense and Sensibility: Remarks on the Distinctive Dynamics and Strangeness of One's Own Body]. In L. Jäger (ed.), *Mentalität und Medialität,* 35-46. Münich: Fink Verlag.

Bolter, Jay David. 1984. *Turing's Man: Western Culture in the Computer Age.* Chapel Hill: University of North Carolina Press.

_____ 1991. *Writing Space: The Computer, Hypertext, and the History of Writing.* Hillsdale, NJ: Lawrence Erlbaum.

_____ 2001. Identity. In T. Swiss (ed.), *Unspun,* 17-29. New York: New York University Press. Available online: <http://www.nyupress.nyu.edu/ unspun/samplechap.html.>

Borgmann, Albert. 1984. *Technology and the Character of Contemporary Life.* Chicago: University of Chicago Press.

_____. 1999. *Holding Onto Reality: The Nature of Information at the Turn of the Millennium.* Chicago: University of Chicago Press.

Brasher, Brenda. 2001. *Give Me that Online Religion.* San Francisco: Jossey-Bass. See also http://www.muc.edu/~brashebe/online%20religion.htm.

Chesebro, James, and Dale A. Bertelsen. 1996. *Analyzing Media: Communication Technologies as Symbolic and Cognitive Systems.* New York: Guilford Press.

Craddock, Fred. 2001. Sermon, Board of Extension (Videotape 23). General Synod/Assembly of the United Church of Christ and Christian Church/Disciples of Christ. Kansas City, Missouri, 13 July.

Curd, Martin and J. A. Cover. 1998. *Philosophy of Science: The Central Issues.* New York: Norton.

Dahan, M. 1999. National Security and Democracy on the Internet in Israel, *Javnost-the Public,* VI (4), 67- 77.

Descartes, Rene. [1637] 1972. Discourse on the Method of Rightly Conducting the Reason in the Sciences. In *The Philosophical Works of Descartes,* Elizabeth S. Haldane and G.R.T. Ross, trans., 81-143. Vol. I. Cambridge: Cambridge University Press.

_____. [1641] 1972. Meditations on First Philosophy. In *The Philosophical Works of Descartes*, Elizabeth S. Haldane and G.R.T. Ross, trans., 133-99. Vol. I. Cambridge: Cambridge University Press.

Dreyfus, Hubert. 2001. *On the Internet*. New York: Routledge.

Eisenstein, Elizabeth. 1983. *The Printing Revolution in Early Modern Europe*. Cambridge. Cambridge University Press.

Ess, Charles. 1995. Reading Adam and Eve: Re-Visions of the Myth of Woman's Subordination to Man. In Marie M. Fortune and Carol J. Adams (eds.), *Violence Against Women and Children: A Christian Theological Sourcebook*, 92-120. New York: Continuum Press.

_____. 1999. Critique in Communication and Philosophy: an Emerging Dialogue? *Research in Philosophy and Technology*, Vol. 18. Pp. 219-226.

_____. 2000. We are the Borg: the Web as Agent of Cultural Assimilation or Renaissance? <www.ephilosopher.com/120100/philtech/philtech.htm>

_____. 2001a. Introduction: What's Culture Got to Do with It? Cultural Collisions in the Electronic Global Village, Creative Interferences, and the Rise of Culturally-Mediated Computing. In Charles Ess (ed.), *Culture, Technology, Communication: Towards an Intercultural Global Village*, 1-50. Albany, NY: State University of New York Press.

_____. 2001b. *The Word online? Text and image, authority and spirituality in the Age of the Internet*. Special issue, "The Net: New Apprentices and Old Masters / Nouveaux Horizons, Vielles Hgmonies," *Mots Pluriels et grands themes de notre temps. Revue l'ectronique de Lettres ^ caractre international*. 19 (Octobre/October 2001). <http://www.arts.uwa.edu.au/MotsPluriels/MP1901ce.html.>

_____. 2002a. Borgmann and the Borg: Consumerism vs. *Holding on to Reality*. A review essay on Albert Borgmann's *Holding on to Reality*, special issue of *Techne*. <http://scholar.lib.vt.edu/ejournals/SPT/v6n1/ess.html>

_____. 2002b. Communication and Interaction. In Luciano Floridi (ed.), *The Blackwell Guide to the Philosophy of Computing and Information*. Oxford: Blackwell.

_____. 2002c. Cultures in Collision: Philosophical Lessons from Computer-Mediated Communication, *Metaphilosophy* 33 (1/2): 1-25.

Ess, Charles and Fay Sudweeks. 2001. On the Edge: Cultural Barriers and Catalysts to IT Diffusion among Remote and Marginalized Communities, *new media and society* 3(3): 259-69.

Ess, Charles, Robert Hodgson, and Scott Elliott (eds.) 2000. *New Voices, New Views: Thinking about Bible Study in the Twenty-First Century*. (Conference proceedings). The American Bible Society, Research Center for Scripture and Media.

Facione, Peter. 1990. *Critical Thinking: A Statement of Expert Consensus for Purposes of Educational Assessment and Instruction*. American

Philosophical Association, "The Delphi Report." ERIC document, ED 315-423. Millbrae, California: The California Academic Press.

Gibson, William. 1986. *Neuromancer*. New York: Ace Books.

Goodenough, Ursula. 1998. *The Sacred Depths of Nature*. New York, Oxford: Oxford University Press.

_____. 2001. Vertical and Horizontal Transcendence, *Zygon: Journal of Religion and Science* 36 (1): 21- 31

Goodenough, Ursula and Paul Woodruff. 2001. Mindful Virtue, Mindful Reverence, *Zygon: Journal of Religion and Science* 36 (4): 585-95.

Gould, Stephen Jay. 1999. *Rocks of Ages: Science and Religion in the Fullness of Life*. New York: Ballantine.

Gorniak-Kocikowska, Krystyna. 1996. The Computer Revolution and the Problem of Global Ethics, *Science and Engineering Ethics* 2: 177-190.

Gregersen, Niels Henrik and J. Wentzel Van Huyssteen. 1998. *Rethinking Theology and Science: Six Models for the Current Dialogue*. Grand Rapids, MI: Eerdmans.

The HarperCollins Study Bible. 1993. New Revised Standard Version, with the Apocryphal/Deuterocanonical Books. A New Annotated Edition by the Society of Biblical Literature. Wayne A. Meeks, Jouette M. Bassler, Werner E. Lemke, Susan Niditch, and Eileen M. Schuller (eds.). New York: HarperCollins.

Harding, Sandra. 1998. *Is Science Multicultural? Postcolonialisms, Feminisms, and Epistemologies*. Bloomington and Indianapolis: Indiana University Press.

Harris, Roger, Poline Bala, Peter Songan, Elaine Khoo Guat Lien, and Tingang Trang. 2001. Challenges and Opportunities in Introducing Information and Communication Technologies to the Kelabit Community of North Central Borneo, *new media and society* 3 (3): 271-296.

Hayles, Katherine. 1999. *How We Became Posthuman: Virtual Bodies in Cybernetics, Literature, and Informatics*. Chicago: University of Chicago Press.

Heaton, Lorna. 2001. Preserving Communication Context: Virtual Workspace and Interpersonal Space in Japanese CSCW. In Charles Ess (ed.), *Culture, Technology, Communication: Towards an Intercultural Global Village*. 213-240. Albany, NY: State University of New York Press.

Helm, Paul. 1999. *Faith and Reason*. New York: Oxford University Press.

Hillis, Ken. 1999. *Digital Sensations: Space, Identity and Embodiment in Virtual Reality*. Minneapolis, London: University of Minnesota Press.

Hongladarom, Soraj. 2001. Global Culture, Local Cultures and the Internet: The Thai Example. In Charles Ess (ed.), *Culture, Technology, Communication: Towards an Intercultural Global Village*, 307-24. Albany, NY: State University of New York Press.

Ihde, Don. 1975. A Phenomenology of Man-Machine Relations. In W. Feinberg and H. Rosemont, Jr. (eds.), *Work, Technology, and Education:*

Dissenting Essays in the Intellectual Foundations of American Education, 186 -203. Chicago: University of Illinois Press.

_____. 1993. *Philosophy of Technology: An Introduction.* New York: Paragon House.

Pope John Paul II. 1998. *Fides et ratio* (Faith and Reason), Encyclical Letter to the Bishops of the Catholic Church. Available online: http://www.cin.org/jp2/fides.html.

Jones, W. T. 1969. *A History of Western Philosophy. III: Hobbes to Hume*, 2nd edition. New York: Harcourt Brace Jovanovich.

Kitcher, Philip. 2001. *Science, Truth, and Democracy.* Oxford: Oxford University Press.

Klee, Robert. 1997. *Introduction to the Philosophy of Science: Cutting Nature at Its Seams.* New York: Oxford University Press.

Kourany, Janet. 1998. *Scientific Knowledge: Basic Issues in the Philosophy of Science.* 2nd edition. Belmont, CA: Wadsworth.

Landow, George. 1992. *Hypertext: the Convergence of Contemporary Critical Theory and Technology.* Baltimore: Johns Hopkins University Press.

_____ (Ed.) 1994. *Hyper/Text/Theory.* Baltimore: Johns Hopkins University Press.

Levine, Amy-Jill. 2001. Personal communication.

Levy, Pierre. 1997. *Collective Intelligence: Mankind's Emerging World in Cyberspace*, trans. Robert Bononno. New York: Plenum.

Lindberg, David C. 1992. *The Beginnings of Western Science: The European Scientific Tradition in Philosophical, Religious, and Institutional Context, 600 B.C. to A.D. 1450.* Chicago and London: University of Chicago Press.

Lyotard, J.-L. 1979 [1984]. *The Postmodern Condition: a Report on Knowledge.* G. Bennington, B. Massumi, trans. Minneapolis: University of Minnesota Press.

Mehl, James V. 2000. Drawing Parallels With the Renaissance: Late-Modernism, Postmodernism, and the Possibility of Historical Layering, *The Midwest Quarterly: A Journal of Contemporary Thought* (XLI: 4 - Summer): 401-15.

Miller, Kenneth. 2000. *Finding Darwin's God: A Scientist's Search for Common Ground between Science and Religion.* New York: Cliff Street Books.

Moravec, Hans. 1988. *Mind Children: The Future of Robot and Human Intelligence.* Cambridge: Harvard University Press.

Mullins, Phil. 1996. Sacred Text in the Sea of Texts: The Bible in North American Electronic Culture. In Charles Ess (ed.), *Philosophical Perspectives on Computer-Mediated Communication*, 271-302. Albany, NY: State University of New York Press.

_____. 2000. Notes on Bible Study, Critical Thinking and Post Critical Thought. New Voices, New Views: Thinking about Bible Study in the Twenty-First Century. A conference hosted by the Research Center for

Scripture and Media of the American Bible Society. New York City, February 11.

Negroponte, Nicholas. 1995. *being digital*. New York: Knopf, 1995.

Nietzsche, Frederick. [1888] 1988. *Twilight of the Idols*, in *The Portable Nietzsche*, edited and translated by Walter Kaufmann, 465-563. New York: Penguin Books.

Noble, David F. 1999. *The Religion of Technology: The Divinity of Man and the Spirit of Invention*. New York: Penguin.

O'Leary, Stephen D. and Brenda E. Brasher. 1996. The Unknown God of the Internet: Religious Communication from the Ancient Agora to the Virtual Forum. In Charles Ess (ed.), *Philosophical Perspectives on Computer-Mediated Communication*, 233-69. Albany, NY: State University of New York Press.

Ong, W. J. 1981. *The Presence of the Word: Some Prolegomena for Cultural and Religious History*. Minneapolis: University of Minnesota Press.

_____. 1988. *Orality and Literacy: The Technologizing of the Word*. London: Routledge.

Pagels, Heinz. 1988. *The Dreams of Reason*. New York: Simon and Schuster.

Peat, David.1990. *Einstein's Moon: Bell's Theorem and the Curious Quest for Quantum Reality*. Chicago: Contemporary Books.

Peterson, Michael, William Hasker, Bruce Reichenbach, David Basinger, eds. 1997. *Reason and Religious Belief*, 2nd edition. New York: Oxford University Press.

Pine, Ronald C. *Science and the Human Prospect*. Online edition: http://www.hcc.hawaii.edu/~pine/Book2.htm.

Rahmati, Nasrin. 2000. The Impact of Cultural Values on Computer Mediated Group Work. In Fay Sudweeks and Charles Ess (eds.), *Cultural attitudes towards technology and communication: Proceedings of the Second International Conference...Perth, Australia, 12-15 July 2000*, 257-74. School of Information Technology, Murdoch University: Perth, Australia.

Ropolyi, Laszlo. 2000. Some Theses about the Reformation of Knowledge. Internet Research 1.0: The State of the Interdiscipline (First Conference of the Association of Internet Researchers), University of Kansas, Lawrence, Sept. 17.

Rosemont, Henry. 2001. *Rationality and Religious Experience: The Continuing Relevance of the World's Spiritual Traditions*. With a Commentary by Huston Smith. Chicago and La Salle, Illinois: Open Court.

Sample, Tex. 1998. *The Spectacle of Worship in a Wired World: Electronic Culture and the Gathered People of God*. Nashville: Abingdon Press.

Sandbothe, Mike. 1999. Media Temporalities of the Internet: Philosophies of Time and Media in Derrida and Rorty, *AI and Society* 13 (4): 421-434.

Schick, Theodore. 2000. *Readings in the Philosophy of Science: From Positivism to Postmodernism*. Mountain View, CA: Mayfield.

Shrader-Frechette, Kristen, and Laura Westra (eds.). 1997. *Technology and Values.* New York: Rowman and Littlefield.

Sobchack, Vivian. 1995. Beating the Meat/Surviving the Text, or How to Get Out of This Century Alive. In Mike Featherstone and Roger Burrows (eds.), *Cyberspace/Cyberbodies /Cyberpunk: Cultures of Technological Embodiment,* 205-14. London: Sage Publications.

Sokal, Alan and Jean Bricmont. [1997] 1998. *Intellectual Impostures: Postmodern Philosophers' Abuse of Science.* London: Profile Books.

Sorrell, Roger D. 1988. *St. Francis of Assisi and Nature: Tradition and Innovation in Western Christian Attitudes toward the Environment* New York: Oxford University Press.

Stone, Allucquere Rosanne. 1991. Will The Real Body Please Stand Up?: Boundary Stories About Virtual Cultures. In Michael Benedikt (ed.), *Cyberspace: First Steps,* 81-118. Cambridge: MIT Press.

Sveningsson, Malin. 2001. *Creating a Sense of Community: Experiences from a Swedish Web Chat* (doctoral dissertation). Linköping, Sweden: The Tema Institute—Department of Communication Studies.

Sweet , Leonard. 1999. *SoulTsunami: Sink or Swim in New Millennium Culture.* Grand Rapids, Michigan: Zondervan.

Taylor, Barbara Brown. 2000. *The Luminous Web: Essays on Science and Religion.* Cambridge, Boston: Cowley.

Toulmin, Stephen. 1990. *Cosmopolis: the Hidden Agenda of Modernity.* New York: The Free Press.

Wertheim, Margaret. 1999. *The Pearly Gates of Cyberspace: A History of Space from Dante to the Internet.* New York, London: Norton.

_____. 1998. Faith and Reason. http://www.pbs.org/faithandreason/.

Wheeler, Deborah. 2001. New Technologies, Old Culture: A Look at Women, Gender, and the Internet in Kuwait. In Charles Ess (ed.), *Culture, Technology, Communication: Towards an Intercultural Global Village,* 187-212. Albany, NY: State University of New York Press.

Willard, Dallas. 1999. Jesus the Logician, *Christian Scholar's Review* 28 (Summer): 605-14.

Winograd, T. & Flores, F. 1987. *Understanding Computers and Cognition: a New Foundation for Design.* Reading, MA: Addison-Wesley.

Critical Thinking: Keynote Address

1

Reasoned Judgment and Revelation: The Relation of Critical Thinking and Bible Study

Peter A. Facione

Very few really seek knowledge in this world. Mortal or immortal, few really ask.

On the contrary, they try to wring from the unknown the answers they have already shaped in their own minds—justifications, explanations, forms of consolation without which they cannot go on.

To really ask is to open the door to the whirlwind.

The answer may annihilate the question and the questioner.

—Marius the Vampire

Reason is a light that God has kindled in the soul.
—Aristotle

Reason, however sound, has little weight with ordinary theologians. —Baruch Spinosa

For humans the impetus toward thinking is as natural as is an eagle's impetus to fly. Birds have wings and no one asks them should they fly. Yet, although humans have minds, we sometimes wonder whether or not we should think. Our research on the aspect of critical thinking called "truth-seeking" shows that many endorse the notions that some questions are too frightening to ask and that they actually seek reasons to support their preconceptions rather than evidence to the contrary. Some thoughts are simply too disturbing to be entertained, and some matters too sacred to be scientifically investigated. On the other hand, the overall disposition toward reasoned judgment is strong. Can we reconcile our natural inclination toward reasoning with the risks that cherished beliefs may be discovered to be unfounded? We are all aware that these tensions are no place more evident than in the frequent and bitter clashes between reason and religion.

It appears far easier for eagles to learn to soar than for humans to learn think well. Learning to make well-informed, reasoned judgments requires years of reflective practice, patient mentoring, and broad education. Perhaps this explains the cynicism of a William James who said, "A great many people think they are thinking when they are merely rearranging their prejudices." David Ben-Gurion commented, "Thinking is strenuous art—few practice it; and then only at rare times." Bertrand Russell suggested, "Most people would die sooner than think; in fact, they do so." Winston Churchill said "Men occasionally stumble over the truth, but most of them pick themselves up an hurry off as if nothing had happened."

Why do we humans often favor the familiar over the true? Moses Maimonides said, "Men like the opinions to which they have become accustomed, and this prevents them from finding truth, for they cling to the opinions of habit." Or is the courageous pursuit of reason and evidence wherever they may lead simply a fool's adventure fraught with hazards far more serious than mere discomfiture? The ancient fable of the boy, Icarus, who flew too close to the sun with his wings of wax and feathers, warns of the grave consequences that come from pridefully overreaching our human capabilities. Are there places where our minds should not explore, ideas that would melt our mental wings, thoughts we should not think? Is it, as Ann Rice's character, Marius the Vampire, suggests, that to truly ask is to risk the whirlwind?

Perhaps. But, eagles have wings and we have minds. For humans not to think for fear of being confounded would be akin to eagles deciding not to fly for fear of falling. Before asking how critical thinking may relate to the study of the Bible, let us first be clear on what we mean by "critical thinking," and how it functions in other aspects of life and living.

Studies of how humans think, and particularly how they conceive of the accessibility of truth, suggest that there are different levels or maturational stages of **cognitive development**. Patricia King and Karen

Kitchener, building on the earlier work of Perry, developed a seven stage model of reflective judgment For illustrative purposes we can simplify their model and add descriptive names of our own devising, as indicated in Figure 1. Most adults function in most contexts as trustfully comfortable or as committed skeptics. As we study and gain experience in an area of specialization we can become more nimble perspectivalists and, in time, skilled evaluators.

Seven Stages of Cognitive Development

(1) "The Naive Observers"—Knowledge is absolute, concrete, and available. The only proof needed is direct personal experience. Things are as they appear to be.

(2) "The Believers"—Truth may not be directly known, but all is knowable. All problems have solutions, but we must find them. Clearly, some people hold true beliefs, others don't. Authorities are the best sources of right answers.

(3) "The Trustfully Comfortable"—Authorities know everything that can be known at this point in time, but the evidence is incomplete on some things, even to authorities. So, beliefs that feel right are the ones to hold. Ultimately, the solutions to all problems will be known.

(4) "The Committed Skeptics"—All people are limited in their knowledge, and uncertainty is real. External validation of any knowledge is impossible. So-called authorities are just as limited as all the rest of us. In fact, life's problems may not be solvable at all. In reality a problem's structure, parameters, and criteria for resolution are seldom clear.

(5) "The Nimble Perspectivalists"—Facts and truth exist, but only in context. Ill-structured problems abound. Any theory or perspective is as good as any other. Knowledge is what you think from where you are. Proof and evidence are entirely domain-dependent. Unfortunately, alternative interpretations cannot be compared.

(6) "The Skilled Evaluators"—Some arguments, perspectives and theories are better than others. Uncertainty is real and context is important. But there are levels of criteria to guide evaluation. To form judgments about ill-structured problems, one must compare evidence, opinions, and arguments across contexts.

(7) "The Sage"—Knowledge contains elements of uncertainty, and opinion is subject to interpretation. Yet, justifiable claims about the relative merits of alternative arguments and claims can be made. We (not just I) can assert with justifiable confidence, that some judgments are more reasonable, warranted, justifiable, sensible, or wiser than others.

Figure 1

Just knowing that there are more advanced stages of development will not be sufficient for us to move up through the levels. Rather, the reflective realization that our assumptions about knowing are somehow inadequate leads to the kind of dissonance that opens the door to cognitive growth. With intelligence and some guidance we can learn to reason in more sophisticated ways. But we must be challenged to do so. Perhaps that is one of the greatest lessons of the Book of Job. Job is comfortable in his belief that the good will prosper and the evil will suffer misfortune. He sees himself as a blameless man, worthy of God's blessings. So when evil befalls him, Job must wrestle with his fundamental beliefs. He questions his most basic assumptions about justice, about the loyalty of friends and family, about his own virtue and godliness. The Book of Job is replete with the cognitive dissonance that the problem of evil presents to thoughtful believers. Job personifies our doubts and our fears. Ultimately faith in God's wisdom and omnipotence is presented as the wisest response. The naïve assumptions with which Job, like the rest of us, begin, cannot be sustained once they challenged and honestly evaluated in the light of that challenge.

Engaging in reasoned judgment about what to believe and what to do requires the skills and the disposition to think critically. During the decade of the 80's a great many educators and theoreticians concerned themselves with efforts to clarify the meaning of the expression "critical thinking." Certainly, the importance of critical thinking as an educational goal drove some of that effort. In 1990, after two years of intense work using the Delphi method, a working consensus among international experts from several disciplines was attained. The conceptualization was later verified independently in research involving other educators as well as government policy makers and employers.

Critical thinking is characterized as the cognitive process of forming reasoned and reflective judgments about what to believe or what to do. The process can be engaged in by an individual, or by a group of people in collaboration with one another. At the core of the process of critical thinking are the *cognitive skills of interpretation, analysis, inference, explanation, evaluation, and self-regulation.* See Figure 2.

The *disposition* toward critical thinking is the consistent internal motivation to use those skills to form reasoned judgments. This disposition can be understood in terms of seven habits of mind: *truth-seeking, open-mindedness, analyticity, systematicity, inquisitiveness, confidence in reasoning, and cognitive maturity.* See Figure 3.

Critical Thinking Cognitive Skills and Sub-Skills	
Interpretation	• Categorization
	• Decoding Sentences
	• Clarifying Meaning
Analysis	• Examining Ideas
	• Identifying Arguments
	• Analyzing Arguments
Evaluation	• Assessing Claims
	• Assessing Arguments
Inference	• Querying Evidence
	• Conjecturing Alternatives
	• Drawing Conclusions
Explanation	• Stating Results
	• Justifying Procedures
	• Presenting Arguments
Self-Regulation	• Self Examination
	• Self Correction

—The Delphi Report, 1990

Figure 2

The question for undergraduate education is how to challenge and nurture students toward the development of their critical thinking in an ever-expanding range of academic and societal contexts. The goal is to prepare students who are willing and able to think. The same question in graduate professional schools translates into the formation of reflective practitioners with sound, professional judgment. In the study of the Bible, the question becomes how to apply our God-given skills at forming reasoned judgments to the sacred writings in ways that are intellectually honest and fair-minded.

One of the best illustrations of the integrated use of critical thinking skills, along with a display of excellent critical thinking dispositions, appears in the film *Apollo 13*. The scene that many may recall is the challenge issued to the ground engineers of NASA when they were told to design a filter to recycle oxygen for the stranded crew in their disabled lunar module. The problem was well defined, yet entirely novel and very high-stakes. The engineers were told exactly what supplies and equipment the astronauts had on board and had to make the filter using only those things.

But a scene that may be even more illustrative is the one during which the problem is initially identified and framed. For if people began

> **The Disposition Toward Critical Thinking**
> **Seven Factor Analysis**
>
> **Truth-seeking**: Courageously desiring of best knowledge in any context, even if such knowledge fails to support or may undermine one's preconceptions, beliefs or self-interests.
> **Open-Mindedness**: Tolerant of divergent views, self-monitoring for possible bias.
> **Analyticity**: Demanding the application of reason and evidence, alert to problematic situations, inclined to anticipate consequences.
> **Systematicity**: Valuing organization, focus and diligence to approach problems of all levels of complexity.
> **CT Self-confidence**: Trusting of one's own reasoning skills and seeing oneself as a good thinker.
> **Inquisitiveness**: Being curious and eager to acquire knowledge and learn explanations even when the applications of that information are not immediately apparent.
> **Cognitive Maturity**: Prudence in making, suspending, or revising judgment. An awareness that multiple solutions can be acceptable. An appreciation of the need to reach closure even in the absence of complete knowledge.
>   —The California Critical Thinking Disposition Inventory
> **Figure 3**

working on the wrong problem, surely grave consequences would have resulted. At first ground control staff, not experiencing the gyrations of the space craft itself, hypothesized that there was an instrumentation malfunction, that the space craft's antenna had been damaged, or that the craft might have been struck by a meteor. However each of these is rejected based on the evidence. For example, Astronaut Jim Levell (played by Tom Hanks) declares at one point, "If we'd been hit by a meteor we'd be dead by now." Then, cautiously but with resolve he rightly interprets the visual evidence of a gas being vented into space and correctly analyzes the situation as being the result of a ruptured oxygen tank. A look at the instrument panel confirms this judgment. Everyone involves then draws the next obvious and grim inference, namely, that without oxygen the probability of the crew's survival is extremely low. Once they have reasoned through all of these steps to the formulation of the problem and the evaluation of its significance, the people on the ground, guided by the executive (self-regulation) function displayed by Gene Kranz (played by Ed Harris) and the crew in the disabled space craft as well, begin to generate and evaluate, with creativity and urgency, the possibilities that would lead to a safe return of the Apollo 13 craft and her crew of three.

Given the above understanding of critical thinking as the application of a set of core cognitive skills to the formation of reasoned judgment, a natural process driven by the human disposition toward critical thinking, there emerge three fundamental postures that critical thinking can appear to have relative to religion and the study of the Bible. The first is the use of reason as a means to better understand the Bible. The second is the function of reasoned inquiry as an independent process by which truth is sought, a process that often bumps up against one's religious beliefs. And the third is as an antagonistic process by which some criticize the Bible as a possible source of genuine evidence, theories, methods, and standards of truth. For convenience we can name the three roles "Faithful Servant," "External Agent," and "Hostile Antagonist."

Critical Thinking as Faithful Servant

Anselm and Augustine used their religious faith to understand the world and they conceived of reasoned judgment as a tool whereby to understand their faith. Both prayed that they would be able to comprehend the truths of their religion better by using the powers of their reason. The expression "faith seeking understanding" characterizes their approach. As we seek to understand the meanings of the holy texts, as we search for guidance in the Bible for how we should relate to one another as sons and daughters of God, and as we explore the mysteries of the relationship between humans and the Divine, we use our critical thinking skills and are guided by our faith commitment. A simple verse can be the source of profound insight and the object of serious analysis. We will draw inferences from the pages of the Bible for how we should live, and we will evaluate events and ideas in the light of the fundamental understandings we have about the world that we have derived from our study of the Bible. We will correct one another's misinterpretations and misguided understandings as we acquire a more thorough knowledge of the holy texts and of the standards of their proper analysis.

The exact interpretations advanced may vary over time as we become better informed, through careful linguistic, anthropological, and cultural scholarship. Yet this does not mean that we have abandoned earlier truths, rather that we have learned the limits of our previous understandings, grounded as they were, in a less than full historical knowledge. So, for example, instead of thinking of Genesis as if it were a simple chronology composed by one author, we find that it is, in fact, an edited joining of two or more oral renditions of the creation. Yet the fundamental message comes through. The story of Adam and Eve, rather than being an early global census, it is about human nature. It affirms our prideful human tendency to overreach ourselves with mixed results, and our equally human tendency to deny responsibility for our acts. In Jewish tradition, generally, it's a story about growing to an adult realization of both the limits of human beings (we are dust, we will die, childbirth is painful) and our powers (we give up individual immortality for species immortality, we can work to sustain ourselves). In a way, this is a story about taking responsibility for ourselves and seeing the necessity to use our minds to solve problems, for we do not dwell in a Garden of Eden.

We also learn, using our critical thinking skills in the service of faith, that Jesus' parables and the other Biblical narratives have the power to shape our core understandings of who we are and how we should live. Narrative is perhaps the most powerful teaching tool for humans. Far more so than abstractions that languish in the web of theoretical constructs, themselves the productions of a maze of assumptions about the world, stories can be remembered and recounted by nearly everyone. The American Bible Society provides a video dramatizing the parable of The Good Samaritan, <*http://www.newmediabible.org/1goodsam/default.htm*>. The accompanying questions, audio clips, and pictures engage the web-site's visitors in thinking about the parable and its meaning in their lives. Critical thinking is used in this web-site with the clear intention of supporting the reading of the Bible as a faith document with important messages for life today. Consider as well the story of Jesus walking on the troubled waters of Lake Galilee. The story brings vivid images to mind of storms and men in mortal danger. The story tells us that trust in the Lord will see us through even the most desperate of times. When all about us are falling, when we feel as though we are about to drown in a sea of trouble, Jesus is there, reaching out toward us, to pull us to safety.

Critical Thinking as Independent Agent

Reasoned judgment, applied as it is by truth-seekers to the business of understanding the natural causes of things, establishes the apparent limits of what can be known by the eyes of faith alone and what can be known by the light of natural reason. Not everything requires a supernatural explanation. And since predicting and controlling natural phenomena is dependent on being able to explain the how and the why of things in terms of natural causes that men might learn to manage, critical thinking plays an absolutely vital role. Unfortunately, saying that things happened because the Lord wills them does not allow one to predict what will happen next. While religion can be an important source of consolation, its way of seeking to explain things cannot feed the hungry, cure the sick, nor launch a space craft. And while it is true that the Lord loves us all, it may not be true that the Lord wants so badly that one high school basketball team should defeat the other that He (or She) causes one team to make baskets and the other to trip and lose the ball out of bounds. The Jesuit adage, "Pray like everything depends on God and work like everything depends on you," seems to characterize the role of critical thinking as external agent.

The film, *The Name of the Rose*, revolves around this independent agent function of critical thinking. The protagonist, Brother William of Baskerville, played by Sean Connery, finds the mysterious deaths of several monks engaged in hand copying ancient manuscripts were due to natural events, not to demonic possession. Brother William then follows a most useful methodological principle that has came to be known as "Ockham's razor." (William of Ockham, a philosopher who wrote during the Fourteenth Century advised thinkers of his time always to prefer explanations that relied upon fewer, rather than more, assumptions.) Relying on this basic principle of explanatory parsimony, the character in the film, Brother William of Baskerville, declares, having found that one of the mysterious deaths was either a suicide or murder, "no need for the devil at all." One might urge that suicide and murder are, themselves, evidence of demonic forces. Yet, it is hardly necessary or useful to advance such a metaphysics in order to explain the deaths under investigation.

Did Jesus really trod dry-footed on the surface of a roiling Galilean lake? Well, not if all we know about physics is true. But is that really the important thing? In fact, if some card-carrying dualistic thinker, seeing everything as "black or white," and perhaps harboring ambitions to replace Quasimoto as Chief Inquisitor, were to demand that we accept the story of a man walking on a fresh water lake as the literal truth, we might all find ourselves at a loss for how to react. And if our lives and fortunes were at stake, some of us would indeed find it not unreasonable to suspend, at least for this one case, what is generally known about the specific gravity of an adult human and the surface tension of lake water. Yet if we were persuaded that not to do so would be to imperil our immortal soul, perhaps such an acquiescence would seem indeed to be correct outcome of the process of reasoned judgment. Or we might wonder, and not without good reason, about the whole notion of the soul, where it comes from, and whether it really makes any scientific sense.

Critical Thinking as Hostile Antagonist

For Voltaire, like Russell, Marx, Sartre, and many others, the third posture seems to emerge inevitably from an understanding of the second. For how could reason as an independent agent, forever remain, or be regarded as, simply neutral? The film, *Inherit the Wind*, is based on the true story of a teacher who loses his job because he was teaching about evolution. The film is the dramatic reenactment of his trial. In the end, the defense attorney, Clarence Darrow, played by Spencer Tracey bundles together into his briefcase Charles Darwin's *The Origin of the Species*, and the Holy Bible, saying "The Bible is a good book. But it is not the only book." Reasoned judgment is not a force one can turn on and off at will. It is an engine in its own right and those with a strong disposition toward critical thinking and well developed critical thinking skills cannot help but use those skills to try to better understand all the dimensions of life and living, including the spiritual dimension. A religious person might rightly ask why, if the Creator endowed us with the power to reason, would it be other than right that we should turn our reason toward trying to understand our Creator. Thomas Aquinas, for example, argued that it is right for human beings to use their power of reason to come to understand as much of God as might be possible by examining creation and developing a natural theology. Yet, when Galileo pointed his telescope toward the heavens, what he saw lead him to realize that Aristotle's notion that the sky was made of concentric crystal spheres was, not to put too fine a point on it, nonsense. The analogy is telling, for we cannot know what will happen when we turn the power of reasoned judgment full bore at the cherished notions we derive from our study of the Bible. But, the one thing we cannot, in conscience, do without risking the ire of the Creator is to fail to use the gifts we were given. It would be wrong of us not think.

The Delphi conceptualization of critical thinking provides not only that the reasoners seek to determine what to do or what to believe, but that they do so by giving reasoned consideration to evidence, context, concepts, methods, and standards. Giving reasoned considerations

> "Critical thinking is the process of purposeful, self-regulatory judgment. In this process we give reasoned consideration to the evidence, context, conceptualizations, methods, and criteria by which those judgments are made."
>
> —The American Philosophical Association Delphi Report: *Critical Thinking: A statement of Expert Consensus for Purposes of Educational Assessment and Instruction*, 1990. ERIC Doc. NO.: ED 315 423
>
> **Figure 4**

to these means, at the meta-level, to subject these very elements to analysis, interpretation, and evaluation. In other words, part of excellence in critical thinking is to do such things as analyze the quality of the evidence, evaluate the appropriate applicability of the criteria, interpret the conceptualizations and reconsider the analysis of the contexts of judgment. Just as in a jury trial good defense attorneys seek weaknesses in the theory, evidence, methods, and standards of proof advanced by the prosecuting attorneys, so do good critical thinkers stand ready to challenge the methodological, epistemological, and metaphysical assumptions upon which judgments are based.

The troubled waters need not be the liquids that form Lake Galilee. Instead they could be the deep and dangerous intellectual waters upon which one hopes to sail as one ventures with critical thinking into the study of the Bible. It is no accident that Martin Luther called reason "faith's greatest enemy." The battle lines are drawn sharply. Concerning religion Bertrand Russell said, "There is something feeble and a little contemptible about a man who cannot face the perils of life without the help of comfortable myths." In that famous scene from *Inherit the Wind* when the word "day" is opened to the possible interpretation that it might refer to a period of time other than 24 hours, we see the tumultuous affect of the collision of reason with what is taken to be revelation.

When we try honestly to reconcile what we have come to believe through the teachings of religion and the study of the Bible with what we have learned through reason and experience, an intellectual storm of fearsome proportions often begins to churn. The classic conflict of evolution as a scientific explanation and the literal reading of Genesis is but one illustration. Other examples with perhaps even more important societal consequences include debates about the meaning of the marriage as it relates to homosexual couples and conflicts about abortion or the use of harvested fetal stem cells in potentially lifesaving medical research.

Can the three become one?

The most fundamental assumption of the rationalism that has driven western philosophical thought for more than two and a half millennia is that all reality, in the final analysis, operates according to principles that make sense. The quest to know and to explain are rooted in the idea that human inquiry is not a pointless effort to discern the caprice of irrational gods and demented demons, but an investigation into an ordered universe. The causal relationships may be extraordinarily complex and subtle. Entropy, uncertainty, and random motion may be elements in the final explanation. But in the end, truth is one because reality is one.

This basic presupposition of western rationalism is echoed down through the centuries not only by atheists and agnostics, but by believers as well. In *The Idea of a University* John Cardinal Newman offers two maxims: "Truth cannot be contrary to truth." And, "Truth often seems contrary to truth." When the truths of science and reason appear to contradict the truths of the Bible and revelation, either one's science is incomplete or one's revelation is a mistaken interpretation. For if truth is fundamentally one, we have every reason to hope that truth-seeking and God-seeking are not inconsistent vocations. Instead of fearing, squelching, or assaulting reason, persons of faith can give full play to reasoned judgment. The challenge, however, is not to settle for using reason in a mediocre way. We should strive for the highest developmental level of reflective judgment attainable, either individually or as a thinking community, namely the level of the sage.

On February 9, 2000 NBC aired a show in the series "The West Wing." The President of the United States, played by Martin Sheen, wrestles with the question of capital punishment. The scriptwriters tell the story so that the question has philosophical, religious, ethical, political, legal, personal, emotional, and historical dimensions. In one scene a learned rabbi advises a presidential aide. The rabbi explains that Talmud sanctions capital punishment in a number of cases, as for example as a punishment for a rebellious son. The Talmud also sanctions slavery, says the rabbi. He goes on to explain that these views may have represented the best wisdom of their times, but that they are not ethically or culturally acceptable any longer. He urges the aide to advise the President to commute the condemned man's sentence. The wise advice the devout rabbi has offered is by no means a rejection of his Talmudic heritage but a manifestation of its deepest meanings in the context of current problems and understandings. In the rabbi's decision we see reasoning having come full circle. For the rabbi is not using reasoning simply as a tool in the service of his faith's propositional beliefs, nor as a neutral agent, nor as a hostile critic, but as a tool to reflectively reinterpret the core meanings of the sacred text in a situation where knowledge includes uncertainty and yet justifiable claims can and, in this example, should be made.

At the level of the sage the second and the third postures critical thinking takes toward the study of the Bible, that of independent agent and hostile antagonist, will, in the end, merge with the first relationship, that of faithful servant. But the faithful servant role must change as well. For critical thinking, truly understood, will retain its edge. Reasoned judgment, if well practiced, has the potential to reunify its triune responsibilities. It serves best not simply when it interprets from within, but when it explains independently and when it evaluates objectively. Anything less would stifle the potential of reasoned judgment to lead to a deeper understanding; it would not be critical thinking, rather it would be sophistry and intellectual dishonesty.

Using the Bible to Foster Reasoned Judgment

In addition to the Society's orientation toward social justice, the Jesuits have historically been known for their erudition and advancement of higher learning. Like the wise rabbi in the earlier example, Jesuits have used reasoned judgment as a formidable tool in the service of faith and justice. Those who have experienced their educational philosophy of reflective engagement and reasoned inquiry often recount having learned to think in their schools and colleges. Not that the Society of Jesus has a corner on the market, by any means, but there are some important pedagogical similarities between its approach and the approach of many of the finest teachers of thinking from the time of Socrates on through to the present. The strategies to foster and strengthen critical thinking skills are well known, as are the things that one can do to nurture critical thinking habits of mind. The lists in figures 5 and 6 below summarize those.

To teach thinking one must have something to think about. The Bible makes for excellent material. It is a richly complex text, open to multiple interpretations, with profoundly deep and conflicted historical, religious, philosophical, and cultural roots. It is at once familiar and yet

Five Suggestions for Nurturing Reasoned Judgment

1. Expect and reward intellectual virtue.
2. Evaluate thinking processes, not results only.
3. Present information from the bottom up, explaining why, not just what or how.
4. Replace rote training with thoughtful mentoring.
5. Build a culture of reasoned, fair-minded, evidence-based thinking.

Figure 5

not at all transparent. It speaks to matters of tremendous human significance, yet often in ways that are deceptive in their apparent simplicity. The relationship between the study of the Bible and critical thinking is a two-way street. Teachers of reasoned judgment have long realized that the problems we face in the future do not come to us in the tidy disciplinary boxes and rigidly compartmentalized areas of study. Thinking that blends the insights of many disciplines and that wisely considers the often divergent standards and conceptualizations of ethics, religion, science, and politics is called for far more frequently than one might at first imagine. The quick and simple solutions, pat answers, and unreflective application of brittle truisms of the past are often inadequate to the task.

We are in the early years of the realization that genetic engineering will have potentially life-altering consequences for our species, if not our entire planet. To reason well about the genomics revolution in science and in social policy, will be to test the limits of our conceptualizations and methods; it will cause us to reconsider standards and

To Teach Critical Thinking Skills

Model CT skills and dispositions.
Create a culture of inquiry.
Diversify contexts of judgment.
Reward and challenge.
Guide reflection on the thinking process.
Engage people in thinking well.
Ask "Why?"

Figure 6

redraw the boundaries of what we imagine to be possible and, indeed, thinkable. It will call for the best in our capacities and disposition toward reasoned judgment. For the person of faith, it will be potentially as troubling as the discovery that the Sacred Mystery is not an anthropomorphic being seated on a golden throne just above the crystal sphere that seems to obstruct our earthbound view of Heaven. And none of this implies that we should lose our faith. Only that we cannot afford to abandon the best gift God has given us, namely our reason.

Conclusion

Only if the human mind is truly free to think and to apply to the study of the Bible and the practice of religion all that is known by the light of natural reason and experience, with all the risks and all the uncertainties that critical thinking as reasoned judgment implies, can we humans ever be assured that our seeking for salvation and our seeking for wisdom have the potential to be reconciled.

References

Apollo 13, Ron Howard, director.1995. Tom Hanks, Kevin Bacon, Bill Paxton, Gary Sinise, Ed Harris. MCA Universal.

Bartlett, J., and Kaplan, J. (Eds.). 1992. *Bartlett's Familiar Quotations, Sixteenth Edition*. Boston: Little, Brown and Company.

Dingle, C. (Ed.). 2000. *Memorable Quotations: Philosophers of Western Civilization*. San Jose: Writers Club Press.

Facione, N., and Facione, P. 1992/2000. *The California Critical Thinking Disposition Inventory and Manual*. Millbrae, California: The California Academic Press.

Facione, P. 1990. *Critical Thinking: A Statement of Expert Consensus for Purposes of Educational Assessment and Instruction*. American Philosophical Association, "The Delphi Report." ERIC document , ED 315-423. Millbrae, California: The California Academic Press.

Inherit the Wind, Stanley Kramer, director. 1960. Spencer Tracey, Fredric March, Gene Kelly, Harry Morgan. MGM.

Scherer, D., et. al. 1979. *Introduction to Philosophy: From Wonder to World View*. Englewood Cliffs, NJ: Prentice-Hall. Reprinted by The California Academic Press, Millbrae, CA. 2001.

Sherrin, Ned (Ed.). 1995. *Oxford Dictionary of Humorous Quotations*. Oxford: Oxford University Press.

King, P.M. and Kitchener, K. S. 1994. *Developing Reflective Judgment: Understanding and Promoting Intellectual Growth and Critical Thinking in Adolescents and Adults.* San Francisco: Jossey-Bass.

Newman, J.H. *The Idea of a University.* 1933. New York, London, Toronto: Longmans, Green and Co.

The Name of the Rose, Jean Jacques Annaud, director. 1986. Sean Connery, F. Murray Abraham, Christian Slater. Twentieth Century Fox.

Phillips, B. *Great Thoughts and Funny Sayings.* 1933. Wheaton IL: Tyndale House Publishers.

Rice, A., *The Vampire Lestat.* 1985. New York: Ballantine Book.

The Encyclopedia of Philosophy, Paul Edwards, Editor in Chief. 1967. New York: Macmillan Publishing Co. Cf. Entries on Anselm, Thomas Aquinas, Aristotle, Augustine, Martin Buber, Charles Darwin, William James, Martin Luther, Moses Maimonides, Karl Marx, Bertrand Russell, Jean Paul Sartre, Baruch Spinoza, Francois-Marie Voltaire, and many other topics and individuals mentioned in this essay.

Critical Thinking within Biblical Texts

2

Bible Reading AND Critical Thinking[1]

Christof Hardmeier

Introduction: Torah as Memorial Literature

First I will explain my main thesis: the biblical books and text records are something like a distinctive kind of memorial literature. This can be seen most clearly in the Torah of Moses, which is represented in Deuteronomy 1-30 as a speech. In the later Exile (between 550—530 B.C.E.), this speech was conceived from a literary standpoint as the opening of the so-called Deuteronomistic History. It is especially important to notice here the fundamental fact and character of a narrated speech (Hardmeier 2000b, 63f.). The text is a matter of narrated speech insofar as it is introduced as such in Deut. 1.5: "On the other side of the Jordan, in the land of Moab, Moses undertook to expound this Torah, by saying: ..."[2] Additional narrative insertions which point to the continuation of the speech can be found in Deut. 5.1, 27.9, and 29.1, following headings later added in 4.44 ff. and 28.69.[3] In any case, Deut. 31 then narrates how Moses established his successor Joshua as the one to lead the immigration and take possession of the land to the west of Jordan (31.1-8) and that he (Moses) then wrote down "this Torah" (31.9) as just recited in Deut. 1-30.

1. Orality and literacy in the Torah

From a transmedial[4] viewpoint, the decisive fact is that a Torah teaching is produced and presented in Deut. 1-30 as an oral speech—

just as in a Readers' theatre. Indeed, you can say it is about a theatrical production put into writing, just like music put into a score. Here a double-transformation which underlies this Torah speech is of fundamental significance: 1) at work here—as shown above—is a narrated speech; 2) this narrated speech is passed on as a written speech. We need to consider both transformations briefly.

Firstly, narration is a—indeed, the—linguistic means to perform remembering[5]. In other words, narration, as a form of acting, is the primary way of performing recollection. But to be sure, what is narrated in the framework of Deut. 1-30 is, on the one hand, exceptionally minimal: on the other hand, it is extensively eloquent and "speaking." Especially as compared with our usual expectations of narrative, here an absolute minimum is narrated—and even this, so far as the details are concerned, is only indirectly given: at the age of 120 (Deut. 31.1), Moses expounds the Torah (Deut. 1.5) in the vicinity of Beth Peor (3.29; cf. 4.46) in the land of Moab (1.5). It is the last day of his life (cf. 1.37; 3.27, and 34.1, 4f.) and the day before Israel crosses the Jordan under Joshua's leadership (cf. 9.1 with 1.38f.; 3.27f., and 31.1-8). This last day of Moses—as an ideal type that will determine everything—on the evening before taking possession of the land on the other side of the Jordan appears in the narrated speech as the continuously invoked "today." What is narrated or remembered here is not a past world represented in colorful, vivid images. We learn nothing, for example, regarding the weather on this definitive day or what the landscapes surrounding Beth Peor or Mount Pisgah looked like. Even Moses' grave remains unknown (34.6). The photo album for this last day is empty. An almost perfectly empty picture of this day—the day in which the Torah is conveyed—is sketched in a highly abstract fashion, without any visual components whatsoever.

This abstract, non-visual narrative thus recalls in an almost oversized way the process of teaching by way of argument and dialogue and makes present to the readers or audience the orality of unfolding the Torah. What is remembered and made present is thereby in the first place how Moses expounded the Torah, as if the readers and listeners were themselves to stand or sit before him. It is the speech-event itself that is made present, to let the reader/listener participate quasi-directly in experiencing Moses as speaker/writer and attending to his speech.[6] Hence, the main object of the narrative and recollection in Deuteronomy is the exemplary performance of a Torah teaching—that is, the rhetorical event of teaching in which the how of the argumentation and especially of the talking about God, as a Torah-adequate form of discourse, is itself vividly performed in the context of the imminent crossing of the Jordan.

Alongside this transmediation of the Torah speech by narrative embedding, we must further consider a second transformation: the narrated fact that, according to Deut. 31.9, this just-presented Torah was written down by Moses. We should keep in mind here especially the goal of this writing down. According to Deut. 31.11, "this Torah" should be read aloud every seventh year during the Feast of Tabernacles (cf. Deut. 16.13). Thus, Moses' narrated speech has been indeed conceived as literature, but as a literature that is constructed to be read aloud to an audience. This second transformation of writing down a narrative is thereby intended for the performative presentation and repetition of Moses' oral Torah teaching—and not to serve as a documentation of a past that is then simply added to archival records ad acta. Writing down the oral teaching is also not for the purpose of preserving the history of the beginnings of Israel as a people, in order to confirm its identity (Assman 1992, 30f., 197f., 212ff.). Rather, everything is arranged in order to let the performative process of the Torah teaching become present in the medium of writing and the narrative recollecting—and, periodically, to bring the listening public into the narrated scene in such a way that it participates currently in the "today" of these beginnings. Also, according to Deut. 17.18f., the king is to read continually in this Torah throughout his entire life: this constant learning process is to keep up the proper attitude of respect for God and thus not to fall victim to a hubristic overestimation of one's own capacities (17. 20, see 8.11, 14, 17f.). In this sense, at stake here in the biblical literature is—to my knowledge, for the first time—a unique cultural-historical phenomenon of a memorial literature. This literature roots its constitutive orality and procedurality in the form of a double transmediation in both the narrative recollection and the medium of script. It aims at shaping the right relationship with God as a vivid and life-promoting process of orientation which is guided by the Torah taught orally to be heard. That is, the relationship with God will be continuously (re)constituted in this orality and performative way of recollection.

2. Moses' Torah Teaching:
THE CORE OF A PERFORMATIVE THEOLOGY

For its own part, however, this formal principle of ongoing vivid recollection, which brought forth the biblical memorial literature in the fashion outlined above, is now the constitutive form of thought of

Moses' Torah teaching itself. His "lecture" for its part makes use of narrative recollection in the context of instructing and preparing the people for the immigration into the land of their fathers. In the narrated world of Moab—that is, in the framework of his ideal-type speech—Moses focuses on Israel's crossing the Jordan in Deut. 9.1: "Hear, O Israel! To day you are about to cross the Jordan to come in and dispossess nations greater and mightier than you: large cities with walls sky-high."

In the background of this preparation is the concern with the possible fear of the people in the face of this highly risky undertaking (which needs to be established in greater detail). But the main issue in Deut. 9.1ff. is the question to whom the success of taking the land is to be ascribed—God's helpful presence within the undertaking or Israel's own righteousness? To forestall the possible misapprehension that the people's own righteousness and rectitude could be the decisive factor for Israel's success, in Deut. 9.7ff. Moses refers back to commonly-experienced events—the problematic experiences of God with his people and the people with their God even since Egypt, at Horeb and then on the journey from Horeb to Moab. Recalling earlier experiences, in Deut. 9.7ff. Moses establishes that from the Exodus to the arrival in Moab, the people of Israel have been a stiff-necked and stubborn people (Deut. 9.6b), a people that has only created difficulties in their relationship with God and thereby continuously angered and enraged him: "Remember, never forget, how you provoked YHWH your God to anger in the wilderness: from the day that you left the land of Egypt until you reached this place, you have been continuously rebellious with YHWH" (MW).

It is not only in Deut. 9.7ff. that Moses refers back in his Torah speech to these sorts of mutual experiences between God and Israel at Horeb and since the arrival in Moab. In addition to this teaching speech at 9.8-10.11, there are four further recollections of Horeb in Deut. 1.6-18; 4.(9) 10-14; 5.4-31 and 18.16-20 (Hardmeier 2000b, 65-67). Beyond these, Deut. 1.19-3.29 looks back to the difficulties and successes which God and Israel lived through between Horeb and Moab (Lohfink 2000). First Deut. 1.19-46 is a paradigmatic recollection of how and why the first attempts to take the land west of the Jordan failed. In Deut. 2.16-3.7 Moses then draws out before their very eyes how and why the taking possession of land east of the Jordan succeeded through the proper relationship with God. Both experiences are recalled and made present as paradigmatic experiences in Moses' Torah speech.

The function of this recollecting within the teaching discourse is made clear in Deut. 3.21f. Moses reminds the audience of what he told Joshua, the designated leader of the immigration into West Jordan, following their taking possession of the lands east of the Jordan (Deut. 2.16-3.7) and after the distribution of the land to the tribes there had been completed (Deut. 3.8-20): "'There your (own) eyes saw all that YHWH your God has acted[7] towards these two kings (i.e. King Sihon and King Og). So shall YHWH act towards all the kingdoms into which you shall cross over. Do not fear them, for it is YHWH your God: he it is who will battle for you.'" What is essential here are three points: first, the emphasis on the fact that these events were eye-witnessed is what is recalled here—that is, first-hand experience with the working of God, and second, the construction of an analogy with the future. Along with these at the center as well is the vivid impression of how God has acted and how God will act in order to substantiate the analogy in a comprehensible way. Third, we must consider the aim of the text in making these events vivid in this way: establishing these events as vivid acts is to inspire the people listening not to be afraid of the imminent undertaking—of crossing over into the lands west of the Jordan—and to have no fear in the face of the risks involved.

With regard to the mode of communication, what is decisive here is that God's cooperation, as it cultivates confidence, is not taught as a dogmatic claim. It is not said abstractly, "because God is benevolent and gracious" or "because God is the Lord of history, God will battle for you." Rather, through the performative recollecting of paradigmatic experiences of past attempts to take the land, Moses makes Joshua and the people aware vividly of how the imminent undertaking could succeed through the right relationship with God. In this way—a specific way with regard to conveying theology and the word of God—Moses teaches what one otherwise calls biblical trust in God. He recalls God's cooperation in the open, highly risky undertakings of the past—and in fact as an experience the people themselves have gone through. This allows Moses to make vivid and plausible how the imminent taking possession of the land can be dared without paralyzing fear but rather with expectations of success, despite comparable risks.

I have a fundamental theological suspicion (one that has grown increasingly compelling for me over the past few years) that we possibly cannot talk about the God of the Hebrew Bible and Christian Scriptures in any other way than in just this mode of performative recollection, a mode of communication that creates analogies and parables for the present and future by establishing similes with past events. This means: in a narrative form of recollection which is applied to a continuously corresponding practice in the present and future. At the very least, Jesus' parables telling of the Kingdom of God follow this same text-pragmatic model. Along with these, only the prayer in the form of a direct address to God in the familiar "thee" stands as a genuinely linguistic form of biblical belief. Both forms of articulation, however, allow God to become present and symbolically comprehensible in a performative act only. These forms are thereby perfectly consistent with the fundamental prohibition against graven images, which, in my opinion, also forbids any discourse about God in the form of dogmatic concepts or theoretical descriptions of God's being or nature.[8] The memorial character of biblical literature and its striking characteristic of presenting the relationship with God primarily performatively is thus anything other than a superficially formal accident or, as it may be, an arbitrary choice of the medium. On the contrary, at stake here is a fundamental theological fact, one that fully takes into account the first and second commandments of the Decalog—above all, from the perspective of the adequate mode of communication involved. This fact must be most carefully kept in mind as we consider the possible ways of presenting the biblical text and its message in electronic media.

2. Bible Reading as Critical Thinking

I now come to my second thesis: bible reading as a specific kind of critical thinking. I would like to initially elaborate how a particular form of critical thinking is at work in this biblical recollecting and making present—a recollection and remembering that focus centrally on a relationship with the invisible God that is strictly bound to specific situations. Basically, it is a narrative form of thinking, but has a narrated speech as its specific performative form: and, as we have seen, this form is constitutive for this kind of critical thinking, especially with regard to the relationship with God, indeed, for talking about the biblical God at all. This kind of thinking is further to be distinguished from the theoretical and conceptual forms of thought characteristic of philosophy, as well as from the empirical/descriptive and/or mathematical/scientific forms of symbolic comprehension of reality as a web of connections and relationships. In diverse ways, these philosophical and scientific forms of thought symbolically reconstruct worlds, states of affairs and entities, in order to be able to engage with them as objects. By contrast, the memorial form of thought found in biblical literature is concerned instead with a practical kind of critical thinking—one which fosters and brings about a realistic perception of risks and opportunities in otherwise disturbing situations and in the face of troubling problems: it does so by minimizing a "closing of the mind" that results from either fear or hubris. In doing so, this memorial thinking thus also stands outside the hermeneutical correlation between pre-judgment and grasping reality—because at stake here is a kind of thinking *coram deo*, that is, a thinking actually faced with the invisible personal Other of God and exposed to his non-disposability[9] in a directly performative relationship with God. This thinking will be shaped and kept up through a permanently vivid recollection of this relationship by both reading/listening to and remembering the texts of the Bible and drawing analogies to one's own situation. It is a "belief-thinking" that, as Paul says, emerges from hearing (Rom. 10.17 and Gal. 3.2) and, according to Deut. 6.6-9, is to pervade everyday life.

1. PARADIGMATIC experience, biblical narrative, and "fear-critical thinking"

To develop this thesis I return to Moses' Torah. What Moses recalls in Deut. 3.21 for Joshua and the assembled people is intended, as we have seen, to eliminate fear in the face of the dangers surrounding the imminent crossing over into the lands west of the Jordan. As God has acted towards Kings Sihon and Og east of the Jordan—so God will act towards the kingdoms in the west. As the successful taking possession of land in the east was possible through the right relationship of respect for God, so God will also "battle" in the west for those addressed in this speech: hence they need not fear. I wish to emphasize here that one thinks in a paradigm of experience connected to a specific situation. As this example shows, significant experiences of self, time, and God are paradigmatically thought together in a form that binds them together in narrative—in order to minimize fear of the future. In this connection, the teaching discourse itself also makes this model of recollection explicit as a key episode in Deut. 2.26-36. There Moses had already presented how a complex tapestry of activities resulted in the successful subduing of the king of Hesbon. In Deut. 3.21f. Moses refers back to this Sihon-episode as an encouraging experience of God and self that is then—according to 3.22—to minimize fear in the face of crossing the Jordan.

The model of recollection in Deut. 2.26-36, however, will be effective as a narrative figure of thought and achieve its meaningfulness only if all interactive aspects of the remembered episode are thought and perceived together. This point is of a piece with the fundamental preconditions of this form of biblical thinking in narrative models. Only then can we more fully understand from Deut. 3.21f. just in what way God will "battle" for his people in the future. In the episode in Deut. 2.26-36, it is especially striking that this episode emphatically begins from Moses' entirely peaceful request: he simply wants to cross the territory of Sihon of Hesbon, and compensate the foreign king for any provision of food and drink (vss. 26-29).[10] In verse 30, however, Moses recalls the fact that for his part, the king of Hesbon refused this request. Moses explains this refusal as the result of God's having stiffened Sihon's will and hardened his heart.[11]

But this hardening of the king's mind is not only a matter of psychology: as we are about to see, this psychological stiffening also leads to a kind of narrowed and mistaken perception of reality and future. This misperception of a peaceful resolution opens then for Israel the decisive opportunity precisely to take possession of Sihon's territory incidentally and accidentally, despite the initial peaceful intentions, and rather more as the gift of God (vs. 31). On the political level, the effect of the foreign king's hardened heart is recalled in vs. 32 as a pre-emptive strike: "And Sihon . . . took the field against us at Jahaz." (MW).[12] That is, Sihon's perceptual distortion manifests itself in Moses' model of recollection as a warlike and violence-laden pre-emptive measure that resulted from the king's fear of being threatened. It is this fear of threat—being able to distort perceptions—that prevents Sihon from seeing the peaceful resolution of conflict that Moses proposed. Sihon's fear of threat, which misled him into a military over-reaction, is thereby not only the form in which God in effect gave the king "into the hands" of Israel, though they only wanted to cross his territory peacefully. Sihon's fear is also the decisive weak point, such that he could be defeated and his entire domain captured, because his fear had blinded him. Here I cannot further explore the subsequent recollection of the destruction of the spoils of war in 2.34, thus dedicated in this way to the God who had "battled" alongside Israel. This destruction involves exemplary connections that will be taken up in Deut. 7.1-5.[13]

But primarily the Sihon-episode in Deut. 2.26-36 is the paradigmatic model of experience for the argument intended to encourage the people of Israel in Deut. 3.21f.: the argument that God will "battle" for God's people again in the future. On the one hand, it shows Israel's primary offer of peaceful engagement and fair compensation in dangerous undertakings pregnant with conflict. It is the recommended first choice. On the other hand, the model makes it vividly credible that in such undertakings other factors are also at work: such factors—for example, the reactions of the potential enemy—are either entirely unpredictable and non-disposable[14] or hardly predictable, much less open to Israel's control. The paradigmatic episode ascribes these factors to the cooperation and acting of God. In this way, it is precisely the unpredictable mistakes in the enemy's reaction, such as those of Sihon, which can become even violent and threatening—but at the same time, these mistakes open up unexpected opportunities. In the Sihon paradigm, an entire stretch of Moabite territory falls into the hands of the people crossing and leads to an unexpected result, because the people, in their trusting openness to God, did not let themselves be intimidated through Sihon's fear-inspired aggression as they did in Kadesh-Barnea (Deut. 1.26-28) due to the misunderstood report of the scouts.[15]

One could denote this narrational paradigm of thought in Moses' Torah as "fear-critical" thinking. This kind of thinking—rooted in the performative relationship with God—preserves its openness to new situations as it likewise preserves the sense for unexpected opportunities under conditions of violence and within contexts defined by fear and uncertainty. In this way, at work here is an elementary form of critical thinking which is at the same time a practical thinking oriented to specific situations. It is schooled through an on-going work of recollection and shaped by an actualizing remembering[16] of biblical paradigmatic experiences. It brings about presence of mind to do the right things at the right moments in solidarity with and with respect for others, as well as being sensitive to environments and collateral effects. The main function of this way of thinking through analogous models of experience consists in critically reflecting on the component of fear in risky undertakings pregnant with conflicts, and arousing a cool-headed trust in indeterminacies and non-disposabilities, which, when considered without fear, also hold unexpected opportunities. In such narrational models of experience is defined in a vivid and comprehensible way what can be called trust in God: a trust that minimizes the distortions brought about by fear of the future and of threat, and opens one's eyes for a cool-headed realism about the future.

2. Self-critical thinking in narrative models of recollection

This fear-critical function of narrative thought, as it performatively sets the Torah of Moses "on stage," is also to be understood above all as having an essential self-critical function. As a last example, I will now examine this function in that part of Moses' speech in which he prepares the people directly for crossing the Jordan and considers the imminent taking possession of the land in the West. This is part of the speech in Deut. 9.1ff. which I mentioned at the outset (see 80): "Hear, O Israel! Today you are about to cross the Jordan to come in and dispossess nations greater and mightier than you: large cities with walls sky-high." The following verses in Moses' address then take up the problem, and the danger that the people could ascribe to their own rectitude and righteousness the expected success in expropriating the land (9.4). This understandable temptation to take exclusive credit for their successes also leads to distorted perceptions that could centrally endanger any future undertakings. This is because, in claiming exclusive credit for themselves, there is the danger of losing sight of all the other factors contributing to the success that are not within the control and influence of their own will and action, but which nonetheless decisively contribute to the success of such a project as the imminent taking possession of the land.

Over against this classic dangers of hubris or neurotic delusions of grandeur, Moses presents three arguments. First, he recalls in 9.3 that God will prepare the subduing of other peoples through his own acts—as the teaching speech remembering the Sihon episode has already made vividly clear, and is recalled in 3.21 for Joshua's and the people's encouragement. Second, Moses deepens this argument in 9.5, insofar as it will be the other nations' own unfairness and wickedness that will prepare and enable the taking possession of their land.[17] Here Moses refers back in this second argument precisely to the self-destructive dimension of the Sihon model. Sihon had unfairly rejected Moses' proposal of peacefully crossing the alien territory, and thereby fell victim to his own fear of being threatened. Deut. 2.30 denotes this self-destructive misperception of Sihon as a stiffening of his spirit, i.e., his will, and hardening of his heart by God[18] which results in his wickedness, attacking Israel (2.32) instead of letting them cross his territory peacefully. This was (and according to 9.4-6 will be) how Israel took possession of the land with God's help.[19]

But now, in 9.6, Moses warns his own people against such stubbornness as it could threaten the success of taking the land in the West because of hubristic self-appraisal: " ...because you are stubborn!"[20] And this is his third and most important argument to counter the destructive danger of taking exclusive credit for success: he turns it self-critically on his own public. To substantiate the argument, in 9.7ff. Moses launches anew that narrative model of thought whose function and distinctive characteristics we have become familiar with in Deut. 3.21f. and in the Sihon episode in 2.26-36. Moses recalls with emphasis ("remember, never forget!") that Israel showed a rebellious attitude towards God during the entire sojourn in the desert, now behind them, and thereby continuously provoked God to anger. In 9.8-23 Moses lays out the paradigmatic situations in which this rebellious attitude manifested itself in a series of conflicts between God and Israel in the past, in order then to underscore conclusively in 9.24 his global assertion of 9.7, using the same words.

The paradigmatic examples of conflict in the past are brought into the debate in 9.8-23 in the form of narrative models of recollection. The first—so to speak, the prototype—of all cases of rebellion is broadly set out in 9.8-21. It is the break with God on Horeb itself, in which Israel broke the first commandment by making an idol, even before Moses had come down the mountain with the tablets. In 9.22, three further— highly compromising—episodes are recalled which are named solely through their localities (i.e., without explaining or even indicating the situation itself), episodes in which further provocations and rebellions against God were committed.[21]

For thinking in narrative models of recollection, however, what is most decisive is the naming of the last instance of earlier rebellions— the example of "Kadesh-Barnea" in 9.23. Granted, this case is also not unfolded narratively—in contrast with the violation of the first commandment on Horeb itself (9.8-21). Nonetheless, Moses thereby refers back to the example of both self-experience and experience of God which he presented in great detail at the beginning of his speech in Deut. 1.19-46. There, Moses has the people recall why the first attempt, started from Kadesh-Barnea, to immigrate into the land promised to their ancestors (cf. Deut. 1.20f.) failed miserably. More precisely, he recalls two efforts, each of which failed, but for different reasons. According to Deut. 1.22-33, the first attempt failed because the people—despite the promising reports of the scouts—were too afraid and refused to risk setting off.[22] In the second attempt (1.41-45), the people thoughtlessly overreached themselves (cf. 1.41 and 1.43) and attempted an armed incursion. But this incursion was contrary to God's prophetic directive (cf. 1.42f.) and because of their mistaken underestimation of the enemy, the people endured a bitter defeat (1.44).

What is important in these episodes in Deuteronomy 1 is their theological dimension, which is then taken up exclusively and in exactly the same words in Deut. 9.23. Both the unwillingness of the people to set off for the "good land" in 1.26 and their flouting the prophetic directive in 1.43 not to enter into the land with military force and against the will of God are generalized in both verses with the same words as "rebellion" against "YHWH's mouth" by flouting his directives. Thus this specific phrase in 1.26b and 43b ("and you rebelled against/flouted YHWH's directive")[23] receives the function of a unifying denominator for the disrupted relationship with God. Just this common denominator reappears in the recollection of the example of Kadesh-Barnea in 9.23—both in exactly the same words and as its essential meaning. This latter context, to be sure, in taking up the episodes of crisis at Kadesh-Barnea goes one step further in its concentration on the theological dimension of the disrupted relationship with God by differentiating the narrative proof of Israel's rebellious attitude exactly following both of the failed undertakings started from Kadesh-Barnea. On the one hand, in Deut. 1.32, Moses evaluates the fearful refusal to set off for the good land as showing lack of faith or lack of trust in God: this evaluation is then taken up in the chain of proofs in 9.23, precisely to make the point: "you did not put your trust in him" (MW). On the other hand, at the end of verse 23, Moses recalls that the people did not "listen to the voice" of YHWH—as was precisely the case in the second failed attempt to take possession of the land, as elucidated already in Deut. 1.42f.

3. Typological generalizations, narrative "TERMS" and abstractions

By way of concluding this thread of my argument, there are two important aspects of this form of narrative thinking and its critical function to bring to the foreground. The first illustrates the narrative unfolding and recalling of different cases of continued rebellion in Deut. 9.8ff., in what way this narrative thinking develops typological universalizations and abstractions, and thereby sets up a distinctive species of narrative "terms" and definitions. The Kadesh-Barnea episode makes especially clear how the levels of narrative abstractions and construction of "terms" mesh hierarchically.

On the one hand, Kadesh-Barnea in Deut. 9.23 functions in the context of 9.7-24 as a case among cases which generally demonstrate Israel's notorious attitude of rebellion against God and defines this casuistically (cf. 9.7 and 9.24). In this way, Moses' effort to establish a definition further achieves a higher level of narrative abstraction in 9.7-24. For an entire chain of paradigmatic experiences of the disrupted relationship with God is called up in order to demonstrate and define the stiff-necked and rebellious attitude of Israel. Apart from 9.8-21 the episodes themselves, however, are not made present here in their narrative vividness. As with the other place-names in verse 22, "Kadesh-Barnea" becomes an abstract "term of episode". This "term" consisting in a place-name denotes and recalls something that, for its part, comprehends an entire model of recollection that is unfolded as particular case in Deut. 1.19-46 only.

On the other hand, these episodes in Deut. 1.19-46—as we have seen—define in part what it means to put one's trust in God and not to trust in God (v. 32), on the model of the missed opportunity to set off for the land in 1.22-33. And in the other part, the example of the willful push to take the land in 1.41-45 demonstrates what it means to fail to listen to the voice of God, disobeying his prophetic directive. With regard to both definitions, past experiences of both self and God are stylized and, in a step-by-step process, universalized into a species of phraseological terms. Furthermore, both the fear-ridden unbelief in 1.22-33 and the failure to obey God's directive in 1.42 are—as we have shown—already reduced to a single common denominator in 1.26 and 43: "to be rebellious against/flouting YHWH's directive." And just this more general phraseological term for breaking with God in Deut. 9.23 is subordinated for its part to the still more general concept of Israel's rebellious attitude over times in 9.24 (see v.7). For here Kadesh-Barnea, as a term for an episode, designates one of the diverse examples in which Israel was rebellious against God and provoked God to anger again and again as it is generalized in 9.24 and 7. For this reason Moses can designate Israel—at the highest level of narrative abstraction and with an entire chain of similar examples at hand—as a "stiff-necked," i.e., a stubborn "people" in Deut. 9.6b. Thereby this most general term for the broken relationship and misdirected attitude towards God is demonstrated through a comprehensive recollection of the entire desert sojourn in 9.7ff. and defined by way of various cases of rebellion since Egypt and Horeb—cases which, for their part, are only called up as terms for episodes and not retold themselves.

4. Closing the circle of the narrative ARGUMENTATION

With this I now come to the second and final aspect of this narrative thinking in the context of the Kadesh-Barnea episode—an aspect that leads us back to the self-critical and fear-critical function of this thinking. I have tried to make clear above that Israel's stubbornness is Moses' third and most important argument in Deut. 9.6, in order to keep Israel from the temptation of taking exclusive credit for the anticipated success of taking the land. But now, if the episodes of the first failed attempts, as described in Deut. 1.19-46, should also be found among the proofs of this stubbornness in 9.23—this would close the circle of the narrative logic and argumentation at work here.

Especially the illustration given in Deut. 1.22-33 makes clear that the first effort to cross over into the land west of the Jordan failed because of the fear and mistrust of Israel. In Moses' view, this fearful refusal was rooted in a lack of belief and trust in God (1.32). But it is also telling that in this failed attempt—as is also true in the Sihon episode—a grave distortion of perception is at work. In 1.27f., Israel's refusal to set off is traced back to grumbling in the tents. What the scouts reported of the good land (1.25) was transformed behind the curtains of the tents into a horror trip. In the promised land there were stronger and taller people, like the Anakim, and cities with walls sky-high (1.28): these constructions in the people's fantasy then occasioned mistrust and fear (1.27f.). As in the case of Sihon, at stake here in this case as well is a self-generated fear of being threatened, which sees only the difficult and threatening elements of the future. While in the Kadesh-Barnea episode this fear disables Israel's willingness to immigrate into the land—this same kind of fear in the Sihon episode misleads the king into making an ill-advised pre-emptive strike. 1.22-33 is concerned with a case of making oneself stubborn as a result of failing to trust God; in the Sihon episode, it is God who harden the foreign king's heart which results in his unpredictably aggressive reaction to the Israel's peaceful request.

Conclusion

Space prevents further consideration of the fear-critical function of this narrative form of thinking and its performative models of self-experience and experience of God. Let me sum up:

1. I hope that it has become clear how this narrative thought process works as an orality that is intentionally written down as literarily-conceived orality—and, correspondingly, how it has generated a memorial literature.

2. It was then incumbent upon me to show that this genuinely "theological" thought process, as situated in the vivid relation and

encounter with God, is a distinctive form of critical thinking. Recalling the biblical models of this thinking again and again, as practically oriented to a specific situation, may hold open by analogy a realistic view of the future and may preserve the daily-life orientation from both fateful distortion of mind inspired by fear and fatal delusions rooted in a presumptuous attitude. Preserving such recollecting thought and drawing analogies then opens the clear-headed and concrete view of the right thing to do at the right time, a view that arises time and again within the categorical indeterminancy and non-disposability[24] of the future to which we are exposed as immutably as we are exposed to the invisible God witnessed in the biblical scriptures, to be recollected again and again by reading and hearing.

3. I have tried to make clear that this critical thinking, with its effect of illuminating the future, remains strictly bound to the performative replaying of the biblical models of self-experience and experience of God as *fides ex auditu* ("faith coming from hearing").

4. It then follows that "Bible reading" and this particular kind of critical thinking coincide as a performative act: we must keep this distinctive, indeed definitive, performative coincidence of reading and critical thinking in mind when we seek to transpose biblical literature into film and electronic media.

Notes

[Translated by Charles Ess and Christof Hardmeier, with assistance from Armin Siedlecki, Philosophy and Religion Department, Drury University]

1. I am very grateful to Charles Ess for the struggle of empathic advices and persistent questions on terms and phrases we discussed extensively to sharpen the sense of this contribution in English as clear and precise as possible.

2. English translations are the author's own but following closely the translation of Weinfeld (1991). Non-amended translations will be designated as "MW".

3. We can ignore here the remaining narrative insertions in 4.41-43, 10.6 f., and 27.1,11: see Hardmeier (2000b, 64, note 11).

4. The term "transmediation" means either the putting of orality into script and/or the change of communication mode such as the transposition of a speech in a narrative discourse by embedding it in a narrative framework, resulting in a "narrated speech" in contrast with an "indirect" or "reported" speech" which is told without being quoted as such.

5. This choice of term as a noun is highly non-idiomatic, but it is most precise because it captures the active sense of recollecting what is decisive for understanding the genuine function of narration.

6. Here the hermeneutic fact that the reader/listener completes the text is not meant and such an impression is to be avoided.

7. The Hebrew expression *'asah l^e* means a neutral, not a hostile acting on sb/sth as the usual translation with "*do to sb/sth*" suggests.

8. This can be shown with reference to the book of Job; see C. Hardmeier (2003).

9. This non-idiomatic term has to be explained. Non-disposability is the translation of the German theological term "Unverfügbarkeit" and means something that escapes one`s disposal ("Verfügungs-Gewalt") so that it cannot be mastered or controlled in any way, because it is categorically not at one`s disposal to influence it. In everyday life, non-disposability will be experienced as chance, accident, surprise or hazard, as event and something that really happens beyond one`s imagination and anticipation.

10. Moses taught this model of a diplomatic and peaceful strategy by remembering the crossing of the land of Edom (and Moab) in Deut. 2.2-8; see 2.9 and 29.

11. The Hebrew text says that God has "hardened the heart" of Sihon. It has to be noted that 'mind' and 'thinking' are in Hebrew localized in the heart (and not in the head): see H. Wolff (1990, 68ff.).

12. Notice the highly misleading translation of this verse in the Contemporary English Version, © American Bible Society (CEV): "We met Sihon and his army in battle at Jahaz!" This translation suggests a (primary) initiative of Israel for the battle and hides the sense of the Hebrew text, which undoubtedly means a primary aggression of the king against Israel as it is translated above verbatim.

13. The great problem of the banning (translated in CEV with "utterly destroying") of people (Hebr. haram) cannot be discussed here. It has to be noted that this practice was something like a consecration of the spoils to God by destruction and figures in the deuteronomistic theory of history as the reverse of the unconditional loyalty to God when Israel was successful in defeating enemies.

14. The adjective term "non-disposable" is used in the same way as the term "non-disposability" as it is explained in note 8.

15. See Josh. 2.9-11! Here Rahab of Jericho revealed to the scouts that the "heart" of the peoples in the western territories "is taken out of them" (v. 11 = discouraged) due to the message of both: of YHWH's support in the Exodus and of what Israel has done to the two kings, Sihon and Og, in the east of Jordan. According to Josh. 2.9b, above all, this discouragement is explicitly the way God proceeded to deliver the territories and peoples in the west to Israel's disposal (see also Deut. 2.31f.!). On the other hand, in Deut. 1.28 we find exclusively the same phraseological "term" of "taking the heart out of *sb*" as in Josh.

2.11. But in Deut. 1.28, the discouragement is that of the Israelites themselves due to their own grumbling misinterpretation of the scout's report about the "good land".

16. For the non-idiomatic term "remembering" see note 4.

17. The Hebrew terms rasha´/ rish´ah (unfairness and wickedness) are the counter-concept of *sædæq/s^edaqa*, that means rectitude and righteousness.

18. To the "heart" as center of mind and thinking see above note 10.

19. This paradigm is to be found *mutatis mutandis* in Joshua 10 (and 11). Because of making peace with Israel (Josh 9.15ff., see Deut. 2.26-29) the Gibeonites were attacked by the surrounding rulers of the western territories (Josh 10.4, see Deut 2.30.32) so that Israel overcomes the aggressors with God's help (Josh 10.9f., see Deut. 2.33) by supporting the attacked Gibeonites (10.6f.). This supporting military expedition and the following combat missions (Josh. 10.16ff.) result in taking possession of the whole territory of the aggressors (10.40-42) as in the paradigmatic episode in Deut. 2.26-36: see especially v.34f.

20. Note the opening word *qashah* (hardening, stubborn) used as in Deut. 2.30.

21. The episodes named by the locality of taking place are told in the other books of the Pentateuch but with regard to the history of biblical literature in a younger version: for Taberah, see Num. 11.1-3, for Massah, Exod. 17.1-7 and for Kibroth-Hattaavah, Num. 11.4-34.

22. It is important to see that this fear of setting off for the land results from the distortion of perception caused by fantasies of horror grumbled in the tents of the people; see below.

23. See the translations of Deut. 1.26b; 43b and 9.23b in Weinfeld (1991, 141, 146, 399).

24. For the meaning of this term see note 8.

References

Assmann, J .1992. Das kulturelle Gedächtnis. Schrift, Erinnerung und politische Identität in frühen Hochkulturen, Munich: C.H.Beck.

Hardmeier, C. 2003. New Relations between Systematic Theology and Exegesis and the Perspectives on Practical Theology and Ethics, paper for the International Symposium "Reconsidering the Boundaries Between Theological Disciplines," 12-15 October, Heidelberg, Germany (will be published in 2003).

———. 2000b. Das Schema´ Isra´el in Dtn 6,4 im Rahmen der Beziehungstheologie der deuteronomistischen Tora, in Mincha. *Festgabe für Rolf Rendtorff zum 75. Geburtstag*, ed. E. Blum, 61-92. Neukirchen-Vluyn: Neukirchener Verlag

Lohfink, N. 2000. Narrative Analyse von Dtn 1,6-3,29, in Mincha. *Festgabe für Rolf Rendtorff zum 75. Geburtstag*, ed. E. Blum, 121-176. Neukirchen-Vluyn: Neukirchener Verlag

Weinfeld, M. 1991. Deuteronomy 1-11. A New Translation with Introduction and Commentary, *The Anchor Bible 5*, New York, London, Toronto, Sydney, Auckland: Doubleday.

Wolff, H. W. 1990. *Anthropologie des Alten Testaments*, 5th ed. Munich: Chr. Kaiser

3

A Biblical Defense of Critical Thinking

Byron Eubanks

In 1974 two California men petitioned the Federal Communications Commission (FCC) to limit religious broadcasters' use of reserved educational FM radio and TV channels. The FCC denied their petition (RM-2493) in 1975, but somehow a rumor connected well known atheist Madalyn Murray O'Hair with this petition. Religious broadcasters and organizations enlisted supporters to send petitions to the FCC opposing RM-2493. Well-meaning Christians flooded the FCC with as many as 8000 petitions a day in ensuing months and years. By the late 1980s the FCC had received some 30 million pieces of mail opposing this bogus threat to religious broadcasting. How much time and energy have Christians spent on mailing 30 million letters and collecting untold millions of signatures on petitions? How much tax money has the FCC spent on processing this mountain of mail and trying to stop this runaway train? How much credibility have Christians lost by crying wolf when the wolves were off attacking somewhere else? With the advent of e-mail this hoax has taken on new life and continues to circle the globe generating misdirected ire and gobbling up misspent resources.

This is but one case in which a small dose of skepticism and checking a few facts could have redirected Christian zeal into more productive endeavors. A little critical thinking can go a long way toward being wise as serpents and harmless as doves. Many Christians readily use the critical thinking skills they have developed through their education and work experience in the expression of their faith. They assume that loving God with all one's mind means using all one's mental skills and faculties to serve God. Others, however, have a view of faith that renders suspect any reliance on human reason in religious matters. I will offer no analysis of the origins of this view of faith (but interested readers can turn to Noll 1994, Moreland 1997). Rather, I am concerned to undermine any resistance those who accept this view might offer to teaching critical thinking in a church context. I assume that one effective response to such resistance would be to show that rejection of critical thinking is not well-founded biblically. This paper is an initial attempt to do just that.

In what follows I first consider biblical passages that might be interpreted to support the view that faith and critical thinking are incompatible. In subsequent sections I consider passages that support a faithful use of critical thinking either by example, by directly commanding critical thinking, or by indirectly commanding critical thinking as an implication of some other command. For the purposes of this paper I am working with a broad or inclusive definition of critical thinking. By critical thinking I have in mind ordinary mental attitudes and activities like being cautious about accepting claims to truth, especially when those making the claims have something to gain or seem overly eager to win acceptance of their claims; asking for evidence or wondering what would count as evidence for such truth claims; using arguments to persuade or to defend one's beliefs or actions; and looking for common reasoning mistakes in arguments.

Possible Biblical Objections to Critical Thinking

One passage I have heard used in ways that come very close to challenging the legitimacy of critical thinking is Proverbs 3:5-6: "Trust in the Lord with all your heart and lean not on your own understanding. In all your ways acknowledge him, and he will make your paths straight" (NIV). Often those quoting this passage are calling for an exercise of faith and rejection of any faithfulness implied by dependence on human effort. Such a call to faith is commendable. Indeed, these verses and those that follow (v. 7: Do not be wise in your own eyes; fear the LORD and shun evil.) at least warn against any intellectual arrogance that would displace God in favor of the sufficiency of human reason and understanding. If the choice is between a humble trust in God and an arrogant trust in human reason, it is clear which the wise person will choose.

However, the book of Proverbs as a whole assumes that faith and an arrogant misuse of human reason are not the only two options. One need merely consider the many facets of wisdom in the book to see that this is so. Kidner identifies five word groups connected with wisdom in Proverbs (Kidner 1964, 36f.). (1) Wisdom comes through *instruction* or *training*, by *correction* and *reproof.* (2) The wise person is a person of *understanding* and *insight*, one who can *discern between* good and evil. Wisdom includes (3) *wise dealing*, (4) *shrewdness*, and *discretion.* Though shrewdness can degenerate into scheming, Proverbs "is largely concerned to show that the godly man is in the best sense a man of affairs, who takes the trouble to know his way about, and plan his course realistically." (Kidner 1964, 37). (5) The wise person is also a person of *knowledge* and *learning.*

In contrast to the wise, Proverbs shows us the fool. This can be the simple person who is gullible, easily led astray, too ready to believe what he is told. The simple person is not mentally disabled but is one who through sheer laziness or weak character is unwilling to take on the discipline required of one who would gain wisdom. Three different words are commonly translated "fool,"[1] but the passages in which they occur paint a composite picture of one whose trouble is at heart a spiritual and moral one. The fool likes his folly, returning to it like a dog to vomit (26:11). His laziness stems from rejecting the fear of the Lord (1:29). He is not self-critical and can hardly imagine himself mistaken ("a hundred stripes for a fool accomplishes less than a rebuke to a discerning man," 17:10). The fool has no patience for searching out wisdom (17:16, 27), and he "feeds on" ideas without discrimination (15:14), taking pleasure in opinion rather than seeking understanding (18:2).

So while we do well to heed the warning against intellectual arrogance, the book of Proverbs hardly teaches that trust in God and using one's critical capacities are wholly incompatible. Indeed true wisdom begins with the fear of the Lord. It is this fear of the Lord that motivates development of genuine wisdom and use of divinely given mental capacities.

In 1 Corinthians 1-4 Paul uses strong language to put worldly wisdom in its place in relation to the divine wisdom expressed in God's plan for human redemption. "Where is the wise man? Where is the scholar? Where is the philosopher of this age? Has not God made foolish the wisdom of the world?" (1:20) "For the foolishness of God is wiser than man's wisdom, and the weakness of God is stronger than man's strength." (1:25) "But God chose the foolish things of the world to shame the wise; God chose the weak things of the world to shame the strong." (1:27) "Do not deceive yourselves. If any one of you thinks he is wise by the standards of this age, he should become a "fool" so that he may become wise. For the wisdom of this world is foolishness in God's sight." (3:18-19a) Some might take Paul's attack on worldly wisdom as a general condemnation of all human reasoning or at least as raising suspicions about the need for critical thinking among believers. Moreland, for example, says some conclude that human reasoning and argument are especially futile for evangelism (1997, 58f.).

A closer look at Paul's extended argument, however, indicates that boasting about wisdom may have been central to the divisions that plagued the Corinthian church. First, Paul identifies several groups in the church, each of which claims to belong to Paul, Apollos, Cephas, or Christ. Second, it seems clear that these groups boasted of their champions. Paul reminds them that God chose the lowly so that no one could boast in God's presence; the only boasting should be in the Lord (1:26-31). He tells them not to boast about human leaders (3:21), not to be puffed up in favor of one against another (4:6), and not to boast about what they have received as a gift (4:7). Third, the source of this boasting seems to be an infatuation with wisdom. Paul reminds the Corinthians that his own preaching focused on the cross of Christ and was not delivered with eloquent words (1:17). The power of his message depended on its content, not on his persuasive skills and oratory (2:1-5). The content of Paul's message, a crucified Christ, is folly to Greeks and a stumbling block to Jews, for the former seek wisdom and the latter miraculous signs (1:22-23). Over the course of his argument Paul uses "wisdom" in two negative ways and in two positive ways (Barrett 1968, 67f.). Negatively it refers to eloquence or skillful speech (1:17, 2:1, 5) and to the kind of worldly reasoning which would find the notion of a crucified Christ an impossible contradiction (1:25, 26, 3:19). Positively, wisdom refers to God's divine plan of redemption (1:21) and the substance of that redemption (1:30, where wisdom is related to righteousness, sanctification, and redemption). Human wisdom on its own would never devise such a plan, for instead of finding a way for humans to ascend to God, in the divine plan God reaches down to humans through the incarnation (Barrett 1968, 55). No reasoning based on the assumption of a metaphysical first mover would ever lead one to incarnation and crucifixion.

What are we to make of all this talk of wisdom? First, "the high incidence in these three chapters of this otherwise infrequent word group, plus the fact that in most cases the word is used in a pejorative sense, is a sure indication that this is a Corinthian way of speaking, not Paul's." (Fee 1987, 48) Paul's language and the argument itself suggest that the Corinthian believers had become enamoured with wisdom and fine speech and were championing various leaders as teachers of wisdom. Though Paul never accused Apollos of fault, it may be that Apollos's oratorical skills (Acts 18:24f.) or the polished speech of other itinerant teachers helped move the Corinthians in this direction. It seems likely they had begun to think of the gospel as an expression of wisdom, worldly wisdom in Paul's view. If so, then the divisions in the church were crucial because their cause was a false theology in which a triumphant wisdom excluded the cross or displaced it from its place of priority (Fee 1987, 50).

In this context, Paul's attack on wisdom makes perfect sense but cannot rightly be taken as a blanket condemnation of human reason. If it were, Paul would himself be guilty, for obviously he carefully constructs an argument to persuade the Corinthians of their error. Too, Paul's other letters, especially Romans, hold a wealth of examples of his use of careful reasoning. The record in Acts also makes clear that Paul routinely used arguments (likely based on scriptural premises) to convince the Jews that Jesus was the Messiah (e.g., 9:22, 13:16-47, 17:16-31, 18:4, 19:8-10). Some take Paul's statement that at Corinth he decided to "know nothing . . .except Jesus Christ, and him crucified" (1 Cor. 2:2) as an indication that he changed tactics after failing to convince the Greeks in Athens. However, there is no indication in Acts that in Athens he departed from his usual habit of presenting the gospel to Jews first and then to any who would listen. And Luke's description of Paul's work in Corinth suggests no change in approach: "Every sabbath he reasoned (διελέγετο) in the synagogue, trying to persuade Jews and Greeks" (Acts 18:4). When describing his preaching in Corinth, Paul more likely intended to contrast his preaching, which emphasized content and the crucified Christ, with that of itinerant teachers, who were more concerned with persuasive rhetoric and with whom the Corinthians were comparing him, than with his preaching before and after Athens (Fee 1987, 92). The error at Corinth, common for both the Greeks and the Jews, ultimately was taking pride in a worldly wisdom instead of glorying only in the crucifixion. So, much like the message of Proverbs, Paul's attack was on an idolatrous use of wisdom, not on human reasoning per se.

A context of false teaching also lies behind Paul's warning to the Christians at Colossae not to be taken captive through hollow and deceptive philosophy (2:8). Christian students often mention this verse at some point in their first philosophy course, and it takes little imagination to expect its use to oppose a church sponsored critical thinking class. Paul's description of this philosophy (it depends on human traditions, basic principles or elemental spirits of the world, and denies Christ) and the letter as a whole indicate that he likely has a particular heresy in mind. So, this verse should not be interpreted as a general condemnation of philosophical study. Nor does it support a rejection of critical thinking. For one thing, philosophy and critical thinking are not identical. Though critical thinking is intrinsic to philosophy as a discipline, it is by no means the sole property of any discipline. Second, and more importantly, Paul's warning actually requires the Colossians to exercise critical thinking. To avoid being taken captive they would have to have a cautious skepticism of preaching and teaching. They would have to be able to test the content of all teaching, consider its implications and connections with other teachings, and evaluate new teachings in light of accepted doctrinal criteria. Instead of challenging critical thinking, this passage demonstrates why believers need to be adept critical thinkers.

Biblical Examples of Critical Thinking

I have already mentioned Paul's practice, described in Acts, of trying to convince Jews that Jesus was the Messiah. Luke's descriptions in Acts (9:22, 13:16-47, 17:2-3, 16-31, 18:4, 19:8-10) do not detail Paul's interactions with the Jews, but we may safely conclude they involved more than proclamation alone, more than mere statement that Jesus is the Christ. Luke uses several related words (e.g., συμβιβαζω [prove conclusively], διακατελεγχομαι [show convincingly], and επιδεικνυμι [confound completely]) which imply a rational process of persuasion, though one based on scriptural assumptions. Luke's description of Paul's preaching in Acts 13 reveals more proclamation than explicit argumentation. But even this proclamation involves a selection of scriptures which his hearers might be expected to accept as pointing toward Jesus as the Christ. This is not to claim that the results of Paul's preaching depended on his logical skills, but it is fair to conclude that in addition to proclamation and working of signs, persuasion and debate were routine in Paul's contact with Jewish opponents.

In Acts 15 the disagreement over circumcision provides another clear example of the apostles' use of argumentation. Initially, Paul debated with the Judean Jews who advocated circumcising Gentile converts (15:2). After the leaders in Jerusalem had debated the issue (15:7), Peter lays out an argument, which settles the controversy (v 7-11). For premises he reminds his audience of his own experience of being sent to Cornelius, a Gentile. Their demonstration of the gift of tongues clearly showed God gave them the Holy Spirit. This implies God cleansed their hearts by faith. In this God made no distinction between Jew and Gentile. If salvation is through grace in Christ, then to require Gentiles to submit to circumcision (a yoke also burdensome for Jews—see Acts 15:10) is to put God to the test. Here we see an argument derived not from Scripture but from religious experience and from theological considerations themselves requiring several inferences.

In the later chapters of Acts, Paul's defense of his actions before the Roman and Jewish authorities clearly show his awareness of the role of evidence in supporting legal judgment and his awareness of the need to tailor his defense to his audience. For example, he purposely drives a wedge between two factions of his accusers when he identifies with the Pharisees and their hope for the resurrection (23:6). And his repeated defenses at Felix's court are models of orderly recitation of the pertinent facts (chs. 24-26). Based on a reading of Acts, there is no evidence that the early Christian leaders saw any intrinsic incompatibility between using human critical faculties and having a vibrant Christian faith.

The preeminent model for all Christian living is of course Jesus himself. Any biblical defense of critical thinking that failed to find a friend in Jesus' own actions would be sorely lacking. In a recent article, Dallas Willard makes a convincing case for seeing Jesus as the greatest human thinker bar none (1999). He builds his case around four representative examples of Jesus' use of logic in the gospels. These four examples will serve our purpose well, too, though additional examples are readily available.[2]

Matthew 12:1-8 tells of the Pharisees accusing Jesus and his disciples of violating the Sabbath by plucking and eating grain while walking through the grain fields. Jesus responds by building an argument around two counter-examples and a quotation from Hosea. In the first example, Jesus reminds them of the story of David and his men eating bread set aside for the priests. In the second he notes that temple priests are not considered guilty, though they violate the work limits associated with the Sabbath in the course fulfilling their temple duties. The point of the Hosea quotation, "I desire mercy, not sacrifice," is that they have both misunderstood scripture and the nature of God. The way in which the argument is incompletely stated allows a variety of interpretations of the application of the counterexamples to the situation at

hand.[3] But clearly Jesus assumes his audience can see the relevant application, draw the appropriate implications, and discover their hypocrisy.[4]

While Willard does not discuss it, immediately following this
episode Matthew describes another striking example of Jesus' use of
argument—in an encounter in which opponents lay a trap for Jesus concerning the Sabbath. "Is it right to cure on the Sabbath?" they ask, having planted a man in need of cure. Jesus uses a brief but pointed argument to reveal their hypocrisy and evade their trap. He begins by assuming they would agree that were one of their sheep to fall in a pit on the
Sabbath, they would lift it out. But a human is much more valuable than
a sheep. So, by implication, if it is lawful to do good to the sheep, it is
surely lawful to do good, in this case to heal, a man on the Sabbath. To
confirm this conclusion, he heals the man's hand. This good act stands
in sharp contrasts to the Pharisees' evil act of trying to trap Jesus on the
Sabbath. Again, Jesus assumes his hearers will understand the argument
and see their hypocrisy.

Willard's second example is Luke 20:27-40. The Sadducees confront Jesus with a *reductio ad absurdum* argument against belief in resurrection. If, by the practice of Levirate marriage, a woman were to suc-
cessively marry seven brothers, then by implication she would be the
wife of all in the resurrection, and this is absurd. In response Jesus first
rejects their assumption that practices like marriage will be the same in
the resurrection as they are now. Then he offers a counter argument in
support of belief in resurrection. He begins with something the
Sadduccees would accept as fact: Moses called God the God of
Abraham, Isaac, and Jacob. In fact, in the Exodus account, God identified himself so to Moses. But at the time of Moses' encounter at the
burning bush, these patriarchs were long since dead. But to be their God
is to be in covenant relationship with them. And "one cannot very well
imagine the living God communing with a dead body or a non-existent
person and keeping covenant faithfulness with them." (Willard 1999,
609) The conclusion is obvious: if God is the God of the living, then
there must be a resurrection.

The episode immediately following in Luke's account is Willard's
third example—one in which Jesus uses a bit of logic to lead his hearers toward a new view of Messiah. Referring to Psalm 110:1, commonly understood as a reference to Messiah, Jesus asks how Messiah can be
David's son if David calls him Lord. The intended inference is that
Messiah cannot be merely David's son and thus not merely a political

deliverer. Messiah must be something higher, something more than they had considered.

Willard's last choice is an example of Jesus' teaching from the Sermon on the Mount, Matthew 5:29-30. Jesus' instruction to those tempted to lust is to gouge out the offending eye or cut off the offending hand. Better to be maimed than to remain whole yet go to hell. Willard sees this as a kind of *reductio* demonstration of the need to surpass the righteousness of the Pharisees and teachers of the law (v. 20). If the goal of their righteousness were to avoid doing anything wrong, then consistency would lead to the drastic measures Jesus suggests. But Jesus' point is surely not that his audience should actually dismember themselves, for this need cause no change of heart and mind. The point is to get beyond this kind of righteousness, "beyond, where compassion or love and not sacrifice is the fundamental thing." (Willard 1999, 610) Whether or not one agrees with the details of Willard's interpretation the point remains that any attempt to understand Jesus' teaching here must take account of the *logic* of this whole section of his teaching on the Law.

Consider also one example of critical thinking by early converts at Berea (Acts 17:10-12). These Bereans are praised because they welcomed Paul's message. Yet they did not hear uncritically. They "examined the scriptures every day to see if what Paul said was true." Their belief followed on this considered reception of the gospel. Here the Holy Spirit apparently worked through their testing of Paul's message to accomplish conversion. There is no naive reception here, but a demonstration of the kind of wisdom the writer of Proverbs had in mind.

In a recent article, Steven Austin and Mark Strauss provide a superb example of a need for this kind of testing today (Austin & Strauss 1999). They examine the statements of several popular teachers and authors (Hal Lindsey, Grant Jeffrey, J.R. Church, Gary Stearman, John Hagee, Peter Lalonde, and Paul Lalonde) that an increase in the rate of severe earthquakes is evidence that the return of Christ is near. These authors cite sources to support their claims, though the source information is incomplete and does not allow one to trace their documentation. Austin and Strauss show that the most complete catalogues of earthquakes demonstrate that the incidence of severe earthquakes regionally and world wide was greater in the first half than the second half of this century. Readers and hearers of these teachers and preachers would have to search more than just the Scriptures to discover their errors,[5] but the incomplete documentation should be a red flag warning of suspect claims.

The examples of critical thinking identified in this section are hardly all that can be found in the gospels and Acts. But these few show clearly that Jesus and his most prominent followers routinely constructed arguments and expected their hearers to have at least some abilities in critical thinking. They present no formal theories of logic, nor do they call attention to formal features of arguments. By example, though, they demonstrate that people of faith can also be people of careful thought.

Commands to Think Critically

In this section I identify passages which explicitly command hearers/readers to exercise some element of critical thought. These passages do not identify critical thinking skills by names familiar in an academic setting, but they do call for kinds of careful thought and discernment at the core of any inclusive definition of critical thinking. I will briefly consider eight passages, six linked by their common use of one Greek word, δοκιμαζω. This word is translated variously as "test," "examine," "prove," "approve," and can emphasize either the process of testing or the approval that results from testing (Arndt & Gingrich 1952; Kittel 1964).

In 2 Corinthians 13:5 Paul begins the concluding section of a long argument defending his apostleship (an argument he assumes the Corinthians can follow) by telling the Corinthians to examine themselves to see whether they are in the faith, i.e., to see whether Christ is in them. The point of this self-examination is that, given Paul's role in their coming to the faith, their passing the test of genuine faith implies that Paul passes the test of genuine apostleship. The self-examination commanded here is not a test of logical validity but it does assume an ability and willingness to both understand and apply a criterion of genuine faith. This in turn assumes a level of self awareness and commitment to honesty that allow, even require, one to recognize and avoid self-deception or biased judgment of one's experience and beliefs. Such self-awareness and honesty are the heart of critical thinking. Of course, discerning the difference between genuine and counterfeit faith is not something that happens independently of the Holy Spirit. And, given the previous discussion of Paul's argument in 1 Corinthians 1-4, we know that Paul was well aware of the danger of relying on human wisdom alone. The point here, though, is that the Holy Spirit may and often does work through human thinking to accomplish its work. Here Paul assumes at least that they are compatible.

Galatians 6:4 shows that Paul recommended a similar self-criticism to his Galatian readers as well. Having contrasted the life of sin and the life of the Spirit (5:13-26), Paul gives concrete examples of the latter. A spiritually mature person is one who restores those who have fallen into sin, one who is aware of his or her own tendency to sin, one who helps others carry their burdens, and one who does not have an inflated view of self (6:1-3). Such a person must "test his own actions" rather than compare them to others' actions. Again, such testing assumes an ability to compare Paul's model of Christian living with one's own behavior and honestly judge the degree to which the latter imitates the former.

In Ephesians 5:10 this same Greek root (here in participle form— i.e., δοκιμαζοντεσ occurs in the context of a challenge to believers to live as children of light. The second half of Ephesians (chapters 4-6) contains many concrete examples of behavior appropriate for children of light, but in 5:10 Paul tells the readers to find out, discover, try to learn what pleases the Lord. No matter how many specific examples are listed, Paul knows that it is not possible to cover every possible action or situation. So, inherent in the life of faith is an examination of every course of action to see if it would please the Lord. We could reasonably expect this to involve evaluation of the conceived action in light of reflection on relevant Christian moral instruction as well as what one believes about the nature of God and his intention for human living. The skills of recognizing implications, identifying relevantly similar cases, and of imagining possible outcomes of actions would serve one well in such evaluation.[6]

Paul tells the Thessalonians to "test everything" (δοκιμαζετε) so they can hold on to the good and avoid the evil (5:21). The immediate context (v 19-20: Do not put out the Spirit's fire; do not treat prophecies with contempt.) suggests a need to discern between genuine and spurious expressions of the Holy Spirit and between false and true prophets. No specific test or criterion is identified, though other passages (e.g., 1 Cor. 12:3) indicate a theological test based on one's beliefs about the nature of Jesus or a test based on what builds up the church. Realization that claimed spiritual gifts and prophetic utterances can be false calls for a cautious skepticism on the part of believers. Such skepticism stops short of cynicism and is a central attitude of critical thinking (Brookfield 1987, 21f.).

In 1Timothy 3:10 the object of testing is not self or a possible course of action, but candidates for the office of deacon. Presumably, Paul intended prospective deacons to be tested in terms of the description of character in the previous verses. The criteria presented (worthy of respect, sincere, not indulging in much wine, not pursuing dishonest gain, keeping hold of deep truths of the faith with a clear conscience) do not allow for a quick and easy test of observation. Such testing requires careful attention to behavior as well as drawing inferences about motives and judgments about the way in which one lives out one's beliefs. In practice such testing is more intuitive than explicit, but even intuitive judgments may rely on critical thinking skills functioning tacitly rather than overtly.

The last of the passages that use the same root for "test" is 1 John 4:1. Writing in a context in which false prophets are a problem, John calls for caution in accepting prophetic utterance as evidence of the Holy Spirit's presence, for ungodly causes are possible, too. So, testing the spirits, and by implication the prophetic utterances and the prophets themselves, is called for. Here the criterion is explicitly theological: they must confess that Jesus has come in the flesh (4:2). False prophecy may take many contemporary forms. Then or now, applying a theological test requires a careful attention to the content of the utterance, ability to see beyond the obvious and uncover unstated assumptions and implications of the explicit message, and ability to compare the message and all it implies with accepted teaching. Again, a healthy skepticism must be assumed as well. That Jesus anticipated this kind of problem is evidenced by his repeated command to "watch out that no one deceives you" (e.g., Mt 24:4).

Finally, two passages call for elements of critical thought other than testing. First, in 2 Tim 2:1-7 Paul uses three analogies (soldier, athlete, and farmer) to teach the nature of Christian service. Paul tells Timothy to reflect on these, for the Lord will give him insight (v. 7). The word νοει is translated "reflect," "consider," "think on." Such reflection suggests looking for connections with the broader content of Paul's teachings and for behavioral implications. The most interesting point for our purposes, though, is Paul's assumption that the Lord uses human reflection as a means of revealing insight. Second, the writer of 1 Peter tells his readers to be prepared to give an answer or "apology" (απολογιαν) to any who ask the reason (λογον) for the hope that believers have (3:15). Such an answer need hardly entail a carefully argued defense of the faith; a simple testimony of personal experience might be sufficient. That the answer is provided with gentleness and respect (v. 16) seems to preclude any hard-nosed apologetic that seeks to bowl over the audience with the strength of its logic. Still, the command surely allows for a carefully thought out and developed response presented with sensitivity to the audience in hopes that God can use it to win over the hearers.

The passages considered in this section demonstrate that not only are faith and critical thinking compatible but that some element of critical thought is essential to Christian living.

Indirect Commands to Think Critically

In this final section I briefly discuss two instances from Jesus' teaching in which he implicitly calls his followers to use their minds. In his teaching on the cost of discipleship (Luke 14:25-35) Jesus uses two illustrations to help communicate his point, i.e., that "discipleship requires a conscious advance commitment, made with a realistic estimate of the ultimate personal cost." (Expositor's Bible Commentary 262). First, imagine someone wants to build a tower. No one, at least no sensible person, begins such a project without first weighing the cost of construction against the financial resources available. Failing to exercise sound financial judgment means one risks being unable to complete the project and having to listen to the jeers of others. Second, imagine a king at the brink of war. When confronted with an opposing army twice as large as his own, only a fool would not weigh carefully whether diplomacy would not be more prudent.

Jesus surely did not intend to suggest that deciding to be his disciple was merely a matter of making a cost/benefit analysis. But these illustrations do suggest that the decision to follow him is one that should be made only after careful thought. Both illustrations imply a careful weighing of options and possible outcomes of choices. Estimations of construction costs and military strength require fairly high levels of thinking. Those considering whether to become Jesus' disciples are not told to stop thinking but, by implication, to think carefully what their decision may require of them.

Later in Luke's account (16:1-9) Jesus tells a parable of a dishonest manager called to give an account by his employer. Seeing no prospects of future employment, the manager writes off a portion of his employer's debtors' accounts. Surprisingly, Jesus commended the shrewd or prudential way this manager used wealth to gain friends against an uncertain future. It is the manager's prudence, not his dishonesty, in virtue of which he serves as a model for Jesus' disciples. Following in Luke's account, Jesus teaches that trustworthy handling of worldly wealth is prerequisite to being trusted with true riches (10-12), that it is not possible to truly serve both God and money (13), that God has values different from humans (14-15), and that choosing to live in luxury while ignoring the needy at one's door may have unexpected eternal consequences (parable of Lazarus, 19-31). In light of the context's emphasis on proper use of money, the initial parable's emphasis on prudent use of money is clear even if some details remain murky.

Prudent stewardship requires both the proper attitude toward money (it makes a good servant and a poor master) and careful use. These teachings primarily emphasize proper attitude, but proper use is implied, and proper use often requires or at least benefits from critical thinking. Consider this story printed in popular magazine ("Playing on Sympathy" 2000). After a twenty-five year old Bostonian told her friends and family she had ovarian cancer, fund raisers brought in over $40,000. Later, an investigation following an anonymous tip revealed she did not have cancer and had spent the money on liposuction and a new car. Less fraudulent opportunities for charitable giving abound, but many organizations spend high percentages of money raised on administrative costs with little actually going to relieve human need. A prudent steward will recognize that gifts carelessly given may express the proper attitude toward money yet fail to accomplish any good. A touch of skepticism and even minimal investigation of facts allows one to avoid fraud and more efficiently direct one's giving so as to accomplish its intended effect.

Conclusion

The passages discussed above hardly exhaust the biblical materials relevant to critical thinking. The nature of God in whose image humans were created, the nature of humans as physical, mental, and spiritual beings, the nature of faith, the effects of sin, and more should inform our understanding of what it means to live faithfully as Christians in our world. However, if I have fairly interpreted these passages, then there is clear evidence that (1) faith and critical thinking are not incompatible, and (2) critical thinking when used without a sinful arrogance can aid one in understanding biblical teaching and expressing one's faith in action.

Notes

1. Kidner associates the simple, the fool, and the scoffer as variations on a theme.

2. For example, Jesus' response to the charge that he casts out demons by the power of Satan includes several counter examples (Mk 3:20-27). And his rationale for calling the Pharisees hypocrites assumes that people would understand the inconsistency between their actions and their charge that Jesus didn't keep the law (Mk 7:1-13).

3. Willard takes the lesson of the David story to be that meeting significant human need can justify doing what ritual law forbids (1999, 608). Yet in the narrative, the disciples are hardly in danger of starvation. The point seems rather that the Pharisees' whole approach to scripture is suspect. Further, since Jesus is greater than David, just as he is greater than the temple (v. 6), and since an exception is made for David and his companions, an exception should be made for Jesus and his companions. The Expositors Bible Commentary (1976-1992) makes a compelling case for this interpretation in the context of the argument as a whole.

4. Willard suggests, quite plausibly it seems to me, that the incompleteness of the argument is intentional (1999, 607). The incompleteness of Jesus' arguments allow the hearers to come to the truth on their own, to achieve an inner understanding that is far more effective than it would be had Jesus made the logic of the argument so explicit as to force the conclusion on his hearers. [Editor's note: Compare this description of Jesus' use of incomplete argument with the Bachmans' discussion of "enthymematic" reasoning, as first recommended by Aristotle, p. 120.]

5. Strauss argues convincingly that their reading of Matthew in regard to earthquakes is wrong, too.

6. In Romans 12:2 the ability to discern God's will follows the transformation that occurs when we cease conforming to the world and have our minds renewed by God. In Philippians 1:10 Paul prays on behalf of the Philippians for increased love and insight that will result in an increase in their ability to discern actions approved by Christ.

References

Arndt, William F. and Wilbur Gingrich. 1952. *A Greek-English Lexicon of the New Testament and Other Early Christian Literature*, Fourth Revised and Augmented Edition. Chicago: University of Chicago Press.

Austin, Steven A. and Mark L. Strauss. 1999. "Are Earthquakes Signs of the End Times?" *Christian Research Journal* 21 (4): 30-39.

Barrett, C.K. 1968 (1987). *The First Epistle to the Corinthians* (New York: Harper & Row; reprinted Peabody, MA: Hendrickson). (Page citations are to the reprint edition).

Brookfield, Stephen D. 1987. *Developing Critical Thinkers: Challenging Adults to Explore Alternative Ways of Thinking and Acting.* San Francisco: Jossey-Bass.

The Expositor's Bible Commentary: with the New International Version of the Holy Bible. c1976-c1992. Frank E. Gaebelein, general editor; associate editor, J.D. Douglas. Grand Rapids : Zondervan.

Fee, Gordon. 1987. *The First Epistle to the Corinthians.* Grand Rapids: Eerdmans.

Kidner, Derek. 1964. *The Proverbs: An Introduction and Commentary.* Chicago: Inter-Varsity Press.

Kittel, Gerhard (ed.). 1964. *Theological Dictionary of the New Testament,* vol. II. Grand Rapids: Eerdmans.

Moreland, J.P. 1997. *Love Your God With All Your Mind.* Colorado Springs: NavPress.

Noll, Mark. 1994. *The Scandal of the Evangelical Mind.* Grand Rapids: Eerdmans.

"Playing on Sympathy." 2000. In "That's Outrageous," *Reader's Digest* (February), 33. From article by Sacha Pfeiffer and Mac Daniel, *The Boston Globe.*

Willard, Dallas. 1999. "Jesus the Logician." *Christian Scholar's Review* 28 (Summer): 605-14.

Three Contemporary Perspectives on
Critical Thinking and the Bible

4

Let the Reader Understand: Biblically Disciplined Thought in Light of the Interrogative Model of Reasoning

Susan Bachman, Ph.D. and James Bachman, Ph.D.

Introduction

"Critical thinking" means "careful thinking," and biblically disciplined thought is careful thought. In our Lutheran tradition, the old dogmaticians emphatically asserted that reason is God's gift and a tool to be used in the understanding of Scripture. The use of reason as a tool "to hear, apprehend, and ponder the words of Scripture includes also the observance of the laws of language (grammar) and the laws of human thinking (logic) as used in Scripture, for God has adopted the human tongue and the human manner of thinking" (Pieper I: 197-198). Martin Luther famously spoke of reason as the Devil's harlot, but Lutherans and other Christians sometimes fail to note Luther's assertion that those who blunder in grammar and logic "must necessarily also blunder in theology" (Pieper I: 198).

John Locke expressed what many people think is common sense about reasoning: it comes with the human territory at creation and it is not a human invention. To reason well people do not need a logic teacher like Aristotle. In his famous Essay, Locke declares that "God has not been so sparing to men to make them barely two-legged creatures, and left it to Aristotle to make them rational" (Essay Concerning

Human Understanding, Book IV, XVII. "Of Reason." 4). Yet, the structured models of reasoning that Aristotle and his successors, including Locke, have proposed help us reflect upon and employ the power of reason that God has given. In recent years Jaakko Hintikka has proposed an interrogative model to help describe how reason functions. We find this model helpful in a variety of domains of human thought ranging from science to law to ethics to theology. Here we use the model to illuminate how biblically disciplined thought engages with Scripture.

In part 1 we present and illustrate the model's main insights. In part 2 we use the model to reflect upon the changes that electronic media are bringing to the study of Scripture.

The Interrogative Model

Introductory Notes

If we are not careful, two different uses of "reason" and "reasoning" may confuse our discussion from the beginning. The interrogative model is not a theory concerning special powers that some faculty called Reason may or may not have. The model does not probe whether a faculty called Reason or Intuition can be a reliable source of information for inquiries. The model does not require that Reason be the final word on how to choose among the many sources of information available to human inquiry.

The interrogative model instead examines two fundamental reasoning activities that appear to lie at the foundation of inquiry. One is the activity of gathering information, an activity modeled as the posing of questions to sources. The other is the activity of logically processing available information to see what can and cannot be inferred from the available information. The model offers insights into similarities and differences between the two activities, into the continuous interaction of the two activities, and into the kinds of rules that govern correct and effective pursuit of the two activities.

A comment attributed to Luther helps illustrate what the interrogative model is and is not concerned with. In the Table Talk Luther is reported to have said, "Reason that is under the devil's control is harmful, and the more clever and successful it is, the more harm it does. We see this in the case of learned men who on the basis of their reason disagree with the Word. On the other hand, when illuminated by the Holy Spirit, reason helps to interpret the Holy Scriptures" (71).

Luther criticizes those who appeal to reason as though reason has special insight for overruling what God reveals in Christ and Scripture. When, however, reason is led by the Holy Spirit to be subservient to the Word, reason helps us interpret the Holy Scriptures. Roland Bainton offers insight into both Luther and reason.

> The reason why faith is so hard and reason so inadequate is a problem far deeper than logic. Luther often railed at reason, and he has been portrayed in consequence as a complete irrationalist in religion. This is quite to mistake his meaning. Reason in the sense of logic he employed to the uttermost limits. At Worms and often elsewhere he asked to be instructed from Scripture and reason. In this sense reason meant logical deduction from known premises; and when Luther railed against the harlot reason, he meant something else. Common sense is perhaps a better translation. He had in mind the way in which man ordinarily behaves, feels, and thinks. (1950, 172)

The interrogative model concerns itself with the activity of gathering information (related to but more complex than traditional talk about "known premises") and with the activity of inferring conclusions from available information (traditionally studied as "logical deduction").

Bainton speaks of "common sense" as the "reason" that beguiles and misleads. "Common sense" points to a complex of often unexamined premises and deductions that people develop in dialog with their culture and their individual experiences. Such thinking is often unexamined and undisciplined. This is Luther's "harlot." Christian faith challenges people to let their "common sense" be corrected, shaped, and illuminated in a disciplined dialog with Scripture and with the communal wisdom of those, both past and present, who have lived in the faith.

Rudiments of the Model[1]

To keep reflections concrete we begin with a biblical passage from which the title of our essay comes.

Mark 13:14 ῞Οταν δὲ ἴδητε τὸ βδέλυγμα τῆς ἐρημώσςεως ἑστηκότα ὅπου οὐ δεῖ, ὁ ἀναγινώσκων νοείτω, τότε οἱ ἐν τῇ Ἰουδαίᾳ φευγέτωσαν εἰς τὰ ὄρη,

Mark 13:14 "But when you see the desolating sacrilege set up where it ought not to be (let the reader understand), then let those who are in Judea flee to the mountains; (RSV)

So that readers may understand this essay, if not the passage, we ask you to pause and imagine how an individual or a group might begin to examine and interpret this passage. What will individuals who have little experience or background in reading Scripture begin to do? What will those who have much experience and background begin to do? Perhaps jot down something of a description of what you think is likely to begin happening.

Two Activities in Reasoning

The interrogative model suggests that you will discern two main activities in the work individuals and groups might begin to undertake in an attempt to understand Mark 13:14. On the one hand, people will seek information that might help them understand the passage. On the other hand, people will use logical inference to sort and sift the conclusions about the passage that might be supported by the available information and/or to discover what missing information might be helpful toward more completely understanding the passage.

The model names and defines two activities—two different actions or steps—that are fundamental to reasoning:

Interrogative steps seek, gather, and select information for whatever inquiry is being undertaken. Information-seeking is modeled as addressing questions to sources.

Individuals and study groups may well pause over this puzzling passage in Mark's Gospel and ask themselves questions like the following:

- What has come just before or just after this peculiar verse? What is the immediate context?
- What in the world is a "desolating sacrilege"? Does the term appear elsewhere in Scripture or other ancient literature?
- Who is speaking? Are these the words of Jesus? Why, in what looks like a quotation of Jesus' oral teaching, would the phrase "let the reader understand" appear?
- How should we who live far from Judea and its mountains understand the verse's advice? Does it speak about events now past or events yet to come? Does it have application to us? What does it mean to flee to the mountains?

These are only a few of the questions that might be asked. Many of us have been in study groups where such questions begin to be raised. Most of us have felt some frustration with group work when apparent flights of fancy raise what look like irrelevant questions and/or too quickly answer the questions that come to mind. At times, however, we discover that someone else's question startles and amazes us, opening up new lines of thought and possibilities for understanding. Typically, in the case of puzzling passages, people take time out to consult commentaries, dictionaries, histories, or knowledgeable experts to gather information and to pursue threads in depth.

Interrogative steps open up possibilities for gathering information that may offer insight into the passage. Information gathering, however, continuously interacts with the other reasoning activity, the activity called "logical inference."

Logical inference steps deductively draw out what is contained in the information made available by interrogative steps.

As information begins to be sought and gathered, we naturally draw together both spoken and unspoken information to see what conclusions may be possible. Consider, for example, the reasoning that might go on concerning "let the reader understand" in Mark 13:14. We have already noted that people might raise questions concerning who is speaking and why such an injunction might appear in the middle of oral instruction. We can imagine available information being drawn together in a variety of ways. Notice now how two commentators provide instructive examples of drawing together information on the way to interestingly different conclusions:

- Bruce Vawter (1969) begins by gathering information to answer another of the questions we mentioned above, "What in the world is a desolating sacrilege?" He asserts, as do many scholars, that Jesus is referring to "Dan 9:27, 11:31, 12:11, and what was meant there was the desecration of the temple in 167 B.C. by the Syrian king Antiochus IV Epiphanes (cf. 1 Macc 1:54, 6:7). . . ." (II: 167). Vawter does not say, but he expects his readers to find plausible that Jesus' reference to the desolating sacrilege would immediately bring the words of Daniel and the events of 167 B.C. to vivid remembrance in his disciples' minds. Jesus can then say, "Let him who reads take note!", meaning that whenever the disciples read or remember Daniel and the events of 167 B.C., then "what had occurred in Maccabean times will once more be a sign" (II: 167).

Vawter has brought together, on the one hand, explicit information about Daniel and Maccabean times and, on the other, unspoken information about how an oral reference to earlier writings and events could remind people like the disciples how they from time to time hear/read/ponder those writings and events. Putting this information together, Vawter offers a way to think of "let the reader understand" as a natural part of Jesus' instruction.

- Dennis Nineham, in his commentary on Mark, sketches a different line of reasoning. He draws our attention to "St Luke's version, which is clearer than St Mark's. . . ." (1963, 351). He does not explicitly say, but he expects us to think with him that Mark is somehow connecting Jesus' words with specific events in history such as "A.D. 40 when the Emperor Caligula came within an ace of having his statue set up in the temple at Jerusalem" (Nineham 353) or perhaps "the destruction of Jerusalem and the temple in A.D. 70" (Nineham 354). He puts these considerations together to conclude that "clearly these words [let the reader understand] can never have formed part of a spoken discourse" (354).

Nineham has brought together, on the one hand, explicit information concerning Luke's Gospel and the course of history experienced by the early church, and on the other, some less explicit information concerning how "let the reader understand" sits uncomfortably—not naturally like Vawter—in the midst of oral instruction. He develops the information to suggest that the most plausible interpretation is to think that people passing on the tradition of Jesus' words were alerting their hearers/readers to a connection that could be made between Jesus' instruction and events the church had now experienced.

Experienced interpreters of the Gospels will be aware of a number of different variations in the ways in which people try to understand Mark 13:14. Our purpose is not to assess the many variations, but to observe that two reasoning activities are continuously interacting: information, both explicit and not so explicit, is brought into play, and the information is structured through logical inference steps to show how a conclusion follows from the information that has been put into play.

The Activity That Makes the Difference

Many people mistakenly think that they are not good at logical, deductive inference. Logic sounds mathematical, specialized, and not close to everyday thinking. But the interrogative model points out that most people process complexes of available information efficiently and with remarkably few errors. And the errors we do make are often quickly corrected when we dialog with other people. Human beings "calculate" or "add things up" or "draw conclusions" all the time in their thinking. They do so quickly and with little conscious attention to what they are doing.

When difficulties present themselves in our thinking, or when people disagree, the problem more often than not lies with discovering what information is being used in the inquiry, not in discerning what conclusions the information supports. This is a very important observation. The difficulties occur because we are constantly using not only the explicit information that has been noted in the reasoning but also much unspoken information that, as we say, we are "taking for granted." Inferences that are thought to be difficult, "brilliant deductions," turn out, on examination, to be surprising and brilliant because they use unspoken information that not everyone had realized might be available for the inquiry. Inferences that are thought to be odd or "stupid" also often turn out, on examination, to be in dispute not because of bad logic but because unspoken information is being taken for granted that many would not grant.

A further problem that makes people think logical inference is difficult is that while we regularly and successfully employ logical inference, difficulties arise in giving precise accounts of what we do. Structured modeling and examining of inference has a long and continuing story going back thousands of years. Students must apply themselves carefully when they come to study and employ systems of explicit logical inference. Nonetheless, the basics of logical inference are well understood. The adaptation of logical inference to digital electronic circuitry in computers shows the difficulty but also the mastery human beings have of logical inference. As we shall see, it is the other activity in reasoning—seeking, gathering and selecting information—that has always resisted systematic mastery.

These reflections lead to further insights that the interrogative model offers concerning human reasoning.

Argument Sketch, Analysis, Evaluation, and Construction

Argument Sketch

The interrogative model observes that ordinary oral and written expressions of inquiries are incomplete sketches of what are usually indefinitely complex investigations. The role of tacit information, "taken for granted," accounts for much of the sketchiness of human communication.

We leave much information unspoken, because to make explicit reference to all the relevant information involved in our thinking is neither possible nor necessary. We are often safe in assuming that the community within which we pursue our inquiries shares a wide range of common information assumed to be true. Husbands and wives, for example, do not need laboriously to explain to one another why tonight they are agreeing to eat at Denny's instead of Chez Pierre. Underlying such a decision are complex questions, answers, and inferences involving available money, culinary preferences, and what is needed for nutrition, relaxation, and the savoring of a fine meal.

Use of tacit information, however, can also lead to miscommunication because there is never complete agreement within even the smallest communities concerning what can be taken for granted. The problem becomes much more complicated as we move from local communities to communities that embrace more and more diversity of experience and background.

James Voelz refers to the use of sketches in biblical material with the word shorthand. He writes that "no text is really as 'complete' as one would like to think. Every text is shot through with 'shorthand' and nonliteral usages. It is in the detection and filling in of these that most 'mischief' occurs in interpretation and where most disagreement takes place" (1995, 339). When knowledge of background information, presuppositions, or understood principles is attenuated or lost, then shortcuts in communication and reasoning will create problems. In these circumstances sketches of our own or others' thoughts need to be fleshed out more completely. With biblical texts the fleshing out of the sketches sometimes takes us beyond the limits of information available to us today.

Aristotle noted and explained some of the dynamics of inquiry sketches by means of the Greek term enthymeme. In his Rhetoric Aristotle praises enthymematic reasoning. He notes that argument from examples can be effective, but arguments in which the audience on its own completes some of the reasoning—the enthymeme—can "excite the louder applause" (I.1356b25). [Editor's note: Cf. Eubank's discussion of Jesus' use of incomplete argument, p. 109, note 4.]

Enthymemes are sometimes thought to be intentional shortcuts in arguments intended to conceal steps of reasoning, for ill or for good. But all communication and reasoning is, of necessity, enthymematic.

Because human thought involves continuous use of sketches, the interrogative model distinguishes between analyzing a sketch, evaluating a sketch, and constructing a new or enhanced line of reasoning based on or in reaction to one or more sketches.

Argument Analysis

Analysis is the foundation for evaluation and construction. Analysis of an oral or written sketch requires sympathetically filling out a sketch in more detail. Analysis, in the interrogative model, is defined in the word's literal Greek sense, a "taking apart." Whereas in some uses of the word "analysis," argument evaluation is included, the model's use of "analysis" is limited to the careful and sympathetic revealing of what is operating in an argument sketch. The goal is to supply some of the unspoken interrogative and logical inference steps to make it evident that if the all the supplied information is accepted, the ultimate conclusion must also be accepted. Analysis typically forces a search for tacit information that enables inference links to be made between the information explicitly supplied by the investigator and the steps needed to arrive at the ultimate conclusion. Analysis gives the benefit of the doubt to an argument sketch, but it also prepares the way for critical evaluation.

Argument Evaluation

Evaluation assesses correctness and excellence of the interrogative and logical inference steps. Evaluation can expose how information needed for inferences continues to be missing. Evaluation asks whether and how the information in play is reliable. Evaluation points out when mistakes have been made in inferences. Furthermore, evaluation asks the important question whether the information provided is the best available and the approach being taken in the inquiry is the best way to proceed.

Argument Construction

Analysis interacts recursively with evaluation and construction. The attempt through analysis to give a more complete sketch of an inquiry enables evaluation to identify strengths and weaknesses in the investigation. Exploitation of strengths and attempts to overcome weaknesses lead to newly constructed, more detailed sketches. Newly constructed sketches can then be further analyzed and evaluated until sufficient depth and accuracy for a given purpose is achieved. The newly constructed material may then be artistically or stylistically shaped for the envisioned situation or audience.

Creative Chaos and Closure

The model observes that often, at the beginning of an inquiry, much of the information that will be needed is missing, and initial accounts of the inquiry will be very sketchy. A typical strategy in the beginning stages of an inquiry will be rapidly to amass a large quantity of possibly relevant information. The result is often a riot of information that can leave many participants feeling that the inquiry has become chaotic. Persons inexperienced with the subject under discussion may perhaps create more chaos than experienced inquirers, but even seasoned inquirers are well advised to allow a certain amount of "creative chaos," to enlarge rather than restrict the quantity of information that is initially brought to and allowed at the table.

Historically, teachers of rhetoric have studied the first steps in communication and inquiry under the classical canon of *inventio*, or discovery. Aristotle and others have suggested that serious investigators need to explore "commonplaces" or common-sense insight in some organized fashion, like a checklist, to ensure adequate exploration of information that may be available for an inquiry. Exploring or visiting the "commonplaces" has meant examining similarities and differences, historical precedents, previous mistakes and errors, and the like. (See Corbett [1990] for an accessible summary of classical rhetoric and the "commonplaces.")

The model points out that while logical inference[2] is a well-defined and well-understood activity, information seeking is not easily governed or understood in terms of well-defined rules. Consequently, especially in inquiries that involve challenging puzzles, we may need to employ a variety of strategies for seeking, gathering and selecting information. Inquiry requires creativity and inventiveness because no hard and fast rules can assure that we rightly handle the problems of seeking, gathering and selecting information. When people agree upon premises or information, they rarely disagree about conclusions. Differences of opinion come about mostly because people often are not on the same page as to what information is acceptable or agreed upon in an inquiry. The role of tacit, unspoken information in reasoning is also a fertile source of disagreement, because people are often unwittingly employing diverging sets of tacit information. Again, we return to this very important insight of the interrogative model of reasoning: the activity that makes the difference is the seeking, gathering, and selecting of information.

The activity of seeking, gathering, and selecting information cannot be characterized by strict rules that must always be followed. Still, we can identify some strategies that typically help improve our success at discovering the information we need. Following are some examples of how inquirers need and use strategies for information seeking:

- Past familiarity with a subject and background knowledge about it can be valuable. Past familiarity—ours or others—means we have a larger store of possibly relevant information available to us. We are well advised to consult this store of special information. Sometimes the ability to spot recurring or distinctive patterns helps us locate relevant and useful information. This ability also is partly a matter of past experience with the subject into which one is inquiring. Among the classical rhetorical canons *memoria* treats the significance of having a store of information available. The model cautions, however, that sometimes this same background knowledge can hinder us if we are confronting genuinely new phenomena, for then our attention to past experience may tempt us to overlook important pieces in the new puzzle. For this reason a new or inexperienced investigator may sometimes bring a fresh perspective to a stalled inquiry by asking questions that are unexpected yet insightful.

- *Logos*: Aristotelian "Appeal" to Knowledge, Truth, Accuracy
  Inquirers in most cases have to wrestle with questions concerning the reliability of information and of the sources of information. In scientific inquiry the strategy of repeating an experiment to make sure that results are consistent within a meaningful error range is one response to this concern. The strategy of getting a "second opinion" to cross check information from two different sources is another example. Aristotle examined some of these strategies under the heading of *logos*.

- *Ethos*: Aristotelian "Appeal" of Credibility
  Aristotle also suggested that in many cases attention to the ethos or character of a human source was important. While we may worry about the "Madison Avenue" effect of celebrities hawking everything from Chevy Blazers to religious commitments, such common practices reflect the fact that people often make decisions about complex matters based on who the person is who is advocating for one side or another. In biblical study *ethos* also plays its

part. People who have come to trust a teacher or pastor or theologian or a particular community are more inclined to accept information and lines of reasoning from such sources.

* *Pathos*: Aristotelian "Appeal" of Feelings and Emotions
Aristotle rounded out his discussion of logos and ethos by reference to pathos. He noted that human beings look not only to content and character in reasoning but also to their feelings and whether an approach or message meets a need. The interrogative model treats emotion as one more possible source of information. Sometimes our feelings reliably guide us. Sometimes they do not. These are just some of the many different strategies that have been studied and are available when we come to assess reliability of information.

* Because we are dealing with strategic matters, there is an element of the unpredictable. Sometimes our inquiries confront us with new configurations and surprising answers. In such situations we must be prepared to let ourselves see what is new. If we try always mechanically to assimilate new inquiries to old patterns, then we risk missing some of the most creative and interesting insights we may come upon. So the model advises that inquirers be willing to risk seeking and selecting information that may not initially appear to be relevant or helpful. Keeping the inquiry open to a range of material until a reliable path to closure seems warranted and wise.

* If we can find an analogy between different cases, and if we are familiar with reasoning about one of the cases, we can try techniques from the known case in our reasoning about the new case. Use of analogies in inquiry and argumentation presents many challenges for models of reasoning. The interrogative model locates the power of reasoning by analogy in the ways analogies can help identify apt questions that may provide crucial information for an inquiry.

One of the fascinating mysteries of inquiry is how people manage in the midst of a chaos of possible information to determine what questions to ask, i.e., what missing information is most likely to help. The highest praise is given to detectives or scientists who, through some uncanny knack of questioning, come upon the pivotal question that leads to success. Once the key to a solution is found, people rarely disagree that that certain path was the correct approach. But perceiving how a Sherlock Holmes made his discoveries or how an Einstein knew just how to shape his inquiry so we can duplicate excellence in the future—that is another matter!

A further puzzle concerns how we achieve consensus concerning what information is most relevant and reliable for the task at hand. As the process goes forward, successful inquiries move beyond the chaos of initial information toward closure that brings about a satisfactory conclusion. The model suggests that movement toward closure is governed primarily by strategies for information seeking rather than by hard and fast rules for inference.[3]

2. Reflections on the New Digital Media and Technologies

Excellence in reasoning

In this brief encounter with the interrogative model, we have introduced two important distinctions relevant to the study of human reasoning. The first is the distinction between information-seeking interrogative moves and information-processing logical inference moves. The other distinction has been implicitly at work throughout the exposition, and we now relate it explicitly to the first distinction.

The second distinction concerns the ways in which the two reasoning activities are subject to rules. The interrogative model of reasoning distinguishes between definitory rules for correctness and strategies for effectiveness. The former define the steps admissible in correct reasoning, while the latter suggest ways to make creative use of the steps allowed by the definitory rules.

Consider an analogy between rules and strategies in games, and rules and strategies in reasoning. The game of chess has rules that define how to play—the bishop moves diagonally; the defining rules of basketball specify that teams shall have five players. On the other hand, games also typically have strategies for more effective play (trading your bishop for the opponent's queen will usually strengthen your position; punting on fourth down in football is often advisable). Similarly, reasoning has definitory rules that define how rational inquiry proceeds (affirming the consequent is an incorrect inference move; *modus ponens* is a permissible move)[4] as well as strategic principles for more effective pursuit of rational inquiry (in a truth-seeking inquiry try to use independent sources of information that can be checked against each other).

According to the model, hard and fast definitory rules govern both logical inference steps and interrogative steps in reasoning. But the majority of definitory rules governing everyday reasoning have to do with logical inference. Computers have these definitory rules for inference built into their electronic structure. Undergraduate logic courses often concentrate on systems for studying the definitory rules governing logical inference. (Critics of such courses rightly worry that exclusive study of such rules does not get at the most interesting and important features of human reasoning.) God has built the human mind in such a way that people do not usually break the hard and fast definitory rules that govern their inferences and their interrogative search for information. When such rules are broken, others rather easily discern the mistakes and prompt those in error to correct them.

Strategic principles also govern both logical inference steps and interrogative steps. Strategic principles are suggestive but not determinative, and the most challenging and creative features of reasoning have to do with finding and employing effective strategies. But the model points out that everyday reasoning usually employs logical inferences in relatively simple ways so that knowledge of sophisticated inference strategies is not required. Thus, according to the model, excellence in the art of reasoning mostly depends upon paying careful attention to the strategic principles governing effective questioning rather than upon special knowledge of definitory rules for inference or for questioning. We return once more to that central and significant insight of the interrogative model: The art and excellence in reasoning lies in strategies for information seeking by questioning.

Digital media and reasoning strategies

In light of the account offered by the interrogative model concerning where art and excellence lies in reasoning, we now can ask whether and how the new digital media and technologies will change our strategies for seeking, gathering and selecting information in biblical study. We can also reflect on whether the changes are likely to improve the way in which both specialist and lay readers study the Scriptures.

• The new media enable us to pursue old strategies in more efficient ways. Electronic concordances, lexicons and information databases provide powerful and convenient ways to make available a wealth of information. Both specialists and lay readers have more ready access, not only to original source data, but also to a variety of extended lines of reasoning that various thinkers have constructed on the basis of the available evidence. It is easier to compare strategies with the speed of electronic retrieval.

- The new media multiply the number of "authorities" that individuals and groups can conveniently consult.
- The new media make possible extended, virtual communities alongside traditional face-to-face home communities. People can transcend geographical boundaries and tackle questions simultaneously with others more easily.
- The new media enhance our ability to extend the range—and the chaos—of initial information seeking. Attention to the classical rhetorical canon of *inventio* or discovery is made easier by the new technologies. In so far as this ability enhances the likelihood of our finding information that brings insight, the new media enhance our study of the Scriptures.
- We have seen that a significant problem in reasoning concerns the necessarily sketchy, shorthand, enthymematic nature of our thinking. The new media will not in themselves assure that we carefully analyze and evaluate the tacit information at work in our study. Analysis and evaluation tend more to be depth than breadth activities in thinking. If the new media mainly bring breadth, they may not help us with depth. The chaos brought by greater breadth can prompt deeper analysis and evaluation, but chaos can also lead to impatience and a search for too quick or shallow closure.
- The new media are not likely in themselves to lead to original insight or depth of understanding. Groundbreaking work that brings additional information will still mostly come from the field, for example from archeology or philology or the day-to-day work of pastors and theologians.
- Ingenious insight into what questions need to be asked in new and puzzling circumstances will not come from simply being inundated by a wealth of information. Indeed, the new media may often keep inquiries confined to the paths already laid down and then frozen on digital media such as the CD-ROM. Electronic resources may come to have a quasi-magical authority for many lay people and in that way hinder the development of personal integrity in the dialog with Scripture as well as originality and depth of thought.
- In fact, the ease with which digital searches can be undertaken is currently limiting the range of sources that some investigators will consult. Undergraduate students notoriously are tempted to limit their searches to computer sources. If a suitable range of quality information is available in these sources, well and good, but there are no guarantees. The problem of quality control on the Internet

has been imaged by someone as the problem of getting a good drink of water from a fire hydrant or, worse still, from a gushing sewer.

• In our estimation the way in which digital media foster virtual communities is one of the most serious problems facing the church in regard not only to study of Scripture but also to life in the Body of Christ. The pagan philosopher Aristotle wisely stressed the significance of *ethos*, personal character, in the rhetoric of human thought. Most Christian communities take seriously Christ's promise to be present among those who together gather in his Name. In the midst of the *ethos* created when people gather around the Word, Christians claim also to experience a real, not virtual, presence of their Lord. If communal wisdom guided by the Holy Spirit in a common life is crucial to right understanding of Scripture, then the ill-defined, relatively anonymous, and individualistic nature of the virtual communities fostered by digital media may work against achieving insight brought by life together in the Body of Christ and hence, against the notion of biblically disciplined thought.

Conclusion

Like reason itself, these new tools that extend our reasoning abilities are likely to be both used and abused in the study of Scripture. Ways to distinguish between use and abuse have been and will continue to be matters of contention among students of the Scriptures. Individuals and their faith communities will do well to look deeply into what they believe study of Scripture to be about. If they have a good picture of what biblical study is about, then they can assess what the new digital media and technologies may do to enhance or hinder understanding.

Insofar as it clarifies the nature of art and excellence in reasoning, the interrogative model of reasoning proves itself a helpful tool for pursuing this investigation into the nature of biblically-disciplined thought and the use of the new digital technologies and media.

Notes

1. Detailed information on the model can be found in Hintikka and Bachman (1991), and in Bachman (1995, 1997 and 1998).

2. The interrogative model takes deductive inference to be the reference for understanding what the model calls logical inference. Some other models of reasoning offer extensive discussion of nondeductive forms of inference in order to account for uncertainty in human thought. The interrogative model begins from the fact that no agreement has been reached on how to characterize nondeductive inference. The model agrees with those accounts of reasoning that locate uncertainty in reasoning in the seeking, gathering and selecting of information. When we are unsure about a conclusion, the explanation is to be found either in the fact that some tacit information is at work in the inquiry that needs more explicit examination or that the reliability of some of the explicit information being used is more or less questionable.

3. More details, both about the convergence toward closure and about strategies for interrogative steps, can be found in Hintikka and Bachman (1991), and in Bachman (1995, 1997 and 1998). Sustein (1994) offers an insightful discussion of how people whose theoretical commitments are at odds nevertheless often achieve lower-level consensus concerning specific issues.

4. In human reasoning a few inference patterns, both for valid and for invalid inferences, occur so often that the patterns themselves have come to be identified by traditional names. *Modus ponens* is one of the valid inference patterns, and affirming the consequent is one of the invalid ones. Such patterns are usually represented in shorthand form by letters that represent statements, but sample statements can easily be inserted in order to illustrate the patterns. For example,

Modus Ponens (valid):
If P, then Q.
P.
Therefore, Q.
If it is raining, then the sidewalk is getting wet.
It is raining.
Therefore, the sidewalk is getting wet.

Affirming the Consequent (invalid):
If P, then Q.
Q.
Therefore, P.
If it is raining, then the sidewalk is getting wet.
The sidewalk is getting wet.
Therefore, it is raining.

In the *modus ponens* pattern there is no way to imagine the concluding statement false while imagining the premise statements true. Once we imagine the premises to be true, we can find no way to escape imagining the conclusion true. The inference is valid.

In the *affirming the consequent* pattern there remain a number of ways to imagine the concluding statement false while imagining the premise statements true. We can imagine the if-then to be true and that it is true that the sidewalk is getting wet, while imagining that the sun is shining and it is not raining. Children may be staging a water balloon battle, or a hose may be being trained on the pavement. Because the pattern does not block our imagining that the conclusion (it is raining) is false, the inference is invalid.

References

Aristotle. 1984. *Rhetoric*. Trans. W. Rhys Roberts. The Complete Works of Aristotle, Jonathan Barnes (ed.). 2 vols. Princeton: Princeton University Press.

Bachman, James. 1995. "Appeal to Authority," in *Fallacies, Classical and Contemporary Readings*, Hans V. Hansen and Robert Pinto (eds.), 274-86. University Park: Penn State University Press.

Bachman, James. 1997. "Putting Theories into Practice," in *The Role of Pragmatics in Contemporary Philosophy*, P. Weingartner, G. Schurz, and G. Dorn (eds.), 21-27. N.p.: Austrian Ludwig Wittgenstein Society.

Bachman, James. 1998. "The Ten Suggestions: Putting Theology into Practice," *Concordia Journal*. 24(2): 138-155.

Bainton, Roland H. 1950. *Here I Stand: A Life of Martin Luther*. New York: Abingdon.

Corbett, Edward P.J. 1990. *Classical Rhetoric for the Modern Student*. 3rd ed. New York: Oxford University Press.

Hintikka, Jaakko. and Bachman, James. 1991. *What If . . .? Toward Excellence in Reasoning*. Mountain View: Mayfield Publishing Company.

Locke, John. *Essay Concerning Human Understanding*. Public Domain Internet Text.

Luther, Martin. 1967. Table Talk. Vol. 54 in *Luther's Works*. American Edition. Philadelphia: Fortress Press.

Nineham, Dennis.E. 1963. *Saint Mark*. Baltimore: Penguin.

Pieper, Franz. 1917, 1950-51. *Christian Dogmatics*. 4 vols. St. Louis: Concordia Publishing House.

Sustein, Cass. 1994. "Agreements without Theories." *Iowa Advocate*. 33:2.

Vawter, Bruce. 1969. *The Four Gospels: an Introduction*. 2 vols. New York: Doubleday

Voelz, James. 1995. *What Does This Mean?: Principles of Biblical Interpretation in the Post-Modern World*. St. Louis: Concordia Publishing House.

5

Critical Thinking and the Black Church

Isaac M. T. Mwase, Ph.D.

Introduction

The *Townsend Press Sunday School Commentary* (hereafter, TPSSC) on the International Bible Lessons for Christian Teaching is touted as "the centerpiece of the family of . . . church school literature designed to interpret the Word of God consistent with the divine purpose of living at all levels of human experiences with age-sensitive considerations" (West 1999, iii). Townsend annually publishes a commentary covering the period from September of one year to August of the following year. TPSSC is important for it serves as the primary reference work for those preparing to teach the more than 8,200,000 persons in more than 33,000 churches who are reportedly associated with the National Baptist Convention, U.S.A., Incorporated. The commentary is mainly the product of one writer, an editor, and the usual publishing support systems. William L. Banks, D.Min, was the writer for the 1998-2000 commentaries under review. It is readily evident that the publication team has an intense desire to make the Scriptures relevant to contemporary believers. Such a desire is laudable. As one, however, who has used TPSSC for over three years, I have been left wondering from time to time whether these materials have a sufficiently critical orientation to address the theological and ethical needs of a membership that is becoming increasingly more educated. Is it the case that the content of these materials is such that they satisfy the spiritual as well as the intellectual needs of as wide a spectrum of its readers as possible?

I want to show that TPSSC does attempt to be sensitive to critical concerns: but given an uncritical commitment on the part of the writer to a dispensational millennialist conservatism, what emerges in some of the lessons are uncritical dogmatisms. I will discuss dogmatisms in three key areas: eschatology, the role of Israel in world history, and matters of science and religion. The commentary, however, displays a praiseworthy *critical* orientation on matters that may be designated as Christ and Culture issues. Its sustained critique of the "health and wealth" gospel is vital for a black church that is becoming increasingly affluent. The commentary also provides readers tools for establishing an understanding of the text that helps the reader form appropriate judgments on pressing contemporary ethical issues.

Commentary on each lesson follows a set pattern that include the following[1]: The Unit Title; General Subject with age-level topics; Devotional Readings; Historical Background; Printed Parallel Texts from the King James and the New Revised Standard Versions; Objectives of the Lesson; Points to be Emphasized; Topical Outline of the Lesson; Introduction to familiarize the reader with the context in which the lesson is discussed; Exposition and Application of the Scripture; Special Features that correlate the text with the unique experience of African-Americans; a Concluding Word that anticipates the Biblical Content Emphases; and the Home Daily Bible Readings designed to provide continuity from one lesson to the next.

My perspective on critical thinking and the black church emerges from an examination of selected passages in and issues addressed by the TPSSC. Initially, I want to indicate how critical thinking manifests itself in the commentary. I will follow this with an argument that an uncritical commitment to a dispensational millennialist conservatism forces the commentary to adopt positions that are becoming increasingly suspect to reflective Christians. It seems to me that the commentary fails to recognize that not all Christians are inclined to affirm the particular positions adopted by the writer of the commentary. It disallows what one may call contestability[2], a key element in critical thinking. Contestability is one expression of what Peter Facione has identified *open-mindedness* as one of seven factors that comprise an appropriate disposition toward critical thinking. Facione defines open-mindedness as being "tolerant of divergent views, [a] self-monitoring for possible bias."[3] It is my contention that Sunday School materials should reflect sensitivity to these factors as ones that promote a much-needed critical appropriation of the teaching of scripture. I am going to argue that when discussing such matters as eschatology, the role of Israel in world history, and the relation of science and religion one ought to allow as wide a variety of perspectives embraced by Christians as possible. I conclude by reworking, in a way that promotes critical thinking, a passage that addresses the controversial topic of creationism and its relationship with evolution.

Critical Thinking in the TPSSC

Critical thinking is evident whenever one is aware of prejudices and biases in what one affirms or argues. It demands that one take into consideration all pertinent information before staking a position. If such is critical thinking, then judgment about the presence or absence of this aspect of reflective endeavor becomes a matter of degrees. Two questions, consequently, are of interest in assessing TPSSC. One, to what extent is the commentary paying homage to critical thinking concerns? Two, is there a deliberate attempt by the commentary to promote a critical thinking orientation in the reader?

The Introduction of each lesson's commentary provides a variety of sections to properly orient the interpreter of the lesson text. Most of the lessons have a section on Biblical Background. This section provides etymologies for key words in the focal text and a review of key events related to the text and lesson.[4] The Introduction may also include a section entitled "A Perception of History" or "A Literal Interpretation." The former delves into details of biblical history and the latter insists that a passage under consideration be interpreted literally, an insistence that fails to respect the need to interpret text in a manner sensitive to particular genre. The sections on biblical backgrounds and history are by far the most sensitive to critical thinking considerations. It is here especially that those who insist on a literal interpretation of select passages tend to project an interpretive stance that leads to ill-advised dogmatism.

To demonstrate that the TPSSC *does* include critical thinking, it should suffice here to cite two instances of commentary text that satisfy the kind of critical thinking considerations called for in Sunday School materials. The first example is provided by the introductory section to the lesson for September 13, 1998, which seeks to locate historically the events of the focal texts: Exodus 2:23-25; 5:1-2; 11:1-8; 12:29-32; 15:1-2, 19-21. The specific issue in question is the dating of the Exodus:

> Now scholars are not sure of the date of the exodus event. This is
> partly because the word "Pharaoh" is an official title that was

given to all of the Egyptian kings. One estimate has the beginning of the oppression of the Jews in Egypt occurring about 1550 B.C. This leaves the suggested date of 1447 B.C. for the Exodus, according to the Scofield Reference Bible; about 1491 B.C., according to the Pilgrim Bible for the Exodus. I repeat: scholars are not sure of the exact date of the Exodus. (TPSSC, 15)

The commentary thus expresses the lack of certainty in the scholarly community. Even though it does not offer a late date as an option, it is sufficiently non-dogmatic to allow those who may subscribe to a late dating to proceed into the lesson without feeling slighted or having a sense of being unfaithful to the scriptures.

The second example is found in the exposition on the lesson for December 5, 1999. The lesson text is Matthew 3:1-8, 11-17. The commentary acknowledges differences of interpretation of the phrase, "He shall baptize you with the Holy Spirit, and with fire" (verse 11):

Some scholars make the Holy Spirit and the fire identical, in which case the Holy Spirit burns up the junk that is in our lives. This then would not be hellfire judgment (Lenski), but that burning zeal within us. On the other hand, some scholars believe the fire baptism points to judgment. Christ thus consigns the impenitent to everlasting punishment, for fire speaks of judgment. The context and references to purging and burning *appear* to refer to judgment. *If* this latter is true, it plays havoc with the denomination known as The Fire Baptized Holiness Church. (emphasis added, IM: 1999-2000, 129)

It is not so much the two different interpretations offered that is of interest; rather it is the cautious approach taken in endorsing just one. This is the kind of critical awareness that allows one to commit to a position without necessarily viewing alternate or contesting claims as devious, disingenuous, or unfaithful to the scriptures. It is refreshing when the commentary offers an issue for class discussion without prejudging what position Christians should take.[5] Whenever the commentary approaches texts or issues that are multivalent in such a cautious manner it promotes a critical orientation on the part of the reader. This is good. Unfortunately such is not always the case in TPSSC.

There are passages in TPSSC that discourage and even denigrate challenges to a theologically conservative appropriation of scripture text. A passage that is not as offensive to one's critical thinking quotient[6] (hereafter, CTQ) occurs in the lesson for September 6, 1998. The lesson text is Genesis 3:1-13 and the adult topic is "Humanity's Basic

Cond: Good
Date: 2024-09-17 19:16:46 (UTC)
mSKU: ZWM 69TD
vSKU: ZWV 076182863X G
unit_id: 18336786
Source: ARIELA

ZWV 076182863X G

delist unit# 18336786

xxxxx

Problem." The introduction to the lesson seeks to discredit any interpretive approach to the text other than a literal one. An interpretation of Genesis 3 as myth or etiology is supposed to lead to unwelcome views concerning the authority of the scriptures:

> However, if there is no personal creature such as Satan, we are hard pressed to explain adequately the presence of evil in the world. If there were no individual human beings as Adam and Eve, then we cannot trust the Bible as the Word of a truthful God. Furthermore, the New Testament would be in error for assuming the historicity of the Genesis 3 account, if indeed it is but a myth. (TPSSC, 1998-1999, 6)

The commentary proceeds to offer several New Testament proof texts to buttress the call for a literal interpretation of Genesis 3. It concludes that one does not gain much "by denying the literal, historical Adam, Eve, and the serpent in Genesis 3" (ibid). It is evident in this kind of treatment that the commentary is acknowledging the existence of persuasive alternate readings of the text in question. Even though the commentary dismisses these readings, for their failure to satisfy the interpretive appetite of those who value a pronounced fidelity to the scriptures, it does allow space for the reader to offer an alternative. The specific declaration of the impotence of non-literalistic interpretive approaches could be phrased with a keener sensitivity to critical thinking concerns.[7] Here I have in mind Facione's identification of *cognitive maturity* as one of seven factors that comprise the right kind of disposition toward critical thinking. This is "prudence in making, suspending, or revising judgment, an awareness that multiple solutions can be acceptable." [8] It is surely the case that there are some who read TPSSC who would readily offer a persuasive argument as to why a non-literalist reading of Genesis 3 and its context is preferable over a literalistic reading. This should suffice to commend an even more cautious approach than the one evident in the selected passages.

Critical Thinking and A Dispensational Millennialist Conservatism

It is readily evident that TPSSC is unabashedly committed to Dispensational Premillennialism and theological conservatism.[9] The commentary intermittently celebrates conservatism as a boon rather than a bane for the black church:

It is true that certain Americans have looked down their noses at Black American Churches, and have despised the simple faith in Christ that we profess. What such sophisticated religionists fail to realize is that the *conservatism* of our Black Baptist churches is the very heart-beat of Christianity in the United States. (emphasis added, IM: TPSSC, 1998-1999, 69)

This celebration of conservatism—presumably of a theological and ethical brand—occurs at the close of a lesson on the miraculous healing of Naaman. This lesson is an instance of touting simple faith as being superior to intellectualized faith. Miracles are to be taken at face value. Any interpretive approach that suggests otherwise is anathema.

In the lesson for February 28, 1999, theological conservatism links up with a dispensationalist eschatology for the purpose of inspiring a confident hope in the Christian. The lesson texts are Titus 2:11-14; Hebrews 12:26-29; Revelation 1:17-20; 11:15. The commentary identifies Revelation 1:19 as "one of the most important verses in the Book of Revelation." With obvious approval the commentary proceeds with the following claim:

Most conservative scholars hold that we have here a three-fold outline of the Revelation. First: The things which John had seen include the vision of the glory of the resurrected Christ described in verses 12-18, the Christ who rules and dominates the entire Revelation. It is the Revelation of Jesus Christ—by Him and about Him! Second: The things which are: We believe that chapters two and three, dealing with the Seven Churches, constitute the period designated by the words, "the things which are." Seven churches are chosen to teach us the nature of the moral character of the entire Church Age. Third: The things which shall be (hereafter) are the things described in chapters 4 to 22. And it will be seen that once again Israel takes the spotlight of world history. (TPSSC, 1998-1999, 226)

Conservatism comes forth as a virtue given the frequent occurrence of the phrase, "many conservative scholars believe." (See as well TPSSC, 1998-1999, 364, 427; TPSSC, 1999-2000, 26.)

This dispensationalism at times results in claims that are very contestable. The lesson with the adult topic "Time of Preparing" and the text Matthew 3:1-8, 11-17, has one such claim. The commentary satisfactorily defines "the kingdom of heaven" as "the spiritual kingdom of God in the hearts of men, entered into by the new birth; it is that sphere in which God's rule is acknowledged" (TPSSC, 1999-2000, 127). The elaboration of this definition becomes an exercise in dispensational ger-rymandering. The commentary is adamant that the "kingdom of God" is not the Church. What then is it, "practically speaking?" I cite the commentary at some length:

> When Christ returns to establish his kingdom on earth, he will bring the church with him to help rule with a rod of iron. By not defining "kingdom of heaven,' John and Our Lord suggest they expected their audiences to understand its meaning in the light of Old Testament promises. We repeat: the kingdom of heaven refers to the millennial kingdom, that one thousand year earthly reign of Christ with headquarters in Jerusalem. (TPSSC, 1999-2000, 127).

Identifying the kingdom of God/heaven with the millennial reign of Christ may seem to some students of the Bible as an instance of strange exegesis. What this shows is an uncritical embrace of an escha-tological framework that interprets scripture according to a prescribed view. Such a posture undermines critical thinking on these issues, as related to a responsible eschatology.

It is most fortunate that the commentary is not always this opin-ionated. The lesson for February 13, 2000, "The Joy of Being Prepared," examines Matthew 24:45-25:13. The commentary expresses an awareness that different interpretations can be offered on the Olivet Discourse. It then offers what it believes to be the most accurate inter-pretation of "what is one of the most important passages in the New Testament concerning things to come or last things (eschatology)":

> Today's lesson does not deal directly with the church. It is extremely important that this be kept in mind. Some applications of course may be made to the church and our present time, as is done in our Concluding Word. But suffice it to say here, the Scriptures under study cannot be assigned to the church. The Olivet Discourse is concerned with Israel; it is Jewish in scope, and no mention is made of the church or of the Rapture of the church. Christ deals with the faithful remnant within the nation of Israel, and they are exhorted to watch. See then today's lesson cen-tering upon Christ's return to earth to establish HIS kingdom. (TPSSC, 1999-2000, 217)

The discussion above of the commentary's conservatism and commitment to dispensational millennialism is not intended to dispar-age such an orientation. Rather, I'm inclined to believe that it is more valuable to expose users of the commentary to a wider spectrum of eschatological orientations than to demand a uniform commitment to one contestable eschatological perspective. What I am calling for may not be a key consideration for TPSSC as it is being produced. A prior question that may need to be resolved with regard to such materials is whether they should be prepared as platforms that promote critical thinking among Christians. An affirmative response is called for but an argument to support such a response goes beyond the purview of this project.

Areas that Need a Critical Thinking Approach

TPSSC's commitment to theological conservatism and a dispensational premillennialist interpretive posture undermines critical thinking in the Black church. This is readily evident in the commentary's treatment of a variety of topics of high interest to contemporary Christians. I address issues related to eschatology, the role of Israel in human history, and matters of science and religion. Other areas that could easily justify one's attention are religious pluralism, the authority of scripture, Black Christian identity, and such controversial issues as gender roles and homosexuality.[10] This section does not go much beyond the identification of the problem. The discussion of eschatology and the role of Israel in world history will be understandably brief, given the discussion in the previous section.

Eschatology

It is important to provide the Christian with a reasonable framework for organizing the present and anticipating the future. Eschatology serves that purpose. Scripture has much to say about events related to the end of the world. When Sunday school materials reflect on these texts, they should avoid fanciful and alarmist accounts. On this count TPSSC excels. The materials present a conviction integral to the Christian faith that human history moves inexorably toward some end. They articulate the doctrine of the Second Coming of Christ, while warning both against an other-worldliness[11] common among eschatological fanatics and those who would disregard the doctrine as merely *compensatory*.[12]

In order for a more reasonable eschatology to emerge, some of the prior commitments undergirding TPSSC have to be modified. Is it absolutely necessary to let only dispensational millennialism be the only framework for interpreting relevant scripture texts? I demur. I would like to believe it possible to develop commentary that allows the reader to make her own decision about the end of the world.[13] It should be possible for commentary readers to become familiar not only with dispensational pre-millennialism (this is the view that a glorified Jesus will return to earth and set up rulership over the world for a thousand years after distinct periods when God acts in ways foretold in the scripture), but also a-millennialism (this view interprets the thousand-year reign of Christ in Revelation 20:6 symbolically), and post-millennialism (not as popular as the other two views, this view holds that the thousand-year reign is the period of Christ's reign in the lives of believers). Reflective Christians in the Black church are smart enough to figure out which eschatological interpretive approaches is most in keeping with the biblical materials.

The Role of Israel in World History

This topic could be easily subsumed under the general topic, eschatology. The reason for this independent treatment lies in the special place the TPSSC accords Israel on its pages. Consider this call to fastidious Bible study and the rationale:

> It is impossible to be a good Bible student without an adequate grasp of the place of Israel in God's Plan of the Ages. Furthermore, recognition of the role this nation plays in the scheme of our Sovereign Lord helps to combat the rising anti-Semitism among American Blacks—an anti-Semitism increasing as a result of the influence of Islamic and pseudo-Islamic organizations in our country. (TPSSC, 1998-1999, 103-104)

The perspective that emerges at the close of the lesson for July 11, 1999, is one that could benefit from the critical assessment of those that share not the kind of pro-Israel view it expresses. This reason is sufficiently compelling to cite the relevant passage in its entirety:

> With the influence of Islam growing among Black Americans, saints of color would do well to study again God's choice of Isaac and not Ishmael. Read again the promise the Lord made to Abraham concerning Ishmael (Genesis 17:20), as well as the promise He made to Hagar (Genesis 21:18). God had chosen Abraham to be the head of a special people, Israel, and limited the line after Abraham to Isaac, then to Jacob and his twelve sons.
>
> Now Ishmael caused trouble later, and his descendants are still quarreling with the Jews. Ishmael is the forefather of the Arabs; and Isaac the progenitor of the Jews. Mohammed, the founder of Islam, came from the line of Ishmael. Today, there is still dispute

over the ownership of the land. Present conflict is evidence of a deep-rooted hatred. Diplomats and statesmen (and women, Mrs. Albright) often indicate they are ignorant of the background of the problem or naïve as to the root of the trouble. And worse, they have left out altogether any thought of Satan and his special hatred for Israel. (TPSSC, 1998-1999, 390)

A critical thinking approach to the question of Israel's role in world history should seek to incorporate the perspective of the Arab world[14] and critiques by Jewish theologians about the doctrine of Israel as a chosen people. Discomfort with the key concept of chosenness has been expressed in critical pieces by some who identify themselves with Judaism. The feminist perspective of Judith Plaskow and the post-Auschwitz reflections of Richard Rubenstein are worth one's examination.[15] Critical thinking on a religious perspective about the role of Israel in world history should take into consideration as many relevant accounts as possible. TPSSC fails to do so and in this failure nourishes a narrow, uncritical view.

Science and Religion

Of the myriad issues that occur at the intersection of science and religion, the most provocative is that of cosmogony. The question of the origins of the universe and more specifically the origins of sentient beings seems to polarize theists. A critical thinking approach demands that those who value both the religious and scientific enterprises forge a comprehensive perspective that shortchanges the truth claims of neither enterprise.[16] TPSSC does not appear to make any conscious effort at integrating the key claims of religion and science. An *independence* orientation seems to be the view taken on science/religion. Science is only of value insofar as it remains mum on what are regarded to be cardinal beliefs of a conservative Christianity. TPSSC adopts a supremely dogmatic position on cosmogonical matters, particularly the *ex nihilo* creation of human beings.

It is not surprising that a dogmatic perspective emerges on the relation between science and religion within the context of a study of the book of Genesis. The general introduction to the summer quarter lessons on "Beginnings" signals an unswerving commitment to an exclusive creationist position that finds any evolutionary cosmogony abhorrent. It is worth quoting at length:

The study of "Beginnings" affords us the opportunity to come face to face with the spiritual understanding of our personal existence. There are those who will discuss the causal aspects of the creation and dare to place God in this cause-effect relationship. In a larger sense, we do not need to prove objectively that God created the world if such verification does not graphically alter the way in which we relate to Him. The point is that we as individuals accept by faith God as Creator and Sustainer and go forth to live lives consistent with that understanding. The fact is that when the writers of the book of Genesis (refer to a reputable Commentary dealing with the JEDP tradition) attempted to bring the history of Israel into focus, their compositions were basically confessions of faith relative to how they felt in the presence of God and whether or not the consciousness of God was consistent with their behavior. Humans, having been created in the image of God and housed in a perfect situation under perfect conditions, elected to affirm themselves rather than confirm the image and likeness of God through obedience, and the rest is history.

In any discussion of the creation, those who conceive of humans as emerging from a lower form of life experience difficulty in struggling to live on a moral and spiritual level which verifies that rise from the primeval ooze. (sic) On the other hand, those who embrace the faith that they were created by God dare to live "a little lower than the angels," rather than a little higher than the lower animals. The faith that God created the world and all that is in it is more than an argument, but a commitment; and we go forth to live lives consistent with that understanding. (TPSSC, 1998-1999, 341-342)

An explicit anti-evolution stance takes shape within the context of the lesson on Genesis 1:1-2, 20-25, 29-31 (ibid., 343-358). The introduction to the lesson is entitled "Creation Versus Evolutionism." The lesson advocates creationism as "the doctrine that matter and all things were created, substantially as they now exist, by an omnipotent Creator, and not gradually evolved or developed" (345). It cannot imagine any Christian being a proponent of evolution, understood as "a man-made theory, often taught as scientific fact, which holds that man accidentally evolved or sprung from some supposed original germ" (ibid). Characteristic of dichotomous thinking rather than critical thinking, the commentary sees no distinction between non-theistic and theistic evolutionary accounts.[17] All evolutionary accounts are suspect. Worse, they are "anti-God or anti-Bible" and "automatically evil" (ibid). It is readily evident that hardly any thought is given to those Christians who find the case for a theistic evolution compelling when the commentary espouses such a vitriolic position. A critical thinking approach would want to interpret Genesis in a way that attempts to accommodate Christians variously persuaded about origins.

Introducing Critical Thinking to the Origins Discussion

I conclude this project by reworking several key paragraphs in the lesson on "Beginnings" in a way that is at once sensitive to critical thinking considerations and seeks to promote the same in the reader. My attempt proceeds on the conviction that collaboration is the best approach in the writing and editing of Sunday school materials that are sensitive to critical thinking considerations. Instead of having only one individual write the lessons, assemble a team of writers from a variety of interpretive and theological perspectives to take the lessons written by a member of the team and rework them so that they reflect a high CTQ. A web-based writing and editing plan can be developed and implemented so that God's people become the beneficiaries of quality Sunday school materials. Quality in these materials will be in part a function of an explicit commitment to promote critical thinking in the church.

The column on the left reproduces what appears in the lesson for June 6, 1999. If a team of say three of four interpretive orientations were to rewrite the lesson in a manner sensitive to critical thinking consider-ations, what kind of text would emerge? The right column is what I envision in commentary that promotes critical thinking.

Introduction

CREATIONISM versus EVOLUTIONISM

Creationism is the doctrine that matter and all things were created, substantially as they now exist, by an omnipotent Creator, and not gradually evolved or developed (*Random House Dictionary*). Thus, what Genesis chapter one teaches is accepted as true. Evolutionism is but a man-made theory, often taught as scientific fact, which holds that man accidentally evolved or sprung from some supposed germ. We are not told from whence came this original germ. I should think that any system which is anti-God or anti-Bible is automatically evil—even that concept of evolution which calls itself "theistic." If the system is essentially wicked, what must be its influence in the lives of those who believe the system? And so I am perturbed not only by the dogmatic way in which the theory is taught as if it were fact, but also concerned with the moral effect the hypothesis of evolution has on its advocates.

Evolutionists are quick to call Creationism a religion. But the question of origins is in the final analysis a matter of faith, thus making evolutionism a religion also. Evolutionists would say that their concept "covers

Introduction

A. THE DOCTRINE OF CREATION AND EVOLUTION

For conservative Christianity, Creationism is the doctrine that matter and all things were created, substantially as they now exist, by an omnipotent Creator, and not gradually evolved or developed. This kind of Christianity is most comfortable with a literal reading of Genesis 1-11. It is uncomfortable with the theory of evolution. It eschews the teaching of evolution as a scientific fact, especially that brand that holds that human beings accidentally evolved or sprung forth from single cell life forms that evolved in some primordial organic soup. Some Christians are persuaded that evolution is anti-God, anti-Bible, and evil. The fact of the matter is that there are Christians who manage to forge a synthesis between an evolutionary account of the world and the teaching of Genesis.

Christians need to proceed with care when attempting to interpret the Genesis account and correlate those interpretations with the most reliable claims of evolutionary science. Dogmatism by the Christian who rejects evolution can easily be interpreted by those inside and outside the church as at best uncritical faith and at worst an antiquated anti-intellectualism. Dogmatism by the abrasive non-

more ground than any of the others." We would respond, the Bible claims to cover all the ground. If there is a God—if the Bible is His Word—who would know better than He how things got started? Dr. Henry M. Morris and his colleagues suggest that "the study of science is seriously deficient unless a full and unbiased treatment of scientific creationism is included." Our continued exposition of the Scripture will help the student better understand our position favoring Creationism.

religious evolutionist is equally inexcusable and undercuts the spirit and processes of good science. This said, we should note that most scientists, religious and non-religious alike, are persuaded that an evolutionary framework is the only viable one for the scientific enterprise. There are a few, though, who characterize themselves as scientific creationists who object vigorously. Henry M. Morris is one such scientist and he contends that "the study of science is seriously deficient unless a full and unbiased treatment of scientific creationism is included." Reasonably intelligent Christians will differ in what they believe about evolution, but this should not be reason for name-calling and hostility.

BIBLICAL BACKGROUND

We live in a world confused by the many philosophies and theories about the origin of the universe. The doctrine of creation is denied, and all kinds of ideas are postulated for the beginning of the universe. One of the great doctrines of the Bible is that of God the Creator. There are so many verses dealing with this matter that it is difficult to understand why we do not hear more preaching and teaching about God the Creator. Indeed, all of the "isms" invented by man are but vanity when seen in the light of

BIBLICAL BACKGROUND

The question of the origin of the universe is one that is of keen interest to Christians and scientists, be they Christian or non-Christian. The biblical claim is that the universe came into existence as a result of God's creative activity. One of the great doctrines of the Bible is that of God as creator. This is such a signal and pivotal doctrine that more pulpits and lessons should devote considerably more time to it.

The belief that God is creator is what distinguishes the Christian, in part, from various

the Scripture. Atheism, in its denial of the existence of God, is called foolishness by the Bible. For the atheist, there is no cause for anything, therefore there is no Creator.

Agnosticism, which claims we cannot know about God or His creation, does not want to be told that God says: "Here is the Bible! Take it, read it, and learn of God the Creator." Pantheism strives to make creation a part of God. Pantheists claim God and creation are one and the same thing. Pantheism teaches that God is everything and that everything is God. Thus, the Creator is confounded with what He has created.

Deism teaches that God is Creator, but He has no present relation to the world. God abandoned His creation when He completed it, and saw that everything "was very good." He remains indifferent to the world. The deist thus rejects the Bible, the revealed Word of God. But our Bible background is one which refutes all of these man-made speculations. "In the beginning God"—these four words alone wipe out every "ism" that denies the description of God the Creator as depicted in the Bible.

"isms" evident in today's cultural landscape. Atheism denies the existence of God. Psalm 53:1 declares, "The fool says in his heart, 'There is no God.'" Agnosticism says we cannot know for certain whether there is or there is not a God. The question consequently of the origin of the cosmos and the human race becomes unanswerable. Pantheism teaches that God and creation are intimately interlinked. Some versions actually view them as one and the same thing. They teach that God is everything and that everything is God. The creator thus is indistinguishable from that which is created. Deism teaches that God is Creator, but He has no present relation to the world. God abandoned His creation when He completed it, and saw that everything "was very good." He remains indifferent to the world.

Conservative Christianity rejects all these "isms," atheism, agnosticism, pantheism, and deism. What it prefers is the view that God created the cosmos, *ex nihilo*. This is the view that God created sentient life pretty much as it is today. It rejects as preposterous the suggestion that human life evolved from lower life forms. We must observe that Christians will differ on how exactly God created the world whether *ex nihilo* or by way of evolutionary processes. But all

will view the doctrine of creation
as a cardinal one in their belief
systems. As we offer our interpretation of the Genesis record, let it
be clear that ours is not the final
word on the matter.

Notes

1. My listing is a slight modification of the list that appears in the Preface
of TPSSC.

2. This is an evaluative posture that recognizes that for every affirmation
that such and such is the case, there may be alternative accounts equally compelling. One then holds to what one holds with a great deal of epistemological
humility. One becomes very cautious about making dogmatic assertions.

3. Peter A. Facione, "Reasoned Judgement and Revelation: The Relation
of Critical Thinking and Bible Study," paper read at *New Voices, New Views:
Thinking About Bible Study in the Twenty-First Century, A Consultation
Sponsored by The American Bible Society, Research Center for Scripture and
Media,"* February 11, 2000, New York.

4. The 1999-2000 commentary provides three pages of a preview of concepts and characters. The entry on the Magi is as follows: "(Wise men or magi-
cians) were considered to be sacred scribes among the Jews as persons who
were skilled in divining, and interpreting the hidden meaning of certain passages of Scripture."

5. As an additional example of such critical caution, TPSSC, 1998-1999,
broaches the issue of capital punishment. The lesson is on Romans 13 and uses
adult topic, "Showing Honor, Living Honorably." The commentary urges the
reader not to "fear prayerfully dealing with the issue in your class . . ." (201)

6. CTQ is one's capacity to stake a position without being dogmatic due
to a recognition that some other position may be truer to the reality of a text.

7. The dogmatism implicit in the declaration, "We see nothing to be
gained by denying the literal, historical Adam . . ." could be defused by recasting the claim as follows: "Denial of the literal, historical Adam, Eve, and the
serpent in Genesis 3 betrays the interpretive commitments of our particular
community of faith."

8. See Facione, this volume, p. 64. Earlier I made reference to the factor
of open-mindedness. The other five factors are: truth-seeking, analyticity, systematicity, critical thinking self-confidence, and inquisitiveness.

9. The two together combine to form what I have chosen to call dispensational millennialist conservatism. Several tenets characterize this orientation.
It believes in the inerrancy of the Bible. It believes that the church is going to

be raptured before Jesus returns to earth in some type of visible form to set up a government for a period of a thousand years (TPSSC, 1998-1999, 145). It views the Jewish nation as an important key for eschatology.

10. My decision to discuss eschatology, the role of Israel in human history, and science and religion matters is in response to the frequency of the dogmatism espoused in TPSSC on these issues. It is my contention that Sunday school material should be sensitive to the variety of views that Baptists are inclined to embrace.

11. Those who exhibit this orientation are so persuaded about the reality of heaven and hell to the extent of neglecting those activities vital for human flourishing. They quit working, expecting the church to provide for their needs. The letter to the church at Thessalonica seeks to subvert this orientation.

12. This term appears in TPSSC, 1999-2000, p. 221. The commentary describes the term as the view that says, "because of our low economic status, we dream of the future when things will be better for us. Especially once we are in heaven."

13. When addressing eschatological scripture texts the commentary could recommend and incorporate the approach taken by Erickson (1987).

14. It is very unlikely that Banks seriously considers what it is like to read the passages he cites with Arab eyes. One would expect an Arab hermeneutic to take exception to the claim that Israel's chosenness automatically means that ALL other ethnicities are excluded from divine favor. One can also imagine such a hermeneutic deconstructing the whole idea of a God who plays the kind of favoritism espoused in TPSSC.

15. Judith Plaskow (1991) judges the notion of chosenness as the chief expression of repugnant hierarchical distinctions. She sees in the notion a close association with claims to superiority. Positively viewed, chosenness has been a source of sustenance and survival for Jews. Negatively though, as Reconstructionists are wont to point out, the notion affirms a hierarchical difference that entails privilege and superiority. Plaskow rejects chosenness on two grounds. With most other reinterpretations of election she sees the notion as pass in a world were Jews have to relate to the wider society. It would be most difficult to reconcile chosenness with equality and participation in a pluralistic world. A related reason for rejecting chosenness is the desirability to rid society of hierarchical dualisms. See also Rubenstein (1994).

16. Ian Barbour has proposed a useful taxonomy on the relationship between science and religion. He sees the relationship characterized in one or a combination of four ways: conflict, independence, dialogue, and integration (1990).

17. A distinction between dichotomous thinking and critical thinking is in order. The former approaches issues in "black and white" terms. An issue has only two viable options. It is an orientation that undergirds an "us against them" mentality. In contradistinction, critical thinking recognizes that an issue may

have more than two viable options. It resists the either/or approach characteristic of dichotomous thinking.

References

Barbour, Ian. 1990. *Religion In An Age of Science: The Gifford Lectures.* Vol. 1. New York: Harper & Row.

Erickson, Millard. 1987. *Contemporary Options in Eschatology.* Grand Rapids: Baker Book House.

Plaskow, Judith. 1991. "Transforming the Nature of Community: Toward a Feminist People of Israel," in Paula M Cooey, William R. Eakin, and Jay B. McDaniel (eds.), *After Partriarchy: Feminist Transformations of the World Religions*, 87-105. Maryknoll, NY: Orbis Books.

Rubenstein, Richard. 1994 "Person and Myth in the Judeo-Christian Encounter," in *After Auschwitz: History, Theology, and Contemporary Judaism*, 14-28. Baltimore: Johns Hopkins, 1994.

West, Ottie L. (ed.) 1999. *Townsend Press Sunday School Commentary: International Bible Lessons for Christian Teaching; 1999-2000.* Nashville: Sunday School Publishing Board.

6

Lay Women's Feminist Critical Thinking about the Bible

Elizabeth Dodson Gray

Before I begin, I want to tell you that I was born and raised a Southern Baptist in Baltimore, Maryland. So I come to this discussion of the Bible not as an outsider but as someone deeply steeped in the biblical tradition.

The Rise of Critical Thinking among Feminist Scholars

Feminist critical thinking about the Bible is usually done by academic scholars such as Elisabeth Schüssler Fiorenza, who writes about what she labels "the hermeneutic of suspicion," a woman's tool for reading and seeking to engage thoroughly-male biblical texts (1983). Feminist theology and scholarship in Judaism and Christianity have blossomed into a scathing critique of male generic language, the pervasive male imagery (God-the-Father, God-the-King), and the male-centeredness of traditional theology. The publication in 1973 of Mary Daly's *Beyond God the Father* (1973) introduced many women to a new critical consciousness. Elisabeth Schüssler Fiorenza in New Testament Studies and Rosemary Radford Ruether in Historical Theology pioneered a now-widespread process of recovering the contributions to religion of women, contributions which had been repressed and lost when men alone wrote "his story" as history, gospel and theology.

But I want to focus on the critical thinking embodied in women who are *not* academics, who have grown up within the Catholic and

Protestant biblical traditions, and who are now standing in a mode of critical thinking as they look at their received traditions.

While academic women use jargon that speaks of *post-modern, deconstructionist,* and *androcentric,* these lay women have no such "distancing" vocabulary with which to cushion the shock they feel when they finally internalize for themselves an understanding that the male-centered tradition—and its Bible—were never about them, never about *her,* only about *him.*

Adam's World

You see, we have never been honest about the power there is in naming. Throughout recorded time, men have named the sacred. And they have done it, inevitably, from the standing point of their male body and of male life-experience. It is not accidental that Adam in Genesis is portrayed as naming everything. Men have been the namers.

That naming which men have done is power, the power to shape reality into a form that serves the interests and goals of the one doing the naming.

My book *Patriarchy as a Conceptual Trap* (1982) is illustrated with 65 cartoons, and one of them is a *New Yorker* cartoon by Bill Maul of two men standing outside as snow is gently falling from a dome-shaped sky. The one man says to the other, "Do you think we could possibly be inside someone else's *paperweight?*" (38).

The truth is that we really are within someone else's paperweight. We are within a bubble of assumptions which sociologists call "a social construction of reality." Only recently have we realized that we live in what I have called "Adam's world." This was the title the National Film Board of Canada chose from my writing for the film they made about my work. Adam's world is "a social construction of reality done almost entirely from the standing point of male life-experience, in which the male of the species can legitimately say, "I've named everything, thought everything, *from my point of view!*"

All of us, male and female, who have been born and socialized within Adam's world—we can say "This is the way the world *is,*" because we have never known any other. Only now are we beginning in a small way to know any other world.

A Conceptual Trap

It just happens that Adam's world is a large conceptual trap. A conceptual trap is a way of thinking that is like a room which, once *inside,* you cannot imagine a world *outside.*

In *Patriarchy as a Conceptual Trap,* I have another cartoon, this one of a board room and it shows seven or eight white middle-aged men, almost identical looking, gathered around a corporate board room table and the caption has the man chairing the meeting say, "All the powers that be being present, let us begin."[1]

When everyone in the room is virtually the same in their experience and thinking, there is absolutely no ability available in that meeting to understand what power there is outside that room which should be represented. There are no women, there are no people of color, there are no children, there are no trees, flowers, none of what we call and think of as the natural world.

Adam's world is the conceptual trap which pervades our intellectual and religious history. It is the illusion that when you've seen life from the male point of view, you've seen life from the human point of view.

Adam's world has given us male religion, male theology, male philosophy, male psychology, and male generic language—and a male-centered Bible.

Adam's World & the Naming of the Sacred

How has Adam's world affected the naming of the sacred?

We live in a universe of a 193 *billion* galaxies. Now, if that doesn't blow your mind away, I don't know what will. It is a universe of vast mystery. And yet we humans are fond of taking *our concepts* about all that mystery, and throwing them out on it. It is as though we were attaching Velcro to our concepts and we throw them out, hoping they will stick to things and never come off. "Take that!—I shall call you 'Divine Presence',," we say. "That's my naming, I want you to be— 'Ultimate Reality.'" Paul Tillich spoke about the Ground and Source of Being, which I rather liked. Others named the same great mystery the "Creative Process."

Now how exactly does the process of that naming of the mystery happen in human society? I think another cartoon in my book sketches out the fundamentals of this process. The cartoon portrays a world populated with Smoos, and someone is saying, "It is so!" All the rest of the Smoos say "No," and "No, I don't think it's so!" "No," "Na—Na!"

Then finally one Smoo manages to conjure up a great cosmic Smoo, leering over the horizon and saying in sepulchral tones, "IT. . . IS. . . SO!"And immediately everyone jumps to agree. My husband especially likes the balloon-caption of one little Smoo who is saying, "You damn betcha it is so if HE says it is so."[2]

That's approximately how the process of naming happens. You don't even need a caption sometimes to explain it. The feminist and former Mormon Sonya Johnson satirizes this kind of naming by imitating its posturing. She leans on the podium, coming forward toward her audience, and whispers strongly into her microphone, saying, *"GOD* told *me* to tell you to do it *my* way." Right.

Symbols As a Form of Naming

Paul Tillich was also concerned about how the process of naming the sacred worked. He saw the infinite up there and transcendent, and the finite world down here where we are. What symbols do, according to Tillich, is mediate between us and that infinite, so we can think about it better. Symbols become an enlarged form of naming. And whatever becomes your symbol, it helps bring the infinite world down partway to you, so you can feel closer to it. Then perhaps you feel you can communicate with it.

Tillich went on to observe that whatever you take from the finite world as a symbol is elevated halfway up to the divine. For an example, says Tillich (who was certainly not a feminist), when we choose fatherhood from the finite world as a symbol of the divine, it brings fatherhood halfway up to divinity. Exactly! Most of us have been nurtured on God symbolized as Father and King. These patriarchal symbols of God's power attribute to God authority *as males* have thought about it and wielded it in family and nation—mainly as power-over.

Michelangelo's portrayal on the ceiling of the Sistine Chapel of the creation of Adam by God has become a visual icon of all this. The theological doctrine is encapsulated in the statement that "God created man in his own image." In the first three centuries after Jesus, the early church fathers in their theology wrote a great deal about the *imago dei,* man created in the image of God. It is clear from the picture in the Sistine Chapel both that God is male, and the human is also male: Michelangelo has displayed clearly Adam's flaccid penis as well as God's male muscles and beard.

We have always assumed that the creative energy in this creation story came from the extended finger of the bearded God-the-Father, leaping across the spatial gap to the extended finger of the man Adam. The energy we have imagined at work here is the energy of God to create life. Until God's energy touches him, Adam is but clay or some similarly inert substance. But when that creating finger of God reaches out and touches that hand, we just know that this dormant Adam-figure becomes alive. Yes, we say, God created man, in his own image.

The Narcissus Effect

But if you understand the sociology of knowledge I have been laying out here, you see that *the creative energy really was going the other way,* and that the human male of the species, peering into the cosmic mystery, reached out to create God in *his* own image, the *male* image.

This is the Narcissus effect. Like Narcissus of Greek mythology, the male has seen only himself in the cosmic reflecting pool of ultimate mystery. *Men, you see, have named as absolute what they have really seen only from their own standing point. But these purported absolutes really are illusions, male-generated illusions. They are frauds.*

These pretentious claims of the maleness of God and the human male as being made in the image of God, are really not inclusive of the religious perception of the whole human spirit.

It can dawn upon women finally that the human male, peering into the cosmic mystery, has like Narcissus seen only *himself.* And they come to understand that men have named as Absolute or Ultimate what is really only partial, i.e., what they themselves have seen from their own standing point.

The Hoax

It can dawn upon women that traditional religion, which has purported to be about the human and the mystery of the divine, has instead only been about one-half of the human species and a very large mirror. As in *The Wizard of Oz,* when you pull open the curtain, there is only a little man there with large megaphone. So traditional religion, including the Bible, is cantilevered out over empty space. The empty space is the lack of the voice, the naming voice, of women.

Women's journey into a critical space begins with realizing that this is a great hoax. Sue Monk Kidd in *The Dance of the Dissident Daughter* (1996) has written poignantly of this realization suddenly engulfing her life. Kidd was an award-winning author in *Guidepost* circles when she began her journey. She entitles this passage "Awakening":

The following Sunday, home again, I returned to my own church. The deacons sat together on the front pews. All of them, I noticed, were men. The ministers—three more men—sat in huge chairs up front. I looked from one stained glass window to another. Most of the figures were men.

As the service began, I became acutely aware that every hymn and biblical passage used only masculine pronouns, as if that was all there was. Until then I had accepted that when it said "men" and "brotherhood," that somehow meant me, too. But now, in a place much deeper than my head, I didn't feel included at all.

I realized that lacking the feminine, the language had communicated to me in subtle ways that women were nonentities, that women counted mostly as they related to men.

Until that moment I'd had no idea just how important language is in forming our lives. What happens to a female when all her life she hears sacred language indirectly, filtered through male terms? What goes on deep inside her when decade after decade she must translate from male experience into female experience and then apply the message to herself? What does the experience imprint inside her? . . .

[W]e've been excluded from creating symbol and myth, from the meaning-making process that explains and interprets reality. This has been particularly true within the church. . . .

Now, sitting in church, I was full of questions. Why was God always the God of Abraham, never the God of Sarah? . . .

The congregation stood to sing. Unbelievably, as if all the irony in the world were crashing down at once, the hymn was "Faith of Our Fathers." I tried to sing, but I could not open my mouth. It was as if something had given way in my chest. I lowered the hymnbook and sat back down. I was fighting tears.

Sandy [her husband] bent down and nudged me. 'Are you okay?' he whispered. I nodded, but inside I felt too heavy to move. Until that moment I hadn't fully understood. I was in a religion that celebrated fatherhood and sonship. I was in an institution created by men and for men.

By the time I got home I felt disbelief that I'd not seen all this before—that the church, my church, was not just a part of the male- dominant system I was waking up to, but a prime legitimizer of it.

I was too dazed to be angry. Mostly I felt disillusioned, sad, betrayed. . . .

That afternoon I opened a book I'd recently brought home, Simone de Beauvoir's *The Second Sex.* I read all afternoon. I read how religion had given authority to men. As de Beauvoir put it,

religion had given men a God like themselves—a God exclusively male in imagery, which legitimized and sealed their power. How
fortunate for men, she said, that their sovereign authority has been
vested in them by the Supreme Being.

That night I couldn't sleep. I slipped out of bed and went to my
study. I stood by the window, looking out at the night. The tears
I'd suppressed that morning in church finally rolled down my face.
(1996, 49-51)

At another place in *Dissident Daughter* Kidd writes, *When a
woman crosses a threshold, she knows that something inside her has
shifted, if only slightly. She knows that she is on a different trajectory*
(1996, 106).

The Effect of Critical Thinking upon Women

Our lives as Christian women, who have read the Bible with the
eyes of faith, are never again the same after we realize the hoax. *We cross
some Rubicon, and we discover that this culture, this Adam's world, this
Bible is really not **about** us or **for** us. What we have discovered is that
we are aliens, singing our song in a strange patriarchal land.*

From now on, we read that Bible with intrusive questions in our
heads:

Is this passage really about me, or is it just about men?

Now I know some people at this point ask, "Oh come now! Why
does this bother women?" Let me tell you a story. From 1980 to 1982 I
was consultant to a Presbyterian National Task Force which had been
mandated to update for the national church their theology of stewardship, expanding the notion of stewardship from money and time to
include caring for the environment of our endangered planet. As we
struggled to draft the report, I was asked to write a short but vivid introduction which would focus on the environment. To make it vivid, I
wrote a story about a woman sitting in an auditorium at a conference
seeing a slide show about the environment and having her own
thoughts. You can see what this accomplished for me. I could convey
environmental principles in the slides, while her thoughts carried forward the novel-like human interest story. I read this introduction to the
committee, which had both males and females from both the then-
Northern and Southern Presbyterian Churches before their merger.

After I finished reading there was an uncomfortable silence.
Finally one Southern minister said, "Well, I'll say what most of us are

thinking. The men in my church could never identify with a woman as the main character to begin this report on Stewardship to the whole Presbyterian Church. Men *don't identify* with women."

The chair of the committee, who was himself quite a feminist, said, "You realize you've just burned your credentials as a feminist!"

The minister answered, "I do—but it's true!"

The committee then had to decide whether to ask me to change the story. We finally compromised, keeping the main character female, but I was prevailed upon to add vividly illustrative stories of her husband's interest in fishing in clean lakes and a comparable item about her son's interests, so that men could identify.

Need I say more? Men are very clear that they identify with men, not women. But somehow women are expected to turn their gender-psyches inside out, to identify with men, and not to cause a ripple in their consciousness. So I repeat my first question, *Is this passage really about me, or is it just about men?*

Can I get past all this male language, all this male imaging of God, so as to find some spiritual truth that illuminates my female life?

What do I do with my anger when women are ignored, invisible or denigrated in these heretofore revered passages?

The Denigration of Women

I must speak briefly now about this "denigration" and the problem it is for women when they begin to realize how the denigration of women has permeated their heretofore revered and beloved Christian tradition. Through the thousands of years since Jesus, Christian theology—*not* Jesus—has "named" women in profoundly hurtful ways.

• Women have been named *inferior,* not created in the image of God as males were.

The first three major theologians in the early centuries of Christianity each had a different reason for why women had not been created in the image of God the way men were.

• Women have been named *evil*, daughters of Eve, temptress.

In 1487 the infamous textbook of the Inquisition, *The Hammer of Witches*, said, "All witchcraft comes from carnal desire, desire which in women is insatiable." I find it hard to read that with a straight face. Our daily newspapers and television news programs are constantly recounting the latest male rapes, male incest, male pedophilia, male pornography—everything. Carnal desire insatiable in *women?* Who are we kidding?

• For three centuries in the Middle Ages, women were named *grotesque.*

Read *Carnal Knowing: Female Nakedness and Religious Meaning in the Christian West,* by Margaret Miles (1989) for many years the historical theologian at Harvard Divinity School (see especially "Carnal Abominations" and "The Female Body as Grotesque," pp. 145-168).

• Sex with women (who have been named evil) was also named evil.

That's not surprising. Once you declare women evil and their bodies evil, you have created problems for yourself if you want to have sex with them. Read Ranke-Heinemann (1990).

• Women were named befouled and contaminated because of their natural and sacred embodied uniqueness of menstruation and child birth.

They were declared "unclean" and in Jewish, Catholic and Episcopal traditions they were declared to be in need of a cleansing ritual before they could be readmitted to the sacred space of worship.

Do you understand what that means? It means that God's gift to women of the blood of life, which enables women to birth the next generation of humans (also a gift from God), was declared unclean and defiling—by humans!

You may say, "Well, these are all *old* doctrines. How can they be a problem for women *today?*"

The problem is two-fold. The Christian Church has *never repented* for this dreadful, hurtful theology. *And* the echoes of those old denigrations still resound in women's consciousness.

Let me tell you about this resonance still present in women's psyches. Several years ago my husband David and I were on the faculty of a week-long conference at Kirkridge, the ecumenical conference center ninety miles west of New York City. It was mid-week, so we were beginning to know one another, faculty and participants. We had just finished our collective morning Bible study and were making the transition to a communion service. The passage we had studied together included the account of Jesus and the woman with the "flow of blood" (Mark 5:25-34), and you will remember there was concern about her touch contaminating Jesus.

We were turning our minds and hearts from this biblical account and toward our communion service, when my husband interrupted us with a question. He had just had an "A-ha" insight which arose from the juxtaposition of that Bible passage and this communion service in which we were about to celebrate "the body and blood of our Lord Jesus Christ."

"Do you realize," he asked the group, "that in our religious tradition women's blood *defiles* but *male blood saves?*" This was a new and stunning cognitive connection and it caused him to speak it out loud in a very uncharacteristic way and in a most difficult moment in time.

Everyone froze. There was a stunned silence, and no one (including our worship leader) knew what to do. Then in that silence one of the conference participants, a woman who was an ordained minister in the United Church of Canada, began sobbing with deep, wrenching sobs. Now we really did not know what to do.

I do not remember what happened next, but somehow we made a segue into the communion service. But after the service was over, the woman minister came to us saying, "Do you want to know why I suddenly started to cry?"

"Ever since I've been ordained, in some deep part of my consciousness I have been aware I was standing in sacred space at the altar with a woman's body, a body which had been declared to be unclean in years past by my own Christian tradition. And when you, David, said what you did, it was as though that deep pain was lanced like a hidden boil, so the poison could run out and I could be healed."

Women *are* "in recovery" from being "named upon" in such hurtful ways by our Christian tradition and by the Western culture which was nurtured by that tradition.

Women Standing in a Disturbed Place

These then are some of the issues in many lay women's critical thinking about the Bible, *critical thinking which is not just an academic question but an existential disturber of their faith.* One by one in the quiet of their church pew (like Sue Monk Kidd), in the silence of their bible study and prayer at home, in the depths of their Christian hearts, many women are doing this critical thinking, and standing in that disturbed place. It should be of some concern to us.

Notes

1. Cartoon by Dedini, in Gray (1982, 18). See also cartoon by Stan Hunt, "Gentlemen, Let us pool our expertise," (Gray 1982, 51).

2. Cartoon by Booth, in Gray (1982, 73).

References

Daly, Mary. 1973. *Beyond God the Father: Toward a Philosophy of Women's Liberation.* Boston: Beacon.

Dodson Gray, Elizabeth. 1982. *Patriarchy as a Conceptual Trap.* Wellesley, Mass.: Roundtable Press.

Fiorenza, Elisabeth Schüssler. 1983. *In Memory of Her: A Feminist Theological Reconstruction of Christian Origins.* New York: Crossroads.

Kidd, Sue Monk. 1996. *The Dance of the Dissident Daughter: A Woman's Journey from Christian Tradition to the Sacred Feminine.* San Francisco: Harper.

Miles, Margaret R. 1989. *Carnal Knowing: Female Nakedness and Religious Meaning in the Christian West.* Boston: Beacon Press.

Ranke-Heinemann, Uta. 1990. *Eunuchs for the Kingdom of Heaven: Women, Sexuality, and the Catholic Church.* New York: Doubleday.

Postmodern Perspectives

7

Reading Scripture as Critical-Thinking Christians in the Post-Modern Era

James W. Voelz

I. Introduction

Critical thinking has been defined as "thinking about your thinking while you're thinking in order to make your thinking better" (Paul 1992, 7). Let us apply this approach to sacred Scripture. Let us think about interpreting Scripture—what actually happens when we engage in the process of reading and interpreting the sacred texts of the Christian faith. It is fascinating what we find.

II. The Contemporary Context

As a starting point, let me say that no thinking and no Scriptural interpretation are done in a vacuum. Both are always done within the context of a contemporary world. In our own case, this is no bad thing, by any means. In fact, it is my belief that interaction with our current world—the post-modern world—provides not only an understanding of the necessary context for reading and interpreting the sacred Scriptures at this time; it also provides important clues to arrive at an understanding of what such reading and interpretation actually entails.

But just what is this post-modern general context? What are its characteristics? Many could be enunciated, but I would like to highlight four and to do so by way of contrast with modernism.

The main characteristics of "modernism"—the dominant outlook of the West since the Enlightenment—are the following:

• belief in the superiority of reason,

- belief in the possibility of the objective access to and assessment of data,
- belief in the possibility of comprehensive explanation of whatever is under investigation, and
- belief in the inevitability of progress.

Modern science, especially as popularly understood, exhibits all of these traits.

In our contemporary world, each of these beliefs is questioned; indeed, each is virtually stood upon its head, and that in the minds of virtually everyone in this nation, including, with perhaps an exception or two, everyone sitting in this room. Post-modernism is characterized by:

- increasing distrust of reason and its ability to achieve real understanding,
- lack of belief in objectivity as a possible stance with which to achieve understanding,
- disbelief in the possibility of comprehensive explanation of anything and everything in life, so that all explanation is partial, and
- loss of faith in the notion of "progress," including the loss of belief in the inevitability of progress.[1]

Post-modernism in its extreme forms questions the notion of a "reality out there," separate from any observer/interpreter, even in the scientific realm.[2]

What has been the cause of this move from modernism to post-modernism in general outlook? I believe that the work of Sigmund Freud was key, with his blurring of the distinction between reality outside the observer and projection of the observer's own mind. But perhaps most influential have been the discoveries of contemporary physics—a theme to which we shall also return below. Consider what has happened since the turn of the 20th century in our understanding of the universe around us. In the centuries before, classical physics—and here we use Newton as shorthand for this view—saw the universe as a "normal" place, a world congruent with our personal, everyday experiences.[3]

- Material is solid, energy is not.
- Actions elicit equal and opposite reactions.
- Time is constant, etc.

But since the early 20th century—and we use Einstein as typical and archetypal here—the universe can be and is also seen as a very unusual place, incongruent with our personal, everyday experiences. Consider the following current "facts" of contemporary physics:

- According to Einstein's Special Law of Relativity (1905), as speed increases, time slows down and the length of objects contracts (Jones 1992, 20-9).
- According to Einstein's General Law of Relativity (1915), space is curved (Jones 1992, 59-62) and time slows down in strong gravitational fields (Jones 1992, 76).
- According to Heisenberg (1929), one cannot know both the position and the momentum (= mass x velocity) of a particle simultaneously (Hawking 1988, 54-5; Jones 1992, 159-62).
- According to de Broglie (1925), matter has a dual nature, so that particles have the properties of, and behave like, waves (Gribbin 1984, 86-91; Feynman 1995, 115-38).
- According to Quantum Theory (1920s), the movement of subatomic particles cannot be predicted individually, only plotted statistically (Gribbin 1984, 61-6).
- According to the standard "Copenhagen interpretation" of New Quantum (Wave) Theory (1920s to the present), physical properties have no objective reality independent of the act of observation (Jones 1992, 162-6).4
- And finally, the results of Relativity Theory and Quantum Theory cannot be reconciled to produce a "Grand Unification Theory" of everything in the universe (Jones 1992, 304-14).5

It is not hard to see how these insights provide the foundation to question every aspect of modernism, with its devotion to reason, to objectivity, to totalizing explanation, and to increased understanding of the whole, which is exemplified by the "truths" of Newtonian, classical science.6

III. What This Means for Scriptural Interpretation

A. Generally

What impact should these developments have on us as Christians who are critical thinkers, we who value rationality and the proper assessment of data, conditions, situations, etc.? On the one hand, we can and should react negatively, I believe. We cannot embrace the supposed "insights" of radical post-modernism, especially the "truth" that there is no truth or fact outside of subjective apprehension and that everything is, in fact, completely relative. Aside from the obvious fact that external reality does seem to impinge upon our existence, whether we acknowledge it or not (getting rear-ended unexpectedly in an automobile should convince anyone of that), we, as Christians confess: "I believe in God...." And this is not a confession that we believe in a projection of God (however subjective our understanding of God might be) but that we believe in a reality external to us who has acted external to us in order to affect our lives.

But it is the burden of this paper to contend that contemporary post-modern developments should impact us as critical-thinking Christians positively, especially with regard to two of the insights which it offers. The first is that there is no objective understanding of anything, including written texts. And the second is that there is no comprehensive explanation of anything under consideration, again, also including written texts. The first insight, concerning objective understanding, contends, on the one hand, that all data is situated and, therefore, understood and described only within its context, and, on the other, that all consideration of that data entails heavy involvement by the interpreter. This is not to say that "there is nothing out there which we consider," but it is to say that there is no pure, isolated *Ding an sich* which we consider, and no immediate, non-observer-affected access to such a supposed *Ding an sich*. The second insight (concerning comprehensive explanation) contends, on the one hand, that all explanation is partial and perspectival, and that understanding of reality around us, including texts, can only be achieved through the use of models, which models give an insight into one (or more) aspect of the object of interpretation, and, on the other, that, depending upon which perspective and/or model one uses, the appearance of the data is affected. This is not to say that no type of large-scale understanding can be achieved, but it is to say that paradox is at the heart of all reality, including the reality of texts. Both of these insights are, I believe, worthy to be embraced.

B. Hermeneutically

Hermeneutically, what do post-modern insights, especially the two we have just detailed, mean for us today? Specifically, how do they impact us as we seek to interpret Scriptural texts from a critical-thinking Christian perspective in 2000 AD? In several ways, I believe.

1. Concerning Objectivity:

a. All discourse is situated—contextualized (even as are the data of the reality which it seeks to reflect)—which means that there is no discourse which is a non-context-bound description of reality and, therefore, immediately transferrable to all other contexts. This applies to Biblical discourse, even as it does to all others.

i. On the most fundamental level, this is seen in linguistics. There is no "real" meaning to words as signifiers, neither is etymology any key to the meaning of a word in any given passage, nor is there a solid "general" meaning of a word (Voelz 1997, 109-14). Diachronic linguistic notions, the foundation of etymological exegesis and the notion of "real" meanings to words, is not the basis for textual discourse. On the contrary, synchronic usage is the (normal) basis for textual discourse,[7] viz., words are used with the meanings that are contextualized in time (i.e., they are contemporary) and contextualized literarily (i.e., they are appropriate to the literary co-text). Equally important, syntax bears the same characteristics.

ii. On a "higher" level, this is seen in literary argumentation, or, perhaps better put, in the applicability of a description or of a line of reasoning in a text. Here Hans Frei's masterful book *The Eclipse of Biblical Narrative* is of great help. As Frei shows (1974, 37), in the pre-modern, pre-Enlightenment era, all Biblical texts were seen to be descriptions of reality as such and, therefore, immediately transferrable to the contemporary world.[8] Medieval, and even Reformation, exegesis would exemplify this view. With the Enlightenment, however, things changed (1974, 42-50), and a "wheat and chaff" situation developed; now some of the Bible was seen as conveying eternal, unchanging truths, while other parts were context-bound and should not be applied. This is the view of modernism. It is certainly the view of historical-critical methods and of the Jesus Seminar—indeed, of any method or approach which seeks to establish the "true" religion or preaching of Jesus and assumes that that system of belief or kerygma is immediately relevant and transferable to today.

An articulate example of this approach is taken by Marva Dawn, who, in an essay entitled "Hermeneutics Considerations for Biblical Texts," distinguishes between three kinds of texts:

> (A) Normative or Instructive Texts—those which give basic, fundamental principles which should characterize the people of God.
> (B) Descriptive Texts—those which narrate examples of practices acceptable among the people of God.
> (C) Problematic or Corrective Texts—those which deal with specific problems among the Jews or in the early Church. (1992, 16)

The post-modern insight is that both the pre-modernist and the modernist position are incorrect, because, in fact, all texts are context-bound, making none of them what might be called "transparent" in their meaning and, thus, immediately applicable to a contemporary scene. (Using Dawn's classification, there are no type (A) texts.) This can be seen in the writings of many authors who make sweeping statements of a general nature concerning, e.g., freedom, oneness, and egalitarianism, on the one hand, but, on the other hand, in other situations, put restrictions on what they say. St. Paul does this often, most pointedly in Gal. 3:28 ("There is neither Jew nor Greek; there is neither slave nor free; there is neither male nor female, for you all are one is Christ Jesus"), and 1 Tim. 2:12 ("I do not permit a woman to engage in teaching or to engage in exercising authority over a man/husband, but she is to be in quietness"). Martin Luther does so frequently, as well. It is well known, e.g., that Luther extols all offices of all Christians, contending that no one *Stand* (class) is inferior to any other and that no one person is inferior to any other. Consider his words in the essay "To the Christian Nobility" (1966, 129):

It follows from this argument that there is no true, basic difference between laymen and priests...between religious and secular, except for the sake of office and work, but not for the sake of status. They are all of the spiritual estate, all are truly priests, bishops, and popes.

Yet, Luther can also sound much less egalitarian than this. In his 1527 commentary on 1 Timothy, e.g., he says (1973, 277): "[God] considers this [the teaching of the word] the greatest thing that goes on in the church."

In other words, in the more restrictive passages, authors like St. Paul and Luther might be said (i) to be inconsistent, or (ii) to be accommodating themselves to backward thinking, or (iii) themselves to be bound to older ways, or (iv) to be giving advice which, in this instance, is situational and context-bound.[9] Or, it might be said (v) that the passage is not written by the same man. But a sixth explanation, and, I would contend, a more satisfactory explanation, is somewhat different from them all. That is, a more satisfactory explanation is that sweeping generalizations are not really so sweeping, not so all-encompassing, not so general, after all. They, too, are contextual, spoken within specific, real-life situations, in the end. Thus, e.g., when Martin Luther extols the priesthood of all believers, its value, its freedom, its authority, and its rights, is he not, in his given situation, extolling that priesthood in the face of a Roman Catholic insistence that the church is really the hierarchy of clergy,[10] that laity must be subservient to ecclesiastical authorities, even in matters of the state, and that the Reformation movement was actually quite illegitimate, at its very core? And when St. Paul speaks of our oneness in Christ, no differences between Jew and Greek, slave and free, male and female, might he not be addressing a Galatian context in which barriers for people were common and in which access to and worthiness before God was severely limited by laws of every kind? This is most likely the case, and, therefore, we observe that in a different context, when different concerns arise—in the two cases I have presented, when confronted not by external devaluation but by internal anarchy, or, differently conceived, when confronted, not by a problem of worth but by a problem of organization or of order—the talk of men like Luther and St. Paul is significantly less egalitarian, indeed![11] The context-bound nature of all discourse is the basis of "deconstructive" analysis of texts, which takes as its primary task the de-constructing or "unmasking" of the moves made by authors,[12] when the meaning of texts is assumed to be obvious and when the scope of a text's description (or prescription) is seen to be totalizing or complete. And this observation shifts our focus to the interpretation of texts and to the "moves" interpreters make in dealing with texts, to which we will now turn.

b. Concomitantly, all interpretation of discourse is situated—contextualized—which means that there is no objective interpretation of any text. Otherwise expressed, all interpretation involves an interpreter in a given context, which interpreter is never uninvolved or detached from the process of interpretation. This principle is true for two reasons.

i. First, it is true because of how the process of the interpretation of texts itself proceeds (Voelz 1997, 208-9). Consider that readers/receptors of any text are hardly passive in the reading of any text. First, they activate what they see, making marks on the page "say" something instead of being simply defacings on a sheet of paper. Second, they decipher the words they identify as conveyers of meaning, which includes connecting or matrixing their meanings, dealing with ambiguity, and filling in the shorthand of the text. Third, they interpret the text on a second level, which involves, if it is a narrative, e.g., "reading" the significance of the deeds, situations, conditions, etc. which are depicted, and this with minimal guidance or direction.[13] Finally, interpreters may, if they so choose, interpret on still another level, detecting implications of what is said for the reconstruction of the author's *Sitz im Leben* ["situation/context in life"]. To put the second sentence of this paragraph positively, the readers/receptors of any text play an important, active, role in the process of textual interpretation.

All of this may be viewed in yet another way. Readers/receptors are themselves complexes of beliefs, knowledge, attitudes, ideas, experiences, etc. When they interpret, these are brought into connection with the text as interpretation takes place and proceeds. Perhaps better put, the readers' beliefs, knowledge, attitudes, ideas, experiences, etc., become part of the matrix for textual interpretation, so that nothing is interpreted in a text, unless it is part of a matrix with what the interpreters are as persons. They are, as it were, texts themselves—complementary "second texts," we might say, which are always a factor in textual interpretation.[14] Therefore—and this is the basic point—the interpretation of any given text involves, in actual fact, two texts: the given or "target" text (e.g., the book of Galatians or Genesis), and, as part of the matrix for understanding the target text (as a whole or focused on any of its parts), the so-called "second text" of the person/s doing the interpretation. And it is "against" the features of the "second text" that the target is, in fact, interpreted. Thus, the "significance" that Jesus is divine, perceived in the matrix or collocation of Jesus' miracles in Matthew (11:2-6) will be the result of a further matrix between these activities portrayed and the interpreter's own personal self as text. But different beliefs and different experiences in life could lead to another conclusion, e.g., that Jesus was in league with Satan (Matt. 12:24). The same is true for the perceived "significance" that Jesus was totally human, derived from a matrix of several passages in Mark. Another's personal second text could lead to the conclusion that, as fully human, Jesus Christ was not also fully divine (contra classical Christology) but simply possessed by God.[15] To restate the last sentence of the previous paragraph in the terms here given: the reader's self as "second text" is active in virtually all phases of textual interpretation.

ii. Second, it is true that there is no such thing as objective, non-reader-involved interpretation because of how literature itself is "set up" and "works" (Voelz 1997, 218-21). Here, our focus is upon literary documents and how communication through those documents takes place. We can begin to understand this set-up and working by examining a diagram which details the distinction between the reader, the text, the author, and the story of the text, using a narrative text as the example:[16]

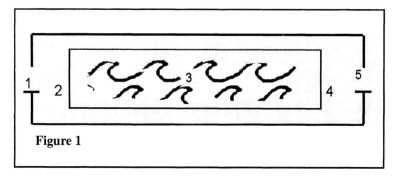

Figure 1

The inner box represents the (physical) text. The actual author (#1) and the actual reader(s) (#5) are concrete entities in the world outside the text, while the action of the story (#3) which constitutes the world of the text, is not physically in the text (not as the marks are on the page) but is depicted or evoked by the signifiers of the text itself.[17] What, then, is the relationship between the readers, on the one hand, and the text, author, and story, on the other? The readers (#5) read the text, and in so doing they (re)construct the author in their own imaginations = the implied author (#2), plus, they bring the story (#3) to life (actualize the text) from the marks which they see on the written page.

But what is on the other side (i.e, opposite) of the implied author (#2) in the scheme: (#4)? The answer is, the obverse of, the complement of, the left side, namely readers of whom the author is conscious, who may also be called implied. And these implied readers stand in the same relationship to the actual readers as the implied author stands to the actual author; they are, again, a construct, not in the real world, and they are detectible (only) in the text.[18] These implied readers are persons, receptors, with that knowledge, those abilities, that competency, which enables them to actualize the text. They are a conception of the author; it is for them which the author writes (though they in no actual fact correspond fully to any actual readers of the text). Who, then, is a valid interpreter of a text? It is the one who conforms to the expectations of the author. It is the one who conforms to the given texts assumptions. It is the one who becomes the implied reader—and only such a one—of a given text. Which means that an objective reading, a non-involved reading of a text is not only impossible; it is not to be desired! Otherwise expressed and more positively expressed, adequate interpretation of a text is not to have no assumptions; rather, it is to proceed with the proper assumptions. Readers are not to have no involvement; rather they are to be involved in the proper way.[19]

The implied author and reader schema, by the way, exercises an important control over the two-text interpretation process described several paragraphs above, because, with the exception of radical post-structuralist interpretation which avowedly "reads against the grain,"[20] only readings which are done by interpreters who seek to conform to the implied reader make "satisfactory" sense out of the "acknowledged" key elements and organizing features of the text. They are, in two words, "more satisfying" as a whole.[21] See Appendix One for a discussion of where one finds the implied readers of the Scriptural text.[22]

2. Concerning Comprehensive Explanation

We now turn to the second of post-modernism's insights, that concerning disbelief in comprehensive, totalizing explanation. According to this insight reality is complex and antinomous, not single and totally coherent. Again, we will focus both upon the characteristics of discourse itself and upon method of interpretation.

a. All discourse is perspectival and partial; it does not convey an easy, comprehensive message and, therefore, an easy comprehensive picture of reality.

The background for this principle is, again, contemporary physics. I have mentioned in the paragraphs above that contemporary physics, characterized by Einstein, contrasts with classical physics, characterized by Newton, in many surprising respects. To review several of the most important: according to relativity theory, time slows down as speed increases; according to quantum theory, matter has a dual nature, exhibiting characteristics of both particles and waves; and the results of both relativity theory and quantum theory cannot, at the present time, be connected or reconciled to produce a Grand Unification Theory or Supersymmetry Theory of everything in the universe.

Two things may now be noticed which are relevant to Scriptural interpretation, the first of which should be familiar, or at least comfortable to most who hear/read this essay.

i. On the one hand, de Broglie's discovery that matter has a dual nature, exhibiting at some times particle characteristics and at others wave characteristics, brought to the forefront the issue of perspective on a very delimited scale. There is no comprehensive, overarching explanation of light in the quantum world.[23]

From one perspective—in accord with one set of experiments—it behaves as do particles; its wave characteristics do not appear. From another perspective—in accord with another set of experiments—it behaves as do waves; its particle characteristics do not appear. In this situation models are needed for explanation (to speak of light as waves and particles is to use models), and several models must be employed. Furthermore, the models do not cohere. They do not fit together smoothly. They are antinomous with one another. One configuration of data will be congruent with one model; another configuration will be congruent with another, and the twain shall never meet. Yet each will provide a valid understanding.

Let me be a little chauvinistic here and say that Lutherans have little problem with this insight. In fact, in many respects, we have been ahead of the curve all along. We are familiar with the contrast between Law and Gospel, and we tend to divide all Scripture into these two contrasting categories. Also helpful is the contrast between *simul justus et peccator* (simultaneously just and sinner) within the Christian life. Even better, exhibiting the antinomous nature of the clash of models, is the Lutheran concept of the Christian as *totus justus et totus peccator* (totally just and totally sinner). We as Lutherans expect these modular understandings of our relationship to God and of the Christian life to be present in the sacred texts.

ii. On the other hand, the general contrast of contemporary physics, whether Einsteinian or Quantum, on the one hand, with classical, Newtonian physics, on the other, provides a clash of models and perspectives on a massive scale. The world of Newton in and of itself assumes an everyday perspective, a human perspective on the ordinary world around us. Its perspective is intuitive, and its data are phenomenological. Its world does not seem odd (time, e.g., is constant), and in it things are as they appear (space is not curved but extends outward).[24] By contrast the universe of Einstein—both the relativity theory universe and the quantum theory universe—in and of itself exhibits characteristics and assumes a perspective which is quite the opposite in all respects. It assumes not an everyday perspective but the perspective of scientists and researchers, and its focus is not upon the objects of our everyday life and world, but, rather, upon distant galaxies and subatomic quarks.[25] Its perspective is counter-intuitive, its data are mathematical, and its world is very odd (there is no gravity, only the geometry of space), with things not at all as they would seem (there is no solid matter; forces are the key). Put another way, the general contrast of the perspectives assumed between Newtonian, classical physics, on the one hand, and of Einsteinian, contemporary physics, on the other, is a contrast of frames of reference and of scale. The frame of reference assumed by, and the scale of, Newton is everyday life as we know it, while the frame of reference assumed by, and the scale of, Einstein is the universe as it truly is.[26]

Now, this situation is seen in the texts of sacred scripture analogically, I would contend. There is an intuitive, everyday, phenomenological understanding of us, of God, and of our relationship to him within these texts—a "Newtonian theology," as it were. And there is a counter-intuitive, universe-as-it-is, non-phenomenological understanding of us, of God, and of our relationship to him, an "Einsteinian theology," so to speak. Let me characterize them for you briefly now, according to four characteristics: God and his actions, the state of humankind, personal salvation, and the Christian life.

First, theology according to the "Newtonian" perspective, Perspective One:

• God and His Actions: According to "Newtonian" perspective, God is revealed as a partner, one who responds to what man does. He is pleased by the sacrifices of people and responds to them (Genesis 8:21: When the Lord smelled the pleasing odor [of Noah's sacrifice] the Lord said in his heart, " I will never again curse the ground because of man...."). He is pleased by all those who fear him and do what is good and acceptable in his sight (Acts 10:35). He is not far from us (Acts 17:27). In this perspective, God changes his mind and can be appealed to to change (see Abraham and Sodom and Gomorrah [Gen. 18:22-33]).

• Humankind's State: In Perspective One, the human state is revealed as bad, but we are not helpless and therefore not without responsibility. We are ignorant (Acts 17:30). We walk in our own ways (Acts 14:16). We are distant from God (Acts 17:27).

• Personal Salvation: In the "Newtonian" perspective, we must in some way respond to our situation and to the approach of God. We can seek after him and find him (Acts 17:27). We are called to repent (Acts 17:30). We are called to believe on the Lord Jesus Christ for salvation (Acts 16:31). We are told to turn to the living God (Acts 14:15).

- The Christian Life: According to this perspective, the Christian life is one of responsible personal action. We as Christians have ability to respond positively and to overcome the evil in our lives. All of the exhortations in Deuteronomy and in the Pauline epistles would essentially fall into this class. Consider this admonition of St. Paul, Romans 6:12-13:

> Let sin never reign in your mortal bodies...Never furnish your members as weapons for unrighteousness in sin but furnish yourselves to God as living creatures from the dead and your members weapons for righteousness for God.[27]

From this perspective, sin in the Christian life is like the black horse which vies with the white horse to pull the ("neutral") charioteer in his own direction. The exhortations are to the charioteer, who has the responsibility to decide in which direction he would go.[28]

This first perspective is phenomenological; it is the view from within our time and from within our daily lives. In general, it is the way things seem from our experience and the way reality strikes us, especially outside times of crisis. It is the way things also seem to outsiders, as one can note in the approaches taken in the evangelism efforts in Acts (see the passages above). This is the "Newtonian" view, "Newtonian" theology, as it were; it is the view of the way religion and our lives strike us day by day.

Now let us consider theology according to Perspective Two, the "Einsteinian" perspective.

- God and His Actions: According to the Einsteinian perspective, God is revealed as creator, elector, savior, and life-giver. He created and creates out of nothing (Gen. 1). He chooses and he says to his people, "...the Lord your God has chosen you to be a people of his own possession...." (Deut. 7:6). He is the creator of the new creation of those who are in Christ (2 Cor. 5:17). His people are made holy and justified by him (1 Cor. 6:11). He gives them life (Col. 2:13)

- Humankind's State: According to Perspective Two, people are revealed as in a hopeless condition. They are lost (Luke 19:10). They are totally in the dark (John 1:5) (Jesus is the Light of the World [John 8:12]). They are sinful (while such, Christ died for them [Rom. 5:8]). Most of all, they are dead (Col. 2:13) and cannot help themselves.

- Personal Salvation: In Perspective Two, this is the act of God alone. We contribute nothing. He died for us (Rom. 5:8); he chooses (John 15:16); he makes alive (Eph. 2:5); he saves (Luke 19:10); he finds those who are lost (Luke 15:1ff).
- The Christian Life: This, too, is God's act, from the view of this perspective. The chief passage here is Romans 7. We are wretched and do what we desire not to do, Paul says. We must be delivered from our body of death, saved by someone else, even when we are Christians! The Christian from this perspective is not much better off than the unbeliever, in some respects. He must still cry with David, "(You) create in me a clean heart, O God" (Ps. 51:10). Or again: "(You) purge me with hyssop and I shall be clean" (Ps. 51:7). From this perspective, sin is like cancer: it ravages the Christian and he is helpless against it. He certainly does not have to be encouraged to hate it, for as Paul says in his despair: "The evil that I do not desire, that is what I do (Rom. 7:19b)...I am a terribly wretched man; who will deliver me from this body of death" (Rom. 7:24).[29]

This second perspective is the eternal one, *sub specie aeternitatis*, which is God's point of view, one might say. It is the one which mature consideration of one's person and of one's situation leads one to; thus, it is the position also of the desperate person who has experienced the depths (cf. Ps. 51). This is the "Einstein" view, "Einsteinian" theology, as it were; it is the perspective of "what is really[30] going on."

How are these two theologies, these two theological perspectives related? Even as Newtonian and Einsteinian physics are related: both are true but both are true on different scales or in different frames of reference. "Newtonian" theology is true from a normal human point of view. "Einsteinian" theology is true from God's eternal point of view. And each is necessary to understand and to function in the world in which we live.[31] Indeed, Luther struggled with this problem until his final day.[32]

Now, the point of our analysis is simply this: there are tremendous advantages to the approach I have here suggested for us as critical-thinking Christian interpreters—exegetes who must learn to respect the "logic" of the writings we interpret, which includes paradox and antinomy, and to respect the "logic" of the Christian life, which includes paradox and antinomy, as well. Two stand out:

- The "Newtonian/Einsteinian" approach helps us to understand ourselves as thinkers and interpreters of texts, no matter which

Christian tradition we are in. Lutherans are "Einsteinian" to the core. Methodists and Baptists are "Newtonian" in their bones.[33] And we all have passages and insights on our side! It also helps us to appreciate each view. "Einstein" has his weaknesses, of course. He can seem irrelevant—too complicated—day by day. "Newton" is more "practical," in the minds of most. But when real explanation is required, "Einstein" simply cannot be beat, I would submit. There are no good "Newtonian" sermons at the side of a child's funeral casket.

• The approach suggested also helps us to be gentle with the sacred text, enabling us to be patient with it, not finding undue difficulties and problems within virtually every part. Could the psalmist say in the same Psalm: "For you have no delight in sacrifice; were I to give a burnt offering, you would not be pleased (Ps. 51:16), in close proximity to "Do good to Zion in your good pleasure; rebuild the walls of Jerusalem, then will you delight in right sacrifices, in burnt offerings and whole burnt offerings (Ps. 51:18-19a)"? (They are only two verses apart!) Yes, he really could; it is likely not another source. It is "Einstein" next to "Newton."

Could Paul the apostle say: "We know that the law is spiritual, but I am carnal, sold under sin (Rom. 7:14), in close proximity to "But now, having been liberated from sin, and having been enslaved to God, you have fruit issuing in holiness and its end, eternal life" (Rom. 6:22)? (They are but one chapter removed from one another.) Yes, he really could; it is not a psychological problem on his part. It is "Einstein" next to "Newton." Indeed, we see the close proximity of these two perspectives in Phil. 2:12-13:

> Therefore, my beloved, as you have always obeyed, so now, not only as in my presence but much more in my absence, work out your own salvation with fear and trembling ["Newton"]; for God is at work in you, both to will and to work for his good pleasure ["Einstein"].

The scriptures use both models and perspectives,[34] of this we must be aware.

In summary, then, for this entire section (point 2.a.), I propose that the sacred scriptures are more complex than you and I as critical-thinking Christians have ever suspected in our wildest dreams. This means that awe and humility before these texts is the proper posture, especially in our day, and that hard work lies before us as we engage in their interpretation. Which brings me to my final point.

b. Finally, I would contend that all interpretation of discourse is perspectival and partial, even as is the discourse of our texts. In the light of the previous discussion I can be rather brief. And here again, contemporary physics is a key. And again, so is de Broglie and his experiments with light. De Broglie discovered in his work that what you look for in a large measure determines what you see and what you do not see. Do you do an experiment in which light will be able to behave as waves? It will behave as waves, and you will not see particle characteristic as you look. Do you do an experiment in which light will be able to behave as particles? It will behave as particles, and you will not see it as waves. In other words, the object of investigation will exhibit different characteristics—some of its characteristics—depending upon the perspective of the observer in each case. And just so it is with texts. Do you come with a dispensational-millennialist perspective and not a-millennial glasses on your eyes? You will find dispensations of God's activity in the text, and a-millennial activity will not appear. Do you come with a Law-Gospel dichotomy as you read? You will find these divisions in the text, and other divisions will recede. Do you feel your sins cannot be forgiven? "...God has laid on him the iniquity of us all" (Is. 53:6) will be to you the purest Law—your sins put him on the tree. Do you look for sins forgiven? "...God has laid on him the iniquity of us all" (Is. 53:6) will be to you the purest grace—your sins were taken to the tree. In the provocative words of the controversial Stanley Fish (1985, 163): "...I did what critics always do: I 'saw' what my interpretive principles permitted or directed me to see, and then I turned around and attributed what I had 'seen' to a text."[35]

IV. Conclusion

My conclusion is short, and it is this. When we think about the thinking which goes on as we interpret written texts, especially the texts of sacred Scripture, we may be surprised to find that our understanding of that process is enhanced by, if not actually enabled by, our current context, the post-modern world in which we live. Modernism's ideals of a detached mind doing objective assessment of data and arriving at comprehensive explanations of what is under consideration is not only passé; it seems to be seriously flawed, not congruent with the process as it actually takes place. And this is good, for with our developing understanding of what interpretation of the text of sacred Scripture actually entails, we are wonderfully situated to take advantage of opportunities presented by our environment to present the Gospel of these Scriptures in the post-modern world of which we are a part.

Appendix One

The Location of the Implied Readers of the Bible

"Where does one find the implied readers of the Bible or of any other text?" The answer of post-modern criticism (Culler 1975, 113-30 and Fish 1976) is, and of the church traditionally has been: One does not find them by looking for an individual, for a reader is not alone. Readers are taught to read. Readers handle language, because they are instructed.[36] Readers develop beliefs and attitudes—a personal or second text— by conversation and discussion. That is to say, readers interpret in a community, with other readers, with other receptors, with those who are their contemporaries, and with those who have gone before. Therefore, readers can become implied readers, only as they are trained to be those implied readers, within a context where the implied reader of a text is appreciated and understood.

A valid interpreter of a text, then, is that person, that man or that woman, who assumes the role required, as it were, by a given text— who becomes the reader implied or called for by that very text. And such a one is formed to assume that role by a community, a community which has assumed that role itself.

But, then, we may ask, Are all community interpretations equal? There is probably no agreement on this answer,[37] and a radical post-modern answer would be definitely, yes! But I would propose the following: that community which has produced, received, and preserved a given set of documents—or, better put, that community whose personal formation includes the production, reception, and preservation of a given set of documents—is likely to teach its members to read those documents in a way congenial to them—that is, in such a way as to find in them what reasonably may be found in them. In such a community there will be, to use terminology we have used above, people who can assume the role of the implied reader of the documents. That is to say, that community's members will possess the competencies for interpretation called for by its documents, for they will operate by a set of beliefs, standards, and knowledge (= personal, second text) congruent with the beliefs, standards, and knowledge of those who produced those documents and, therefore, congruent with the beliefs, standards, and knowledge assumed by the texts themselves. Therefore, to be able to assume the role of the implied reader for a given set of documents, one must be a member of the community of those documents and be taught to read by it.[38]

What does this mean for a reading of the sacred Scriptures? It means, it would seem, the following: As far as the NT is concerned— and for the purposes of the discussion in this Addendum, I will limit myself to it (the OT presents its own unique set of difficulties in this regard [Voelz 1997, 226-9])—these books were produced, received, and preserved by the Christian community.[39] Therefore, that community is likely to teach its members to read these documents in a way congenial to them, to assume, as we have said, the role of the implied reader as they read. And, therefore, to be able to assume the role of the implied reader of the documents of the NT, one must be within the Christian community and be taught to read by it. Put into the terms of this argumentation: as one is in the church and adopts what is confessed (its beliefs, standards, etc.), ones personal text becomes congruent with the personal text of those who produced, received, and preserved those NT texts (Voelz 1997, 221-3).

Notes

1. See McKnight (1988), as well as the thought-provoking essays by several authors in volume 8 of the *New Perspectives Quarterly*, entitled "The Last Modern Century" (1991)

2. Walter T. Anderson, e.g., notes in his provocatively titled *Reality Isn't What It Used to Be* that "constructionist science" knows only "versions" of the world and concludes, "since we are admitting that anything we say about 'out there' is a construct, don't we create 'out there' also?" (1990, 76)

3. Strictly speaking, this way of putting it is true of us modernists in the West. Historically, Newtonian physics was itself revolutionary, contrary to "the appearances," i.e., to what seemed natural to everyday observation. According to James Burke, "Aristotle's cosmological system, which had survived almost intact for two thousand years, was based on a common-sense view of the universe. To the ordinary observer the sky seems to move..." (1985, 132). With Newton's theories, by contrast, "[m]an was no longer at the center of a system created for his edification by the Almighty; the earth was merely a small planet in an incomprehensibly vast and inanimate universe..." (1985, 161). See also Jones (1992, 100-1). For us, however, Newton's revolutionary theory of universal gravitation seems congruent with our everyday understanding of life.

4. The following quote from Gribbin is typical: "...whereas in classical physics we imagine a system of interacting particles to function, like clockwork,

regardless of whether or not they are observed, in quantum physics the observer interacts with the system to such an extent that the system cannot be thought of as having independent existence" (1984, 160).

5. Perhaps the best attempt at unification is so-called "string theory," which involves "superstrings," whose vibrations account for all elementary constituents of nature and the four dimensional space time of relativity (Jones 1992, 313-4). As one might expect, "string theory," which requires ten dimensions, has not achieved general recognition (Jones 1992, 101, 172 note).

6. For a similar but more general argumentation, see Robert E. Webber, who says, "The first and perhaps most fundamental challenge to modernity with its emphasis on reason and the empirical method has come from the twentieth-century revolution in science" (1999, 21) Webber, properly in my view, sees a philosophical revolution and a communications revolution building upon the revolutionary developments in science: "...the new philosophical thought...is a response to the scientific revolution (1999, 22)....The revolution in communication, birthed after 1950, has followed the same trajectory" (1999, 24). One might add a revolution in the social sciences to this list. The revolution in the hard sciences provides the base-line warrant for a revolution in thinking in the other disciplines.

7. There is, of course, the exceptional situation in which old or archaic meanings are specifically selected, but that is another matter and an exceptional case. Equally different and exceptional is technical linguistic usage.

8. Frei also makes this point by saying that in this era, the contemporary world (of, e.g., the 14th century) was seen as of-a-piece with the Biblical world, so that descriptions and assertions made in the scriptures were immediately applicable to the reader of the day (1974, 37).

9. This would correspond to Dawn's type (C) text in her essay on hermeneutical considerations.

10. Cf. the understanding of the church evidenced by Terence Keegan (1985, 20).

11. The same thing is seen in Exodus, which has a discussion of the priesthood of all of God's people Israel (19:5-6), along with a discussion of the more restricted, Aaronic priesthood (28:1; 29:1).

12. Deconstruction does not, of course, mean the destruction of texts and their meaning. For a somewhat lucid introduction, see Phillips (1990).

13. Indeed, the interpreters must also do many other complex operations on this level, including "filling in the blanks" of the story world and matrixing the deeds of the story together for an overall narrative significance.

14. Cf. Paul: "All thinking...is a creation of the mind's work, and when it is disciplined so as to be *well-integrated into our experience*, it is a new creation precisely because of the novelty of that integration" (emphasis added) (1992, 10).

15. No part of an interpretive matrix is unaffected in the process of interpretation. That is to say, the meaning of any given part is affected by the meaning of every other part. Therefore, the meaning of the target text affects inter-

preters as "second text," i.e., their understanding of their experiences, ideas, beliefs, etc. We call this, commonly, "application" (Voelz 1997, 323-5).

16. The diagram presented is my own variation of a standard diagram (see, e.g., Keegan 1985, 94), normally attributed to Seymour Chatman (1978, 146-51).

17. I have made the outline of this somewhat amorphous, because the content of a story will be different when read by different readers or when read repeatedly by the same reader.

18. It may also be said that the detection of the implied reader is accomplished only by a reader in the act of reading.

19. Note that for the sacred scriptures, personal faith would seem to be involved as one characteristic of the implied reader. St. Paul writes "to the saints" (Rom. 1:7). St. Luke tells Theophilus that he writes "that you may know the surety of those matters in which you were first instructed" (Luke 1:4). The role of personal faith in interpretation is, itself, a large issue and worthy of a complete discussion in and of itself (Voelz 1997, 223-6).

20. See Stephen D. Moore's provocative *Post-Structuralism and the New Testament: Derrida and Foucault at the Foot of the Cross* (1994). Such a reading is a dubious enterprise which sees texts as catalysts to personal insight rather than documents which seek communication. It "balkanizes" the use of literature and our understanding of it, reducing virtually all readings to expressions of the will to power.

21. In this and the previous sentence many terms are put into quotation marks. I realize that there is argument over what is "satisfactory" and which readings are "satisfying," but that is the nature of interpretation.

22. As a final comment concerning objectivity, the following may be observed. We said above that two factors are involved in the "non-objectivity" surrounding texts: i. all data is situated and, therefore, gives rise to contextualized understanding, and ii. all consideration of that data entails heavy involvement by the intepreter. The first of our points within this section, viz., concerning textual discourse itself, focused on the former factor and the second, concerning textual intepretation, on the latter. It is important to note, however, that each point does involve both factors. The discourse of any text is actually the result of the interpretation of reality by its author, thus entailing involvment of the author as interpreter, while textual interpretation, taking place (as it does) against the interpreter as second text, finds its data contextualized within the features of that (second) text.

23. It would be true to say that the current understanding of light is "comprehensive" mathematically and in terms of its ability to predict, but such an antinimous understanding is not comprehensive in a "unified" sense, in the sense that there is one overarching model or metaphoric understanding which accounts for all phenomena.

24. But see footnote 3, above.

25. The world of relativity and the world of quantum clash with each other, also on a massive scale, but that is another matter and not relevant to the point at hand.

26. Here the parallel to contemporary physics begins to break down. While the Einsteinian view is more "real" than the Newtonian view, it does not pretend to describe how things actually are in any objective (not to mention literal) sense. This is specifically true of the quantum theory component of what we are calling the "Einsteinian," non-intuitive view. In actual fact, Albert Einstein himself did not personally embrace this understanding of quantum, insisting that finally explanations had to be realist. For this reason, Niels Bohr, with his "Copenhagen interpretation," would no doubt provide a better archetypal figure for contemporary, non-Newtonian physics than Einstein, but he is less well-known generally. Einstein and Bohr carried on a dispute over precisely this point for many years (see Jones 1992, 179-87, including notes). See also note 31, below.

27. See also Deut. 30:11-18a.

28. See Raabe and Voelz (1996), who apply the ideas articulated here specifically to the paraenetic sections of Paul's epistle to the Romans. Their article also discusses the images of the charioteer/white horse/black horse with reference to its Platonic background.

29. More positively put, Paul declares that God is responsible for all of the good within him. He says that he no longer lives; rather, "Christ lives within me" (Gal. 2:20).

30. But see footnote 26, above.

31. Similar is Roger Penrose's observation that Niels Bohr had to balance two quite different pictures of the universe: "...Bohr needed to regard the world at the classical level as indeed having an objective reality. Yet there would be no 'reality' to the quantum-level states that seem to underlie it all" (1990, 280). Of course, in its specific details this observation is not congruent with the characteristics of the theological levels as we have been describing them.

32. See especially William C. Placher's important book *The Domestication of Transcendence: How Modern Thinking About God Went Wrong* (1996), which seeks to demonstrate that Aquinas, Luther, and Calvin all developed systems of theology which struggled with the contrast between the divine and human point of view. Indeed, his presentation of Luther's understanding of *deus absconditus* (the hidden God) and *deus revelatus* (the revealed God) is quite congruent with what is argued in this paper:

> ...Luther was struggling with a legitimate problem of perspective or standpoint. From God's perspective, the pieces do fit together, and one could see God at work, even in the trials of our lives. But no human theologian can occupy that perspective, and so, even to make such confident claims is to reach beyond faith. (1996, 51)

See also his discussion of Calvin's struggles with the problem of the will(s) of God and the question of predestination (1996, 63-4).

33. So are transdenominational movements, by and large: WWJD, Promise-Keepers, Church Growth, etc. They are practical and thus "Newtonian" at their core, for they are designed to help people in their normal, daily lives. Consider, e.g., the opinion of high school student Christy Oberdeck expressed in an article entitled "The WWJD Controversy: An LC-MS Student Speaks Out," printed in the Concordia Seminary student publication *Spectrum* (31 no. 5, February 12, 1999, 3), responding to something asserted in a previous issue concerning WWJD:

> I have a bracelet that I try to wear every day because it is a great reminder for me. A couple times this school year I was tempted to look at my neighbor's paper, when I came to a hard question on a test. But instead of my eyes drifting on the other person's paper they drifted to the bracelet. Once I saw the bracelet, I realized that I was about to do something I knew was wrong, and so I didn't do it.

Here we see "Newton" in all his glory!

34. Another example would be the following: According to St. John, Jesus says: "No man can come to me except the Father draw/pull him" (John 6:44). According to St. Luke, Peter says: "God is pleased by all those who fear him and do what is good and acceptable in his sight" (Acts 10:35). These are not competing theologies; they are an "Einstein"/"Newton" clash.

35. We may note that hearing texts as Law and hearing texts as Gospel is a matter of pragmatics—still another contemporary issue for consideration; it concerns the impact (e.g., accusation, comfort, promise, threat), not the meaning of a text, and it is a special concern of Speech-Act Theory. An author intends an impact for a text (what Speech-Act Theory calls it "illocutionary force"), but it is the readers and interpreters who feel the actual impact of that text (what can be called the actual "perlocutionary force"). And the perspectives of the readers, the interpreters' perspectives—and theirs alone—determine the real pragmatics, the final impact of a text. And that pragmatics may change, virtually every time they read.

Here we Lutherans have been ahead of the curve, I would say again. We have spoken of three "uses"—perhaps better, three "impacts"—of the Law, not three "meanings" of the Law (for the content of the Law does not change, whatever its impact on us might be). And the actual use, the actual impact of a text, is dependent upon the readers of that text, upon the perspectives which they bring.

36. Community instruction encompasses such basic things as grammar. For example, does a ἵνα clause ever convey result in the NT? (The answer is disputed.) It is because of the commonality of community that one can commu-

nicate at all. A community gives us a common understanding of language and of life.

37. See especially Culler (1975, 113-30) and Fish (1976). See also Moore's masterful Literary Criticism and the Gospels (1989, 108Ð30) for an excellent overview of the problem.

38. Note that this analysis does not mean that a text is a "waxen nose," as many who evaluate positions such as this seem to fear (cf. Thiselton 1992, 538-39, 546-50), though it is far more waxen than many do believe. A text, because it is an item of intention, because it is not an arbitrary pattern with no preconceived intentionality, does have the ability to judge the community of which it is a part. In other words, a text can "rise up on its hind legs," as it were, and say to the very people whom it serves: "You are wrong! You must rethink!" And this dialectical relationship between text and community, between the produced and those who produce and who preserve, is seen repeatedly within the history of the church.

39. Note that the question of canon comes immediately to the fore.

References

Anderson, Walter T. 1990. *Reality Isn't What It Used to Be.* New York: Harper.
Braaten, Carl. 1983. *Principles of Lutheran Theology.* Philadelphia: Fortress.
Burke, James. 1985. *The Day the Universe Changed.* Boston: Little, Brown.
Chatman, Seymour. 1978. *Story and Discourse: Narrative Structure in Fiction and Film.* Ithaca, NY: Cornell University Press.
Culler, Jonathan. 1975. *Structuralist Poetics: Structuralism, Linguistics, and the Study of Literature.* Ithaca, NY: Cornell University Press.
Dawn, Marva. 1992. Hermeneutical Considerations for Biblical Texts. In *Different Voices/Shared Vision: Male and Female In The Trinitarian Community,* eds. Marva Dawn et al., 15-24. Delhi, NY: ALPB Books.
Feynman, Richard P. 1995. *Six Easy Pieces: Essentials of Physics Explained by Its Most Brilliant Teacher.* Originally prepared for publication by Robert B. Leighton and Matthew Sands. New Introduction by Paul Davies. Reading, MA: Helix Books, Perseus Books.
Fish, Stanley. 1976. Interpreting the Variorum. *Critical Inquiry* 2: 465-85.
Frei, Hans W. 1974. *The Eclipse of Biblical Narrative: A Study in Eighteenth and Nineteenth Century Hermeneutics.* New Haven, CT: Yale University Press.
Gribbin, John. 1984. *In Search of Schrödinger's Cat: Quantum Physics and Reality.* New York: Bantam.
Hawking, Stephen W. 1988. *A Brief History of Time From the Big Bang to Black Holes.* NY: Bantam.

Jones, Roger S. 1992. *Physics for the Rest of Us: Ten Basic Ideas of Twentieth-Century Physics That Everyone Should Know...and How They Have Shaped Our Culture and Consciousness*. Chicago: Contemporary Books.

Keegan, Terence J. 1985. *Interpreting the Bible: A Popular Introduction to Biblical Hermeneutics*. New York: Paulist.

Luther, Martin. 1973. The Lectures of Dr. Martin on the First Epistle to Timothy. In *Luther's Works*, Vol. 28 (American Edition), trans. Richard J. Dinda, ed. Hilton C. Oswald, 215-384. St. Louis: Concordia.

_____. 1966. To the Christian Nobility of the German Nation Concerning the Reform of the Christian State. In *Luther's Works*, Vol. 44 (American Edition), trans Charles M. Jacobs, rev. and ed. James Atkinson, 115-217. Philadelphia: Fortress.

McKnight, Edgar V. 1988. *Post-Modern Use of the Bible: The Emergence of Reader-Oriented Criticism*. Nashville: Abingdon Press.

Moore, Stephen D. 1989. *Literary Criticism and the Gospels: The Theoretical Challenge*. New Haven, CT: Yale University Press.

_____. 1994. *Post-Structuralism and the New Testament: Derrida and Foucault at the Foot of the Cross*. Minneapolis: Fortress.

New Perspectives Quarterly 8, No. 2. 1991 [The Last Modern Century]. The Center for Democratic Institutions. 10951 W. Pico Blvd, 2nd Floor, Los Angeles, CA 90064.

Paul, Richard. 1992. *Critical Thinking: What Every Person Needs to Survive in a Rapidly Changing World* (2nd edition), ed. A. J. A. Binker. Santa Rosa, CA: Foundation for Critical Thinking.

Penrose, Roger. 1990. *The Emperor's New Mind: Concerning Computers, Minds, and The Laws of Physics*, reprint edition with corrections. Oxford: Oxford University Press.

Phillips, Gary A. 1990. Exegesis as Critical Praxis: Reclaiming History and Text from a Postmodern Perspective. *Semeia* 51 ["Poststructural Criticism and the Bible: Text/History/ Discourse"]:7-49.

Placher, William C. 1996. *The Domestication of Transcendence: How Modern Thinking About God Went Wrong*. Louisville, KY: Westminster John Knox.

Raabe, Paul R. and James W. Voelz. 1996. Why Exhort a Good Tree: Anthropology and Paraenesis in Romans. *Concordia Journal* 22: 154-63.

Thiselton, Anthony. 1992. *New Horizons in Hermeneutics: The Theory and Practice of Transforming Biblical Reading*. Grand Rapids, MI: Zondervan, 1992.

Voelz, James W. 1997. *What Does This Mean?: Principles of Biblical Interpretation in the Post-Modern World*, 2nd edition. St. Louis: Concordia.

Webber, Robert E. 1999. *Ancient-Future Faith: Rethinking Evangelicalism for a Postmodern World*. Grand Rapids, MI.

8

McLuhan and a Critical Electronic Ethos: Contexts in Collision or Harmony?

Donald B. Colhour

Retracing becomes in modern historical scholarship the technique of reconstruction.

—McLuhan (1995, 1)

Culture and Implications of Context

As the media respondent for the conference, my point of view was requested as a media professional, and now an ordained minister serving a congregation. In this chapter, I pay critical attention to a relevant epistemological context for the church in the electronic age. I argue that the rupture of the literate or "critical" church is a consequence of contextual oversight by critical thinkers.

Some additional background is in order. From 1994 to 1997, my research at the School of Theology (New College), University of Edinburgh, Scotland, focused on Marshall McLuhan's doctoral dissertation, completed at the University of Cambridge in 1943. This research, coupled with 25 years of professional media experience, confirmed for me the validity of McLuhan's argument that contextual and historical understanding are essential to assessing the impact of elec-

187

tronic media. The absence of attention to this understanding has allowed electronic media to replace the literate or "critical" church as the place where the community gathers to dialogue, worship and celebrate. The reason for this, I propose, is that the context of the way we communicate has changed.

Electronic media is contextually driven. Its sole allegiance is about delivering the message, regardless of what that message is. The content-driven church is no match for the speed and precision of electronic context. The discussion is not about right vs. wrong. It is about the logic used. In 1943 McLuhan asserted that the decline of the church had more to do with its failure to re-contextualize itself and its structure than the assertion that the world was contaminated by the new technologies.

Structure vs. content as determinants: Gutenberg's contextual inversion

Gutenberg's invention of the printing press suddenly shifted the primary context of logic from hearing to seeing. The advent of the printing press climaxed a long history in the advance of the phonetic (Greek) alphabet and the sudden ability to place multiple copies of the same article into the hands of many individuals brought about the need for reading (literacy). This new logic (linear) recontextualized both the church and the academy, McLuhan pointed out, by inverting the classical trivium (grammar, rhetoric and dialectics) as derived from the "Book of Nature." Whereas the trivium had always been governed by grammar, the advent of mass printing placed dialectic in charge (Colhour 1997, 6) Literacy rates in Germany jumped dramatically after the printing press. Eyeglasses became necessary. The way we perceived the world changed. Monarchs were overthrown in favor of republics. The Protestant Reformation fractured the Roman Catholic Church. Reading texts for themselves, people developed ideas that could not be controlled by the church. When those who protested the church were persecuted, it was Rome who became the object of hatred. Academics changed. Old Logic was out. New Logic was in. Proponents of the new context viewed this dramatic contextual shift as Holy Revelation by Protestants and Holy Degradation by the Roman Church declared apostate.

Now, in the second century of the electronic age, the proponents of the electronic context have declared the "critical" church apostate. Now, with the advent of the Internet and the personal computer, business and culture have been restructured again. As the printing press restructured business, society and the faith of its time, the electronic culture has restructured all of these things in this time. As usual, the established faith(s) are following, but not without great resistance. Then as now, those who adopted the new context found themselves ruling the conversation. To clarify this voice and view, let us look at the following aspects of context.

The Trivium and old logic: The ghost behind the confusion

Dialectics, noted McLuhan, fragmented the educational system into separate schools, which eventually became so separated that they saw themselves as unrelated (1943, ii). The same can be noted for the church. Whereas the church previously saw itself as inevitably interrelated, the shift from grammar to dialectics brought about cultural fragmentation. Groups emerged who saw very little, if any, relationship to each other. In fact, there was great competition and derision among the groups. It was not just the Church of Rome that found itself split. The Church of Scotland (Presbyterian) and the Church of England (Anglican) had very different views of one another. Methodists, Baptists, Congregationalists (Separatists), and Lutherans became more and more fragmented until the number of independent sects seemed destined to defy any hope of proclaiming the faith outside a context of endless argument and antagonism.

McLuhan identified this centrifugal pattern of separation in his 1943 doctoral thesis when, through his retracing, he observed the cause of this fragmentation originated in the shift when the trivium ruled by logic of the ear (old or oral logic) shifted to logic of the eye (new or linear logic). History records this as the rift of the ancients and moderns. McLuhan argues that through the gradual ascension of the Greek alphabet, the trivium was ruled by dialectics rather than grammar as had been the case since time began. This is not to say that dialectics were unimportant to understanding in the old world. It is to say that they were not in contextual control of the learning process. Until Gutenberg, the written word was not primary to communication. What we *heard* was primary.

For the 1800-year reign of literacy, the 400 preceding the advent of electricity were the height of the linear, sequential, alphabetical method, with grammar and rhetoric subservient to dialectic. (Colhour 1997, 15) This sequential context of harmonious Euclidean, visual space of the moderns changed the conversation. The argument for many changed from "what God *said*" to "what God *wrote*." The context of "critical" analysis gave rise to a new academy, a new church and a New World. This context ruled the conversation from the advent of

Gutenberg until the invention of the telegraph when once again the context shifted.

The Context of Electronic Media and Old Logic

The advent of electricity began to turn the tables once again toward inclusive, audile-tactile orchestration of the senses, with the reintroduction of the space of the resonant interval. (McLuhan and McLuhan 1988, 33)

The advent of electricity put our ears back in charge. The ancient trivium of grammar, rhetoric and dialectics would be inverted. Grammar and the logic of the ear would end the visual logic of the book and the alphabet. Just as the Gutenberg galaxy displaced grammar (logic of the ear) as primary and fragmented the unified ancient world into separate school which eventually became so separated that they saw themselves as unrelated, the electronic word reawakened our oral and tribal nature. What has transpired is the collapse of linear, homogeneous contexts. McLuhan pointed this out though his observation of the difference between the modern home environment of integrated electric information and the classroom. He noted, 'Today's television child is attuned to up-to-the minute 'adult' news-inflation, rioting, war, taxes, crime bathing beauties-and is bewildered when he enters the nineteenth-century environment that still characterizes the educational establishment where information is scarce but ordered and structured by fragmented classified patterns, subjects and schedules" (McLuhan & Fiore 1967, 18).

The advent of the printing press upended the ancient world, which was bound together through two books, The Book of Nature (which was never really a book but a concept) and the Bible. That world fractured under the stress of dialectics taking charge of the trivium. Then, just as now, the world seemed to come apart. Then, just as now, the source of truth was questioned. Indeed it came apart so much that separate faith groups, nations and belief systems seemed unable to connect. The homogenous nature of the ancient world evaporated into factions. Now the trivium has inverted once again. Grammar or the magic of utterance is once again in charge. This time, however, the difference is that grammar and dialectics (logic of both the ear and eye) merge at the speed of light and sound to from the super-power of electronic media. This super-power, perceived by some to be controlled by America, is in charge not through the throne, the parliament, the academy or the pulpit, but through the unseen studio transported live into the living room. What is heard on the so-called "idiot box" is believed as gospel. It is believed as gospel, not because it is, but because it combines the two logics of the brain (left and right, visual and oral). This super-power combination has not just upended the third world and its religions. From the beginning it upended the western world ensconced in the Gutenberg Galaxy.

Creeds and dogma developed by the fragmented churches of the Reformation have completely disappeared in the electronic church. Young people are equally lost in the 19th Century paradigms of the reformed churches. Interestingly, faith groups in the New World, which led the reformation and saw themselves in charge of the New World, have been just as terrorized by this super-power of electronic media as the third world. They were leaders, like the leaders of the electronic culture, who realized the power of the technology they were using without realizing the source of the power. McLuhan, in his Cambridge study, uncovered the one theologian, Kierkegaard, who sensed and predicted this electronic shift. The key clue, McLuhan claimed, lay in Kierkegaard's reference to the sinister technology in his *Concept of Dread*, published in 1844, the year of the telegraph line between Baltimore and Washington (McLuhan and McLuhan, 1988, 44). For Kierkegaard, dread was the point of intersection of the nature-determined world and the world of the individual free spirit; the person chose between them.

It is pertinent to note that this was precisely the height of Alexander Campbell's *Millennialist,* the height of the Great Awakening and the apex of the Disciples of Christ growth. Contextually speaking, it could be forcefully argued that the all-inclusive church they envisioned was an equally subconscious reaction by the Campbell-Stone churches to the inclusive, audile-tactile orchestration of the senses that electricity was reintroducing. The open table and believers' baptism made Campbell's Disciples of Christ and Stone's Christian Church the cutting-edge religious organizations of the day. New hymnody (composed on the frontier) in combination with Campbell's early introduction of historical criticism made this non-denomination of associated churches the dot com. religious entrepreneurs of their day. The splintering of the movement by those who refused to accept the new context in the hyper-linear, hyper-literate, hyper-content became The Church of Christ.

But, Campbell's vision triumphed. When radio swept the culture, the Stone-Campbell paradigm was on the wave's crest. Why? Because the Stone-Campbell wave contained classic combination of two side-effects of technology discovered by McLuhan. When confronted with contextual change, both institutions and individuals go through reversal and nostalgia. That was the heart of the Stone-Campbell principal of restoration. Restoring the church to its original structure provided the nostalgia that made the paradigm. So exciting was this paradigm that the Disciples of Christ could hardly keep up with their expansion. In the media capitol of this new world, the marriage was made visible when Wilshire Boulevard Christian Church became the first to build its great cathedral-style edifice in the heart of the carriage trade mansions of Los Angeles. Broadcast by its next-door neighbor, radio KFI, directly across the street from the famous Ambassador Hotel, Coconut Grove and original Brown Derby, Wilshire was the Crystal Cathedral of its day. From this mother church of the Disciples in Los Angeles more than 125 Disciples churches grew. Neither Willow Creek, Saddleback, nor the Crystal Cathedral can claim such a record. Let us take a deeper historical look at why.

A brief history of electronic media and old logic contexts

Electronic culture developed from telegraph to telephone. The photograph developed into moving pictures and coupled together to become the movie. This was the first of the inclusive, audile-tactile orchestrations of the senses and the space of the resonant interval, which really assaulted and fragmented linear Euclidean space. Among the tools of the movie was the microphone.

The microphone and public address systems gave rise to the public electronic crowd, just as the printing press gave rise to the literacy. A defeated but highly literate Germany led the way. *Nostalgia* from a depressed world was amplified through the microphone, broadcast on the radio and enlarged at the cinema. This nostalgia for that time of ethnic purity (which of course never existed) challenged the social context. It gave a beleaguered people hope of regaining their place in a world that had left them behind. While Gutenberg's printing press gave rise to literacy and challenged the non-literate church—the microphone, radio and movie amplified, broadcast and enlarged the voices of Hitler's Germany to the Master Race. World War II erupted.

After this war, television partnered with microphone, radio and movies to let us instantly watch and talk about ourselves. The electronic mirror was born. In the post war 50's that electronic mirror had America reveling in its victories. Anyone not reveling in this victory was blacklisted as un-American. There was even a committee in United States Congress that became the watchdog for this belief. When the 60s Peace Movement used these same tools to organize, propagate and agitate for their bell-bottomed, longhaired, free love crowd—the mirror cracked. Those who had lived through the horror of WWII and the microphone crowds of the 30s and 40s could not imagine that a microphone crowd should be gathered for any reason other than protesting Nazism or Communism. Any other behavior must be subversive. People of color marching for civil rights and students with long hair had no place in this mirror image. This, contextual argument asserts, was the great electronic war of the 60s, which climaxed with the assassination of the King of Camelot, John F. Kennedy, and imploded linear culture into war in the living rooms of America. Billed as Anti-Communist this war changed us even more.

War was no longer something described in history books. It was no longer an abstract concept. It was not insulated or isolated by interpretations created by historians. It was in living color while people ate their TV dinners or had their morning coffee. The reality of war shocked us. In the end we failed to have the stomach for it and our culture was altered. The draft ended. Soldiers who left with flags waving came home to be rejected. The president who started the war would leave office. The president who would follow would be removed. Previously held ideas about who we were and where we were going would be questioned for decades. Conference participant Brenda Brasher described these phenomena this way. "Today, the infiltration of technology into daily life is transforming our patterns of play, work, love, birth, sickness and death such that speaking about cyborgs is not an imaginative plot device but a metaphor that is lived by." What the Christian church (not just the Disciples of Christ) and every other religious organization missed then, and has still missed to this day, is that the source of the powers of technology (as extensions of our body) which affects everything we think, feel and believe originates in the context of its logic.

That same religious community has failed to understand that it was the center of the conversation because it used the logic of the printing press—so it has failed to understand that it is not in the center of the conversation of the post-modern world because it has failed to use the logic of electronic technologies . . . except of course for the radical and fringe anti-modernist conservatives, who now define the terms. To resist is to be displaced. That is what happened. President of the Disciples, Dr. Richard Hamm, noted this reality when discussing the decline in church membership in the 1960s: "Nineteen sixty-eight was the apex of disestablishment, and so it follows that 1968 also marked the beginning of decline in membership for most mainline denominations"(1996, 10).

The failure to assimilate new information systems and the electronic technology in the church's epistemology created a void. Instead of the church being on the cutting-edge of human understanding it rested in its own nostalgia. A new world called secular arose in its place. This world studied and applied the new knowledge that the religious world rejected. Psychology and psychiatry (specifically, contextual studies of behavior) partnered with social science (also contextual in its approach) to fill the understanding gap. For example, Freud studied the role sexual repression played in development (the most taboo subject the church could possible imagine) and Carl Jung developed a theory, which measured perceptual impressions called *gestalts*. Psychology and psychiatry made extensive studies about first impressions and their effects on personal choice. In addition, media studies developed the science of demographics, which uses the knowledge of psychology and psychiatry. Demographics found that organizations also have gestalts. This gestalt or perceptual picture becomes the driving force behind an organization. It also affects who is attracted to the organization. In this electric age, an organization, which wants to be in the center of the conversation, needs to consciously examine its gestalt.

In short, one could say "On the Air = In the Conversation". Broadcasters understand it. Madison Avenue understands it. Conservative Christians and religious fundamentalists understand it. Why can't the so-called mainline understand it?

Summary/Conclusion

In conclusion, we can see if we retrace history back far enough we find answers which elude us when only the present or recent past are reviewed. As a television executive, I was always puzzled at the way the actions and styles of the shows we broadcast became mandates in popular culture and behavior. From the studio drawing boards, scripts and scenes we would weave together and transmit into millions of homes, behavior of those who watched would be altered. Buying patterns for everything could be altered. It was an awesome and powerful medium. Sitting behind the secure walls of the studios, those inside understood that we were in the center of the culture's feelings about itself. People clamored to come to Hollywood. They would stand in line for hours to get a seat in the audience of a recording of their favorite show. All through those years I wondered what gave us such extraordinary power.

It took extracting myself from the Hollywood culture and immersing myself in a foreign culture to satisfy this question.

It was in the basement stacks of the main library at Edinburgh University where McLuhan's little book jumped at me. As I pulled it from the shelf and began to peruse its funny pages of pictures and commentary, the picture became suddenly clearer. This odd little book, which academics poked fun at during the Sixties was not odd anymore. McLuhan's voice and view have points worth considering. His son Eric once told me that the original title of *The Medium is the Massage* (1967) was really *The Medium is the Message*. The printer made an error. When Marshall saw the change he smiled. The metaphor resulting from changing an 'e' to an 'a' captured the undertone of his message. While it was certainly not new that electronic culture had changed everything —my television mind caught the link between the different kinds of logic used to make these shows. It was the absence of this voice and view that was missed when linear academics attempted to analyze what had happened. Our content-oriented, abstract linear paradigm had bit by bit isolated us from our ears for nearly 1800 years. The slow pace of this isolation was evident to very few. There were periods, such as the Grand Renaissance, when people like Erasmus attempted to remind us of the importance of the ancient paradigm. But Gutenberg and the floods of literature it created made us deaf to such voices or views.

After working through McLuhan's little-read *Laws of Media* (1988), which his son Eric finished after he died, I became convinced that this faithful English professor had important things to say. Upon finding the ex-directory number of Eric McLuhan through his publisher, I made the call. The answer will always ring in my ears. Eric said, "I have been waiting for this call for seven years." My response was "What do you mean?" Eric said, "My Father and I always wondered why theologians never caught the connection." That was when he invited me to Toronto. It was in McLuhan's private library that Eric pulled out a dusty black box and suggested that I might find its contents interesting. That was the introduction to McLuhan's never-published nor critiqued Cambridge thesis of 1943, "The Place of Thomas Nash in the Learning of His Time." After a week of digging through this work, it became clear that some important answers to the questions about the influence of electronic media would be answered in this television executive's mind. In the following months it became clear. By combining the different logics of the ear and eye, the electronic medium was contextually superior. Perhaps this short chapter will initiate some new voices and views on this subject.

One final thought. As this book goes to press, the events of September 11 are still fresh in our minds. Many have been asking. Why do they hate us so much? Why do some in Islam perceive that it is being threatened? If we examine these questions contextually, some plausible reasons emerge. The illiteracy at the center of the people feeling threatened signals an absence of the linear logic, which Western Civilization, Christianity and Judaism have embraced for centuries. Islam rejected the printing press and its logic. The most conservative Islamic schools still reject this logic. The only thing taught is the Koran while Christianity, Judaism and the cultures they represent are fully immersed in the logic combinations found in electronic context. Western attitudes, through organizations like CNN and the BBC, penetrate all the cultures receiving their signal at their heart. They invade the home. Western thought, dress and customs and ideas threaten the traditions of not just Islam, but many other cultures. It is in this way that western culture is perceived as terrorist. We propagate our ideas in the homes where the Mosque cannot control the content. This should not be surprising to us. When electronic technologies first appeared in Western culture it too was threatened. People in the West are, to this day, are still attempting to find ways to control the media.

Powerless to stop or contain it, some think the only way to strike back is to attempt to destroy it. The World Trade Center stood as the symbols of the threat Western Civilization represents. When one listens carefully to the voices and views of those who articulate the resentment, one hears the voices and views that these people have been abandoned. Perhaps another voice and view is that they were left out of the electronic age. Historically, kept out of the reformation, democratic government and scientific knowledge by religious leaders, these same leaders are attempting to keep out or control the electronic context. They may think Al-Jazeera News is the answer to the dilemma. Conservative Christians thought that TBN, CBN, Focus on the Family and the 700 Club would be the answer for conservative Christians. The voice and view of contextual inquiry will contend this. Until leaders and educators understand the logic of the electronic media, our cultures will remain in collision. Paying attention to both contexts and logics could build bridges, which would bring all people into the post-modern age without threatening our faith. The key will be religious leaders of all groups working together to insure that all, not just some, are integrated into the electronic paradigm in a positive way. The road to understanding of the many voices and views that abound in the global village begins with (one) understanding the structures and history of utterance, and (two) keeping that understanding grounded in the divinity of our human frame.

References

Brasher, Brenda E. 1996. Thoughts on the Status of the Cyborg: On Technological Socialization and its Link to the Religious Function of Popular Culture. *Journal of the American Academy of Religion* 64(4), 809-830.

Colhour, Donald B. 1997. *The Tetrad in the Works of Marshall and the Relevance of Electronic Context to Religion.* Unpublished dissertation. University of Edinburgh, Edinbrugh, Scotland.

Hamm, Richard L. 1996. *From Mainline to Front Line.* St. Louis: Chalice Press.

McLuhan, Marshall. 1995. *Essential McLuhan.* Concord, Ontario, Canada: House of Annasi Press.

_____. 1943. *The Place of Thomas Nash in the Learning of His Time.* Unpublished dissertation. Cambridge University, Cambridge, U.K.

McLuhan, Marshall & Quentin Fiore. 1967. *The Medium is the Massage.* Singapore: Jerome Agel.

McLuhan, Marshall and Eric E. McLuhan. 1988. *Laws of Media.* Toronto: University of Toronto Press.

9

Hearing the Hum in a Wired World: Preliminary Musings on Virtual Reality and Evangelical Education

Dr. Ben Witherington, III

Introduction

It stands to reason that in an information age, words would be important, and none more so than the Word, but strangely enough, those most responsible for conveying the Word—whether in the church or in the university—have often been slow to get on the Information Superhighway.

Like an Amish buggy on Interstate 40, I suppose some figure that as long as we are on the right road, we will eventually get there. But will there be any 'there' there when we arrive, if we approach technology in an electronically-challenged manner? Will there be any students there when we arrive, if we approach education while suffering from technology-deficit-disorder? If we choose the buggy approach, all the computer-driven delivery systems will be passing us in the *autobahn* lane, and while they may honk and we may wave as they go by, more often than not we are liable to be hit and run over. There is no virtue to being the equivalent of technological road-kill on the Information Superhighway. It is also no good to complain about the distractions of the litter and the gaudy billboards along the information superhighway as an excuse for not traveling at all.

We are already seeing viable education by extension, not only in the old manner of traveling to a remote site, but now by satellite link and downloading and interactive teleconferencing. Will we be midwives to the process, or will we seek to abort the process in favor of older models of delivery? Inquiring minds want to know. And what does any of this betoken for Evangelicalism and its institutions of higher learning which profess to be solidly committed to the Word (even though, to judge by our resources, by which I mean Christian bookstores and CBD catalogs, what we spend most of our time reading is the Christian equivalent to Harlequin romances, sci-fi thrillers [demons from another planet inhabit the study of the Rev. Billy Bob Proverb], and books on how we too may become a viable part of a therapeutic culture dwelling on victimization, repressed memories, and finding the right carousel on which to unload our personal baggage). Does any of this sound like we know what the Word is worth in the Information Age?

Several years ago, in a conference at Asbury Theological Seminary, Leonard Sweet delivered a seminal and challenging lecture on how to drag the church onto the Information Superhighway. In a good deal of what follows I am indebted to him and will be pursuing some of the rabbits he scared up from out of the brush, and seeking to apply them to Evangelicalism and the future of our higher educational pursuits as it pertains to the conveying of the Scriptures. If there is a virus in anything I should say in what follows, I trust that the thoughts will self-destruct or at least breakdown into easily digestible binary codes. *Caveat Emptor.*

Leonard Sweet began his seminal lecture by asking these sorts of questions: Who would have ever imagined that modems, faxes and e-mail would revive the lost art of letter-writing? Who would have ever predicted that the electronic era would bring back the literary arts or make them easier to compose—prose, poetry, music, painting all have become easier to produce, even mass produce in the electronic age. Who would have ever guessed that the 900 numbers would bring back the party line? Who would have ever guessed that not the physical destruction of the Berlin wall, but rather the building of the Internet would do more to destroy the walls between nations and ideological groups than any other single event? As we speak, publishers are dealing as easily with persons and manuscripts in Hong Kong as those next door. National boundaries and walls simply do not exist on the Internet.

Who would have ever figured that in the electronic age, the free lancers, the self-employed, and those who work at home, would make a dynamic new place for themselves in the world of business and education? I have two friends with whom I went to University of North Carolina, Chapel Hill, both are now in their forties, retired from academia and are living comfortably in North Carolina. One is doing freelance leadership training for churches, universities, and businesses. The other was an award-winning philosopher at Notre Dame who has since then become the official philosopher of Walt Disney, and a highly prized speaker on success in life as well as in business and education, making more than $10,000 a lecture. Is this the future of evangelical educators, if not of evangelical education? Will we all become free agents?

Who would guess that electronic culture would make it easier to communicate with remote family members, and in fact put parents *back* in the home more of the time? Perhaps electronic culture is the ultimate Promise Keepers tool. Who would have predicted that in an electronic culture, Americans would spend *more* on books than on any other kind of entertainment, to which all of us who publish say a hearty `thank you Jesus'—but are they actually reading what they buy? More to the point: are they actually buying what they read, or at least understanding what they read? Information—whether from the pulpit, in the classroom, on the e-mail or in print—without transformation availeth nothing. Let the one with two good ears hear what the voice simulator is saying.

John Perry Barlow has said that the invention of electronics will in due course have more impact on our culture than the invention of fire. Indeed, I would say it already is having a greater impact. Which modern person today does not find telephones, automobiles, televisions, computers, and the like indispensable to their lifestyles? And this is good news for the Good News because wires and lines and modems and faxes and e-mails and the rest are mainly tools of conveying words, and they may as well convey the Word, rather than some other sort of communication. If Moses had gone up on Sinai at the end of the 20th century instead of in the 13 or 14 century B.C.E., he would have come back down with a super-VGA-monitor, a super-computer, a Zip™ drive, a lifetime supply of diskettes, and a direct online service—hopefully hooked up properly to heaven. The line to heaven however, unlike AOL, would never be busy. The Ten Commandments would still be the Ten Commandments but they would appear in a form even Cecil B. Demille could not have envisioned.

Lest we think we can avoid dealing with these issues, I beg you to listen to our children. A boy or girl today might look at my old IBM typewriter and say, "Gosh, a printer with a keyboard." There is now nowhere to run and nowhere to hide. If you don't believe me, just move from one place to another in the U.S. and see how long it takes for your junk mail and junk credit card calls to find you again. Not long enough for sure. So will we face the issues that the electronic age raises for us, or will we be like deer in the headlights? This is an especially pressing question for Evangelicals in higher education because in theory we are supposed to be training the future leaders of the church, and it is the church that seems often to be just about the least computer literate organization on earth. What's wrong with understanding WordPerfect™ if we believe in the perfect Word? What then does it mean for the Evangelical institutions of higher learning to get wired, hear the hum, see the vision, capture the image?

Firstly, I think without doubt that we will have to recontextualize our ministries of education. Increasingly this will mean that whether in person or in some viritual form we will have to go to them rather than expecting them to come to us. The old philosophy, "if we build it, they will come," has only limited usefulness in the electronic age. Education by extension, whether in person or by downlink or in some virtual form is and will continue to happen. The question is whether we will take advantage of it? Will we see its obvious promise but also its potential drawbacks such as the lack of personal touch, the loss of personal relationship? Two years ago I taught two classes at Asbury in the TV studio. There were about 80-90 students in the class and the studio only held 30. How did I do this? The class was simulcast to one of our larger lecture halls with interactive link so that the students were able ask questions and I could answer them. The students rotated into the studio so that each student was with me in the studio for one of the three weekly lectures. In the classroom there was virtual Ben; in the studio there was live Ben, and in the long run this will prevent me from becoming a has-been, precisely because I can meet the ever-burgeoning demands of students for required courses in this way without doing so many multiple deliveries of the same courses, and so be freed up to do electives, do more writing projects, and go various places lecturing. In fact, even as I speak here today, I have already spoken twice in Wilmore, Kentucky, to my students today by video tape re-broadcast. Is the picture of the Information Age becoming clearer? In the Information Age we may not need a thousand repetitions of the same lectures on the Bible; we may only need one or two good ones per year with excellent satellite hookups and downlinks.

In my courses now I regularly use the following in addition to traditional lecture material. 1) Video clips from movies. This past week, it was *Jesus of Nazareth, A.D., Cleopatra, Peter and Paul.* Next is *Ben Hur.* In a class on New Testament history and Criticism this works well

to bring the first century to life. (You can do this for educational purposes in the classroom: just don't try to market the video tapes—the
permissions are generally either expensive or not forthcoming as of
yet.) Why is this an important tool? Because we live in an age of predominantly visual learners—the TV/movie/computer screen/Gameboy
generation. 2) I use Powerpoint presentations. I can either do these as
overheads to reinforce the lectures' main points, or I can display it right
off my laptop by plugging it into the 'Vis' box which also provides
access in the classroom to all visual materials programmed for me in the
Technology Center. Indeed, anything on my laptop I can put up on the
screen in the classrooom, including maps, art pictures from the Internet
and much more. 3) I no longer have to fiddle with my slides. Our
Technology Center will simply schedule them and program the time and
classroom for them and when I get to the classroom all I have to do is
turn on the Vis box, and use a clicker and they will come up on the
screen, even though they are three buildings away. 4) Music.
Interestingly enough, we live in a visual age which also has a dominant
aural subculture, the music industry. Music of all forms is more popular
than ever, especially various forms of modern music. Thus with my students, sometimes they get Jesus with jazz, sometimes they get Paul with
rock pizzazz, sometimes they get a depiction of Pentecost with
Prokofiev, and if I'm dealing with all those Texas students they hear
about the straight and narrow while listening to George Strait and Peter
Yarrow. The goal is that the message will be memorable, not trivialized,
and that the student will experience total saturation, learning through
eyes and ears, minds and hearts. If "the heart has reasons that the mind
knows not of," if "the Spirit prays through us with sighs too deep for
words," it will not be enough to offer our students *logos* if we do not
also offer them *pathos*. This is what being a good rhetorician is all
about. We wish to reach the whole person with the whole Gospel, taking every thought and feeling captive for Christ. This requires we use
the whole arsenal of learning tools.

In some ways we Protestants are well behind the Roman
Catholics in these matters. The Catholics are sending missionaries into
cyberspace: they have their own home page on the Internet
(<http://www.vatican.va/>; you can make your confessions while surfing the Net; you can download items from a 30,000 document Catholic
library (<http://www.vatican.va/offices/index.htm>), they have forums
and chat rooms, and people are talking and talking and talking to them.
It is not enough to have your College or Seminary advertise on the

Internet and have a homepage. You must take up virtual residence there in some form. Believe it or not, even the Amish are on the Internet! They have their own homepage called `Ask the Amish' as part of the Pennsylvania Dutch Country Information website (<http://www .800padutch.com/atafaq.shtml>). Are you hearing the hum yet? It may not be the tune you yourself like to hum, but this is one of those hums that we can ill afford to ignore, especially if we still believe in the 'evangelism' part of being an Evangelical.

There is a wonderful new add for MCI that highlights the promise of the Information Age and the use of e-mail. It shows a speech-impaired girl, an old black lady, a young boy and others and says, "On the Internet there is no race, no gender, no age, only minds." Chat rooms are places for disembodied voices to speak, and often they speak like voices crying in the wilderness. They have the freedom to say what they really think under the guise of a screen name. It made me wonder if when Paul said in Christ there is no Jew or Gentile, slave or free, no male and female, he could have envisioned a means of communicating where one's appearance or age or race or gender might mean nothing. If it is true that God gives no face and accepts no face, then the Internet is surely the place both for God and for God's Gospel. Yet there is need for caution—often one cannot tell the tone of an utterance by simply looking at its alphabetical form. A disembodied voice leaves little room for irony or sarcasm or plaintiveness conveyed by tone of voice. This is why printed sermons often come across rather like last week's doughnut—very stale and hard to swallow. One of Mr. Wesley's circuit riders used to say that one of the great ministries to him was provided by the lady who sowed up the armpits of his preaching gown again and again. There is not much room for gesture in a chatroom, and instead of 'read my lips,' you can only urge 'read my text.' In an Internet age, it is no surprise that post-modern deconstructionists are thriving. Their mantra is 'there is only text.'

I find it ironic that Wesleyans and Methodists tend to be behind in many of these technology areas. I was at a meeting recently where one speaker said the problem with the Holiness Movement these days is that there is little holiness and no movement. Today I'm speaking to you about the movement part of the equation. It is not like us to be behind. Consider Mr. Wesley. As Sweet has reminded us, Wesley was open to and in touch with and profoundly influenced by the scientific and technological developments of his day. No man who prided himself on having and using his own electrifying machine in the 18th century could possibly have encouraged us to be the 'People called Technologically Challenged.' Wesley subscribed to the scientific revolution in his day; he was all the time talking about experimental religion; he spent one day a week studying science and metaphysics; he read astronomers, mathematicians, biologists. While many of his fellow clergy and even educators were denouncing people like Sir Isaac Newton, Wesley was calmly using Newton's law and examples from the study of gravity in his sermons. Wesley wrote a compendium of natural philosophy, as it was called then, and a survey of the wisdom of God in creation. Furthermore, Wesley required his preachers to read this new-fangled scientific stuff as well.

If this Wesley—who even then said the world was his parish— lived today, was standing before us, he would ask us why we are here, holding this conference, if we weren't also going to downlink it across the globe so more could benefit and participate? He would be asking us which classes we are offering on the convergence of science and religion and why we aren't requiring the reading of Philip Davies *God and the New Physics* (1990) or some of the more user-friendly works of Stephen Hawking in our theology and philosophy classes?

The Information Age is about convergence of all knowledge; it is about inter-disciplinary cross fertilization; it is about sharing—time sharing, shareware, and the like. In other words, turf wars and tenure, and separate but equal departments had better watch out. If you cannot teach in at least two major fields, you are not likely to be able to escape the coming changes in education. Let each teacher seek to be like the Master teacher—who was a university all in himself. The fat lady is tuning up—and she's about to hum!

Leonard Sweet reminds us that while in the modern age we used to say "What you don't know can't hurt you," today in the Information Age it can be said that what you don't know or what you know wrong can harm, yes, even kill you. In other words, we are in danger from three sides, beginning with, first, *too little* information of the sort we truly need, and second, *too much* "useless information, supposed to fire our imagination" inundating us and overwhelming us. T.S Eliot was more than a little prophetic when he lamented in the earlier part of this century "where is the wisdom we have lost in knowledge, where is the knowledge we have lost in mere information?" (1971, 96). Finally, there is the danger of *wrong information*. In the fullness of time in the Information Age we are enduring massive Biblical illiteracy in the church and at the same time colleges and seminaries are downsizing their Biblical and language requirements more and more. Isn't it time to ask—what's wrong with this picture? What is scarce and at a premium in the Information Age is wisdom, specifically Biblical wisdom, and if our institutions continue to churn out students who are Biblically challenged we are sowing the wind and we will be reaping the whirlwind of theological and moral anomie in the 21st century.

The last place on planet earth that should be downsizing its commitment to Biblical and Theological studies is an Evangelical school. It is this, if anything, which would say to the world we still are an Evangelical institution. What does need to be done differently however is the modes of delivery and the integration of these subjects with the wide variety of other subjects being taught. This is not because the Bible is a textbook on every subject known to humankind; it is because biblical and theological presuppositions and perspectives should inform and transform how we present all our subjects. It is because we wish to reach the whole person as well as the whole world with the whole Gospel.

What Sweet says of the church applies equally to our educational institutions. Because we have failed to be not only an institution of learning but also an institution of unlearning, our intellectual capital has been steadily depreciating in the world. We stand at the bottom of the information and credibility food chain. Rearguard actions or pseudo-scientific studies will not impress many in the Information Age. Evangelicals must be on the cutting edge in every field they are in, and they must be busy about the task of integrating their faith with what we are learning in these fields. An Evangelical institution that does not hold up the tandem of knowledge and vital piety is in danger of losing its public face and witness as well as in danger of losing its very soul and *raison d'etre*. There must be no compromise on knowledge for the sake of vital piety, but equally there must be no compromise on piety for the sake of what may or may not be real knowledge.

Furthermore, Biblical knowledge must be integrated with the other sorts. Hiring faculty who do not reflect this balance in their own lives of knowledge and vital piety is a recipe for danger, if not disaster. It is not enough that they know Boyle's Law: do they also know Moses' Law or the Law of Christ? For what does it profit a post-modern Christian if she gains information in the Information Age, yet loses wisdom and even her soul?

Toxicity is a principle we need to understand in the Information Age. Bad information poisons. Leonard Sweet gives the illustration of a toxin, such as a herbicide, giving a plant bad information, causing the plant to grow faster than its capacity to absorb nutrients allows. It literally grows itself to death. This can happen to churches hooked on growth formulae and it can happen to growing Evangelical institutions. Not all growth is good growth; some can be hazardous to your health. Jesus said "Feed my sheep," not "Count my sheep." In a Calvin and Hobbes' strip, Calvin is touting the virtues of having a monitor which measures the rate at which he chews his gum. The tiger asks, What's the point of attaching a number to everything? Calvin responds: "If my numbers go up I know I'm having more fun and doing well." The tiger sighs and responds: "Science to the spirit's rescue once again."

And while we are at it, have we not in our smorgasbordian approaches to educating fed our students too little of too many subjects with too little retention being the result? No wonder so many get educational indigestion. Better to do a few things well, and give quality education in our strong suites than to pretend we can be all things to all persons. Perhaps in some cases we should go back to calling our universities colleges and let them be truly Christian colleges. We are all too well aware of the devolution from 'Christian college' to 'church-related college' to simply 'college.' At the top academic institution in the state of Kentucky where I live, Centre college, the progression is visible in an iconic sort of way. The original old main building of this once Presbyterian college, founded in the early 19th century, has as its founding motto "Doctrina lux mentis" [Doctrine is the light of the mind]. But on all of the newer buildings on campus. the motto reads "sapientia lux mentis" [Wisdom is the light of the mind]. There is a difference between doctrine and generic wisdom, and we should have the wisdom to know the difference. This change chronicles the decay of piety and commitment to the Word while the school's academic integrity only improved. We could chronicle the same trajectory with Harvard, Yale, and Princeton divinity schools, with each in succession being founded as the Evangelical antidote to the spiritual slippage in the previous one, though none of these institutions by any means have entirely given up the ghost, by which of course I mean the Holy Ghost. One needs to ask why this trend is far more likely to happen to a college than to a seminary or divinity school. I am not entirely certain of the answer to this question but I do know that in the Information Age these trends are likely to accelerate in Christian colleges in the rush to get more and more faculty who have expertise in more and more cutting-edge subjects onto the campus. Character counts, and we should be far more concerned about the Christian character and faith of our faculty, and less worried about the same in the case of our incoming students, unless of course we think it improbable that students can become Christians at a Christian college.

Sweet points us to the example of the Chinese bamboo tree as a model for the future of the church in the Information Age. I would say it is a model for our schools as well. During the first four years after the bamboo tree has been planted, tended, watered there are no visible signs of growth. However, all this changes during the fifth year. During the fifth year the tree grows an astounding 90 feet up in six weeks. What was happening in that first four years was that the tree was putting down deep stabilizing roots, roots that will sustain the enormous upward growth that is to come.

It is my view that now is the time for us to repent of our shallow commitment to the Word and put down deep, stabilizing roots of biblical knowledge, theology, church history, Christian philosophy, original language study. If we do not do this, we will find that our schools will either be blown away by the winds of change in the Information Age, or at least we will find ourselves swaying in whichever direction the wind blows. The answer, my friends, is not blowing in the Wind; it is resident in the Word Perfect. Neither uprootedness nor theological vertigo caused by swaying in various directions are healthy options. On the other hand, if we do return to putting down roots, then we may see enormous growth in the 21st century of a clearly and unashamedly Christian sort. One thing is clear to me from what Sweet and others have said: "good enough" will not be good enough as the Information Age progresses. The world is looking for the Word Perfect, and we claim to know where it may be found.

By way of review, let me remind you of some of the things I have said. One, we must be prepared to re-contextualize our education ministries and get beyond the traditional classroom, using all the means afforded by the electronic culture. I have spoken above of some of the ways this can be accomplished without comprising the integrity of what is delivered in the classroom or turning it into mere entertainment. Two, in the future it is likely that Evangelical institutions will have to look for ways to do multi-tasking—including hiring people who are good in more than one discipline, and who can teach cross disciplinary courses. The future of education is both in more specialized knowledge but also in the convergence and cross-fertilization of all knowledge. This is a natural outcome of the Information Age. Three, growth is not *the* answer to the problems at Evangelical institutions; we must put down deeper roots to endure into the 21st century. Four, in particular we must regrow our Biblical and theological roots as the foundation to and the means of integrating all else we do. Five, faculty hirings must concentrate not first on competencies in a field and secondly on Christian character and faith, but rather the reverse. Character and modeling is crucial to truly Christian education. Six, knowledge and vital piety must be held together with a commitment to excellence in both. There are all too many conservative Christian colleges which have a zeal, but not according to knowledge. They also do not show us the way forward on the Information Superhighway. Seven, all truth is God's truth, and the church and its institutions must not be reactive, but rather pro-active in the Information Age, looking for new ways we can learn from each other. Eight, the Internet provides an opportunity for a meeting of minds and a real discussion of issues without the hindrances of race, gender, appearance, age and the like. The universal Gospel belongs in this medium and is far more likely to do well there than parochial or special interest messages will.

It is my prayer and fervent hope that when we finally hear the hum, and get wired, we will not send mixed signals, but rather remember the words of the one who spoke and it came to pass, the words of the one who said my Word does not go forth from me and return void, remember the one who said that the beginning and end the Alpha and Omega, the first and last word of Christian education is the Word that took on flesh and became the exegesis of the Father among us. If we know and proclaim this, then we will be living not merely in the Information Age; we will be living in the transformation age.

At the February 2000 conference held at the American Bible Society offices in New York, various contributors offered new challenges in regard to the issues addressed in this paper.

One of the more passionate pleas had to do with the fact that while we may be more technologically advanced—we are still theologically challenged in the ways we deal with issues of inclusive language, the imaging of God, and in general, hearing voices other than the traditional ones when it comes to the interpretation and translation and teaching of the Word. Indeed, there seemed to be some anxiety about the fact that the Internet and online teaching seems at this point to be primarily the provenance of more traditional or Evangelical institutions. In short, even if the delivery method continues to advance in a progressive direction, this does not necessarily betoken the content being delivered well as well. This is a point worth pondering, not least because online learning on the Internet does give those who are normally more disadvantaged or disenfranchised an opportunity to participate more fully and freely. But it appears unlikely that the advances in technology can or will or even should prompt a revisioning of the fundamentals of the faith. Scientific advancements and theological inquiry are two very different fields of knowledge, and when they interface the assumptions that drive the former do not necessarily affect the assumptions driving the latter.

Critical thinking about the use of technology for education is of course still in a nascent stage, not least because there are huge issues about intellectual property and what happens to it when it is made available online. Publishers as well are only now beginning to think through the issues so far as copyright laws are concerned. Artists are concerned about the use of a 'cold,' two-dimensional medium to deliver an experience of a three-dimensional object. Can incarnational learning or experiencing, which seems to require presence rather than virtual reality, happen through the Net? Or is the internet just one more rough beast lumbering its way toward Bethlehem, making false messianic claims to save us and deliver us from various educational woes and problems?

However we answer these questions, they are questions well worth pursuing. A final warning however is in order: the critical thinking movement will have to retool itself in various ways to meet the new challenges of the age of technology. It will discover that total immersion encounters with the technology will inevitably, even if unconsciously, change one's basic assumptions about epistemology and what amounts to real learning. In other words, it is not possible to be totally unaffected or totally objective about the media that we all use, even if one tries to study the matter dispassionately. These and other issues must be addressed as we press forward into the new millennium.

References

Davies, Paul. 1990. *God and the New Physics*. New York: Penguin.
Eliot, T.S. 1971. Choruses from "The Rock," in *T.S. Eliot: The Complete Poems and Plays, 1909-1950*, 96-114. New York: Harcourt, Brace and World.

Voices of Caution

10

Images Have Consequences: Preliminary Reflections on the Impact of the Visual on the Word

Terry Lindvall, Ph.D.

"I'd give my soul to take out my mind, hold it under a faucet, and wash away the dirty pictures you put there today."
—Kirk Douglas, *Detective Story*

In developing his theory of cinematic montage, Soviet filmmaker and theorist Sergei Eisenstein, found delight in the serendipity of life, in encountering the unexpected and discovering fresh ways of looking at life and art through a collusion of events and people. On one occasion, he stumbled across the novels of Charles Dickens, haiku poety and the Kabuki theater, all of which provoked an intercourse of ideas (copulative, he called it) and a cultural collision (Eisenstein 1949). What his observations of seemingly disparate moments provided was a means of interrogating a subject under investigation. So I too seek to find the threads that connect several items. But first allow me to open with two parabolic narratives.

In *Breaking the News: How the Media Undermine American Democracy*, author James Fallows recounted a particularly revealing episode about the effects of visual imagery. "CBS reporter, Lesley Stahl had produced a news piece intended to show the internal contradictions

213

between what Ronald Reagan said and what his policies produced." So she "included footage of Reagan speaking at the Special Olympics competition, ... and then pointed out that his administration had cut funding for mental health. She showed him at ceremonies opening a nursing home, and then pointed out that he had opposed public-health funding too." (Fallows 1997, 62)

Soon after the piece aired on CBS, Stahl got a call from a White House official. She was expecting to be chewed out and was amazed when the official praised her. "Why?" She asked, adding: "Did you hear what I said? I killed you." The official explained the reality to her this way (as Stahl later recalled it):

> "You television people still don't get it. *No one* heard what you said. Don't you realize that the picture is all that counts. A powerful picture drowns out the words." (Fallows 1997, 62)

When St. John Chrysostom, the "golden mouthed" preacher of the 4th century, visited a Roman theatre, he was struck with the visual impact of the performance on his memory faculties. In seeking to reform the church, he had exhorted people to pray and eschew the great public sins of gambling, horse racing and the indulgent use of wealth. He questioned the value of pagan culture, seeing it built on the sands of vanity and materialism. But he also warned of the consequences of certain theatrical images:

> If you see a shameless woman in the theater, who treads the stage with uncovered head and bold attitudes, dressed in garments adorned with gold, flaunting her soft sensuality, singing immoral songs, throwing her limbs about in the dance, and making shameless speeches, do you still dare to say that nothing human happens to you then? Long after the theater is closed and everyone is gone away, those images still float before your soul, their words, their conduct, their glances, their walk, their positions, their excitation, their unchaste limbs—and as for you, you go home covered with a thousand wounds! But not alone—the whore goes with you— although not openly and visibly...but in your heart, and in your conscience, and there within you she kindles the Babylonian furnace...in which the peace of your home, the purity of your heart, the happiness of your marriage will be burnt up![1]

My concern here is not so much with lascivious and prurient images, although I may find that a particularly fascinating research area, but upon the place of visual images in inhabiting our memories and in shaping our consciousness, particularly for studying the Bible. In this essay I investigate three interrelated realms that may help us make sense of the place of the visual in studying the Bible: historical Christian perspectives on the image, recent studies in graven imagery and religious piety, and the impact of mediated images on mimesis and memory.

The Early Church and Visual Images

The task of thinking critically about studying the Bible in the 21st century requires that we also think about studying the Bible in earlier times. Although there is nothing new under the sun, we do encounter many innovations, and find, thanks to the insights of Walter Ong and Robert Webber, that different eras have been captivated by different paradigms and their respective rhetoric.[2] We thus do well to return to our classic Christian tradition and attend to the wisdom of other witnesses who enable us, standing on St. Bernard's proverbial shoulders of other giants, to see a little better.

The iconoclastic controversy of the eighth century in which theologians opposed the use of imagery on their understanding of the Commandment against graven imagery found an articulate apologetic in the works of St. John of Damascus. He authored a tripartite treatise entitled *Against Those Who Attack the Divine Images* as a response to those who condemned such works as idolatry. Ultimately, it was the ruling of St. Gregory I who maintained a *via media* between the Iconoclasm and Image-Worship (Bevan 1940, 147).

By the eleventh through the twelfth eras, epochs which art historian E. H. Gombrich labels as the Church militant and the Church triumphant, Pope Gregory the Great had articulated an apologetic for holy aesthetics, namely that painting can teach as well as illustrate religious ideas. "Images lived on in the minds of the people even more powerfully than did the words of the preacher's sermon" (Gombrich 1972, 130). Franois Villon rhapsodized this thought in verses written for his mother in the mid-fifteenth century.

> I am a woman, poor and old, Quite ignorant, I cannot read. They showed me by my village church. A painted Paradise with harps, And Hell where the damned souls are boiled. One gives me joy, the other frightens me ... (cited in Gombrich 1972, 130).

The doctrines of the church and the ideas of the transcendent were conveyed through panel paintings, illuminations, calendar manuscripts, brass fonts and even candlesticks. In the 13th century heavy stones, flying buttresses and vaulted naves spoke as much of the supernatural as did the bishop's own homilies, maybe more so. These cathedrals "gave the faithful a glimpse of a different world. They would have heard in sermons and hymns of the Heavenly Jerusalem with its gates of pearl, its priceless jewels, its streets of pure gold and transparent glass" (Revelation 21: Gombrich 1972, 141).

Sacred stories were told in living sculpture; Gothic stones came to life to breathe truth into the common congregants, who were spectators as much as worshippers. Within one medieval frame, stories of various characters could be combined, a precursor to Chaucerian modes of narrative. The walls of Italian churches were freshly painted to extend the range of medieval story-telling. In Padua, one of the earliest of visual auteurs, Giotto, "followed the advice of the friars who exhorted the people in their sermons to visualize in their mind, when reading the Bible and the legends of the Saints, what it must have looked like ... when the Lord was nailed to the cross" (Gombrich 1972, 152).

By the fourteenth century, Nicholas of Lyra listed three reasons justifying the institution of images for religious purposes in his *Praeceptorium*. The primary reason for incorporating these artistic lessons, sculptures, and paintings onto the altars in the religious community was that while uneducated people could not read words, they could read images on a wall. Second, the sluggish emotions of all people could be more powerfully moved to devotion by things seen than merely heard. And lastly, people forget what they hear, but remembered what they see. Such justification of faith by images was to be echoed five centuries later during the advent of moving images. Nicholas' apologetic for the visual prepared the way for the imminent deluge of images and dramas that would teach and move many congregants. (1981, 1).

These uses of images follow the functions St. Augustine laid down for effective rhetoric, namely that we are commissioned to teach, move, and delight others with every possible means.[3] The fact that the church encouraged such media as illuminated manuscripts to promote contemplation and understanding of the Gospels has been beautifully set forth by Kate Lindemann in this collection of essays. Yet questions and suspicions followed when it came to communicating to and through the eye.

Were not children of the light dabbling unnecessarily in shadows? Or is it that they were helping light to shine out of the darkness that men and women may see? This ambiguity has persisted throughout church history. In 1646, a creative Jesuit priest described an innovation, presumably his own, called the magic lantern, a prototype of the modern film projector, for which he found mischievous uses.

With this magic toy, Father Athanasius Kircher projected dancing shadows of phantasmogorphic images onto sheets of cloth. In an era of alchemy, where science and magic were mixed in imaginative combinations, the good Father's projected images onto a wall in darkened rooms astonished audiences, who stood amazed as they gazed on eerie shadows of phantasmagoria dancing on the curtains and walls. A very devout religious audience of fellow monks was fascinated and amused with his amazing program. Enthralled, that is, until Kircher projected an image of the devil and his cohorts onto a cloud of smoke. Then suddenly, this marvel of the magic lantern was seen to be the "workings of the devil."[4]

This eerie, supernatural "happening" so terrified and outraged his fellow monks that they rushed to exorcise the room and Kircher himself. In desperate attempts to defend himself, Kircher did what any good medieval or contemporary scholar would do: he published a paper. With the impending threat of exorcism or clerical torture for this "catoptric art," Kircher published *Ars magna lucis et umbrae* (The Great Art of Light and Shadow), a scholarly work attempting to demystify the basic apparatus and procedure of making these images with technical explanations and elaborate illustrations (Godwin, 1979). It was a science of optics and reflections, rather than magic and demonic activity. The work explained how light and mirrors worked, not in conjuring up demons, but in using God's wondrous principles found within God's own created universe. But still Kircher put his magic lantern away lest some grand inquisitor should show a more robust curiosity.

Contrary to popular opinion, the Roman Catholic and Protestant churches did not hold an antagonistic stance against motion pictures in their infancy. Many found them as a promising source for preaching, teaching, missionary work and uplift. The Reverend Herbert Jump even published one of the first pamphlets on film, promoting *The Religious Possibilities of the Motion Picture* (1911: see especially Keyser and Keyser 1984) and Lindvall 2001). It wasn't until the early twenties when protestations against sexual immorality and violence in films dominated religious voices. However, before then, the church community believed this was a fresh and new way to communicate the faith. In 1898, Colonel Henry H. Hadley, lawyer and newspaper man turned evangelist, optimistically announced: "These moving pictures are going to be the best teachers and the best preachers in the history of the world"

(Ramsaye 1926, 375). In films of the Passion Play, he recognized the power of this new medium to shape the imagination of all audiences.

Graven Images and Visual Piety

Images have consequences. With apologies to Richard Weaver's *Ideas Have Consequences* (1948), I theorize that the saturation of the tremendous output of visual, rather than oral or literary, communication is shaping our contemporary culture's perspectives on religion. In conjunction with the postmodern characteristic of visual images, we find the reemergence of spirituality as a topic. The fertile union of these two concepts, visual imagery and religion, has yielded a brood of scholarship. The importance of material culture for the study of the Bible in the 21st century is becoming more evident and pressing. Two recent studies provoke us to at least reconsider the neglected significance and relevance of the Second Commandment as it bears upon our image-saturated society.

Lionel Kochan approaches the second commandment seriously and with utmost reverence in his *Beyond the Graven Image: A Jewish View* (1997). Exploring the Biblical prohibition against the use of images as a means of worship, Kochan probes the theological perception of the Jews as a people of the ear rather than of the eye, a people historically tempted to make and worship false idols. Through an appeal to the eye, the graven image attracts the worshipper and endows the false gods with a spurious power and presence, provoking the wrath and jealousy of God. It solidifies and entombs the seemingly transcendent.[5] The danger was always that what is physically constructed and embodied could be confused with what it signifies and become idolatrous. One is grateful for such satirists of these dumb idols as the prophets like Isaiah. (e.g., Isaiah 44:9-20; see also Jeremiah 2:27).

A conception of stone, wood and other brute matter as dynamic and symbolic of the divine is for the Jewish scholar "the greatest conceivable error of which man is capable." (Kochan 1997, 30) This delusion against which the prophets railed is, along with the self-inflicted deception that images can mediate between man and the holy, the danger to which the eye exposes the worshipper. The artifact conceals the reality that it purports to reveal.

The Hebrew prophets repudiated idolatry as a form of rebellion, in that the idol is fashioned by humans as a repository and agent for human hopes, desires, and fantasies. This constitutes no more than a form of self-worship, Kochan argues. God, on the other hand, addresses His people in direct, personal ways, eschewing plastic, symbolic mediation, such as sphinxes, sacred groves, Asherim,[6] etc. The ideal was, and is, direct oral communication between God and His creatures. In contrast to material images, monuments, and mummies is the Mouth Who speaks to the ears.

In the 1933 Gifford Lectures, Edwyn Bevan addressed "Holy Images: An Inquiry into Idolatry and Image-Worship in Ancient Paganism and in Christianity" by drawing upon the early church fathers to establish a biblical understanding of the second commandment. Of particular interest was the post-Manichean (and rhetor) Bishop of Hippo, St. Augustine, who, following Plato, found aesthetic pleasure rooted in the supreme Beauty; but he also found himself squandering his time in the imitations of that beauty, so much that he confessed "I too find my feet caught in these beauties."[7] Such lower beauties became the temptations for idolatry.

Connected to idolatry are the twin vices of sexual license and violence, as evidenced in Asherim, Baal and Moloch worship. Kochan points to the teachings of the Talmud where the seduction of idolatry is likened, because of its pervasiveness and strength, to sexual desire. And no one, Kochan proposes, is immune to its lure. He reminds us that "Eros and Dionysos are Greek and not Jewish heroes—An Eros who converted to Judaism would have to be concerned with marriage, fertility, progeny, and the satisfaction of feminine sexual needs" (98). Art is allowed in the shade of the temple, but it must be remembered that beauty has a moral duty.

While Kochan is able to affirm the Divine creation of the seeing eye as well as the hearing ear (Prov. 20:21), he, like French sociologist Jacques Ellul, favors and esteems the ear to be a necessary corrective to the eye's dominant and potentially corrupting inclinations. In the hegemony of the visual, the ear needs empowerment in the struggle against a static and idolatrous synthesis of divinity, beauty, and secularity. According to Kochan, and the grand company of classic, medieval and recent Jewish scholars he gathers to speak, priority must be given to the receptive ear in the hierarchy of the senses. God, speaking through the Decalogue, demands it.

It is a persuasive and unsettling argument that Kochan articulates, one that reveals profound implications regarding holiness, our relations with God, and the communication of truth for the descendents of Bezalel (Exodus 35: 31ff), descendents such as Christian film professors who dabble in topics on the transcendent and the visual.

David Morgan's *Visual Piety* takes us in another direction, challenging the iconoclastic tendencies of those who would remove the
visual from American religious life (1998). Tracing the history of popular religious imagery from the Middle Ages through the modern period, in works such as Mathias Grunewald's *Crucifixion* and Warner
Sallman's *Head of Christ*, Morgan asks how religious kitsch contributes
to a construction of everyday life.

Built on the premise that a world is a human construction that is
continually designed, built, razed, and redesigned, Morgan argues that
material culture, such as imagery, tries to mend or conceal the ruptures
or suture the gaps of our fallible constructions. In other words, the
images attempt to legitimate and reaffirm one's view of the world.
Devotional images are thus intended to keep chaos and meaninglessness
at bay, by capturing, taming and controlling our image of God.

In his own way, Morgan echoes some of Kochan's concerns. He
argues that the act of looking itself "contributes to religious formation and,
indeed, constitutes a powerful practice of belief" (1998, 3). Thus as part of
the symbolic universe we inhabit, devotional images provide the primary
documents for the scholar investigating how we construct the self.

But Morgan's stimulating study goes farther than showing how
evangelical Protestants, as well as Roman Catholics and those from
highly sacramental traditions, are informed by the cultural politics of
image making and worship. He argues that the "images believers see are
encoded with both their collective religious and their personal identities." (1998, 47) The debate between a romantic view of popular culture
as the creative expression of the will of the people and a cynical view
of popular culture being the hegemonic power of an evil capitalism
wanes in importance in examining the actual practice of believers who
use these images.

In analyzing over 500 personal responses to an inquiry on the
impact of Sallman's *Head of Christ*, Morgan demonstrated the truth of
both positions. In exploring how believers "read the face of Jesus," he
points to the venerable medieval tradition of "symbolic, hieroglyphic,
emblematic, and hermetic imagery employed" for religious and pedagogical ends. Rather than offering an opportunity for a disinterested
contemplation of beauty or transcendence, such an image functions as
an "eminently social" means of constructing, as well as understanding,
one's own piety and religious practice (1998, 45). The sacred image, as
C.S. Lewis would have expressed it in *That Hideous Strength*, both
unmakes and remakes our world.

Ideas formulated through religious and secular iconography will shape the worlds that press upon us. The postmodern culture, awash in images, threatens to outline and to define our identities as social beings and religious beings. For those of us fascinated by or suspicious of cultural trends, these works are essential reminders of the various issues involved in the convergence of Christian faith and visual art.

Museums of the Mind

Our contemporary culture has privileged the image over the word. The word, in Jacques Ellul's language, has been humiliated; it has been supplanted in our epistemology (Ellul 1985, Troup 1998). A pervading belief is that knowledge is acquired primarily by looking at the world through visual representation. The ascendancy of a technological image-based culture has redefined our social relations and our views of reality. We like to watch, as Jerzy Kosinski's character Chauncy in *Being There* repeatedly confesses.

Our cultural obsession with watching has been documented, with the average US household keeping the television set on for more than seven hours a day (Nielsen 1998, 16). As Gary Edgerton writes:

> There are slight variations depending on age, race, gender, socioeconomic and educational background, but, by and large, the typical person in the United States viewed four hours and nine minutes of television a day in 1998 (Nielsen 1998, 17).

Put another way, the characteristic babyboomer will spend nine full years in front of the TV by the time he or she turns 65 (Edgerton 1999, 10).

A condition within communication studies known as the "cultivation effect," contends that the more time people spend watching television, the more they misperceive the real world as being isomorphic to the prefabricated vision of life as presented on TV (Gerbner 1973; Gerbner and Gross 1976a). So Edgerton notes:

> The pervasiveness of the cultivation effect is not hard to understand when one considers that the average American child now spends 900 hours in school each year, and 1,460 hours in front of the television set. What is alarming about these totals is that much of this viewing is unsupervised. In 1960, only one out of ten households in the United States had more than one television set; today the figure is three out of four, and 50% of children between the ages of 6 and 17 have TVs in their own bedrooms. (1999,10)

A leading media expert, Dr. Ellen Wartella, Dean of the College of Communication at the University of Texas, recently outlined the long-term impact of media violence. She noted that viewers of all ages learn aggressive attitudes and behavior over time; they also become emotionally desensitized toward real violence while simultaneously growing ever more fearful of becoming victims themselves (Edgerton 1999, 10f.). Such research lends itself to a suspicion of contemporary cultural images as the primary channel of values and attitudes.[8] (Yet the spiritually and morally impoverished images have been with us always; there is nothing new under the sun.)

The image suggests and adumbrates its own consequences. In response to the claims that the impact of the image is negligible or nugatory, one only has to examine one's own experiences. The human mind is more akin to a picture gallery than a debating chamber, with ideas and memories clothing themselves in images?

Marcel Just and Patricia Carpenter of Carnegie Mellon University referred to the working memory as "the blackboard of the mind."[9] In technically viewing an image, they found that we find particular sections of the primary visual cortex analyze different visual characteristics. It synchronizes activities of physical seeing and cognitive understanding simultaneously.[10]

Lesions in the visual cortex produce what is known as blindsight, an inability to understand any visual information. These are people who can "see" but not "comprehend." We have in our culture, such moral blindsight, a rupture of seeing and understanding. Semir Zeki, professor of Neurobiology at the University of London, wrote that in blindsight, people are "unaware of what they have seen, they have not acquired any knowledge. In short, their 'vision'...is quite useless" (Zeki 1992, 74). These are the kind of people who see the movie *Titanic* more than once.

The etymology of *aisthesei*, the Greek root of 'aesthetic,' stems from the root ideas of perception—in both body and mind. Aesthetics must include moral discernment as well as insightful judgment regarding matters of beauty and taste. The apostle Paul spoke clearly about these things: "Whatever is true, whatever is honorable, whatever is right, pure, lovely, and of good repute, if there is any excellence and if anything worthy of praise, let your mind dwell on these things" (Phillipians 4.8) What our minds dwell upon is rarely the exquisite landscape sermons of a Jasper F. Cropsey[11] or the moral illustrations of William Hogarth, but upon legions of commercials for what is false, ugly, and superficial.

Walt Whitman, passionate poet of the Potomac, wrote:

There was a child went forth every day,
And the first object he'd looked upon, that object he became
And that object became part of him for the day or a certain part of
  the day,
Or for many years or stretching cycles of years. (1954, 20)

Everything the child saw became a part of him. Yet no longer does the modern child wondrously encounter early lilacs, third-month lambs, tidy and fresh-cheeked girls (as Walt meant that), the flying sea-crow, or his or her own parents; the child meets hours of commercials.[12]

The culture of mediated images, particularly in its deleterious influence on children, has troubled various religious leaders including Pope John Paul II. He had warned that young people

Enchanted by the instruments of social communication and defenseless against the world and adult persons,...are naturally ready to accept whatever is offered to them, whether good of bad...They are attracted by the "small screen" and by the "large screen"; they follow every gesture represented on them, and they perceive quicker and better than anyone else, the emotions and sentiments which result. Like soft wax on which every tiniest pressure leaves a mark, so the child is responsive to every stimulus that plays upon his/her imagination, emotions, instincts, and ideas. Yet the impressions received at this age are the ones destined to penetrate most deeply into the psychology of the human being and to condition, often in a lasting way, the successive relationship with self, with others, and with the environment.[13]

That children collect images for the galleries of their minds is obvious; how they marshal and arrange them, how they make sense of their moral and religious world, is more crucial. Psychologist Robert Coles' personal study of children and movies, "Seeing is not Believing" revealed how children creatively select, generalize and interpret movies, feeding them into an overall paradigm of moral understanding (1986). Yet, Coles investigated the consequences of such films as *A Raisin in the Sun*, *To Kill a Mockingbird*, and *Star Wars* among minority children raised in strong Christian homes. Where there was a solid foundation of faith and goodness, these children could see through and understand the images, images with and images without bottoms, or moral foundations.[14]

We collect and mount provocative images in the museums of our minds. For those fortunate enough to breathe in the glories of the natural world and to soak in the beauties of beloved families and friends, portraits of goodness hang in our memories, both as reminders of an ideal and warnings to our tendency to stray into evil. For those surrounded by mediated advertisements and commercials, prospects for mental or aesthetic health do not augur well. According to David Marc, the "shifting role of human memory in everyday life may provide clues to the stunning problems of shrinking attention span and lack of historical consciousness which seem to be plaguing education, and subsequently, the entire sphere of public life in America."[15] He points out that television functions for most as a "throbbing public memory....By manufacturing norms and by announcing the parameters of acceptable manners, styles and language usage, it stimulates and constricts behavior, setting contexts and expectations for future events" (1993, 127).

The poetic observation by Whitman is a harbinger of two image-conscious authors: Kenneth Boulding and Rene Girard. Boulding, in a classic little book entitled *The Image*, maintains that the way people behave depends on the image or images they hold, consume or inhale, with the corollary that if we change someone's images, we may change their behaviors.[16] Ideals of perfection are gleaned from the media, manufactured norms that abet dissatisfaction of the self, depression and low self images.[17]

Rene Girard argues that desire is mimetic, that is we learn what it is we want by watching what others want (Girard 1996). The devil, liar and father of lies, who promised Adam and Eve that they could be like God, sets an agenda for the eyes, who tempts and seduces with vain longings and desires, through the power of images. Much like the profaning film, *Devil's Advocate*, one is tempted by the forbidden fruit images of the Big Apple. Through the lust of the eyes for wealth, power, fame, etc., movies have become mediated billboards for both products and philosophies.[18]

A key point made by Girard, derived from experimental psychologists on imitation, verified that "imitation precedes consciousness and language" (1996, 277). Thus, what we see sets an agenda for what we think about and how we act. In a positive theological sense, the oral communication and writing of the Gospels followed the historical witness of the Christ events. The consequences of those visible, public events ("what was from the beginning, what we have heard, what we have seen with our eyes, what we beheld and our hands handled...we also proclaim to you" (I John 1:1-4) were the radically transformed lives of saints and martyrs. However, the spectacle of watching many of those saints beheaded, crucified, and martyred in the Coliseum introduced a more brutal scene for imitation for the Roman mobs, provoking a more insatiable appetite for bread and circuses.

The consequences of watching more contemporary and symbolic worlds of violence and eroticism are more devastating than many have realized. George Gerbner and Larry Gross found that those who watch more television "see the real world as more dangerous and frightening than those who watch very little" (1976b, 556). Excessive viewing tends to make one more suspicious, more fearful and less trusting of others. Columnist William Raspberry once indicated the key problem regarding TV violence was that we as a culture "*want* it." The wanting of worthless images, again and again, is a constant, addictive danger. Yet such repetitive images cannot satisfy. They speciously promise fulfillment, but cannot deliver.

So, too, Arnold P. Goldstein, director of the Center for Research on Aggression at Syracuse University, thrust the issue of television violence into the foreground: the only people who question the link are the media people themselves. What troubled him most was

> ...the bystander effect. You know, the Kitty Genovese syndrome. Televised violence increases the degree of callous-ness and indifference to actual violence. People who watch TV violence become less helping toward the victims of violence and display more tolerance for higher and higher levels of aggression. (Goldstein 1996, x)

Ironically, such a truth was played out in the finale of Seinfeld, in which the four stars were arrested for callous indifference to their fellow man.

Professor Victor Cline of the University of Utah has argued that pornographic images are analogous to heroin or morphine addiction (1985, 13). Dr. James L. McGough of the University of California, Irvine, corroborated such findings, indicating that "Experiences at times of emotional or sexual arousal get locked in the brain by the chemical epinephrine and become virtually impossible to erase" (Cline 1985, 15). The Vagus nerve, ending in the gut, is where experiences of intense fear, raw emotion and erotic excitement trigger the brain to record and imprint the image, to have and to hold from this time forth. "Priming" occurs in the brain when a "recent experience forms a nonconscious residual memory." Images "prime" our brains to detect items related to that perceptual experience, and tease them to want it again (Azar 1998). Thus advertising tactically addresses our often unconscious desires.

In the complexity and diversity of molecular nerve cells lies a mystery of perception, understanding, imprinting, priming, and motivating. We are wonderfully and fearfully made, especially fearfully. Future research may yet demonstrate the dual power of salient images and an obsessed imagination in showing that images do have isomorphic consequences, that they actually function as the "narcotics of the soul."

I am curious about the nature and functions of the visual, especially in what I believe is an epistemological hegemony of the image. The second commandment seems to recognize this creeping, consuming power of an image to dominate our imagination, and therefore to dictate our modes of thinking and acting. If not shaping our entire thought processes, it at least works in our present age for setting agendas for our reflections and desires. In a collection of essays on pictorial stereotypes in the media, Paul Martin Lester titled his work *Images That Injure*, and echoed the sentiments of Walter Lippmann's formulation of "pictures in our heads." As Lippmann wrote "Whether right or wrong...imagination is shaped by the pictures seen....Consequently, they lead to stereotypes that are hard to shake." (Lippmann 1965 (1922), 59, cited in Lester 1996, ix). And these images are mostly mediated, rather than direct images.

Yet images can recommend goodness. Even mediated Images can potentially heal. In his defense of images in the eighth century, St. John of Damascus wrote his three treatises *Against Those Who Attack the Divine Images*. In them, he cited ecclesiastical patriarchs like St. Basil, commenting that "You see that praising the saints glorifies God: the memory of the saints brings joy and salvation to the people. Why do you wish to destroy it? This remembrance is accomplished through sermons and images" (1997, 37). What is key in St. John's commentary is the crucial positive role played by visual images in memory. For him, both sermons and images served the same purpose: namely as St. Basil wrote: "Both painters of words and painters of pictures illustrate valor in battle; the former by the art of rhetoric; the latter by the clever use of the brush, and both encourage everyone to be brave. A spoken account edifies the ear, while a silent picture induces imitation" (1997, 38-9).[19]

The American Bible Society's Mediated Scriptures

In a study on the integration of the formal expression in El Greco's religious images with the subjective experiences of the viewers,

Amy Heebner sought to bring forth a universal theoretical explanation: "If a work of religious painting succeeds in achieving a fusion of meaning and form, it must still be summoned to life by the viewer's consciousness" (1999, 16). Heebner asserted the salience of spectatorship on engaging and interpreting the "living experience" of artistic images. The significance of receiving works of religious art (versus what C. S. Lewis (1961) called "using" them) was that it opened the reflecting viewer to the "numinous" (Otto 1923). However, the role of mediated visual religious images leads viewers to a consciousness of a variety of meanings, rarely in the realm of the numinous.

Research done by William Brown and Benson Fraser on the mediated products created by the American Bible Society helps us to connect the memory and mimesis studies with the study of the Bible in the 21st century (Brown et al, 1999). In a series of studies on the mediated Bible products of the American Bible Society, Fraser and Brown analyzed audience responses to the visual translations that also revealed the subjective hermeneutic at work. The organization's mission statement to translate the Scripture accurately and "without interpretation and commentary" was challenged by their research findings (1999, 22). The very process of representing the written word with moving pictures and sound implies an interpretative process.

Brown and Fraser surveyed audience response to the ABS's visual translations, examining the nature and functions of three creative visual interpretations, and their effects upon the audience. In seeking to assess expectations of ABS video users, they conducted 75 in-depth interviews by phone and in person and then conducted focus group studies. The various demographic samplings included people along ethnic, geographical, and denominational lines: from the northeast, southeast, Midwest, and west; those who were Caucasian, African-American, Hispanic, and Asian; Roman Catholic, Southern Baptists, United Methodists, and Assembly of God. In 25 interviews they targeted preteen and teenagers. In another set of interviews they targeted 60 opinion leaders and gatekeepers of educational products in both CD-ROM and video forms.

What they sought to do was to assess the users' expectations of and responses to the ABS Scripture video and CD-ROM products. They discovered that many video Bible products had been used by Christian educators and leaders, and those associated with the ABS generally had high quality expectations. However, satisfaction of the products did not include older teenagers and experienced CD-ROM users. A majority in the tests in California and the northeast preferred "Out of the Tombs," reflecting a preference for the MTV style of music video. "Out of the Tombs" was the most confusing and hardest to interpret, with many participants expressing that the "*imagery and music overpowered the narration*" and viewers not understanding much of the symbolism. However, older teenagers liked this "interpretation" more than the other videos. The study participants in general expressed that all genres were appropriate for communicating Scripture given the right audience, with the exception of the "thriller" or "horror" genre of "Out of the Tombs."[20] However, in these visual products, *the oral/written biblical story was diminished.*

What is important here for our study however is this salient fact: that the visual and musical aesthetics overwhelmed and dwarfed the narrative and thematic. Responses were akin to a Dick Clark Bandstand program of "I'd give it a three because it has a good beat and I can dance to it." The research indicated that more focus should be given to the message than the artistic expression, *if the goal is to communicate biblical narratives.*[21] If, however, the intent is to provoke, stimulate, rouse, kindle, incite, fuel or whet one's curiosity and interest—in true parabolic fashion—then the obscure symbolism and hidden lessons of the narrative may be the appropriate strategy. As the Bible was produced as a literary work from an active oral tradition, its translation into the contemporary vernacular of visual media opens up connotative aspects of the biblical signs and symbols.

The question of diversity of interpretations through the visual parable opens other possibilities and challenges. To mix metaphors, a veritable Pandora's box of Rorschach tests allows audiences to see what they want to see. Yet Walter J. Ong pointed out the same dissidence of dissent, to use Edmund Burke's phrase, occurred when the private reading of Scriptures afforded by the Reformation and the invention of the printing press. Such reading encouraged not only a difference of perspective among believers, but fostered divisiveness of competing propositions. Silent reading "forced the individual into himself and out of the tribe" (Ong, 1981, 272) Both print and mediated images can lead to many interpretations. However, an image also makes a concrete decision for its viewers; it freezes and locks in a specific image associated with the text in the memory. This is why one should produce a hundred biblical films by a multicultural variety of writers, directors, etc. A diversity of faithful artists might yet provide worthwhile, insightful and competing perspectives on the stories of the Bible.[22]

Finally, what concerns us is the consequence of images, particularly in the nature of obtrusion of the visual on the Word and its effect upon the memory. What alternative paths does an image lead one down that a word would not? Does the attractiveness or perceived eroticism of the actor provoke lust? Does the seeming affluence of the material image invite envy or covetousness? Is there implied the notion of an ethnocentric standard or norm? Is it that historical memory is shaped by a frozen or embalmed visual image? Or is it that some superfluous detail will obsess a spectator? Does an image re-structure the human as a product, promoting more of an I-it relationship rather than Buber's ideal I-Thou, by objectifying and concretizing human beings? Does an image incite idolatry more than words do? Without being an iconoclast spewing jeremiads at the media, one must attend carefully to what Stuart Ewen called *All Consuming Images*, simulacra images without bottoms or references that dictate not only what we know and think about, but how we think about it (Ewen 1988). Otherwise, we are continually conformed to the image of Adam, rather than transformed by the renewing of our minds to the *imago Dei* (Genesis 5:1-3; Romans 12:1-2).

Yet even with this possibility for misunderstanding, the Scriptures show how God used a graven image of a serpent to bring healing to His people. Whoever looked up and gazed upon it, "he shall live." While the image of the brazen serpent prefigures the spectacle of Jesus being lifted up on the cross, it still stands as potential idolatry. So much so that by Hezekiah's time, it was necessary to bring it out of the image archives and destroy it.[23]

In the heart of Steven Spielberg's powerfully wrenching film, *Amistad*, African slaves receive an illustrated version of the Bible (images anachronistically represented as those of Gustav Dore) from a dour-looking assembly of Congregational abolitionists.[24] In Spielberg's film, the protagonist Yamba and his fellow Mende prisoners turn the pages of this visual holy book. They observe that here are other people who have also suffered, especially this one man who seems to have done nothing wrong to anyone; in fact, he seems to have helped and healed people. Lifted up on a cross, he seems most unjustly treated. But that is not the end. There is more to this terrible story. He seems to go to a better, even a wonderful, place. The pious pictures lead, remarkably, to an understanding of the Gospel and to an awareness of Yamba's own political predicament in light of this other illustrated story.

What is fascinating about this tremendous scene is that it raises the same questions of the nature and roles of religious imagery in our

cultural history. Without rallying to the side of the iconophiles or icono-
phobes, we must find that messy, but crucial, middle wisdom that
enables us not only to dwell in a Land of Pictures, but to be able to discern the signs of the times and even communicate through them. Rather
than being consumed by images and having our hermeneutics dictated
by a mediated hegemony of images, it is time to do what Michael
Warren has recommended in a title to his provocative book, namely to
engage in *Seeing Through the Media*, that we might both resist and be
renewed through the power of the Holy Spirit (Warren 1997). May
those who have eyes, see.

Parabolic Postscript

In May, 1997, a whistle-blowing watchman in a Swiss bank saved
Holocaust era documents from shredding at the Union Bank of
Switzerland; the security guard, Christoph Meili, broke bank secrecy
laws by saving files that were records of Jewish properties. "I was convinced that documents were being destroyed illegally. I wished to prevent the Swiss people from suffering harm and to make the documents
and actions know to the public." Meili acknowledged that the inspiration for his act came after seeing the movie, *Schindler's List*, which con-
victed him into taking responsibility and doing something. "I am convinced I did the right thing and moral thing. I'm a Bible-reading
Christian and regard Jews as my brothers" (CNN, 1997). Images have
consequences.

Glossary

PET SCANS ("positron emission tomographic techniques reveal
that blood flow in the brain shifts" to different locations depending on
whether an auditory or visual task is being performed) "Mind and
Brain" by Gerald D. Fischbach of Harvard Medical School in *Scientific
American* 1992: 54.

Notes

1. Søren Kierkegaard ironically bemoaned the fact that preachers were
not as effective as poets and actors in their respective rhetoric. "Whereas, alas,
the Christian proclamation at times is scarcely heard, all listen to the poet,
admire him, learn from him, are enchanted by him. Whereas, alas, people quickly forget what the pastor has said, how accurately and how long they do remem-

ber what the poet has said, especially what he has said with the help of the actor!" (1996, 47)

2. Ong 1967; Webber 1999. Also worthy of discussion is Garrett Green's study of theology and the religious imagination as an attempt to sanctify the imagination (1989).

3. Augustine 1958, 142. In this work, Augustine articulated the key philosophy of Christian humanism, i. e., that "every good and true Christian should understand that wherever he may find truth, it is his Lord's" (54); as well as his insights into the use of "neutral" means of communication, i.e. rhetoric or, by extension, film, for the glory of God. This concept has become known as "Egyptian gold." ("When the Christian separates himself in spirit from their miserable society, he should take this treasure with him for the just use of teaching the gospel" [75].)

4. The subject matter of Kircher's spectacle provides support for those who argue that it is the content and not the medium itself.

5. See Bazin (1967, 9-16) for a critical perspective from a Roman Catholic film theorist on the analogy of embalming the dead as a progenitor of film making.

6. The *Asherim* are the female counterparts to Baal; see. Exodus 34:13; I Kings 15:13; 2 Chronicles 19:3, 33:19; and Micah 5:14.

7. Augustine. (1960, x, 34, 53). Pope Gregory I reprimanded Bishop Serenus of Marseilles whose flock had zealously smashed images: "Whence, for the heathen especially, a picture takes the place of a book...If anyone desires to make images, do not forbid him; only prohibit by all the means in your power the worshipping of images." Quoted in Bevan (1940, 126).

8. A remarkable children's book, *The Wretched Stone* (Allsburg 1991), satirizes the deleterious social and psychological effects of TV on a fellowship of sailors. An old seminary professor of mine would always cite research on television effects and passivity done at UCLA (which I have never been able to locate) that indicated that people use fewer brain waves watching television than when sleeping. It may be part of Academic Legend, but it is a humorous insight.

9. Goldman-Rakic (1992, 111). Gerald D. Fischback of Harvard Medical School has also written that "positron emission tomographic techniques reveal that blood flow in the brain shifts" to different locations depending on whether an auditory or visual task is being performed (1992, 54).

10. In contrast to Immanuel Kant, who believed that these two faculties were, respectively, passive and active, research seems to indicate an immediate coordination.

11. See, for example *Autumn—On the Hudson River* (1860). Of special note is James F. Cooper's recently published *Knights of the Brush: The Hudson River School and the Moral Landscape* (1999).

12. Whitman envisioned the highly-kinetic popular mediated culture as he continued: "Whether that which appears so is so, or is it all flashes and

specks? Men and women crowding fast in the streets, if they are not flashes and specks—what are they?" (1954, 20)

13. Pope John Paul II (1979, 46). More recently see Pope John Paul II (1999). John Paul II said that people have the natural propensity to live in peace and in harmony with God, with their fellow human beings, with themselves, and with the whole of creation. If movies become interpreters of these values, they could become the "place of reflection, of calling to values, of invitation to dialogue, and of communion" (1979, 46). However, this objective seem both distant and ethereal. Therefore, the Pope himself suggested the formula to reach it: "In his complex and mysterious reality, it is necessary that the human person become the reference point for quality films proposing culture and universal values." It must be a cinema that keeps people in mind, "every person, one and indivisible," because if on the contrary, it only considers "some aspect of the impressive complexity of the human being, it inevitably ends up being reductive, and ceases to be a beneficial cultural service."

14. For those who argue that we receive deep wisdom from the alternative moralities of the image-making industries, Marshall McCluhan frequently retorted: " Even mud gives the illusion of depth."

15. Marc (1993 3). Citing Hans Magnus Enzensberger (1974), Marc laments that we "can no longer think of our minds as our own because mass culture, with its endless barrage of styles, suggestions, moral codes, and so on, has become the context for all our thinking." We are constrained by a "mind-making industry," one that construct our collective and personal memories. Marc, however, has hope for religious peoples: "people who sincerely believe in sacred books or in the presence of supernatural forces are less susceptible to electronic media manipulation," and sees the religious traditions rolling back the influence of the "secular, materialist juggernaut of electronic media." (3) See also Lipstiz (1990).

16. "The meaning of a message is the change which it produces in the image" (Boulding 1961, 7).

17. A *New York Times* press release entitled "Television changes body image of girls in Fiji, study indicates" reported how eating disorders and diet consciousness for teenage girls entered the South Pacific culture with the advent of television in 1995 (1999, 3).

18. And the only way this brutal, consumerist cycle is broken, and obsessive desire controlled, argues Girard, is in suffering, the Cross, the Sacrifice that shows us a higher way, a better desire. (What is one of the great ironies of life is that in terms of "mimetic desire," our "desires are copied from models or mediators whose objects of desire become our objects of desire" (1996, 3). (And, many times, we live a life we ourselves would be tempted to covet if we saw someone else living it.)

19. "What more conspicuous proof do we need," opined St. John, "that images are the books of the illiterate, the never silent heralds of the honor due the saints, teaching without use of words those who gaze upon them, and sanc-

tifying the sense of sight?" (39) And later, he argued: "If you speak of pagan abuses, these abuses do not make our veneration of images loathsome. Blame the pagans who made images into gods! Just because the pagans used them in a foul way, that is no reason to object to our pious practice" (63).

20. Appropriately, most of those located in the southwest and Las Vegas liked the "Father and Two Sons" best as it was the easiest to follow and could be understood even without a prior knowledge of the parable. Those who disliked "The Father and Two Sons" tended to dislike country music. Over 3/4 of the participants felt the singer's movements were funny and distracting and too much visual footage focused on her. A few leaders felt the movements were sexually suggestive and inappropriate for a teenage audience in a church setting. A number of teenagers laughed at the depiction of "wild living" at what seemed to be a Burger King indoor playground. "The Visit" was universally disliked by teenagers across socio-economic and cultural backgrounds, even by African American youth. A few leaders reported that this video was effective in women's retreats, especially among those who related to the joy of childbirth.

21. Viewers generally regarded the narration as a direct translation and the visual imagery as a contemporary interpretation of the text. Most participants recognized that ABS products followed Scripture closely and were faithful to the texts, and believed that ABS maintained a high level of integrity. One of the most seemly recommendations was for ABS to consider developing product with a longer shelf life, i.e. for elementary age culture which is not as ephemeral as teenage culture.

22. By studying the variety of "Jesus" films, from the silent *Passion Plays* (1898), *From the Manger to the Cross* (1912), and Cecil B. DeMille's influential *King of Kings* (1927) to the more recent versions of Campus Crusades' *Jesus* film and Visual Entertainment's books of *Matthew* and *Acts*, we see "faces" of Jesus that challenge one another. For a remarkable multimedia study of this phenomenon, consult Yancey (1998).

23. See Numbers 21:4-ff and 2 Kings 18:4. Also see Lindvall and Quicke (2001, 2f.).

24. In actuality, a group of Yale Divinity School students called upon the Reverend George Day, a former professor of the New York Institute of the Deaf and Dumb, to help Mende prisoners learn how to read and write, especially concerning the doctrines of the Christian faith. Using sign language, sermons, prayers in the Mende language and simple pictures, he did enable them to both learn the Gospel and how to write sentences from it.

References

Allsburg, Chris Van. 1991. *The Wretched Stone*. New York: Houghton Mifflin.

Azar, Beth. 1998. Cited in Cline (1995), Note 2.

Augustine. 1958. *On Christian Doctrine,* trans. D W. Robertson, Jr. New York: Bobbs-Merrill.

_____. 1960. *Confessions.* New York: Image Books.

Bazin, Andre. 1967. The Ontology of the Photographic Image. In *Que-est-ce que le Cinema?* ed. and trans. Hugh Gray, 9-16. Berkeley: University of California Press.

Bevan, Edwyn. 1940. *Holy Images: An Inquiry into Idolatry and Image-Worship in Ancient Paganism and in Christianity.* London: George Allen.

Boulding, Kenneth E. 1961. *The Image: Knowledge and Life in Society.* Ann Arbor: University of Michigan Press.

Brown, William J., Fraser, Benson P. and Lindvall, Terrence R. 1999. A Holy Critique: Examining Visual Translations of the Bible. Unpublished Paper presented at the National Communication Association Annual Conference, Chicago, November 5.

CNN. 1997 US News Story page, May 7. URL: <http://www.cnn.com/US/9705/07/swiss.guard/index.html.>

Cline, Victor. 1985. Psychologist Cites Porn's Effects on Children, Men. *National Federation for Decency Journal* (November/December): 13.

Coles, Robert. 1986. Seeing is Believing. *American Film* 11 (7) (1986): 26-32, 58.

Cooper, James F. 1999. *Knights of the Brush: The Hudson River School and the Moral Landscape.* New York: Hudson Hills Press.

Cropsey, Jasper F. 1860. "Autumn—On the Hudson River" (painting).

Edgerton, Gary R. 1999. With Eyes Wide Open: Five Fundamental Considerations for Living in the Media Age. *American Arts Quarterly* (Spring): 9-15.

Eisenstein, Sergei. 1949. *Film Form: Essays in Film Theory,* ed. and trans. Jay Leyda. New York: Harcourt Brace Jovanovich.

A Father and Two Sons. 1995. A CD-ROM program based on the story of the Prodigal Son, Luke 15.11-32. New York: American Bible Society.

Fischbach, Gerald D. 1992. Mind and Brain. *Scientific American,* September, 54.

Ellul, Jacques. 1985. *Humiliation of the Word.* Grand Rapids: Eerdmans.

Ewen, Stuart. 1988. *All Consuming Images: The Politics of Style in Contemporary Culture.* New York: Basic Books.

Fallows, James. 1997. *Breaking the News: How the Media Undermine American Democracy.* New York: Vintage.

Gerbner, George. 1973. Cultural Indicators: The Third Voice. In *Communication Technology and Social Policy,* eds. George Gerbner, Larry Gross, and William H. Melody, 555-73. New York: Wiley.

Enzensberger, Han Magnus. 1974. *The Consciousness Industry.* New York: Seabury.

George Gerbner and Larry Gross. 1976a. Living with Television: The Violence Profile. *Journal of Communication,* 26, 173-199.

_____. 1976b The Scary World of TV's Heavy Viewers. *Psychology Today* 9 (11) (April): 41.

Girard, Rene. 1996. *The Girard Reader*, ed. James G. Williams. New York: Crossroads.

Godwin, Joscelyn. 1979. *Athanasius Kircher: A Renaissance Man and the Quest for Lost Knowledge*. London: Thames and Hudson.

Goldman-Rakic, Patricia S. 1992. Working Memory and the Mind. *Scientific American*, September, 111-17.

Goldstein, Arnold P. 1996. *The Psychology of Vandalism*. New York: Plenum Press.

Gombrich, Ernest H. 1972. *The Story of Art*. London: Phaidon Press.

Green, Garrett. 1989. *Imagining God*. Grand Rapids: Eerdmans.

Heebner, Amy L. 1999. Aesthetic Experience and Religious Painting. *Journal of Visual Literacy* 19(1) (Spring 1999): 1-20.

John of Damascus. 1997. *On the Divine Images*, trans. David Anderson. Crestwood, NY: St. Vladimir's Seminary Press.

Keyser, Les and Barbara. 1984. *Hollywood and the Catholic Church*. Chicago: Loyola University Press.

Kierkegaard, Soren. 1996. *Works of Love,* ed. and trans. Howard V. Hong and Edna H. Hong. Princeton: Princeton University Press.

Kochan. Lionel. 1997. *Beyond the Graven Image: A Jewish View*. New York: New York University Press.

Lester, Paul Martin. 1996. *Images That Injure*. London: Praeger.

Lewis, C. S. 1946. *That Hideous Strength: A Modern Fairy-Tale for Grown-Ups*. New York: Macmillan.

_____. 1961. *Experiment in Criticism*. Cambridge: University Press.

Lindvall, Terry. 2001. *The Silents of God: Selected Documents in Silent American Film and the Protestant Church*. Virginia Beach: Regent University Press.

Lindvall, Terry and Andrew Quicke. 2001. *The Brazen Serpent: The Christian Film Industry*. Virginia Beach: Regent University Press.

Lippmann, Walter. 1965 (1922). *Public Opinion*. New York: Free Press.

Lipstiz, George. 1990. *Time Passages: Collective Memory and Popular Culture*. Minneapolis: University of Minnesota Press.

Marc, David. 1993. Mass Memory: The Past in the Age of Television. In *Rhetorical Memory and Delivery: Classical Concepts for Contemporary Communication*, ed. Fred Reynolds, 125-38. Hillsdale, NJ: Lawrence Erlbaum..

McGough, James L. 1985. Cited in Cline (1985), 13.

Morgan, David. 1998. *Visual Piety: A History and Theory of Popular Religious Images*. Berkeley: University of California Press.

New York Times. 1999. Television changes body image of girls in Fiji, study indicates. Press release reprinted in *The Virginian-Pilot*, Sunday, 23 May, Nation and World, 3.

Nicholas of Lyra. 1981. *Last Judgment: Circle of Michael Pacher.* Norfolk, VA: Chrysler Museum.

Nielsen Media Research. 1998. *1998 Report on Television.* New York: Nielsen Media Research.

Ong, Walter J. 1967. *The Presence of the Word.* Minneapolis: University of Minnesota Press.

_____. 1981. *The Presence of the Word: Some Prolegomena for Cultural and Religious History.* Minneapolis: University of Minnesota Press.

Otto, Rudolph. 1923. *The Idea of the Holy.* Oxford: Oxford University Press.

Out of the Tombs. 1997. An interactive story video, music, and study program on CD-ROM based on Mark 5.1-20. New York: American Bible Society.

Paul II, Pope John.1979. Children and the Media. Message for World Communication Day given May 27, 1979, *Origins* 9 (3) (June 7): 33-47.

_____. 1999. The Cinema: Pictures for a Dialogue Among Peoples and a Culture of Peace in the Third Millennium. Vatican City: Pontifical Councils for Culture and for Social Communications. (December 12).

Ramsaye, Terry. 1926. *A Million and One Nights.* New York: Simon and Schuster.

Troup, Calvin L. 1998. Include the Iconoclast: The Voice of Jacques Ellul in Contemporary Theory and Criticism. *The Journal of Communication and Religion* 21:1 (March) 22-46.

The Visit. 1994. A CD-ROM program based on the story of the visit of Mary, Mother of Jesus, to Elizabeth (Luke 1. 39-56). New York: American Bible Society.

Warren, Michael. 1997. *Seeing Through the Media: A Religious View of Communications and Cultural Analysis.* Harrisburg, PA: Trinity Press International.

Weaver, Richard. 1948. *Ideas Have Consequences.* Chicago: University of Chicago Press.

Webber, Robert. 1999. *Ancient-Future Faith.* Grand Rapids: Baker.

Whitman, Walt. 1954. "There Was a Child Went Forth," in Oscar Williams (ed.), *The Pocket Book of Modern Verse*, 20f. New York: Washington Square Press.

Yancey, Philip. 1998. *The Jesus I Never Knew: A Video Resource for Small Groups.* Grand Rapids: Zondervan.

Zeki, Semir. 1992. The Visual Image in Mind and Brain. *Scientific American* (September), 69-76.

11

Scripture Study in the Age of the New Media

Michael Palmer

Not long ago, a student of mine described a Bible study software package she had recently purchased for about one hundred dollars. This software package, which advertises itself as a PC-based "reference library," contains complete texts of four versions of the Bible, cross reference resources, a Bible dictionary, an encyclopedia, two commentaries, word study reference works, and biblical language reference helps. It also includes maps, study guides, a reading plan, and a photo collection of notable geographical sites from the ancient Near East. It even provides a place for "personal notes." My student described this new acquisition not with the excitement of someone who has made a remarkable discovery but in a matter of fact way, almost as a parenthetical aside in an on-going conversation.

This incident is noteworthy not for being unusual but precisely because it typifies a generation of young adult students of the Bible who stand poised at the outset of a new millennium. She, like her contemporaries, is aptly described as a child of the digital age (Honen 1999). Conversant and comfortable with personal computers and a host of software applications, she knows how to communicate electronically and has surfed the Internet for business, research, and recreation. Thanks to the technologies of digitization and computer-mediated communication (most strikingly evident in the Internet and the World Wide Web) she enjoys almost immediate access to resources the likes of which could hardly have been imagined in the middle of the twentieth century. Primary sources like the Dead Sea scrolls, vast holdings of discipline-specific secondary professional writings, 3-D topographical maps of the ancient Near East that permit "virtual" travel and exploration are all readily available to her. It is hardly surprising, then, that she sees nothing remarkable about owning a "reference library" of Bible software.

This student belongs to the same faith tradition that I claim as my own. But her approaches to Bible study as well as the circumstances in which she encounters the biblical text and related resources bear only a weak resemblance to those familiar to me from my childhood nearly half a century ago. Considering the sheer quantity of available materials, their variety and quality, as well as the sophistication of the technological devices and related software that grant quick, easy access to them, the advantages all lie with my student. Moreover, these advantages will undoubtedly only increase in the foreseeable future. However, I do not draw the comparison simply to applaud the substantial advances in Bible-related digital technology. Rather, I am concerned to identify and examine certain ways the new media foster attitudes and behaviors that militate against attempts to sustain what is valuable in the way particular faith traditions (such as my own) have studied the Bible. I shall clarify my thesis at the end of the next section after setting forth some of the salient features of traditional Bible study.

I

Thinking back on the practice of Bible study as I knew it in my childhood, I have more distinct memories of the *occasions* of study than I do most of the specific content. By this I mean that although today I consider myself to be biblically literate, I have (with certain notable exceptions) few distinct memories of studying specific passages in the Bible. But I do recall with considerable clarity the occasions—the places, the ebb and flow of time, the interpersonal dynamics among friends and family—in which Bible study became a cherished activity.

The places were familiar and conducive to human interaction: homes, Sunday school classrooms, the church sanctuary. In these places, spatial relations assumed concrete meaning. My peers and I measured near and far not in abstract units of feet and yards but in categories of immediate experience: lounging on the sofa next to my mother in the living room of our home listening to her read a narrative from the Bible; sitting on a chair, elbows on knees, across the Sunday school room from a teacher during the instructional time; or occupying just a certain pew in the church sanctuary during the Sunday worship service or the mid-week Bible study.

Time, too, was reckoned qualitatively, in palpable rhythms whose meter almost never synchronized precisely with the movement of the clock's hands. Depending on the type of activity and my own readiness, time might stand still or drag or march or slip away quickly. For my childhood peers and me, time allotted for Bible stories ended almost before it began, whereas time for reciting our "memory verses" contracted or expanded according to whether we had diligently attended to our homework. Bible study among certain adults whom I knew and respected was decidedly unhurried. They seemed to delight in it with a level of appreciation and discernment that exceeded my childish reach. The pace of their study was leisurely, sauntering, more often circuitous than goal oriented, in keeping with their contemplative and conversational approach toward confirming or challenging various interpretations of biblical passages.

My perception of the substantive message of the Bible was also shaped by the particular *way* the message was presented. Both in small group settings and in congregational worship, the Bible was commonly read aloud. Hearing the words in the distinctive cadences and intonations of the readers who enunciated them lent intelligibility and authority to the text.[1] One of the few distinct memories I have of encountering a specific passage of the Bible is linked forever to the occasion of hearing it. Even now, many years after my grandfather's death, I recall clearly his resonant voice reading from the gospel of Luke at the annual Christmas gathering of our extended family. Moreover, pastors and teachers used their active presence as a medium for teaching, and what they taught emerged partly from the words they uttered but also partly from physical cues such as the way they held the Bible, gestured to emphasize a point, furrowed their eye-brows questioningly, nodded in affirmation, or touched a neighbor's hand or arm as if to invite special consideration for a certain idea.[2]

Walter Ong has correctly observed that the field of biblical study has generated what is undoubtedly the most massive body of textual commentary in the world (1982, 173). This fact had little significance for the faith community that I knew in my childhood, where study resources were limited in quantity and modest in quality. The best of the abundant printed resources to which Ong was no doubt referring were either housed at locations far removed from my community or too expensive for most parishioners. Consequently, when members of my faith community studied the Bible, they relied heavily on pastors, teachers, and senior members in the congregation for guidance, expecting them to confirm or challenge their reading of particular passages. Auditing the various exchanges among adults, my peers and I gleaned insights about the meaning of biblical narratives, discerned the rudiments of the faith community's theological commitments, and assimilated its hermeneutical assumptions. Equally importantly, we were exposed to the collective wisdom of the senior generation, this wisdom being something different from the accumulation of discrete data or isolated propositions. In short, pastors and other senior members of the faith community safeguarded and mediated the transmission of the biblical text.

Devotional and confessional Bible study as I remember it functioned not only as a source of enlightenment and encouragement to individuals but also as a way of integrating the individual into the faith community.[3] Incorporated as it was into the rhythms of daily life and habits of the people, it represented one of the principal recurring occasions for encountering one another in homes and in the church. Studying the Bible with friends and relatives provided a doorway for entering into trust relationships and a forum for transmitting acquired knowledge and wisdom from one generation to the next. In this way it strengthened the faith community.[4]

If the preceding recollections have identified salient features of traditional Bible study, the question naturally arises whether these features are safeguarded and strengthened, left unchanged, or threatened and undermined by technological developments in the age of the new digital media. I believe the last alternative accurately represents the current state of affairs and this in two ways. First, the new media, for all their potential to make available the best and most extensive biblical resources, encourage users to blur the distinction between the act of gathering information and the process of reflectively, contextually making sense of information. Second, the most rapidly developing facet of the new media and the one with the most potential to transform contemporary life—the Internet—encourages forms of anonymity and social isolation that threaten to estrange people from their faith community, the relevant social context in which traditional Bible study occurred. In following two sections, I make the case for these claims.

II

In "Redeeming the Time," an article promoting use of computers and software in Bible study, Nick Nicholaou argues that using time efficiently is one of the primary reasons to consider acquiring Bible-study software. To support his thesis, he cites a pastor of a large California-based church who claims that as a result of using Bible-study software he was able to reduce his weekly sermon and Bible study time significantly: "[Bible study software] saves me a lot of time . . . My own experience is that through the more focused use of Bible-study software, God can guide me to the message he wants me to communicate in nearly half the time" (2000, 21). Setting aside the impertinent question of how one measures the rate at which God communicates a message, this pastor (and by extension the author) leaves no doubt that when it comes to studying the Bible speed and efficiency are both possible and desirable.[5]

Of course, "redeeming the time" is a biblical expression, a fact Nicholaou clearly wishes to exploit. By appropriating these words from the epistle to the Ephesians and making them function as the title of his essay, he invokes the authority of Scripture to support his thesis. But exegetically his interpretation fails. In the biblical context, the reader is admonished to redeem the time, "because the days are evil" (5:16 NRSV). In one sense, of course, the case for not wasting one's resources (including available time) is unimpeachable. But exploiting the Ephesians passage as a proof text to justify the use of Bible-study software is a dubious strategy. To begin with, the justificatory clause, "because the days are evil," hardly supports the view that economy of time was upper-most in the biblical writer's thinking. In all likelihood, "redeeming the time" has more to do with engaging the prevailing culture circumspectly, adopting a more deliberate and thoughtful posture toward all of life's tasks, and evaluating one's choices in terms of what finally matters. In other words, precisely because the days are evil, people of faith should first and foremost reflectively evaluate their deeds in the light of ultimate concerns. This reading of the biblical passage leads to a rather different orientation toward Bible study software and other new-media dependent Bible study resources than the one suggested by Nicholaou. Particularly for people of faith, who approach the biblical text devotionally or confessionally, it shifts the emphasis away from one question and toward another: away from "Do the new digital media allow me to use my time in the most economical way?" and toward "Do these media facilitate understanding the biblical text?"

Contrary to current popular opinion, the two questions are not synonymous, Moreover, the answer to the second question is not inevitably affirmative. In this connection, and by way of illustration, consider once again my student's recently acquired "reference library" software. Like other similar packages intended for general retail consumption, this product is not a true Bible study suite but simply a bundle of discrete products packaged to give the illusion of forming an integrated unit. Moreover, its components vary widely in quality and applicability to specific audiences. For instance, one of the language resources, Brown, Driver, and Briggs' *Hebrew and English Lexicon of the Old Testament*, a standard reference work well-known to scholars, is too technical for anyone who does not already know biblical Hebrew and is therefore of little use to general readers. At the other extreme, Matthew Henry's commentary, one of the two complete commentaries included in the software package, is an antiquated reference work (really little more than a historical relic) and has no place in a twenty-first century reference library.[6] In addition, although the package offers four versions of the Bible (KJV, NIV, NKJV, ASV) only one of them (NIV) even remotely lays claim to being a credible contemporary version; two others (KJV, ASV) contain dated idioms and do not reflect the best current scholarship; and one (NKJV) suffers the ignominious distinction of being the only modern version whose translators intentionally reverted to an inferior edition of the underlying manuscripts.[7] These deficiencies will not be readily apparent to uninformed customers inclined to view the purchase price as reasonable in comparison to the cost of printed materials purchased separately. But when they become apparent, the users will discover that the package, far from offering instant enlightenment, actually exacts a heavy cost in money (to buy it) and time (to install it and laboriously discover its limitations).

To be sure, specific deficiencies in Bible study software can be addressed in up-graded versions and in new products. Strategies for improvement seem likely to follow two primary tracks. Along the first track, users can expect to see more and better attempts at creating truly integrated software packages. The second track leads straight to the Internet, where users can expect to find increasingly comprehensive resources. Quite simply, in every area of biblical inquiry, the Internet will make more information available more quickly than anyone acquainted with traditional Bible study fifty years ago could ever have imagined.[8]

These two tracks—one leading to more powerful, integrated software suites for PCs, the other to the Internet—are not identical and not precisely parallel.[9] Nevertheless, they are related, and each in its own way supports the thesis asserted earlier, that the new media blur the distinction between the act of gathering information and the process of reflectively, contextually making sense of information. Thus, the track leading to integrated Bible study software packages promises several appealing features. Because future software suites will be designed to

run on the latest generation of computers, they (compared to their pred-
ecessors) will perform more responsively and will have higher audio-
video resolution and other features that generally enhance their multi-
media capability. The best ones will function interactively and provide
access to local databases. They will also provide links to the second
track, the Internet ("the information highway"), which in turn will grant
access to large remote databases and facilitate forays into virtual reality. The latter will permit users to do such things as take virtual-tours of
first-century Palestine, participate in virtual-digs at archaeological sites
in the Near East, or virtually-rediscover the Dead Sea scrolls. Most
importantly, however, improved Bible study software suites and
Internet applications/sites will be developed for users having specific
needs or abilities (e.g., middle-school children, adult learners, scholars)
or will contain self-selection features designed to accomplish the same
kind of discrimination among users. In short, they promise to be eminently "user friendly."

The question, of course, is whether "user friendly" equates with
"promotes understanding." New media proponents claim that it does.
Indeed, in their estimation, the information revolution as it relates to
Bible study resources represents a major improvement over traditional
approaches.[10] The best new software suites, so the argument goes, will
select, categorize, filter, organize, and order the data they make available. By performing these important manipulations on the data they will
quickly, seamlessly, and colorfully present the most relevant information to the user, who will then presumably be optimally positioned to
understand what is so presented.

But this argument is specious. An integrated software suite or an
Internet site might well perform its functions flawlessly and exhibit the
results in an eye-catching graphical interface and yet fail to promote
true understanding if it fails to promote a searching, critical assessment
of the information it so pleasingly presents on screen. In other words,
digital Bible study products that do not engage the user's capacities for
critical reasoning (capacities for analysis, synthesis, logical evaluation,
and reflection) will not lead to true understanding—regardless of how
much information they make available, regardless of how many organi-
zational and filtering functions they perform, and regardless of how
invitingly they present the data. Thus, for instance, locating and viewing a crisp digitized image of an ancient artifact, archaeological site, or
map of the ancient Near East is not the same as grasping the historical,
social, political, or religious significance of those items. Understanding

these things within the context of their worldview involves more than gathering information about them; it also requires critical assessment. Similarly, having ready computer access to a biblical passage, even if presented in several contemporary versions and juxtaposed with the relevant Greek or Hebrew text, is something different from reading that passage attentively, in context, with a critical, interpretive eye.

Proponents of digital technology, of course, contend that the new media offer a better prospect of transforming learners from passive recipients to active choosers and critical thinkers than do traditional forms of study (Solomon 1992; Ehrmann 1995). The argument has two parts. The first involves the claim that traditional Bible study follows a parochial and authoritarian model that impedes the development of critical thinking skills.[11] The traditions and social dynamics described in the preceding section appear antiquated and constraining. The new digital media, according to its proponents, represent the best prospects for liberating learners from arbitrary authority and parochial perspectives. Moreover, the new media, they claim, free us from the accidental confinements of space and time. Students of the Bible no longer have to depend on deficient holdings in local church libraries or public libraries but are able to travel to the world's best archives, libraries, and museums with the click of a button, selecting at will the materials most suited to their needs. (Prior to the digital revolution, presumably, students of the Bible suffered from a poverty of information, particularly from too little exposure to the best scholarly resources.) The second part of the argument says that the new media actually do promote critical thinking by providing access to certain kinds of information, such as a wide range of scholarly opinion.

In certain respects, of course, the first part of the argument is not without merit. If a Bible study leader, Sunday school teacher, or pastor lacks appropriate education to address difficult interpretive questions or holds simplistic or dogmatic positions, parishioners (particularly young adults) will understandably feel liberated by having access to wider sources of information through digital media. Also, students of the Bible old enough to remember when study resources were limited in number and quality will view the ability to retrieve versions, commentaries, and other study helps electronically from remote sites as a godsend.

But what seem to be liberating factors do not come without cost. One such cost appears in the way digital riches produce what Albert Borgmann calls "a deceptive sense of facility" (1999, 209). Thus, for example, the beginning Greek student who gains instant access to an electronic database that definitively identifies the form of every word in the Greek text of the New Testament may well feel liberated from the cumbersome process of committing roots of words to memory and painstakingly coming to terms with the declensions of nouns, conjugations of verbs, and the logic of syntax. But the difficult, sometimes tedious, processes that such facility allows one to skirt constitute the inescapable preconditions for becoming truly conversant with the original language of the New Testament. Similarly, with regard to study of the English Bible, what seem like constraints on freedom—reading and re-reading the biblical text, setting aside time to patiently examine and evaluate secondary sources, attentively attending to a teacher's or pastor's exegetical comments—are often actually the disciplines and practices of engagement within which information is most likely to become knowledge. In the home or in the church, these may include devotional disciplines like reflecting on the meaning of a certain biblical passage, prayerfully participating in a liturgy as part of a worship service, or meeting with a group of friends to discuss the social justice implications of a certain passage of the Scripture.

By contrast, having unfettered access to vast amounts of data encourages the false impression that the sheer ability to locate particular items of information in an electronic database or on the Internet counts as *knowing* what one has thus located.[12] But information is not the same as knowledge. Information is homogeneous. Discrete bits of digital information can be assimilated to the fields of any sophisticated database. Knowledge, by contrast, always takes an articulate form. It arises from patterns of justification, and these in turn find their place in larger epistemological and social contexts. When people seek knowledge but get information instead, it is because they have lost sight of this principle that knowledge requires a context of justification and explanation. In decades past, parents, extended family, and the church community provided the relevant context of justification and explanation within which traditional Bible study took place. When study resources were rare, parents, teachers, and pastors read the Bible to children, teenagers, and other adults. Within the limits of their education and life experience, they commented on and illuminated the text. Through their explanations and responses to questions, they made the text intelligible and brought it to life in particular places at particular times—which is to say, within a spatial and temporal order that expressed their faith community's distinctive traditions and social structure. Norman Maclean, author of the celebrated novella *A River Runs Through It,* recalled just such practices from his childhood in Missoula, Montana: "After breakfast and again after what was called supper, my father read to us from the Bible or from some religious poet such as Wordsworth; then we knelt by our chairs while my father prayed. My father read beautifully. He avoided the homiletic sing-song most ministers fall into when they look inside the Bible or edge up to poetry, but my father overread poetry a little so that none of us, including him, could miss the music." With apparent regret, Maclean says, "I need hardly tell you that families no long read to each other. I am sure it leaves a sound-gap in family life"(McFarland and Nichols 1988, 84, 22).

In "Scriptural Literacy," Peter Feuerherd makes the case that basic biblical literacy has been declining for a number of years. "Almost every American has at least one Bible," Feuerherd notes. "Yet, public opinion surveys show, for many, it is a kind of treasured heirloom hidden away in an attic gathering dust, much of its content an inscrutable mystery. Relatively few have a working knowledge of its content."[13] Feuerherd quotes pollster George W. Gallup as saying, "We revere the Bible, but we don't read it." Gallup's research shows that the numbers of those who read the Bible at all have declined from 73 percent of the population in 1990 to just 59 percent in 2001. Moreover, among those who read the Bible, most are doing it alone; only about 14 percent participate in a regular Bible study group. These findings are intriguing in light of the fact that digital media in general, and the Internet in particular, have experienced explosive growth during the decade of the 1990s, the same period that Feuerherd discusses in his article. Social theorists may someday be able to provide a comprehensive explanation for this convergence of facts. Short of such an account, it may be impossible to demonstrate a causal relationship between the historical trend away from traditional forms of Bible study and the current weak state of biblical literacy. In any event, there is little reason to believe that the new media, glowing promises to the contrary notwithstanding, have had any discernible impact in slowing the decline of biblical literacy. Evidently, the new digital media are not (or at least not yet) the doorways to liberation they are sometimes made out to be (Solomon 1992).

To turn to the second part of my argument—nor is it clear that the new digital media promote active decision making and critical thinking better than traditional methods of Bible study. The claim that they do rests in part on an optimistic assessment of what computers can (or will eventually be able to) do and partly on a faulty view of traditional methods of Bible study.

The promise held forth for digital technologies in general is that they will someday be fully interactive and fully capable of exploiting advances in artificial intelligence. Insofar as the new media relate to Bible study resources (stand-alone PC software and Internet sites), this promise has not yet been fulfilled. The current state of digital Bible study resources, though impressive, largely represents an extension of the kinds of resources already available to scholars in the print medium or by direct physical inspection. Thus, electronic databases extend the reach of lexicons, encyclopedias, and concordances; and compress the time necessary for information searches. Geography programs make it possible to view the terrain of the Middle East with a greater sense of fluidity and "realism" than still photographs, with more flexibility than videos, and with less expense and bother than actually going on location. Museum and archive Internet sites facilely display digitized photos together with brief written descriptions of artifacts that would otherwise require much time and expense to view in person. However, none of these operations fully exemplifies the cognitive processes ordinarily associated with critical thinking.

The significance of this point becomes apparent if we consider how the new media might assist someone who wishes to understand a certain difficult passage in the Bible. As we have noted before, these media are well suited to presenting the text in multiple versions and in its original language; providing access to various study helps of the sort mentioned above; and making scholarly commentaries available. Any or all of these resources can be helpful in developing a rich understanding of the text in question. But for this to happen, the person using them must already possess a fairly high level of critical reasoning skill. Thoughtful, well-reasoned commentaries, for example, can serve as models for responsible interpretation and can thus provide useful points of departure in a complicated process that may eventuate in the reader's arriving at a plausible judgment of her own about the meaning of the biblical text. But merely having commentaries available, without the reader also bringing to the text an appropriate background and mental aptitude, will not yield a rich understanding of the text and will not inevitably enhance the reader's capacity for critical thought. This is so because both the biblical text as well as the commentaries intended to illuminate it represent classic instances of what learning theorists call "ill-structured problems"—problems for which there is no easy, obvious, or single solution (Resnick 1987). A student who encounters five options for each question on a multiple choice examination (and who is also told that in every instance one of the options is the correct answer) does not face an ill-structured problem. The student's problem is straight-forward ("well-structured"): to determine which of the five options is the correct answer to a (presumably) clearly expressed question. But the reader of the biblical text does not necessarily know whether *any* of the commentators has the correct answer to her question(s). Indeed, the fact that eminent Bible scholars sometimes differ over the meaning of important passages constitutes *prima facie* evidence that the text—at least initially, and perhaps indefinitely—is susceptible of being read fruitfully from multiple perspectives. More crucially, she does not necessarily know whether she has posed the correct question(s) to the text itself. Thus, depending on the specific question(s) she asks, one or a few or all or none of the commentators might have the correct answer or a partially correct answer. Part of what it means to be a critical thinker in such instances is to possess both a well developed sense of the importance of formulating questions and a measure of critical reserve (not skepticism, but the willingness and ability to live with ambiguity and indeterminacy). Thus, learning theorists who describe higher order thinking not simply in terms of thinking about and choosing correct answers from among available options but in terms of *problem-finding abilities* (Arlin) or *stages of reflective judgment necessary for dealing with ill- structured problems* (King and Kitchener 1994) will justifiably be unimpressed with claims that certain Bible study media promote critical thinking if in fact those media primarily present multiple stimuli for analysis and reflection. The latter is not unimportant, but it also does not count as a strategy for developing critical reasoning.

Do traditional forms of Bible study fare any better in developing critical thinking skills? It is possible to answer this question negatively but only by assuming that they depend almost exclusively on simple models of rote memorization, transference of information from one person to another, or outright indoctrination. These techniques, of course, have been evident in traditional Bible study and remain a continuing point of concern. But instruction by nurturing and mentoring more aptly define traditional Bible study at its best, and these educational strategies are in fact quite conducive to the development of critical thinking.

Why so? The answer lies partly in the complex nature of critical thinking itself. According to Peter Facione, "Engaging in reasoned judgment about what to believe and what to do requires the skills and the disposition to think critically." In other words, critical thinking—the process of engaging in purposeful reasoned judgment[14]—is not a purely cognitive skill, not purely an act of a facile mind. It also involves a certain *disposition* (or consistent internal inclination) to use one's skills to form reasoned judgments.[15] Facione contends that this disposition is characterized by certain habits of mind, among them truth-seeking, open-mindedness, inquisitiveness, and confidence in reasoning.[16] Now if critical thinking is complex in the way Facione describes, involving both cognitive skill and disposition, we should wonder not only how the cognitive skills are acquired but also how the dispositional features are acquired. Perhaps the case can be made that purely cognitive skills can be acquired by abstract means.[17] But if we take seriously the comments of people like Norman Maclean, quoted earlier, we will conclude that the dispositional aspect of critical reasoning results from nurturing and mentoring—in his case by his father, who read to him, taught him how to pray (not so much by precept as by example), and instilled in him a love of the Bible and poetry. But we must be clear here that the style of instruction involved in nurturing and mentoring is less like transferring information than developing a collaborative, trust-based relationship in which certain kinds of responses can be called forth. In the words of Henry Bugbee, "the sense of responsibility for meaning is the key to the development of the educational potential of the person; and this is evoked" (1974, 4).

The burden of this section has been to show that, for all their potential to make available the best and most extensive resources for Bible study, the new media in certain crucial respects encourage users to blur the distinction between the act of gathering information and the process of critically evaluating that information. (They do this in several ways, such as by creating a false sense of facility or inviting the view that information counts as knowledge.) This tendency to blur the distinction between the two is pernicious because it threatens certain valuable functions of traditional Bible study such as those having to do with the way we orient our lives morally and spiritually. As Stephen O'Leary and Brenda Brasher eloquently observe, "When ... the whole record of human culture is digitized and available on computer databases connected to each other by a global web, our spiritual crisis will remain and even intensify, for we will be forced to confront the fact that no electronic alchemy can turn information into knowledge or into the wisdom that will teach us how to live" (1996, 262).

But if critical reasoning is complex in the way Facione claims, and if the dispositional component of critical reasoning (to say nothing of its cognitive component) is evoked through nurturing and mentoring, then we should expect that the future development of mature reflection on the Bible—reflection of the sort that can engender knowledge and teach us how to live—will depend on the continued vitality and coherence of communities of interpretation, which are the social contexts within which nurturing and mentoring take place. What is the impact of the new media on these social contexts? It is to this question that I turn in the next section.

III

The promise of the new media is that they will both bring about vital transformations of traditional expressions of religion and also foster new forms of religious community, which though different from traditional forms of community, will nonetheless function as legitimate and viable expressions of community.[18] The Internet, we are told, will liberate people from the constraints of geography or isolation brought on by stigma, illness, or schedule, and will allow people to affiliate with others on the basis of common interest rather than convenience (Katz and Aspden 1997; Rheingold 2000).[19]

In support of the claim that the new media foster new forms of community, one can point to Internet sites designed specifically for people of faith. Both Faithnet.com ("a collaboration of Christian communities interacting live on-line") and Beliefnet.com (mission: "To do whatever it takes to help individuals meet their own needs in the realm of religion, spirituality and morality") advertise a wide array of interactive opportunities for people of faith. LifeOfTheWorld.com, a Web site affiliated with Concordia Theological Seminary, claims to provide a single comprehensive source of information with daily scriptures, devotions, and insightful articles about Christ, coupled with news, weather, sports and shopping. *Christianity Today, Inc.* sponsors two venues: an interactive forum called Daily Bible Study Chats ("Join in one of our daily hosted Bible studies. Learn and grow as you open God's word with other believers.") and a posting site called Bible & Theology Message Board ("Add your posting to the thousands discussing doctrine, the end times, and other hot issues."). Those who seek religiously centered entertainment ("products that reflect what we believe in") need only log on to iChristian.com, which claims to have the Web's largest selection of "Bible-centered," entertainment products for the entire family. The list goes on.[20]

Despite the proliferation of Web sites like these, recent assessments cast suspicion on the claims for benefits associated with Internet use. For instance, transformations are beginning to appear in the way people of faith (particularly the young) think about themselves, conceptualize their faith, and relate to other people of faith. These transformations include increased incidences of feelings of isolation and estrangement as well as theological trends toward trends toward fundamentalism and eclecticism. According to *Newsweek*'s John Leland, "This broad pattern of belief—the simultaneous rise of both fundamentalism and eclecticism—accelerates through the Internet. Religious chat rooms and Web sites like Faithnet or Beliefnet act like spiritual supermarkets, offering an assortment of belief systems all within one click. ... The Web's influence will only grow as online faith-based services become more sophisticated, targeting ever more select micro-congregations" (2000, 63).

Concerning community formation, a major empirical study by a research team at Carnegie Mellon University has found that although the Internet is designed to be a social technology it actually reduces social involvement and has other negative psycho-social consequences as well (Kraut et.al 1998). Reviewing the current discussion about the social impact of computer technology, these researchers identified several possible uses of the Internet, including both *asocial* and *social* purposes. *Asocial* uses are ones that make it easier for people to be alone and independent, such as using the Internet to enhance private entertainment, to obtain information from remote sources, to increase technical skills, or to conduct commercial transactions. *Social* uses are ones that allow people to communicate or socialize with colleagues, friends, and family through e-mail or joining social groups through distribution lists, news groups, or MUDs.[21] The Carnegie Mellon researchers found that interpersonal communication—communication for social purposes—is the dominant use of the Internet at home. However, contrary to expectations, they also found that increased Internet use among the study's participants "led to their having, on balance, less social engagement and poorer psychological well-being" (Kraut et al 1998, 1018). These findings struck the research team as paradoxical: Although the Internet is a social technology and although the main reason people use it at home is to facilitate interpersonal communication, increased use of the Internet turns out to correlate with declines in social involvement—less communication within the family, diminished size of people's local social networks, more loneliness, and more depression. Moreover, these correlations seem to be causal, not simply coincidental. "Our analyses are consistent with the hypothesis that using the Internet adversely affects social involvement and psychological well-being. The panel research design gives us substantial leverage in inferring causation, leading us to believe that in this case, correlation does indeed imply causation"(Kraut et al 1998, 1028).

If the Carnegie Mellon researchers are correct, what explains the fact that Internet use causes declines in social involvement and psychological well-being? One explanation begins with the premise that time is always and already full. In practical terms, this means that to do one thing is to displace another. Thus, Internet use, one might argue, displaces time people might otherwise devote to social purposes. A study conducted at the Stanford Institute for the Quantitative Study of Society lends weight to this explanation (Nie and Erbring 2000). The Stanford research team, which considered the social consequences of Internet use based on a large, representative sample of Americans (including both Internet users and non-users), found that as Internet use increases, people spend less time with friends and family. In the words of Norman Nie, the principal investigator, "The more hours people use the Internet, the less time they spend with real human beings" (O'Toole 2000). Fully one quarter of the study's polling respondents who used the Internet regularly (more than five hours a week) reported that using the Internet had reduced their time with friends and family or had detracted from other social events outside the home. Among Internet users who were employed, one quarter reported that the Internet increased the time they spent working at home without cutting back at the office. Those least affected in their day-to-day social interactions were people who used the Internet less than five hours per week; those most affected spent more than ten hours per week surfing the Net. In an interview on PBS's NewsHour, Nie offered this summary: "I think the big story is that . . . the time you spend on the Internet is time that comes out of friends and family and social activity and goes into work and into spending time by yourself on the Internet." Also, "With the growth of bandwidth, we'll move from a state of billboards and print and rough graphics to a true multimedia. And I think we have the beginning evidence that people are going to spend a lot of time on it and that ultimately . . . I think one has to be concerned about . . . the sheer reduction in amount of real social interaction" (Nie 2000, 2, 3).

Displacement is not exclusively a temporal phenomenon; it can be spatial as well. William J. Mitchell, dean of the school of architecture at MIT, has described a kind of spatial displacement that takes place in cyberspace, the digital sphere where "you get from place to place . . . by following logical links rather than physical paths" (1995, 23). The new categories of cyberspace, according to Mitchell, "will turn classical categories inside out and will reconstruct the discourse in which architects have engaged from classical times until now" (1995, 24) From these new categories, Mitchell predicts, a new virtual-city will emerge.

> This will be a city unrooted to any definite spot on the surface of the earth, shaped by connectivity and bandwidth constraints rather than by accessibility and land values, largely asynchronous in its operation, and inhabited by disembodied and fragmented subjects who exist as collections of aliases and agents. Its place will be constructed virtually by software instead of physically from stones and timbers, and they will be connected by logical linkages rather than by doors, passageways, and streets (1995, 24).

The homogeneous virtual-city that Mitchell describes here is neither a place nor a dwelling, but a City of Bits, whose citizens are cyborgs.[22] Certainly, it bears only faint resemblance to the homes or places of worship in which traditional Bible study once flourished, though it has the potential (and in certain respects has already begun) to displace them.

Of course if, as the Carnegie Mellon study shows, the most prevalent home use of the Internet is for social purposes, then the displacement explanation, whether temporal or spatial, only partially illuminates the apparent causal connection between Internet use and declines in social involvement and psychological well-being. For if people use the Internet at home primarily for social purposes then, generally speaking, when they exchange face-to-face social arrangements in real-world places for online social arrangements in the City of Bits they still remain socially engaged, and we should not expect a causal connection between Internet use and declines in social involvement and psychological well-being.

A more searching explanation might well have more to do with the *kinds* of social relationships the Internet encourages and sustains than with the mere fact that the Internet isolates people from what Nie calls "real human beings." In other words, even though in their homes people use the Internet primarily for social purposes, the nature of the social relationships they find there may not be of the same quality as the face-to-face relationships displaced by going online. Put another way, displacement may be the key issue, but not quite in the way initially suggested. Thus whether or not face-to-face social relationships get displaced by the Internet may be an important concern, but the more fundamental concern is whether a certain kind of social relationship commonly found in face-to-face relationships gets displaced by another kind of relationship more prevalent online.

This line of explanation can be developed in terms of a distinction between *strong* and *weak* social ties. Strong social ties are associated with relationships in which people have frequent contact with each other, exhibit deep feelings of affection and obligation, and communicate on a broad range of substantive issues. Where social ties are weak, people have infrequent contact, their social bonds are superficial and easily broken, and they communicate about relatively few substantive issues. Both kinds of ties are useful. Weak social ties, for example, are useful in providing access to information and social resources not readily available in other ways (Granovetter 1973; Constant et al. 1996). But strong social ties are the ones most likely to provide people the support they need to cope with life's important issues and challenges (Cohen and Wills 1985; Krackhardt 1994). Drawing on this distinction between strong and weak social ties, Kraut and his colleagues venture the following explanation: "Perhaps, by using the Internet, people are substituting poorer quality social relationships for better relationships, that is, substituting weak ties for strong ones" (1998, 1029).

This explanation is consistent with the major findings in their study. For example, their research shows that people can sustain strong ties electronically. (Interviews revealed examples of people staying in contact with family members and friends living in remote locations.) However, many online relationships, especially new ones, exemplify weak ties rather than strong ones. (Examples from the study included a man who exchanged jokes and Scottish trivia with a person he met through an online tourist web site and an adolescent who disseminated fictional stories about his underwater exploits to other members of a scuba diving chat service.) Also, making friends online is rare, but even when such friendships do develop they do not counteract overall declines in real-world communication with family and friends (Kraut et al 1998, 1029). Online friendships, moreover, are likely to be more limited than friendships developed in physical proximity, meaning that (compared to friends developed at school, work, church, or in the neighborhood) online friends are less likely to be willing or able to provide assistance with tasks or comfort in difficult times. Even when people try to maintain strong ties by means of digital technology such as e-mail, the nature of the relationship is likely to be different in kind, perhaps even diminished in strength, compared with strong ties supported by physical proximity. In sum: "The interpersonal communication applications currently prevalent on the Internet are either neutral toward strong ties or tend to undercut rather than promote them" (Kraut et al 1998, 1030).

If the findings of the Carnegie Mellon and Stanford studies hold up in the long run, the prospects seem dim for developing forms of digitally based Bible study capable of sustaining complex and thickly textured faith communities of the sort that functioned as vibrant social institutions in the past. Even in cases where Internet users enter cyberspace with no intention of maintaining their anonymity[23]—that is to say, even when they purposefully reach out to other people in order to discuss sacred texts and to communicate candidly and intimately about matters of faith—their efforts are likely to prove unsatisfying in the long run unless they are undergirded and sustained by a network of real-world social relationships. At best, it seems, cyberspace relationships can augment real world relationships, and this in a limited way under special conditions.

Conclusion

It strikes me that from the preceding discussion two challenges emerge. The first is to reinvigorate the study of the Bible and to do so in a way that makes it a central community activity among people of faith; the second is to find an appropriate role for the new media to perform in meeting the first challenge. Part of the difficulty in meeting the first challenge is that the Bible, like the preponderance of documents in the print medium, lacks glamour by comparison to contemporary digital products. In the age of new media, in which colorful surfaces seem to count for more than ideas, the printed Bible is gradually being relegated to the hall desk drawer or the lower shelf of the living room lamp table. Proponents of digital technology, of course, have made breathtaking promises. New media resources, we hear, will revolutionize Bible study by making information and resources available of which earlier generations could only dream. Moreover, they will transform and revitalize community life through the formation of online communities tailored to the needs of specific audiences. But as we have seen, these promises have not yet been met, and this through no lack of effort. It is certainly true that the general public and scholars alike have benefited from the information revolution and that the computer can be a uniquely powerful tool. However, the much welcomed proliferation of digital Bible study resources has so far led neither to increased reading of the Bible among the general public nor to increased overall understanding of its content. For many people, the overall increase in digital data does seem to have had the unintended side-effect of blurring the distinction between the act of gathering information and the process of reflectively, contextually making sense of information. (As pointed out earlier, exposure to data is not a sufficient condition for understanding.) Furthermore, preliminary evidence seems to suggest that Internet use is causally connected with declines in social involvement—hardly an auspicious finding for a medium whose primary home use is said to be for social purposes.

Meeting the first challenge cannot involve assuming the posture of a Luddite. It is neither possible nor desirable either to do away with the new media or to retreat to a time when information was less available. Digital media and digital information alike should be accepted affirmatively and incorporated into the life of contemporary faith communities deliberately, intelligently, and realistically. This requires in the first instance establishing clear priorities. The new media, for all their wonder, should be strictly limited to a supporting role. On the spectrum of means, ends, and ultimate ends, digital technology is often treated as if it were an end in itself, and in some quarters studying the Bible is treated as if it were merely an occasion for the development of sophisticated digital Bible study resources. Community formation, too, is sometimes treated not as an end having merit in its own right but as a problem to be solved technologically (Werry and Mowbray 2000; Preece 2000; Kim 2000). From this perspective, demonstrating that an online community can indeed be established (regardless of how minimal or attenuated it may be) then becomes a reason to celebrate the hardware and software that made it possible. But establishing priorities of the sort I have in mind entails reversing this order. It means placing Bible study and faith community formation in the position of ends eminently worthy of pursuit and relocating the new media to the unmistakable position of means.

Establishing clear priorities in this way (perhaps it is now evident that from an historical perspective the proper expression should be 're-establishing priorities') offers the possibility both of renewing our appreciation for Bible study as a rewarding activity in its own right and of delighting in the remarkable liberty and facility that digital technology make possible. Thus, for example, earnestly and deliberately studying a passage in the Bible is a practice of intellectual engagement that has the effect of deepening one's admiration for the way the new media can make available a remarkable array of relevant study resources. In the context of sustained effort to understand the text, digital study resources would surely be gratefully welcomed. Certainly they could not be spoken of in the casual, almost dismissive way my student spoke about her new Bible study software.[24] Similarly, engaging in a serious discussion of a biblical passage with family members or friends, attentively attending to interpretations advanced by scholars, or reflectively considering the text's moral or spiritual implications in light of a pastor's well-crafted sermon are the kinds of disciplined focus of attention that might well lead one to appreciate more fully the technological wonder of being able to confer via e-mail about the same passage with a friend in another city or revel in the fun and intellectual stimulation of discussing the text with strangers in an Internet chat room.

Establishing priorities in the relationship between the practice of studying the Bible and the digital technology that facilitates that practice implies that this relationship can never be strictly symmetrical and equal. One is always primary, the other secondary. One is always the end for which the other is the means. Stated more concretely, disciplined engagement with the biblical text, particularly within a community setting, is eminently worthy of our full effort. The new media at their best support and facilitate that end. We should, therefore, measure these media (both the resources they provide and their potential for transforming community life) by one standard: whether they encourage sustained engagement with the biblical text. In the words of Albert Borgmann, "The task, it would seem, is a matter of commensurating the fluidity of information technology with the stability of the things and practices that have served us well and we continue to depend on for our material and spiritual well-being .... What is needed is a sense for the liabilities of technological information and an ear for the changing voices of traditional reality" (1999, 210). Certainly it would be a calamity to be deprived instantly of all digital Bible study resources. But the perfection of these resources is a penultimate achievement at best. And their perfection will count for little if at the end of the day the earnest study of the Bible itself ceases to be a central, sustaining, and orienting activity in our lives.[25]

Notes

1. In this connection, Walter Ong's comment on the force of the spoken word comes to mind: "The interiorizing force of the oral word relates in a special way to the sacral, to the ultimate concerns of existence" (1982, 74).

2. This description of the bodily cues that facilitate understanding in Bible study groups calls to mind Shoshana Zuboff's description of the interpersonal dynamics among pulp mill workers in which senior employees transmitted knowledge of their skills to their junior colleagues (1988). Significantly, in the 1970s and 1980s, as mills were in the throes of massive modernization efforts that would place every aspect of the production process under computer control, these workers faced problems analogous to those under consideration in this essay.

3. By setting forth the preceding (mainly favorable) description, I am not suggesting that Bible study in the middle of the twentieth century was free of problems and stress points. Dubious hermeneutical assumptions yielded unconventional, eccentric, or anachronistic readings. Proof-texting was an ever-present danger. Differences of interpretation among people otherwise kindly disposed toward each other sometimes erupted into heated exchanges. By the middle of the twentieth century, cultural and technological changes were also already impinging on the process. The transistor radio, the television, and the automobile all made strong claims at a time in which social status and economic aspiration loomed large. In the increasingly busy climate of the post-war years, reflective people were compelled to question how or whether devotional Bible study as they had come to practice it could continue to play a central role in their lives.

4. My experiences were hardly unique. Setting aside certain specific differences of theology, liturgy, and worship, the general features of Bible study described here are recognizable in the practices of other people of faith throughout the country during the same period. As it was for my own friends and family, Bible study among many others was contextual rather than abstract, empathetic and participatory rather than objectively distanced.

5. Nicholaou's emphases on speed and efficiency are perfectly in keeping with the times. A decade ago, Alvin Toffler called attention to the accelerated pace of change and anticipated its consequences when he predicted that the world's next fundamental confrontation would not take place between East and West, nor North and South, but between "the fast and the slow." (1991) (Toffler was referring to global economies, but his analysis also seems pertinent for individuals and subcultures.) More recently, James Gleick advanced a related claim: "We are in a rush. We are making haste. A compression of time characterizes the life of the century now closing" (1999, 7). According to Gleick, the leading edge technologies are the ones governed by "Moore's Law," named after Gordon Moore, the founder of Intel who, in 1965, predicted that microchip miniaturization would lead to a doubling of computer power every eighteen months (Gleick 1999, 77).

6. It is not unreasonable to speculate that, since the text is in the public domain, the software developers included it only because they could add a title to the package without incurring an obligation to pay royalties.

7. For a more detailed analysis of these and other versions, see Kubo and Walter (1975).

8. In the words of Albert Borgmann, "The ideal limit of hyperreality is encyclopedic completeness" (1992, 88). This assessment of the new media coincides with Borgmann's broader analysis of the promise of modern technology: "Technology, as we have seen, promises to bring the forces of nature and culture under control, to liberate us from misery and toil, and to enrich our lives. . . . As a first step let us note that the notions of liberation and enrichment are joined in that of availability. Goods that are available to us enrich our lives and, if they are technologically available, they do so without imposing burdens on us. Something is available in this sense if it has been rendered instantaneous, ubiquitous, safe, and easy" (1987, 41). Also see chapter 8 "The Promise of Technology" and chapter 9 "The Device Paradigm" (1987) and his earlier description of availability in "Technology and Reality" (1987, 62). Borgmann provides other important treatments of technology (1972, 1978): his most extensive treatment of information technology appears in *Holding On to Reality, The Nature of Information at the Turn of the Millennium* (1999).

9. The process of improving stand-alone Bible study products will likely eventuate in the disappearance of such products in the strict sense (i.e., as true stand-alone products) since their ultimate "improvement" will lead developers to connect them to large databases on the Internet.

10. Some technologists and educational theorists advance the claim that electronic media are the preferred, if not only, instruments for reforming educational institutions and practices. Some attribute extraordinary capabilities to the new media and even speak of the computer's call (Hannafin and Savenye 1993, 26). Others admiringly describe the computer as the electronic doorway in educational restructuring (Solomon 1992, 327).

11. The idea is that in traditional models of education one (or a few) authority(ies) dispense information at their pleasure to others who must accept what they are offered. To illuminate this relationship, Oblinger and Maruyama employ the "factory model," in which students presumably are the workers and instructors the bosses (1996, 3). Borgmann, who is critical of this view, invokes ancient imagery from the book of Genesis. "In the traditional circumstances of education, as the proponents of technological information see them, the teacher is someone like Joseph, the governor of Egypt under the Pharaoh. The students are like Joseph's brothers who come asking for provender and must accept whatever Joseph parcels out" (1999, 205).

12. By way of analogy, consider the following telling incident from a public school setting recounted by David Pepi and Geoffrey Scheurman. They describe a college student who, as a requirement for a professional education course, had constructed a poster dealing with a contemporary educational problem. According to their account, the poster, which mainly presented comments from people across the country who had been discussing the topic through an electronic newsgroup, was eye-catching."The technology-enhanced beauty of the poster was breathtaking, and we spent the better part of a 10-minute encounter talking with the student about the various applications that contributed

to its aesthetic appeal. What we found troubling was how difficult it was to shift the discussion to the substantive issues the poster raised. When we finally asked the student to tell us about the nature of the dialogue on the issue, her response was immediate: I got it off the Internet. Looking at one of the more provocative statements, one of us asked about the context in which the comment was made. It was on a newsgroup on the Internet. We asked, Well, who made the statement? Where did he or she come from? Peering closely at her own poster, the student replied, I think he was from Seattle; I guess he's a teacher or something. I got it off the Internet" (1996, 232). Pepi and Scheurman lament that the student seemed to have understood the purpose of the assignment as using technology to collect information rather than as addressing the credibility of the information or the nature of the arguments. In this day and age when scripture resources are so widely available through the Internet, we should not be surprised to find cases in which students of the Bible similarly confuse the task of acquiring information with the higher order critical thinking process that leads

13. Among the findings Feuerherd (2001) cites are the following: Despite all the controversy about its placement on the public school walls, most Americans can name only half of the Ten Commandments; many Americans believe that the Sermon on the Mount was delivered by Dr. Billy Graham and that Joan of Arc is the name of Noah's wife; 80 percent of Christians who claim to be "born again" believe that the saying "God helps them that help themselves" (coined by Ben Franklin) is a quotation from the Bible; less than half of Americans, about 40 percent, read the Bible every week; and about 40 percent erroneously believe that the entire Bible was written after Jesus' birth.

14. The APA Delphi report describes critical reasoning as "purposeful, self-regulatory judgment. In this process we give reasoned consideration to the evidence, context, conceptualizations, methods, and criteria by which those judgments are made" (Facione 1990).

15. The California Academic Press, which has developed an assessment instrument called The California Critical Thinking Disposition Inventory (CCTDI), defines the disposition to think critically this way: "There is a characterological profile, a constellation of attitudes, a set of intellectual virtues, or, if you will, a group of habits of mind which we refer to as the overall disposition to think critically." "The ideal critical thinker is habitually inquisitive, well-informed, trustful of reason, open-minded, flexible, fair-minded in evaluation, honest in facing personal biases, prudent in making judgments, willing to reconsider, clear about issues, orderly in complex matters, diligent in seeking relevant information, reasonable in the selection of criteria, focused in inquiry, and persistent in seeking results which are as precise as the subject and the circumstances of inquiry permit." See their site at <http://www.calpress.com/cctdi.html>.

16. Facione's schema actually incorporates seven dispositions toward critical reasoning. He explains these seven habits as follows: Truth-seeking: Courageously desiring of best knowledge in any context, even if such knowl-

edge fails to support or may undermine one's own preconceptions, beliefs or self-interests; Open-Mindedness: Tolerant of divergent views, self-monitoring for possible bias; Analyticity: Demanding the application of reason and evidence, alert to problematic situations, inclined to anticipate consequences; Systematicity: Valuing organization, focus and diligence to approach problems of all levels of complexity; Inquisitiveness: Being curious and eager to acquire knowledge and learn explanations even when the applications of that information are not immediately apparent; Self-confidence in Reasoning: Trusting of one's own reasoning skills and seeing oneself as a good thinker; Cognitive Maturity: Prudence in making, suspending, or revising judgment, an awareness that multiple solutions can be acceptable, and an appreciation of the need to reach closure even in the absence of complete knowledge. [See Figure 3, p. 64, this volume. —Ed.]

17. I doubt that this is actually so but do not feel compelled to develop an argument at this point.

18. O'Leary and Brasher seem to acknowledge this point: "[W]e are willing to risk the claim that religious discourse on the global network shows signs of a new and vital response to the anomic condition that Philip Rieff has characterized as 'post-communal culture,' in which the breakdown of traditional social and religious institutions results in atomization and alienation of the self. While the traditional forms of religion appear to be flourishing in the new electronic forum, subtle changes are taking place and new genres of religious discourse, such as online prayer and cyber-rituals, are emerging" (1996, 243).

19. One of the populations until recently most resistant to trends in new media, the elderly, now seem to be increasingly willing not only to access resources and services online but also eager to seek out social interaction. According to David LaGesse, "The rush online by seniors, now the fastest-growing population of surfers, is just a hint of how technology might transform elderly lives. New products reach beyond the Internet's communication and entertainment features, promising to bolster independence for tomorrow's retirees while helping them fight the isolation and illness that can accompany aging" (2001, 78). Web sites devoted to the social interests of the elderly include <www.aarp.com>, <www.elderhostel.org>, <www.geezer.com>, <www.seniortheatre.com>, <www.seniornet.org>, <www.seniorjournal.com>, and <www. seniors-site.com> (2001, 78f.).

20. O'Leary and Brasher discuss current trends at some length (1996, 248ff.).

21. One of the remarkable incongruities associated with the Internet is that even though people think of it as the most public of all utilities (hardware and software developers and users almost universally believe that it should be allowed to expand without government control and corporate coercion and that it should function both as a vast world-wide public market place for commerce and as a public forum for exchanging ideas) they also believe that this market place/public forum should be accessible with the highest possible degree of pri-

vacy. We are left then with the intriguing notion of an open market place/public forum to which participants come, if not in disguise, at least anonymously—knowing no one and being known by no one. This incongruity shows up in part in the ambivalent view of increasing numbers of Internet users, who want not only to be connected electronically to as many people and places as possible but also to have their privacy protected. Thus, as Peter McGrath points out, "The world of ubiquitous computing raises a number of questions. High among them is the issue of inescapability. 'In practice,' says Livermore, president of enterprise computing at Hewlett-Packard, who says, 'the slogan *Any time, anywhere* means *All the time, everywhere.*' Even greater, though, is the problem of privacy, when pervasive in fact means invasive. There is no precedent for the idea of self-executing devices that are ubiquitous, networked and always on. If your car knows when you're intoxicated, why can't it also inform a police car. If a communicating pacemaker can tell your doctor that you're on the verge of a cardiac event, why can't it also tell your insurance company" (McGrath 2000, 72f.). For some recent analysis of privacy issues in cyberspace, see Branscum 2000; "Cyberprivacy: How Savvy is the Public?"; "Green et al 2000; Levenson 1999; McGrath 1999; Sandberg 1999; "Service Offers Anonymity to Internet Users"; and Szalavitz 1999.

22. One of the twentieth century's seminal short works on dwelling is Martin Heidegger's essay "Building, Dwelling, Thinking" (1992). The term 'cyborg' derives from "cybernetic organism" and applies to artificial and augmented bodies animated by human intelligence. For a fuller discussion of cyborgs, see Mitchell (1995, 182) and O'Leary and Brasher (1996, 254f.). Paul Levenson suggests that the new media lead us to exchange a sense of location and place for an abstract and undifferentiated notion of spatiality and leave us disembodied. "When we are on the Net, we become illustrative of another of McLuhan's concepts. We become virtual—or, in McLuhan's vocabulary, 'discarnate'—meaning that, in cyberspace, our physical bodies play no role in our relationships. We might say that, on line, everybody is nobody. McLuhan noted the discarnate effect of, for instance, talking on the phone, and he wondered what impact the effect has on our morality. The on-line participant is incorporeal in the same interactive way as the person on the phone. Cyber sex, like phone sex, entails no physical risks, but on line we can be angels or devils. Romeos or Mata Haris. No wonder pornography is the best-selling business on the Internet. The Internet liberates not only prior media, but also our libidos" (1999, B11).

23. It cannot be assumed that most or even many people generally go online with the presumption that they will disclose themselves to others in any significant or personal way. Richard Seltzer, for example, believes that anonymity is one of the things that attracts people to the Internet (1995, ch. 7).

24. But neither could they be legitimately viewed as "short-cuts" or "replacements" for the disciplined activity of study.

25. I wish to thank my colleague Gary Liddle for reading and commenting on this essay.

References

Arlin, Patricia K. 1990.Wisdom: The Art of Problem Finding. In Robert J. Sternberg (ed.), *Wisdom: Its nature, Origins, and Development*, 230-43. Cambridge: Cambridge University Press.

Borgmann, Albert. 1992. *Crossing the Postmodern Divide*. Chicago: The University of Chicago Press.

_____. 1999. *Holding On to Reality: The Nature of Information at the Turn of the Millennium*. Chicago: The University of Chicago Press.

_____. 1972. Orientation in Technology. *Philosophy Today* 16: 135-47.

_____. 1987. *Technology and the Character of Contemporary Life, A Philosophical Inquiry*. Chicago: The University of Chicago Press.

_____. 1978. The Explanation of Technology. *Research in Philosophy and Technology* 1: 99-118.

Branscum, Deborah. 2000. Guarding Online Privacy. *Newsweek* 5 June: 77-78.

Bugbee, Henry. 1974. Education and the Style of Our Lives. *Profiles* [University of Montana] 6.4 (May): 4, 5.

Clark, Herbert H. 1996. *Using Language*. New York: Cambridge University Press.

Cohen, Sheldon, and Thomas A.Wills. 1985. Stress, Social Support, and the Buffering Hypothesis. *Psychological Bulletin* 98.2 (Sept): 310-57.

Constant, David, Lee Sproull, and Sara Kiesler. 1996. The Kindness of Strangers: On the Usefulness of Electronic Weak Ties for Technical Advice. *Organization Science* 7.2 (Mar/Apr): 119-35.

Cyberprivacy: How Savvy is the Public? 2000. *Business Week* 20 Mar.: 96.

della Cava, Marco R. 2001. Stress Short-circuits Tech Families' Lives. *U.S.A. Today* 29 Jan, D 1+.

Ehrmann, Stephen C. 1995. Moving Beyond Campus-Bound Education. *Chronicle of Higher Education*, 7 July, B1-B2.

Facione, Peter A. 1990. *Critical Thinking: A Statement of Expert Consensus for Purposes of Educational Assessment and Instruction* [American Philosophical Association Delphi Report]. ERIC Doc. NO.: ED 315423.

_____. 2000. Reasoned Judgment and Revelation: The Relation of Critical Thinking and Bible Study. Presented at New Voices, New Views: Thinking About Bible Study in the Twenty-first Century. A conference hosted by the American Bible Society, New York, New York, 11 February.

Feuerherd, Peter. 2001. Scriptural Literacy. *Record* [American Bible Society]. Apr.-May: 12-13.

Gleick, James. 1999. *Faster: The Acceleration of Just about Everything*. New York: Vintage Books.

Granovetter, Mark. 1973. The Strength of Weak Ties. *American Journal of Sociology* 78.2 (May): 1361-80.

Green, Heather, Mike France, Marcia Stepanek, and Amy Borrus. 2000. Online Privacy: It's Time for Rules in Wonderland. *Business Week* 20 Mar: 82-95.

Hannafin, Robert D., and Wilhelmina C. Savenye. 1993. Technology in the Classroom: The Teacher's New Role and Resistance to It. *Educational Technology* 33.6 (June): 26-31.

Heidegger, Martin. 1993. Building, Dwelling, Thinking, in David F. Krell (ed.), *Basic Writings* (revised and expanded edition), 347-63. New York: HarperSanFrancisco..

Honan, William H. 1999. College Freshmen's Internet Use a Way of Life, But Disparities Emerge. *New York Times*. 25 Jan, A11.

Katz James E., and Philip Aspden. 1997. A Nation of Strangers? *Communications of the ACM*, 40.12: 81-86.

Kim, Amy Jo. 2000. *Community Building on the Web: Secret Strategies for Successful Online Communities*. Berkeley, CA: Peachpit Press.

King, Patricia M., and Karen S. Kitchener. 1994. *Developing Reflective Judgment*. San Francisco: Jossey-Bass.

Krackhardt, David. 1994. The Strength of Strong Ties: The Importance of Philos in Organizations, in Nitin Nohria and Robert G. Eccles (eds.), *Networks and Organizations: Structure, Form, and Action*, 216-39. Boston: Harvard University Business School Press.

Kraut, Robert, Michael Patterson, Vicki Lundmark, Sara Kiesler, Tridas Mukopadhyay, and William Scherlis. 1998. Internet Paradox: A Social Technology That Reduces Social Involvement and Psychosocial Well-Being? *American Psychologist* 53.9 (Sept): 1017-31.

Kubo, Sakae and Walter Specht. 1975. *So Many Versions? Twentieth Century English Versions of the Bible*. Grand Rapids, Mich.: Zondervan.

LaGesse, David. 2001. Technology Can Lift Barriers for Seniors. *U.S. News & World Report*, 4 June: 78-79.

Leland, John. 2000. Searching for a Holy Spirit. *Newsweek* 8 May: 61-63.

Levenson, Paul. 1999 Millennial McLuhan: Clues for Deciphering the Digital Age. *Chronicle of Higher Education* 15 Oct: B10-11.

Levy, Steven. 1999. Wired for the Bottom Line. *Newsweek* 20 Sept.: 43-49.

McFarland, Ron, and Hugh Nichols, eds. 1988. *Norman Maclean*. Lewiston, Idaho: Confluence Press.

McGrath, Peter. 2000. If All the World's a Computer ... *Newsweek* 1 Jan: 72-73.

_____. 1999. Knowing You all too Well. *Newsweek* 29 Mar: 48-50.

Mitchell, William J. 1995. *City of Bits: Space, Place, and the Infobahn*. Cambridge: MIT Press.

Netting Answers on the Web. *U.S. News & World Report* 4 June 2001: 78,79.

Nicholaou, Nick B. 2000. Redeeming the Time. *Christianity Today* 26 April: special advertising section, 21+.

Nie, Norman. 2000. Internet Disconnect. *NewsHour with Jim Lehrer Transcript.* MacNeil-Lehrer Productions. 16 Feb.. <www.pbs.org/newshour/bb/cyberspace/jan-june00/disconnect_2-16.html, 2>.

Nie, Norman, and Lutz Erbring. 2000. Internet and Society: A Preliminary Report. Stanford Institute for the Quantitative Study of Society (SIQSS), Stanford University in cooperation with InterSurvey Inc. 16 Feb. <http://www.standord.edu/group/siqss/>

Oblinger, Diana G., and Mark K. Maruyama. 1996. Distributed Learning. CAUSE Professional Paper Series 14:14.

O'Leary, Stephen D., and Brenda E. Brasher. 1996. The Unknown God of the Internet: Religious Communication from the Ancient Agora to the Virtual Forum. In Charles Ess (ed.), *Philosophical Perspectives on Computer-Mediated Communication,* 233-269. Albany, NY: State University of New York Press.

Ong, Walter. 1982. *Orality and Literacy.* New York: Methuen, 1982.

O'Toole, Kathleen. 2000. Study Offers Look at How Internet is Changing Daily Life. Stanford University News Service, February 16.

Pepi, David, and Geoffrey Scheurman. 1996. The Emporer's New Computer: A Critical Look at Our Appetite for Computer Technology. *Journal of Teacher Education* 47.3 (May/June): 229-37.

Preece, Jenny. 2000. *Online Communities: Designing Usability and Supporting Sociability.* New York: Wiley, John & Sons.

Resnick, Lauren B. 1987. *Education and Learning to Think.* Washington, D.C.: National Academy Press.

Rheingold, Howard. 2000. *The Virtual Community: Homesteading on the Electronic Frontier,* revised edition. Cambridge Mass.: MIT Press.

Sandberg, Jared. 1999. Losing Your Good Name Online. *Newsweek* 20 Sept: 56,57.

Seltzer, Richard. 1995. *The Way of the Web.* Electronic book on diskette (IBM-HD). <http://www.samizdat.com/anon.html.>

Service Offers Anonymity to Internet Users. 1999. *News-Leader* [Springfield, Missouri]. 4 Dec:10A.

Soloman, G. 1992. The Computer as Electronic Doorway: Technology and the Promise of Empowerment. *Phi Delta Kappan* 74: 327-29.

Survey Shows Widespread Enthusiasm for High Technology. 2000. NPR Online 2 Mar. <http://www.npr.com/programs/specials/poll/technology.>

Szalavitz, Maia. 1999. Can We Become Caught in the Web? *Newsweek* 6 Dec: 11.

Tenner, Edward. 1996. *Why Things Bite Back: Technology and the Revenge of Unintended Consequences.* New York: Alfred A. Knopf.

Toffler, Alvin. 1991. *Powershift: Knowledge, Wealth, and Violence at the Edge of the 21st Century.* New York: Bantam Books.

Werry, Chris, and Miranda Mowbray, eds. 2000. *Online Communities: Commerce, Community Action, and the Virtual University.* Upper Saddle River, N.J.: Prentice Hall.

Zuboff, Shoshana. 1988. *In The Age Of The Smart Machine, The Future of Work and Power.* New York: Basic Books, 1988.

Middle Grounds

12

Bible Study, Critical Thinking, and Post-Critical Thought: Cultural Considerations

Phil Mullins

It is for us today to realise the difficulties of the modern mind to the full, and for us to accept these difficulties as our problem. (Polanyi 1997 [1962], 93)

Our appreciation of scientific value has developed historically . . . much as our sense of justice has taken shape from the outcome of judicial decisions through past centuries. Indeed, all our cultural values are the deposits of a similar historic succession of intellectual upheavals. But ultimately, all past mental strife can be interpreted today only in the light of what we ourselves decide to be the true outcome and lesson of this history. . . The lesson of history is what we ourselves accept as such. (Polanyi 1964 [1958], 158.)

Before it was fashionable to speak of postmodernism, the scientist-turned-philosopher Michael Polanyi argued that most minds shaped by modern western thought have deep-rooted, culturally destructive dispositions. But it was possible, and indeed incumbent upon us, he contended, to reconsider our patterns of thought and to take a stand today upon the controversies of intellectual history. Through this process, Polanyi argued, we can move toward what he identified as "post-critical"[1] approaches to cultural endeavors. It may seem odd to launch a discussion of Bible study and critical thinking with quotations pointing rather broadly at the cultural problems and possibilities of the modern mind. Nevertheless, it is at just this macroscopic level that I believe much of the account of Bible study and critical thinking, and their possibilities, needs to be told. I try here to frame and unite comments treating Bible study and critical thinking within the context of the history of ideas. I thus begin by characterizing some of the dominant motifs in Bible study in late modernity. Following this introduction, I shift the discussion to describe the contemporary "postmodern" cultural terrain where new digital technology is further recasting many of the commitments of late modernity. In the final section, I review some of the discussions about critical thinking and try to recast some ideas about critical thinking in terms of what, with Polanyi, I call a post-critical perspective.

Interpreting the Bible in Late Modernity

Bible scholars in the middle of the twentieth century in the Euro-American world either accepted so-called "higher criticism" (sometimes termed "scientific," "higher critical" or just "critical" scholarship) or they were convinced that "higher criticism" was anathema. If they were partisans of "higher criticism," this meant they favored "historical-critical" approaches. That is, Bible texts were recognized as much like other ancient texts and should be treated so. Such approaches advocated strongly historicist notions of meaning that became dominant in late print culture (i.e., the nineteenth and much of the twentieth century). Over roughly the last four centuries, the idea developed and took firm root (i.e., became presuppositional for many) that the "original" or privileged meaning of a text is that appropriate to the text's earliest social context. Historicist perspectives try to explain (and some say explain away) any mystery in the text in terms of the earliest communicative milieu. Such an account resolves the text-as-problem into the earliest social context, for it is believed that only in this locus is it possible to definitively delineate meaning.

Although one can find evidence of these or similar hermeneutical commitments earlier (e.g., in the Renaissance), by the nineteenth century they became an underpinning for German historical scholarship and fared well in academic circles for over a century. How and why these commitments came to dominate is an interesting puzzle, but one that I can only allude to here; likely many elements contributed. The Renaissance interest in ancient languages and the past must have contributed. The Reformation's new attention to the Bible also certainly was important. The reformers insisted that the Bible, rather than the prevailing institutional power structure, was authoritative and must shape new cultural institutions. The emergence of pietistic but scholarly study of the Bible in new Reformation traditions was an important outgrowth of such convictions. Pietistic scholarship invited scrutiny of diverse interpretations. As I note later, the emergence of philosophical rationalism with notions about the heuristic value of doubt and the coming of the new science also have helped shape hermeneutical commitments. Finally, I expect that the mere proliferation of printed texts, after the sixteenth century development of movable type, contributed to the notion that texts belong to a particular social context.

By privileging a particular social context, the "original context of meaning," the notion of meaning as part of every social context for a living text became philosophically complicated in modernity. Is tradition no more than the accumulated residue of misconstruals piled on a kernel of authentic meaning? What is the connection between the privileged meaning context and the meaning contexts that follow? How does one get into the so-called hermeneutic circle? One of the most celebrated late modern philosophers, Martin Heidegger, spent much effort in *Being and Time* to show that we always already are in the circle and the problem is getting disposed or attuned in the right way (Heidegger 1962, 194f.). Most of these questions about meaning can be reformulated as questions about the nature of history itself. What does it mean to acknowledge that understanding history is always an affair located in history? Are there in fact multiple locations within history from which to seek an account of past events? Should one assume that any account of the past made from within a place in history can provide impersonal, universal knowledge? These kinds of broad questions historical-critical Bible scholars have struggled with in the modern period; even more often, philosophers and theologians have wrestled with them and Bible scholars have tried to take over particular accounts to provide a foundation for their work.

The notion of a "sacred" text is a problematic notion to modern historical-critical scholars. In essence, acceptance of historical-critical approaches to the Bible has entailed radically reconstituting the "sacredness" (to a community) of the Bible, in the interest of understanding the Bible in a particular social context. Rudolph Bultmann, in the middle of the twentieth century, perhaps offers the most straightforward example of such a reconstitution. He represents the way in which historical-critical suppositions led to philosophical and theological questions, like those noted above, which ultimately had to be addressed. As Stephen Gunter notes, Bultmann sharply separated the faith of the New Testament from the worldview of the New Testament, and he recognized this worldview as sharply different than the modern worldview (Gunter 1999, 41). Surely Bultmann was correct that worldviews seem to differ in different eras and cultures, but what Bultmann believed this pluralism called for seems much more dubious today. He announced a program for demythologizing the New Testament, which is a strategy for picking out the understanding of existence found in the New Testament while not being mislead by the imagery of the social context of the writers. As Stephen Gunter puts it, "it is a method of interpreting the mythological understanding of humanity held by the New Testament so that it becomes comprehensible to its hearer and compels one to make a decision 'for oneself' with regard to the proclamation that has been heard" (1999, 41). Under the influence of existentialist thinkers, Bultmann thus claimed the Bible has in disguised form a certain existential relevance or power for today. The "sacredness" of the Bible was recast in the dress of existential philosophy or a theology predominantly shaped by existentialism.

Bultmann provides a good late modern example of an aspect of what Charles McCoy terms the dominant "Constantinian paradigm"[2] so often found in Western Christian theology, and secondarily in scholarly Bible study: a currently attractive philosophical perspective (in this case existentialist thought) is borrowed and becomes a vehicle with which to organize or transform the blooming, buzzing confusion and diversity of human action. The plurality of human belief and practice found in history and in cross-cultural exploration is recognized only as a "problem" which requires discerning some underlying structure, essence or human potential that at least in principle overcomes the problem. With this Rosetta stone, imperial proclamations can be made which suggest that theologians "assume that they occupy a transcendent perspective, an ontological peak, outside and above the limited perspectives of historical and social location" (McCoy 1980, 29) The problem here is that we forget we are in history—and often a particular fashionable philosophical perspective seems to aid this forgetfulness on the part of theologians and Bible scholars. McCoy suggests the diversity of history ought to offer an occasion for reforming the commitments of persons and communities but this is hampered by our readiness to move forward with ontological generalizations.

It is not only the mid-century thinking of philosophically inclined, historical-critical modern Bible scholars like Bultmann that today seems tortured. Modern conservative Bible scholars across the divide from Bultmann who were dead set against "higher criticism" seem equally strange. Such interpreters, very common in Bultmann's era but also still present today, were not "uncritical" in the sense that they refused to reason, but they reasoned in ways that did not presuppose historical-critical assumptions. But most often those who take more literalist approaches to the Bible are heirs to centuries of print culture in which mass literacy and the transparency of texts are presumed. They rarely explore the ways in which print culture's presuppositions inform their views. The Bible for literalists is imagined not as a complex historically fixed document that must be existentialized, but as a beacon capable of producing illumination visible across the ages to those who diligently attend to it. In late print culture, the printed word, and perhaps especially the printed Bible, is often tacitly presupposed as an unmediated representation of what is. That is, the Bible is taken by literalists to be "revelation" from God, and to so identify it solves many interpretative problems. To respect, honor and understand God's intentions primarily requires better quality attention to a text.[3] In a certain sense, for the literalist, the complications of social location and diversity are overcome by overlooking them. The "problems" of history—problems for figures like Bultmann—are not on the radar screen because there are, for literalists, different underlying assumptions about what a deity is — that is, in particular how God, as an active and revealing deity, works in history. Many of the literalist assumptions about what past events are and the nature of our access to them are akin to figures like Bultmann. Stephen Gunter suggests "fundamentalist literalism that insists on certainty and factuality is itself a narrow expression of modernism, a victim of historicism. The irony is that this conservatism is predicated on the historical assumptions of modernism" (Gunter 1999, 68). The objectivist outlook of literalists, one that holds there are simple facts that can guide us to absolute certainty, is the naïve byproduct of a scientistic culture. In such a culture, science is a dominant force, although the presuppositions, methods and conclusions of science are simplistically misrepresented in the culture's worldview. It is just this sort of misrepresentation that has dominated Western culture under the influence of the Enlightenment in much of the twentieth century.

Finally, let us gather together the historical-critical and objectivist literalist approaches to the Bible by borrowing a sympathetic note or two from Umberto Eco's analysis about the history of ideas of interpretation. Both approaches, in Eco's schematization assume "that to interpret a text means to find out the meaning intended by its original author or - in any case - its objective nature or essence, an essence which, as such is independent of our interpretation" (Eco 1995, 205). Each approach is a permutation of an interpretative option grounded in "epistemological fanaticism" and is "instantiated by various kinds of fundamentalism and various forms of metaphysical realism..." (ibid).

The Great Change: Emerging Postmodern Hermeneutics

In the last third of the twentieth century, there emerged in the Euro-American academy a great awakening in literary and philosophical studies that produced enormous interest in language, literary critical theory and methodology, philosophy of science, sociology of knowledge and communication studies. We now call the literature generated by this movement "postmodern" philosophy and cultural studies for it seems to have displaced many of the literary and philosophical concerns and assumptions of mid century.

There is much discussion, of course, about what "postmodern" thought is and how it is distinguished from what preceded it. David Griffin has suggested that "*postmodernism* refers to a diffuse sentiment rather than any common set of doctrines—the sentiment that humanity can and must go beyond the modern" (2000, x). Extending the logic of this comment, James Mehl, a Renaissance historian, has argued that there is a new historical self-consciousness at the end of the old millennium and the beginning of the new. Ours is a period of rapid cultural change and it is perhaps best understood, according to Mehl, with a model of a similar period, the Renaissance. The present transitional time should be seen in terms of what he calls a "layered development" in which both the modern and the new are intertwined (2000, 411). Lyotard, in *The Postmodern Condition: A Report on Knowledge*, pointed to the problem of meaning in contemporary culture in his famous one line effort to specify the "postmodern" cultural mood: "I define *postmodern* as incredulity toward metanarratives" (1984, xxiv). He spoke of the "obsolescence of the metanarrative apparatus of legitimation" (ibid). Grand narratives seem to have lost plausibility; they no longer work very well to integrate society and inspire and justify action. On a note akin to Lyotard's perspective, Griffin followed up, in his discussion of contemporary philosophical and theological thought, his claim that postmodern sentiment aims to go beyond the modern: it is, he argued, important to distinguish deconstructive, relativistic or eliminative postmodern thought from revisionary or reconstructive postmodern thought. Deconstructive thought aims to upset or eliminate "various concepts that have generally been thought necessary for a worldview, such as self, purpose, meaning, a real world, givenness, reason, truth as correspondence, universally valid norms and divinity" (Griffin 2000, xi). Reconstructive thought

> seeks to overcome the modern worldview not by eliminating the possibility of worldviews (or "metanarratives") as such, but by constructing a postmodern worldview through a revision of modern premises and traditional concepts in the light of inescapable presuppositions of our various modes of practice. (*ibid*)

The suggestions of all of these cultural critics are helpful for understanding something of the ambience of contemporary culture and the changes in the late twentieth century that led to it. If, however, I had to select a single axis around which to organize thinking about the emergent reorientation that is associated with so-called postmodern literature and culture, I would point to an epistemological stance that has shifted significantly since the middle of the last century. At least in the West, many cultural leaders and intellectuals no longer believe that knowledge is or can be fully objective and impersonal. Nor is there confidence that a growing edifice of knowledge is assuring that human kind is "making progress." This does not necessarily mean that science is less important in shaping culture and human outlooks; in fact, I believe science and technology is perhaps more important in molding human beliefs and practices as we enter the new millennium than it was in the middle of the twentieth century. As I note below, new digital communications technology is likely reinforcing if not helping to create, the post-objectivist cultural mood. What, however, seems most definitive is that the cultural images suggesting what knowledge is, how it is formed, and who it serves have shifted significantly over the last fifty years. Knowledge has became widely recognized as socially generated, paradigm dependent, and permeated by interests and allocations of power. It is this sort of epistemological change that has lead philosophers and religious thinkers toward what Giffin sees as the twin paths of deconstructive and reconstructive appropriations of the modern.

The early phase of the literary and philosophical great awakening that we now call postmodern thought (i.e., literary and philosophical writing from roughly 1970 to 1990), came, in rich first world societies, at almost the same time as the widespread emergence of the personal computer. The computer is what Jay David Bolter terms a "defining" technology. By this he means that it is redefining the human role in relation to nature. The human being is now acquiring new definition as an "information processor" while nature is becoming "information to be processed"(1984, 13). Digital tools have now become widely available and used for communication. More and more, North Americans are socialized to use and accept the computer and cyberspace, the world of networked computers, just as they do the telephone or other now second-nature communication tools. The computer has complemented and sometimes supplanted other communication tools. As interactive, integrated digital communication artifacts proliferate, the tacitly held values and the mental habits of earlier print culture are being transformed; they are migrating toward what Myron Tuman terms "online literacy" (1992, 22). Our larger sense of what "communication" involves, our ideas about what "reading," and "writing" and "listening" are, and ultimately our notions about the nature of "knowledge" are leveraged by our practices using the computer.

As we enter the new millennium, what can be called digital culture has begun to supplant the culture of print; slowly, across the world, this successor to book culture is taking shape as phenomena such as electronic writing and the World Wide Web have proliferated. The mental habits of those exposed to digital communication have begun subtly to shift from the tacit dispositions that print culture nurtures. The emergence and proliferation of networked computers has produced the contemporary super-saturated information environment. The seedbed within which digital tools could quickly take root was, of course, the world of broadcast media which already had come to shape popular culture by the late twentieth century, reinvigorating our sense of the aural and pictographic. Tex Sample offers an important insight about emergent culture when he identifies what he terms "spectacle" as a primary artifactual type or category in contemporary culture:

> Spectacle is a basic and indigenous practice in electronic culture whenever we find a full-blown use of image, sound as beat, and visualization. Indeed, it is the augmented power of these electron-

ic factors that enhances a spectacle's capacity and makes it even more captivating. (1998, 57).

Sample has in mind, as a model of the spectacle, primarily rock concerts, sports events, public celebrations and similar events in which people gather and become emotionally engaged as they focus on a common object. The spectacle is an increasingly common occasion or practice through which we make or discover and enjoy meaning. Clearly, the popularity of the spectacle owes much to the broadcast and film industries. I suggest, however, that it is the virtual world of integrated, interactive digital media that is another increasingly important domain of the spectacle; perhaps the virtual world soon will be regarded as more spectacular than the non-virtual world of special electronically mediated events. Digital communication artifacts, proliferating by the minute in cyberspace, gravitate toward the spectacle. It seems likely that spending more time online leads people to expect that which is meaningful to have more features of spectacle—including participation via the interactive dimensions of online communication.

The online environment is one in which postmodern epistemological commitments readily become second nature. In cyberspace, it is easy to recognize that "information" is grounded in a particular social context and rests upon certain presupposed values and visions; it is clear that interests shape information, and information aims to produce certain effects which inevitably fit into some political context. For example, the way in which advertising has come to be so much a part of "information" provided (whether you like it or not) on the Web readily illustrates this. But our sense of the perspectival and socially grounded nature of information in the electronic world is broader than the simple case of crass advertisement.. The birth of digital culture seems to have dovetailed seamlessly with the emergence of literature and philosophy that is articulating postmodern perspectives.

Postmodern digital culture is an interesting and confusing climate within which study and promotion of the Bible is occurring in the opening decade of the twenty-first century. The renaissance in literary studies influenced scholarly biblical studies, giving birth to a variety of scholarly approaches to the text. This effectively undermined naïve historicist approaches supported by many Western academics in late book culture (Jim Voelz' essay in this volume draws a similar conclusion). However, it had little effect on some theologically conservative Bible studies other than perhaps to deepen ideological divisions. A more literalist interpretive approach can be blended with spectacular use of the Bible (e.g., in worship) in ways that merely reinforce existing interpretative habits. Digital tools themselves, of course, also create many new questions for Bible study, questions such as those about the possibility and legitimacy of "transmediated" text (see, for example, Lindvall's discussion in this volume.) Not only serious philosophical questions have emerged from the digital revolution, but also new complications in the cultural politics of religious diversity have emerged as digital tools begin to serve the many different institutional religious masters with different agendas. For some, digital tools are no more than a new avenue for marketing, and nothing sells like high technology products with the imprimatur of the sacred text.

Biblical studies and Bible-related cultural initiatives are radically pluralistic today. Insightful (and somewhat blunt) statements such as the following by Bible scholars identifying the limitations of the recent paradigm for Bible study are not hard to find:

> The pervasive modern emphasis on the objective recovery of the ancient context in which biblical texts were produced has had the double effect of obscuring the significance of the Bible in contemporary Western culture and of turning the Bible into an historical relic, an antiquarian artifact. It has also produced a modern biblical scholarship that, for many, has become a curatorial science in which the text is fetishized, its readings routinized, its readers bureaucratized. Moreover, historical criticism has implicitly veiled the historical character of biblical scholarship's entanglements with modernity and has therefore left unexamined its own critical and theoretical assumptions as well as the cultural conditions that produced, sustained, and validated them. (Aichele et al 1995, 2).

As we enter a new millennium, there is no broadly shared new paradigm about how to study the Bible or how the Bible might be a resource in postmodern culture. Psychoanalytic, feminist, structuralist, deconstructive, rhetorical and many other approaches to reading the Bible are extant today. Is such pluralism a threat or an opportunity or both? Certainly, it has been an opportunity insofar as it has allowed a thousand flowers to bloom, including some non-Eurocentric flowers. But the danger of such sporting is that it at least seems that the logic of affiliation and the grounds of continuity get lost when there is only diversity and the politics of interpretation.

Critical Thinking and Post Critical Thought

Can critical thinking reorient us in the postmodern digital world? Can it knit together the many efforts in digital culture to use (or exploit) the Bible as a sacred or simply an old text? Can it lead us to a new paradigm to supplant the historical-critical paradigm or the twin paradigm approach (historical-critical versus literalism) that seemed to dominate before the emergence of postmodern literature and digital tools? I am not convinced that such questions can be directly and simply answered. Nevertheless, the context of their emergence can be highlighted in a way that is illuminating. Below I comment on the possibilities of "critical thinking" understood at three different levels.

Some, of course, hope that "critical thinking," understood simply as developing logical acumen, can be used to tether the postmodern digital world which seems to move in all directions at a gallop (the Bachmans' article in this volume seems close to this hope). It seems likely that honing logic skills cannot accomplish this, if by "tether" one nostalgically hopes ultimately to recover the sort of knowledge-stable world of late print culture. The postmodern digital world is a place of radical plurality and rapid transformation. Human attention has a center, but that which is at the periphery can and quickly does become central in a world shaped by networked computers. The meaning of "meaning" has shifted away from notions in which texts could be imagined as containers with stable content inside. In a digital era, "meaning" increasingly points to a kind of absorption in the immediacy of the multi-sensate spectacle. We seek and savor participatory feeling rather than critical distance. Lindemann (see her essay in this volume) sees the potential to transform this new interest in participation into meditative reading; she hopes to see some of the traditions of earlier illuminated manuscripts reborn in the web page. Surely, however, radical plurality and rapid transformation as features of the web world work against meditative reflection. In fact, a fast moving, multi-sensate electronic reading/writing/thinking environment hampers the germination of critical questions about electronic artifacts. The web environment is unstable or volatile by nature. The emphasis in such reading/writing/thinking space is upon revision, malleability and/or the center-infinite periphery connection that can be quickly transformed. Admittedly, for many nurtured rather exclusively by book culture (i.e., most intellectuals), cultivating logical acumen is a strategy that has great appeal in the face of the rush of digital multimedia and the uncertainties of postmodern ideas. Logic seems just the medicine called for to make digital culture

become a more rational space. And it remains true that study of fallacies and logic can no doubt support rational discourse. But such an
approach is one that fundamentally misreads the epistemological
changes embedded in the shift to postmodern digital culture.

In the last decades of the twentieth century, a critical thinking-
across-the-curriculum movement emerged in many colleges and universities. The movement has been broad based—more so than efforts
simply to renew the teaching of logic—since it draws extensively upon
research in areas such as cognitive and moral development. It has
aimed, in a wide-visioned sense, at improving human ability to form
reasoned and reflective judgments. Peter Facione, an articulate
spokesperson for this movement, has pointed out that critical thinking
broadly understood works to nurture a disposition toward such values
as truth-seeking, open-mindedness, inquisitiveness and reliance upon
analytical and systematic approaches to inquiry (see Facione's article in
this volume). He suggests that nurturing a critical thinking disposition
relies upon the cultivation and refinement of cognitive skills, including,
but not limited to, drawing logical inferences.

It seems clear that this broad-based critical thinking-across-the-
curriculum movement is an effort in colleges and universities to encourage institutions to take seriously the development of what once was
termed the generally educated, intellectually curious person. Higher
education has increasingly become a domain of technical and specialist
training. But educational institutions at lower and higher levels do not
seem, on a wide scale, to inculcate in students a commitment to disciplined inquiry. The Socratic notion that life should be examined now
seems to many in Western culture a strange dictum. Narrowness of
interest and limited inquisitiveness (i.e., the failure to seek a coherent
account of things) enfeeble institutions and have deleterious consequences in the civic arena. Supporting a movement that works across
the curriculum to inspire and invigorate inquiry seems to be a natural
and commonsensical affirmation, at least for educators. How could
there be opposition to values and practices that ground educational
institutions? However, the critical thinking movement needs to avoid
nostalgia for book culture and to appreciate both the strengths and
weaknesses of postmodern digital culture. Most importantly, it needs
what I term a post-critical vision of reason in order properly to situate
an appreciation of critical faculties and inquiry. I turn in the following
discussion to comments on these matters.

In many ways, postmodern pluralistic suppositions about knowledge and ecstatic notions about meaning are a relief from the narrow scientific objectivism of late modernity produced by Enlightenment ideals
reinforced by print. Such postmodern suppositions foster creativity and
wariness about the subtle ways in which cultural and/or political hegemony works. Notions of meaning that move beyond the narrowly rational open us up to riches of symbol and sense that have been diminished
and deprecated in modernity. Too frequently, however, postmodernists
celebrate a vision of knowledge as altogether relative and subjective.
Such a vision remains within the same frame of reference that produced
objectivism in the culture of the Enlightenment. Is knowledge objective
and correspondent to an external world or subjective and reflective of
human interests and struggles for power and meaning? This question is
posed by many today but it is primarily an answer masquerading as a
question. It invokes two values or metaphysical and epistemological
frames of reference and assumes that they cover the options. Why must
knowledge be either objective or subjective? Why must thinking about
human efforts to orient ourselves in the world be linked only to an ideal
of absolute impersonality or the absence of such an ideal? Why must we
take truth to be correspondence to external affairs or merely the reflection of the power politics of interpretation?

Western culture began developing this bifurcated way of constru-
ing matters at the beginning of modernity when Descartes separated
mind and matter and recommended doubt as the principle that can help
the extraordinarily capable reasoning mind find truth. The separation of
mind and matter leads to peculiar visions of the human and of our participation in the rest of the created order. We imagine ourselves as fundamentally separate and distinct from the environment that nurtures us.
The philosophical tradition came to see even human beings as divided
or separated, hence there emerged "the mind-body problem." Once on
the path set by Cartesian rationalism or its empirical successors, we
have great difficulty imagining the ways in which we are members of
the environing world and of one another. We have no sense of how we
extend ourselves and transform our vision and our identity through our
dwelling in the other. Because we see ourselves as thinking subjects
independent of the world, we overestimate our own capacities for discernment. We don't see how our activity in the world and with our
social companions provides instructive resistance that allows us to
reconstruct our dispositions, but we believe that sheer willful doubt can
purify our vision. Enshrining doubt as the gateway to truth has primari-

ly served, in the modern period, to undermine traditional beliefs and the fiduciary foundations of inquiry. The critical stream of Western philosophical thought has been naïve about the pervasiveness and the function of belief and of communities in which common beliefs and practices form a tradition. Because early science resisted the traditions of the Roman Catholic Church, all traditions came to be viewed as antithetical to critical inquiry. This critical stream of thought has overvalued formalization and has held up an impossible ideal of objective knowledge that amounts to a knowledge independent of any human knowers and of any communities in which such knowers are nurtured and in which such knowledge is valued.

The postmodern epistemological shift has challenged many elements of Enlightenment objectivism, but much postmodern thought continues in the venue that all modern thought has taken. Many postmodernists seem merely to have made a substitution for the high value placed upon suppositions about doubt, critical rationalism and objectivism in Enlightenment culture: the reigning postmodern assumption is that power and interest are inevitably the keys to what counts as knowledge.[4] Just as overestimates of the importance of doubt and mental acuity have led to a misunderstanding of belief and its importance in the modern philosophical tradition, so overestimates of the importance of power and interest are leading today to postmodern misunderstandings of the process of justifying and respecting belief.[5]

Much of postmodern thought seems to share what Charles Sanders Peirce identified as the nominalist cast of all modern thought.[6] In dubbing modern thought "nominalist," Mary Keeler suggests that Peirce was objecting to the philosophical preoccupation in modernity with questions about how knowledge is possible from experience.[7] Peirce wanted to shift the focus of philosophy from the problem of knowledge to broader questions about how meaning is possible in experience. That is, philosophy needs to examine the conditions for meaning to occur; it needs to broadly consider the ongoing, public process of making meaning rather than the narrower concern with the problem of knowledge. Put in ontological language, Peirce's complaint was that modern thought recognizes "but one mode of being, that being of an individual thing or fact, the being which consists in the object's crowding out a place for itself in the universe, so to speak, and reacting by brute force of fact, against all other things." (CP 1.21) Peirce held that rather than one mode of being there are three: "They are the being of positive qualitative possibility, the being of actual fact, and the being of law that will govern facts in the future." (CP 1.23) It is particularly the nature of laws (i.e., generalities or "universals") that Peirce held have been misconstrued in modernity, for modern thinkers consider laws, which are essentially predictions about the future, to be "a mere word or couple of words." (CP 1.26) That is, laws or generalities are viewed as in the mind only and as having no existence as independent realities. Peirce thinks this is an impoverished, static account of reality which is grounded in false ideas about representation. Modern and now post-modern thinkers cannot appreciate the evolution of meaning because they undervalue signs, reading them in a dyadic rather than a triadic scheme. For most moderns and postmoderns, meaning is not always unfolding in the sign process, but is either an objective or a subjective phenomenon. Such a misconstrual of signs, Peirce thinks, reflects the modern commitment to a single mode of being. The "nominalism" of modernity, as Keeler puts it, is concerned with the "assumption that we can capture meaning in representational structures (of any kind)..." (1998, 169). Human beings, especially in modernity and now in post-modernity, seem too readily to believe that particular representations are final or privileged, but such privileging serves primarily to impede further inquiry. Peirce tries to set forth a system in which the growth of meaning is central; his emphasis is upon a triadic method of logical investigation that focuses upon the way in which signs work in an ongoing cycle. As Keeler notes, "nominalism leaves our individual views hopelessly relative," while Peirce's approach counters individualism and relativism: "the essential continuity of experience, giving it coherence and tendency, in which meaning is always a possibility in the future, is the fundamental theoretical hypothesis of Peirce's pragmatism...." (1998, 170). Peirce's thought is through and through fallabilistic even while affirming the importance of careful reasoning: pragmatism invites us to build meaning "by provisionally believing that we have captured meaning in concepts and categories—while continuing to examine them critically, from as many points of view as possible" (Keeler 1998, 171).

If a critical thinking movement is to be truly helpful for sorting thorough some of the questions about the Bible in digital culture, I expect that the study of how to cultivate a critical thinking disposition will needs to be enriched by the development of a broader post-critical and semiotic philosophical perspective. That is, the critical thinking across the curriculum movement needs to be informed by incisive criticisms of the patterns of philosophical conceptions found in modernity and in emerging postmodern digital culture. But we must go beyond mere criticisms of the philosophical presuppositions of the last several centuries. We must hammer out basic elements of a constructive philosophical stance that gets around the philosophical cul de sac, in which we have and continue to wander. I believe that the philosophical work of two thinkers, Michael Polanyi and Charles Sanders Peirce, are particularly helpful for both criticizing the critical tradition of modern thought and for reconstructing the modern tradition.

As I noted at the beginning of this essay, "post-critical" is Michael Polanyi's term for the turn that he believes is necessary in the Western tradition of thought. As Jerry Gill puts it, Polanyi, like many postmodern thinkers, is not a foundationalist, although "he continued to maintain that there is a viable grounding, albeit of a different sort, for human cognitive activity" (2000, 8). What Polanyi does is look for that grounding in the tacit foundation of explicit knowledge. That is, Polanyi argues that we need a new and broader notion of knowledge and the process of knowing. In Keeler's terms used above to describe Peirce's reorientation of philosophy, Polanyi shifts the account of the problem of knowledge to a broader account of meaning. Such a new account acknowledges both the explicit (that before the mind's eye which can be formalized) and the subsidiarily held foundation of beliefs and skills (i.e., beliefs internalized as human capacities to respond) upon which a person relies for achieving any explicit or focal knowledge. Polanyi argues that doubt is not heuristic and that belief is the norm in human affairs; belief or patterns of belief always undergird particular dispositions for human response. That is, a fabric of belief not explicitly known but tacitly relied upon, underpins human response, and that includes the disposition we term a capacity for critical thinking or inquiry. Belief, however, must be related to a tradition of thought and practice that serves as its foundation. Skill in reasoning and the capacity to be reasonable can only grow in the soil of a particular tradition.[8] In Polanyi's view, that soil must support independent thinking, even when such thinking goes against the grain. Such independence is possible when the members of a community affirm (i.e., the living tradition of the community makes clear) that there are realities not dependent upon your or my opinions about them, realities that can be known and about which there can be agreement eventually, even though the meaning of such realities grows and develops in history.[9] A post-critical stance is one that must recover from the typical postmodern embarrassment that surfaces when talking of "truth." Although certain notions of "truth" (e.g., simple correspondence) are not viable, this does not mean that the insistence of realities can be dismissed; the public character of knowledge and the universal intent found in the commitment of serious investigators must be respected. Rather than discarding "truth," it is necessary to re-root it in human responsibility and human communities. A post-critical perspective embraces a certain wonder before the world as well as a deep curiosity about the world. It values inquiry even while recognizing that discoveries bear indeterminately upon the future; the veridical aspect of meaning always points ahead of us.

Finally, let me put the case for a post-critical turn in semiotic terms, an idiom that comes from the constructive thought of Charles Sanders Peirce. The emerging digital era appears to be a time that calls for the re-evaluation of reason and critical thinking along with it; such a reevaluation must situate reason within the broader framework of semiosis, the operation of signs in the world. Michael Raposa provides a straightforward account (drawn upon the often-obtuse Peirce) of semiosis:

> Semiosis is an interpretative process that involves the continuous production of new signs, each itself subject to further interpretation. Human experience, from the simplest sensations and emotions to the most complex judgments about states of affairs, takes the form of semiosis. (1999, 143)

Objects, events and ideas in the world give rise to signs that shape (i.e., they make an impact or impression upon) persons as well as succeeding events. Such impressions (of signs upon us and the world) themselves become succeeding signs giving shape to further impacts in an on-going continuum. It is the breadth and the depth of such a semiotic perspective that recasts some of the philosophical dualisms of modernity. A semiotic perspective rescues the philosophical tradition from some of the metaphysical and epistemological axes that have become presuppositional for asking critical questions: subjective-objective, phenomenal-noumenal, body-mind, percepts-concepts, mind-matter—these and other axes are recast in Peirce's triadic framework. Objects give rise to signs; signs represent objects in some respect to those persons or things whom signs impact or impress. Such persons are linked through the sign to the object. But the impact or impression made upon persons or things becomes a sign in the ongoing flow of time. This triadic semiotic perspective, although it initially seems a complicated scheme, helps us see human critical powers in their broadest context. Human reason is our effort to coordinate and control the impact of signs in human communities; it is the primary vehicle through which we struggle to be responsible members of a particular interpretive matrix. Human beings are forever engaged in sign or sense reading endeavors as well as sign or sense giving responses. We live in a meaningful world and participate in the change and growth of meaning. While our sign reading is certainly subject to error, it is also the case that critical thought or inquiry provides our access to the continuity of signs.

If we hope to develop critical thinking as a disciplined commitment to inquiry that can help us appreciate the Bible in an era of digital communication, we need to explore the triadic logic of a semiotic perspective. Such a post-critical semiotic perspective will take us beyond the historicist versus literalist debates about the Bible of late modernity. But it will also move us beyond the sort of postmodern perspective that rediscovers the Bible at the price of collapsing meaning into the politics of power and interests. Critical thinking about the Bible that is grounded in a post-critical and semiotic perspective will recognize that inquiry is an ongoing endeavor grounded in the richness of tradition, an endeavor in which the growth of meaning unfolds in history.

Notes

1. Note that this is the subtitle for Polanyi's *Personal Knowledge* (1964). The discussion especially in the last section below makes an effort to set forth what "post-critical" means.

2. McCoy (1980, 69ff.). McCoy has much more to say about the Constantinian paradigm than I do here. Among other things, he points out that this is an outlook that often shrinks the interest and attentiveness of theologians to institutional Christianity and to academic accounts of religious faith. This outlook fails to examine and understand the varied religiosity in the dynamic historical environment other than to regard it as a problem. Such an outlook is preoccupied with formulating doctrines for a particular religious tradition. Faith or faithful living outside the enclave (i.e., action informed by other narratives, symbols and centers of value) is "secular" or at least the business of disciplines other than theology. The variety of human believing remains hidden or at least uninteresting other than as a threat. Once that variety is rediscovered, questions about appropriate methods for theological analysis become central. McCoy proposes a "covenantal or federal paradigm" which he suggests is "in continuity with the biblical Christian heritage, yet capable of coping with the pluralism and liberation of the emerging global culture" (77). Speaking as a Christian, using his federal paradigm, he sees the variety of human commitments as an opportunity rather than a threat.

3. See my essay "Sacred Text in the Sea of Texts: The Bible in North American Electronic Culture" (Mullins 1996, 280-284) for further discussion of psychodynamics of literalism.

4. It is something like this substitution that I think leads that master of the well-turned phrase Stanley Hauerwas to remark that "postmodernism is a far too comforting story for alienated intellectuals" (1999, 109).

5. Succeeding paragraphs discuss elements of what Polanyi regarded as a "post-critical" philosophy. One of those elements is clearly a new vision of the process of knowing and the nature of knowledge. Polanyi worked on the problem of knowledge in 1958 *magnum opus, Personal Knowledge*. But clearly there are other thinkers who share Polanyi's effort to effect a major shift in the philosophical tradition. In a recent book, *A Philosophical Testament*, Marjorie Grene (1995) has an excellent discussion of the postcritical account of knowledge as justified belief. Grene argues that the assumed categorical difference between knowledge and belief, running through the Western philosophical tradition since Plato, is problematic: we must correct the presumption that knowledge is necessary and universal and belief is contingent and parochial, and that the two have no connection with one another. As an alternative, Grene argues, we must "look at the knowledge claims we make and see how they are structured if we take them, not as separate from, but as part of, our system of beliefs" (1995, 15). She then proceeds to discuss what is involved in justification as a complex historical-social, rational and commitmental process. Grene is very clear that this reconception of knowledge is not merely a move to "subjectivize." She is a realist who holds that an authentic biological realism undercuts the dualistic approaches popular since Descartes. She defines her realist position as built on two theses: human beings exist within a real world and are surrounded by it and shaped by it and human beings are real. These fundamental affirmations she says are essentially an effort to get beyond the subject-object split and the split between in-here and out-there which "makes nonsense of a world that is living, complicated, messy as you like, but real. I am myself one instantiation of that world's character, one expression of it, able also, in an infinitesimal way, to shape and alter it" (1995, 114). As this comment implies, it is also important to recognize that the postcritical turn involves a re-visioning of what a person is and that includes our relation to nature and our fellow creatures. Grene summarizes matters this way in her "ecological epistemology" (1995, 26):

> . . . as human reality is one version of animal reality, so human knowledge is one species-specific version of the ways that animals possess to find their way around their environments. Granted, our modes of orientation in our surroundings are peculiarly dependent on the artifacts of culture. Culture mediates between ourselves and nature, and given the multiplicity of cultures, we appear, so far as we can tell to possess, or to be able to acquire, a very much greater variety of paths of access to reality than can members of other species. Now culture, and the artifacts of culture,

are of course of our own making and in the last analysis we accept their authority only on our own recognizances. But culture, rather than being a mere addendum to nature, a fiction supervenient on the naturally induced fictions of perception—culture, on our reading, while expressing a need inherent in our nature, is itself a part of nature. (1995, 144)

6. Charles Sanders Peirce argues that philosophy since Descartes has been extraordinarily nominalistic: "Thus in one word, all modern philosophy of every sect has been nominalistic." See volume 1, paragraph 19 (as well as the general context, paragraphs 15-27) of Pierce (1931-58), *Collected Papers of Charles Sanders Peirce*, ed. Arthur W. Burks, Charles Hartshorne, and Paul Weiss. 8 volumes. (Cambridge: Harvard University Press, 1931-58), cited hereafter in parenthesis by volume and paragraph (CP 1.19). I am suggesting that much of so-called "postmodern" thought simply continues this trend. It overcomes certain Cartesian problems but remains nominalistic. Below I suggest briefly what this nominalism consists of, although I cannot treat this large topic with any depth here. In the previous paragraph, I have briefly outlined the dubious substitutions that postmodern thought often seem to make for the values of Enlightenment thought. Identifying the "nominalism" of postmodern thought is another way to levy the same sort of criticism. That is, the nominalistic presupposition of much postmodern thought leads to misunderstandings of the process of justifying belief.

7. Mary Keeler (1998) provides a helpful general account (that I follow here) of Peirce's alternative to modern nominalism. Peirce actually goes back and reworks Scotus in order to become a particular kind of realist (see 1.16-1.26). It is beyond the scope of this essay to try to set forth in depth what Peirce means by either his scholastic realism or his charge that modern philosophical perspectives are nominalist.

8. This seems to me the best sense of what Augustine and his followers have affirmed in linking faith and reason. "Faith seeking understanding" is an acknowledgment that understanding is possible only when grounded in trusting appropriation of a grounding context.

9. Tradition and independent thought are not at odds; independent thought or free inquiry prospers within traditions that support it through an appropriate metaphysic and an appropriate governance structure within the community. I have in mind something like the best of the scientific tradition. Science teaches the importance of inquiry. It also values novelty even while it supports both rigorous procedures for discourse about the results of inquiry. In some ways these several values of scientific ideology and practice are held together (as mutually reinforcing) by the metaphysic of science which emphasizes the interesting realities of the cosmos are knowable but are not dependent upon any individual's opinions about them. For the ideas sketched in this paragraph, I am relying on the account of science provided by Michael Polanyi and Charles Sanders Peirce. The best brief summary of the way tradition and free

inquiry work together in science is Polanyi's "The Republic of Science: Its Political and Economic Theory" (1968, 49-72). This essay is also on the Web, <http://www.mwsc.edu/~polanyi>. Although it is an early essay, Peirce's brief "The Fixation of Belief" (available in almost every anthology of Peirce's writing, in CP 5.358-87, and on the Web, <http://www.peirce.org/writings/ p107.html>) provides a clear statement about how a certain conviction about reality grounds scientific work. Peirce's 1903 Harvard Lectures are an interesting later account of science in terms of logic. See Turrisi (1997) for both the lectures and commentary.

References

Aichele, George, et. al. (The Bible and Culture Collective). 1995. Introduction, *The Postmodern Bible*, 1-19. New Haven: Yale University Press.

Bolter, Jay David. 1984. *Turing's Man: Western Culture in the Computer Age*. Chapel Hill: University of North Carolina Press.

Eco, Umberto. 1995. Unlimited Semeiosis and Drift: Pragmaticism vs. Pragmatism, in Kenneth Laine Ketner (ed.), *Peirce and Contemporary Thought: Philosophical Inquiries,* 205-221. New York: Fordham University Press.

Gill, Jerry H. 2000. *The Tacit Mode: Michael Polanyi's Postmodern Philosophy*. Albany: SUNY Press.

Griffin, David. 2000. Introduction to SUNY Series in Constructive Postmodern Thought, in Jerry H. Gill, *The Tacit Mode: Michael Polanyi's Postmodern Philosophy*, ix-xiii. Albany: SUNY Press.

Grene, Marjorie. 1995. *A Philosophical Testament*. Chicago: Open Court.

Gunter, Stephen. 1999. *Resurrection Knowledge: Recovering the Gospel for A Postmodern Church*. Nashville: Abingdon.

Hauerwas, Stanley. 1999. Surviving Postmodernism: The University, the Global Market, and Christian Narrative, *Soundings*, Vol. LSSSII, No. 1-2 (Spring/Summer 1999): 107-125.

Heidegger, Martin. 1962. *Being and Time*. Trans. John Macquarrie and Edward Robinson. New York: Harper & Row.

Keeler, Mary. 1998. Iconic Indeterminacy and Human Creativity in C. S. Peirce's Manuscripts, in George Bornstein and Theresa Tinkle (eds.), *The Iconic Page in Manuscript, Print, and Digital Culture*, 157-93. Ann Arbor: University of Michigan Press.

Lyotard, Jean-François. 1984. *The Postmodern Condition: A Report on Knowledge. Theory and History of Literature*, Volume 10. Trans. Geoff Bennington and Brian Massumi. Minneapolis: University of Minneapolis Press.

McCoy, Charles S. 1980. *When Gods Change: Hope for Theology*. Nashville: Abingdon.

Mehl, James V. 2000. Drawing Parallels With the Renaissance: Late-Modernism, Postmodernism, and the Possibility of Historical Layering, *The Midwest Quarterly: A Journal of Contemporary Thought* (Vol. XLI, No. 4 Summer 2000): 401-15.

Mullins, Phil. 1996. Sacred Text in the Sea of Texts: The Bible in North American Electronic Culture, in Charles Ess (ed.), *Philosophical Perspectives on Computer-Mediated Communication*, 271-302. Albany: SUNY Press.

Pierce, Charles Sanders. 1931-58. *Collected Papers of Charles Sanders Peirce*, eds. Arthur W. Burks, Charles Hartshorne, and Paul Weiss. 8 volumes. Cambridge: Harvard University Press.

Polanyi, Michael. 1997 [1962]. History and Hope: An Analysis of our Age, in R.T. Allen (ed.), *Society, Economics and Philosophy: Selected Papers—Michael Polanyi*. New Brunswick: Transaction.

_____. 1964 [1958]. *Personal Knowledge: Towards a Post-Critical Philosophy*. New York: Harper Torchbook.

_____. 1968. The Republic of Science: Its Political and Economic Theory, in Marjorie Green (ed.), *Knowing and Being: Essays By Michael Polanyi*, 49-72. Chicago: University of Chicago Press.

Michael L. Raposa. 1999. *Boredom and the Religious Imagination*. Charlottesville: University Press of Virginia.

Sample, Tex. 1998. *The Spectacle of Worship in a Wired World: Electronic Culture and the Gathered People of God*. Nashville: Abingdon Press.

Tuman, Myron C. 1992. *Word Perfect: Literacy in the Computer Age*. Pittsburgh: University of Pittsburgh Press.

Turrisi, Patricia Ann. 1997. *Pragmatism as a Principle and Method of Right Thinking*. Albany: SUNY Press.

13

On Scrolls and Screens: Bible Reading between History and Industry

Eep Talstra

1. Introduction

Producing and using texts for centuries has been a combination of particular arts. That is, there always has been an interrelationship of various human skills: writing, reading, constructing knowledge and building communities of readers interested in that knowledge. In our times, new technologies and new media turn the arts of the production and the usage of texts more into some kind of an industry. Produce and distribute the types of information any kind of user might ask for. This transformation evokes a series of questions: what does this change mean, particularly with respect to biblical studies? Can industry take over fully from arts? Is information just another word for knowledge? Can arts be imitated? What will happen to the reader? Both from the side of the Sciences (Toulmin 1990; Bolter 1984) and from the side of the Humanities (Steiner 1997), scholars exhibit mixed feelings: does not 'knowing more data' end up in 'understanding less of human life'?

I work with the Bible, computing, and methods of biblical studies: I see my contribution here in approaching these changing fields from the view of the humanities and biblical scholarship. Traditionally one can, in my opinion, distinguish in the humanities four types of arts in handling texts, i.e. the work of the Scribe (to produce or copy), the Librarian (to store and distribute), the Scholar (to analyze) and the

Reader (to understand and react). It will be clear that in labeling these skills with the word Arts, I am not particularly referring to arts in the classical sense of the word, i.e. the basic disciplines of education, the 'artes liberales,' such as 'grammatica,' 'rhetorica,' 'arithmetica.' The reference is in terms of techniques, the traditional human skills and procedures applied to share knowledge using written texts. So the question provoked by the new electronic media is: How will we in our own time produce, store, distribute, analyze and understand texts? Will these media, as some fear, turn all knowledge into a matter of private consumption? What will it do to the interaction of knowledge and social communities? The claim I want to make in here is, first, that the interaction between the Scribe, the Librarian, the Scholar and the Reader, even when substantially influenced by the new media, continues to be basic to the process of reading and communication; and second, that the new media though successful in imitating the role of the Scribe and the Librarian, have not yet been very helpful in designing effective tools to assist the analytical work of the Scholar or the hermeneutical interest of the Reader. In the public domain the new electronic media basically restrict themselves to imitating the Scribe and the Librarian, i.e., copying and distributing textual data. So the basic question is: how can one construct additional tools to help the Scholar in analyzing a text and the Reader in entering dialogue with the electronic texts presented to them?

2. From Arts to Industry: changing attitudes

To start reflection on the effects of the new techniques I list the traditional arts or skills with an attempt to describe what is changing now and what the effects might be on the study of texts, especially of biblical texts, in modern culture.

2.1. The art of copying and commenting: the Scribe

What changes: *the format and the distribution of texts.*

Changes in this area already were made by the transition from manuscript to book, that is, making copies without starting a new tradition of errors. We see changes occurring again with the transition from book to digital manuscript: is it a copy of a book or a copy of a text? At the moment the book format is still being imitated electronically, just as the first cars had to look like carriages. But it will change. Perhaps future documents will emphasize their presentation of a line of argumentation and store the information used in files to be reached by links. As with ancient manuscripts, copies of texts again may become just private, i.e., they can be altered, comments can be added, etc., by the individual: you start your own conversation with a text, inserting notes and suggestions for answers.

Effect: Changing the art of copying (the ancient Scribe is now a command: "copy x into y") will also change the role of the library.

2.2. The art of searching and collecting: the Librarian

What changes: *the library function of storing and retrieving.*

As well, retrieving will turn into a command: "search and get file x". At the moment this function is quite popular in Internet facilities. You become your own librarian. The Web feels like a worldwide extension of your private library. But also the limitations are clear. What is the value of the information presented? For biblical study one can retrieve only existing scholarly opinions: classical philological data, traditional textual interpretation and translations, i.e., the current academic mixture of knowledge and opinion. Nevertheless, the electronic extension of one's desk and one's library will have great impact in terms of the accessibility of texts.

Effect: Changing the art of collecting and retrieving (the classical library) will change scholarship.

2.3. The art of argumentation: the Scholar

What changes: *The impact of knowledge is shifting* from the established religious or learned communities into the private area or into the domain of ad-hoc communities of people sharing the same interests for a while, as long as they are in the same mailinglist. In this way new areas of sharing knowledge and of intellectual dialogue will arise. But where? Now there always has been a useful tension between truth and text: one is reading and one performs the act of appropriation (Thiselton, 1992). That is, one agrees, or disagrees, or one applies the text in a new context, perhaps be even running against a text's original intentions. This type of arguing with a text, however, always has been located in a community of readers and connected to the authority of the group or accepted by the group (in terms of religion, science, arts, morality, etc.). In academic theology this tension is visible between reading the biblical text as material for theological argumentation, and reading a biblical text as material for the history of religion. In a community of believers the text may function in different ways too: it may vary from the absolute authority on the one hand, to, on the other hand, the elderly friend inspiring you. New media will not remove these ten-

sions and the variety of opinions, but they may change the social group
or the academic tradition as a framework to rely upon. New media will
stimulate a more private style of reading, much more than the transition
from manuscripts to printed editions already did. With respect to biblical studies it will also produce access to a variety of text types. That is,
the contemporaneity of reading traditions will become much more visible, e.g., Protestants reading the Hebrew text of the Jewish tradition,
Catholics reading the Latin versions and Orthodox readers using the
Greek tradition of the Old Testament. At the same time, other text traditions also will become easily accessible, such as ancient Hebrew
inscriptions (Renz & Röllig, 1995), expressing a type of religion different from the Old Testament. As an effect it means a challenge for existing communities and authorities of bible reading and interpretation. We
see examples of such challenges in the media hype concerning the Dead
Sea scrolls, in headlines such as: Find the 'truth' about Christianity
'hidden' in these texts! Attack the authorities that try to keep historical
'truth' a secret! etc.

Effect: the easy access to a variety of texts and text traditions will
change scholarship and education. It will stimulate the study of 'intertextuality' and 'canon.' Questions will arise, such as: Which collection
of texts will continue to function as a canon on which to found ideas and
communities of readers? Where will authority or tradition go if you no
longer can point to a particular, physical book, saying: That is my, or
our, Bible? (Mullins 1996). It will mean much more discussion between
texts, traditions and choices made by reading communities (churches)
in past and present. Thus the position of the reader will change.

2.4. The art of reading: the Reader

Even with the new media, the reader, of course, will remain as the
addressee of all text production and distribution. What changes: the
position of the individual reader in front of the information hurricane. It
is important to stimulate modern readers to find a way out of the ideological rhetorics of the new media. First, rhetorics of the new media
start from a technical redefinition of the ancient art of reading. Reading
in terms of computer programming is to identify a character in a text,
store it into the machine's memory and wait for a program instruction
to do something with it. Or: reading is scanning a text and storing it as
an image of the physical text we had. Due to the instruments used, reading becomes collecting information in terms of data, rather than in terms
of meaning. Secondly, there is a strong attempt to commercialize the

reader. In modern idiom the reader is nowadays renamed as the user or the web-surfer, which actually means: our potential customer. It implies that 'reading' is assimilating to, for example, the act of 'buying a car' or 'driving a car,' rather than to the act of 'intending to go somewhere.' Thus the Web has its own rhetorical conventions, related to commercials, working with much color, much noise, much competitive talking. Negatively put, the Web is changing the art of writing and reading into the art of persuasion and seduction of special target groups. Positively put: this is identical to what ancient rhetorics always tried to do, so what has changed after all? No doubt, human reading remains what it is: an intellectual process using linguistic and literary conventions. However, the new media themselves will tend to simplify reading: from constructing knowledge to handling data or information. Since more material from various intellectual and religious traditions will be available, texts with an authority based on tradition will face more difficulties. On the other hand, this certainly will mean an interesting challenge. We may be able to have an open debate on valuable traditions of religion and knowledge. Part of the historical debate about canon and community probably will be reopened. If traditional communities of reading have quality, it will show.

3. New Media, Bible and critical thinking

3.1. What do new media mediate? Virtual texts in a virtual world?

A concern: the new media, if not dominated by market and money alone, will give opportunity to reopen ancient options: a public discussion as in the market place of an ancient city. People will have an easy access to textual data and to the electronic location of the debate. Exchange of data and opinions is becoming possible by direct contact and by direct access. In this way today's readers have more texts at their disposal, from a greater variety of Christian or other religious groups. Will it be helpful? Confusing? At the moment the new media seem to reduce the act of reading to the processing of information. The direct exchange of data through the Web requires reformatting of texts to make them fit for storing and transportation. To my regret too much of the energy spent at this moment in the area of computers and the humanities is only dedicated to formatting and reformatting. How to make my texts transportable?

What we need is to provide readers with tools that can analyze texts, compare texts and make readers aware of the historical interaction of texts and their readers. Only when the readers would have analytical tools that can do more than just 'retrieval,' they will have occasion to find new ways in the domain of texts, communities and canon. However, at the moment too much of the existing Bible software only produces a (quick) echo of traditional scholarship: scholarly tools copied from existing dictionaries or grammars, fundamentalist or evangelical comments, copied from existing books, but no newly made analyses, and certainly no possibility for the user to experiment with analyses him/herself. See the comments made in this volume by Susan and James Bachman: 'The new media may in fact favor older, less critical scholarship that has fallen into the "public domain".' The modern media lack a modern concept of Reading. They are mainly imitating the work of the Scribe and the Librarian, not helping Scholars and Readers with the process of analysis and reception. This means that the presence of much more electronic reading materials not yet has been matched by many more computerized tools for textual analysis. In terms of contents or scholarly demands one must say: in the area of Bible and computing we tend to ride quicker horses, instead of inventing better cars.

A hope: new tools for textual analysis of biblical texts of many ancient and modern traditions would help us in the debate on intertextuality and canon that is coming up by the new media. The very existence of the electronic media provokes and intensifies hermeneutical questions. These questions regard the relationship of texts and reading communities. There is no such thing as a neutral text containing just 'information.' Why do people read biblical texts? Not only to be informed about the ancient religions, but also to have the experience of an invitation to participate into the texts' world and into the worlds of the community of readers. Theologically it means: Bible reading is the experience of an invitation to participate into an history of criticism and hope. This would be my way of phrasing what Christof Hardmeier calls in his contribution 'biblical literature as memorial literature.'

Now biblical texts demonstrate, by the very process of their tradition, what the roles of Scribes, Librarians and Scholars have been. They all were also Readers, members of communities analyzing and applying texts in new contexts. In a way the era of the printed book, by its concentration on the final product, the printed text, has obscured these different roles. It is possible that the new era of the electronic manuscripts, their great variety and the emergence of various ad-hoc reading communities, will force us to become aware again of these different roles. My intention is to make clear that methods of bible study in the 21st century will find new ways to respect the roles of the Scribe, the Librarian, the Scholar and the Reader. The era before the book and the era after the book will demonstrate considerable similarities. I intend to demonstrate some of these ideas by examples of Bible texts, their classical and modern usage and the kind of modern aids for readers that I have in mind.

3.2. Real texts in a real world

Reading has an analytical element, i.e., the decoding of information. Reading also has the element of appropriation, i.e., the application of a text into the context of one's life, as a community or as an individual. Reading processes influence and change texts: this has been the case before the invention of printing. This situation may return when the electronic versions of texts become the main medium. Biblical texts by their format and tradition types demonstrate and reflect the interests of groups that were both the addressee and also were engaged in transmitting the texts. This process is not to be evaluated negatively. This is how tradition works. It needs the contribution of the Scribe, the Librarian, the Scholar and the Reader. In my view the use of new techniques and new media may change these roles, but they will continue to play their part in the continuing process of reading and interpreting biblical texts. Reflection on the process of textual transmission both in ancient and in modern electronic times is necessary to help today's religious communities to understand themselves as part of a continuing tradition. They receive texts and also hand down textual traditions and traditions of reading. Therefore, biblical scholarship of the 21st century should reject the idea that reading is only picking up information, by reducing a text to data and statements. Rather, the modern media should be used to help bible readers to take part in the hermeneutical processes to which both texts and readers belong. Modern readers should not be left in isolation behind their private screen. A reader needs to have access to the communities that were based on and still base their existence on ancient texts.

In the following, I present some examples of the interaction of texts and reading communities. These are examples of the ancient hermeneutical processes of textual tradition, which in my view still are valid in biblical studies of the new century. I am not suggesting that we should only copy these processes into the new century. The point is that we will have to find new ways to accept these hermeneutical processes

as operating alongside the methods of the era of printed books, i.e.
methods of literary and historical criticism. In terms of methodology I
consider, for example, exegetical models proposed by feminist theologians, or by theologians representing more traditional, confessional
groups in the Christian tradition, to be expressions of the same
hermeneutical processes.

Therefore we should enter the new era by also looking back into
the times before the era of the printed book and ask the question, How
did real texts work in a real world?

3.2.1. Adapting a text: the interaction of the Scribe and the Librarian

Comparing the Massoretic text of the Old Testament with texts
from the Qumran collection and the traditions of the Septuagint,
Samaritan or other Versions reveals something of the process of writing
and transmitting texts. The question here is not only a text-critical one,
i.e., could we possibly define the original text? More important is the
hermeneutical question: can we understand the theological processes
that are connected with the activity of transmitting texts? In the context
of the new electronic media this question will continue to be crucial.
Examples are cases where a Qumran text agrees with an ancient version
of the Hebrew Bible against the Massoretic text of the Hebrew Bible.
This happens in the manuscript called 4QpaleoExm (a Qumran scroll
in ancient Hebrew script that contains the text of Exodus 6-37). In Ex.
32,10 both the Samaritan tradition and the Qumran text have added a
verse that is likely to have been borrowed from the more or less parallel text of Dtn. 9,20. It is Moses' statement about God's wrath against
Aaron, which in the Massoretic text does not occur in Exodus 32.

In the edition by Patrick W. Skehan et al (1992, 124ff.) the
Qumran text is presented like this (the underlining of the section added
is mine):

4QpaleoEx^m

Col. XXXVIII   Exod 32:10-19 ... 25-30
    top margin
1 או]תך]לגוי : גדול]ובאהרון התאנף יה]וה : מאד : להשמידו
2 וי]תפלל:משה:בעד.א]הרון   [ ] [ ] va[cat
3 י]ה]ל .משה .את] פנ]י]   ויאו]מר.למ]ה]יהוה.יהר.א]פך[

1 yo[u]to a great nation. [And with Aaron was YH]WH very
angry as to destroy him.
2 And [pr]ayed Moses on behalf of A[aron ...]
3 And implored [.... he sa]id: Wh[y,] YHWH does burn [your
wr]ath?

Reading and copying clearly also meant adapting the text. The
idea seems to have been that texts should match. A textual corpus should
be consistent. A similar example in the same manuscript is the text of
Deuteronomy 1,9-18 being added to Exodus 18, 24v. (Tov 1992, 98).

What is the hermeneutical process? One sees the interaction of the
Scribe and the Librarian, entering a process of both collecting and
adapting texts. One could call it an act of protection. The goal seems to
be to protect a reader from the confusion that may arise from the existence of multiple texts and textual traditions. Our task? New electronic
media should make this process visible, by making the data available
and linking the various texts. This would help students understand the
interaction of texts and communities of readers.

3.2.2. Interpreting and expanding a text in translation: the
interaction of the Librarian and the Scholar

In Jewish tradition one finds some of the Greek translations
expressing a clear theological point of view with respect to a problem
posed by the Hebrew text. An example is the story of the Syrian general Naaman in II Kings 5. How can he, just having converted to the God
of Israel, be allowed to accompany his king to the temple of Rimmon
and bow down there for an other god? And why is it that Elisha is ready
to give his permissive answer: 'Go in peace'? The Hebrew text of II
Kings 5:18 narrates that Naaman is asking forgiveness in advance, arguing: May God forgive me when I bow down in the temple of Rimmon,
since it is my duty to accompany the king there:

נִשְׁעָן עַל יָדִי וְהִשְׁתַּחֲוֵיתִי בֵּית רִמֹּן בְּהִשְׁתַּחֲוָיָתִי בֵּית רִמֹּן
יִסְלַח נָא יְהוָה לְעַבְדְּךָ בַּדָּבָר הַזֶּה :

"With the king leaning on my arm I will bow down in the temple
of Rimmon. In my bowing down in the temple of Rimmon may
YHWH forgive his servant for this." (translation ET)

It is interesting to see that the main LXX tradition presents an
argument for Elisha's permission. It has a slightly different text (Rahlf
[1935], 1979). The expression 'my bowing down' in the Hebrew Bible

has changed into 'his bowing down.' The reading: ἐν τῷ προσκυνεῖν αὐτόν corresponds to a Hebrew construction of the type: infinitive + pronominal suffix בְּהִשְׁתַּחֲוָיָתִי (see also BHS critical apparatus). This text implies that Naaman only will be present, but not will bow down.

Montgomery, in his commentary on the books of Kings (Montgomery, [1951] 1976, 379), refers to the Lucian revision of the Septuagint, where Naaman says, he will bow down in the presence of the king, but only will perform this act for the Lord: προσκυνησω ἁμα αὐτῷ ἐγω Κυριῳ τῳ θεῳ μου. 'Then I will bow down, together with him, for the Lord my God.'

A comparable situation can be found in Deuteronomy 4. First it is said (verse 19) that Israel should not serve the sun, the moon or the stars. They are inferior to the God of Israel, since YHWH himself has allotted these heavenly bodies to other peoples to be their gods. Israel, however, is God's personal heritage. (See also Dtn 32,8-9 in LXX and Qumran.) In verse 28, however, it is said that when Israel in the future forgets YHWH, it will lose its land and be forced to go into exile. Living on foreign territory Israel, in spite of being God's people, will serve other gods, man-made gods of wood and stone. (See also Deuteronomy 28, 36, 64.)

Deuteronomy 4:28

וַעֲבַדְתֶּם שָׁם אֱלֹהִים מַעֲשֵׂה יְדֵי אָדָם עֵץ וָאֶבֶן אֲשֶׁר לֹא יִרְאוּן
וְלֹא יִשְׁמְעוּן וְלֹא יֹאכְלוּן וְלֹא יְרִיחֻן:

'And there you will serve gods, products of human hands, wood and stone, that do not see and do not hear and do not eat and do not smell.' (translation ET)

In Jewish interpretation and translation this text caused a debate. How can Moses say that Israel will serve other gods? The Targum Pseudo-Jonathan (Aramaic translation, see Weinfeld 1991) overcomes the problem in translating: "you will serve there the worshipers of the idols". An interesting discussion in Midrash Leviticus Rabba elaborates on the problem. King Nebuchadnezzar (Dan 3,1-12) clearly has carefully studied Moses, for he asks critical questions to the friends of Daniel, who refused to bow down for the king's statue. 'Has not Moses written about you in the Torah, and you will serve manmade gods?' They said to him: 'my Lord king, not to bow down but to serve with taxes.'(Weinfeld 1991, 209: Midrash Leviticus Rabbah, edition Margaliot, 768-69).

What is the hermeneutical process? These examples demonstrate an act of interpretation or appropriation performed by the ancient scholars. The librarian needs to make the traditional library available for Jewish readers in a world speaking Greek; the scholar thinks about the identity of that reading community in that new world. The result of their interaction is to allow the readers of the text to continue to identify with their own religious heritage in a new context of life. The reader is addressed as being part of the Jewish tradition. By adding a more precise interpretation to the text the reader can still be addressed as such. Our task? New electronic media should also make this process visible by presenting the data and adding information about these early reading communities and their texts in a new cultural environment. It would help to understand the needs and the freedom of the ancient reading community and it would help asking questions about appropriation of biblical texts in today's religious communities.

3.2.3. Appropriation and application of a text: the interaction of the Scholar and the Reader

The text of the Septuagint demonstrates that translating a text is not being done just out of historical interest. The translators of the Septuagint sometimes also updated their text, making it into a prophecy that was valid for their own history. A recent study of Van der Kooij (1998) presents a clear example of this process, taken from Isaiah 23. In the prophecy about the destruction of the city of Tyre, the Hebrew text speaks of ships that used to come from Tarshis to Tyre. The Septuagint, however, speaks of ships that used to come in from Carthage (Isaiah 23,1,6, 10,14).

Isaiah 23:1 The pronouncement about Tyre

הֵילִילוּ ׀ אֳנִיּוֹת תַּרְשִׁישׁ כִּי שֻׁדַּד מִבַּיִת :MT

Wail, ships of Tarshish, for it is laid waste, so that there is no house ...

LXX: ὀλολύζετε πλοῖα Καρχηδόνος ὅτι ἀπώλετο

Cry aloud, ships of Carthage, for it is destroyed ...

Isaiah 23:6

עִבְרוּ תַּרְשִׁישָׁה הֵילִילוּ יֹשְׁבֵי אִי :MT

Pass over to Tarshish, wail, inhabitants of the isle!

LXX: ἀπέλθατε εἰς Καρχηδόνα ὀλολύζατε

Depart to Carthage, cry aloud, inhabitants of that isle!

The Greek translation applies the Isaiah text to the Hellenistic period. Carthage was destroyed by the Romans in 146 BCE, at the end

of the third Punic war. Then the Romans took over power in the whole
Mediterranean area. Tyre's power came to an end.

In the tradition of Christian theology one finds similar processes
of appropriation. The Hebrew text, via the Greek and Latin versions, is
read directly as a text expressing Christian faith. An example is Martin
Luther's comments on Psalm 67 (Roach & Schwarz, 1983, 214f.;
Mülhaupt 1962, 313), a song about God's blessing of his people Israel
and his righteous government of the nations.

Psalm 67
Now the earth has given its harvest

Ps 67:7 אֶרֶץ נָתְנָה יְבוּלָה

may God, our God bless us;

Ps 67:7 יְבָרְכֵנוּ אֱלֹהִים אֱלֹהֵינוּ:

may God bless us

Ps 67:8 יְבָרְכֵנוּ אֱלֹהִים

that respect him all the ends of the earth

Ps 67:8 וְיִירְאוּ אֹתוֹ כָּל אַפְסֵי אָרֶץ:

Luther explained the Psalm as a "prophecy about the coming of
Christ and the manifestation of the Gospel to the entire world" [Peticio
prophetica aduentus Christi. et manifestandi euangelii per totum
mundum].

In his comments he clearly reads the text as representing the point
of view of Christian readers. His explanation is inserted into the (Latin)
text. For example in verse 7:

Terra dedit fructum suum quia sine viro sola eum concepit.
[Earth gave its fruit—since without a man she alone conceived
him.]

The 'earth' in verse 7 is the Virgin Mary, who conceived without
a man. A note added to 'Terra' says, "beate virgo peperit Christum
secundum carnem et Ecclesia eundem secundum spiritum" [The blessed
Virgin gave birth to Christ according to the flesh and the Church according to the Spirit].

The appearance of 'God' three times in verses 7 and 8, in combination with a singular verb, means a reference to Trinity, in Luther's
interpretation.

With more subtlety the same technique of appropriation has been applied in the text of the oratorio *The Messiah* by Georg Frederic Handel. In this oratorio a collection of biblical texts is sung with reference to Jesus as the Messiah. One example taken from the second part with texts about the suffering of the Messiah. It has an aria with the text of Lamentations 1:12:

Behold, and see if there be any sorrow like unto His sorrow.

However, the Hebrew text does not say: 'his sorrow.' It reads: 'my sorrow':

הַבִּיטוּ וּרְאוּ אִם יֵשׁ מַכְאוֹב כְּמַכְאֹבִי

In this text the devastated city of Jerusalem complains about her own suffering. The text does not refer to the suffering Messiah. It means that in Handel's Messiah we do not only find a selection of texts according to a schema of Christian interpretation. In addition, the reading of a text even has been changed to become an element of that schema of interpretation.

What is the hermeneutical process? The actualization of the text in Jewish or Christian tradition is not only a process of protection or interpretation. It is an example of appropriation. The prophecy of Isaiah is considered to be valid for the time of actual experience by generations much later than the time the prophet Isaiah lived in. The text of the Psalm is considered to express already the theology of the Gospel. The text of Lamentations is considered to refer to Christ ultimately, rather than only to Jerusalem. Our task? New electronic media should also make these processes visible in presenting and comparing the relevant data. What texts do we have, what kind of reading communities transmitted them? This would help understand the hermeneutics of the older reading communities that considered themselves to be the text's addressee.

3.3. Reading in modern scholarship. A critique of Readers and Traditions

As I hope the examples presented here may have demonstrated, textual traditions are shaped by hermeneutical processes of adaptation and appropriation. We have no neutral 'information.' One reaction to this is present in modern scholarly research of the bible, which clearly is strongly connected to the era of the book. The so-called critical scholarship went into the opposite direction, i.e., hoping not to support the theologically motivated processes of adaptation, actualization or inter-

pretation of texts. Rather, the main interest in so-called critical scholarship has been to reveal these processes with the help of analytical tools
of historical reconstruction. And if one sees the effects these procedures
of tradition had on the texts, it is understandable why academic theology since the Enlightenment made the choice not to support particular
theological traditions, but to search for historical data and historical
truth. Biblical studies decided to give up innocence.

More on this topic is presented in this volume by James Voelz. I
question, however, whether his more or less philosophical definition of
modern biblical scholarship does full justice to its intentions. With
many older literary critics the impetus was not just 'belief in the superiority of reason,' as Voelz puts it. It was much more modest and much
more instrumental: if the transmission of religious texts has produced so
much variation and errors, we need an analytical instrument to find our
way back to the beginnings of the texts. Also in the electronic era, we
cannot return behind that point, though we will deal differently with historical reconstruction. For, times have changed. Postmodern scholarship
has given up the search for the ultimate truth to be found in history and
is more inclined to accept the existence of various religious traditions. I
think that this leads to a more modest usage of critical analysis that can
be applied fruitfully in the domain of new electronic media. We need
analytical tools allowing us to enter a dialogue between the various religious traditions about the reading of biblical texts. So where are we
now? Modern, critical scholarship has dismissed the ancient hermeneutical processes as non-scientific. Post-modern scholarship is aware of
the fact that nevertheless we cannot do without them, otherwise we will
turn a living tradition into a museum of ancient religion. So, as the contributions by black theologians, by feminist theology or by more classical, confessional types of theology demonstrate, at the moment we feel
more need to revitalize the old hermeneutical processes of appropriation, since we need them. On the other hand, critical scholarship has
made sure that we have lost our innocence. If you want to be the
addressee of the biblical text you cannot help but to be aware of the
great historical distance.

This is how I think we will enter the new, electronic era. We will
use the tools of critical reconstruction given to us by the era of the book
and apply again the hermeneutical processes of reading and appropriation from the era of manuscripts. Biblical scholarship should remain
independent and be careful not to be led astray by commercial rhetorics
around the Web. After centuries of intense work biblical scholarship has

some right to claim that reading texts is fully different from processing information. The interesting point, however is, that when we decide to use the modern electronic media in an independent way, the enormous power it has will be of great assistance in giving us a fully new access both to the era of the book and to the era of the manuscripts.

3.4. The Tools needed.

The examples presented may make clear what kind of instruments we need for biblical research. Simply retrieving texts and translations, of course, is important to the process of collecting materials and finding scholarly opinions about it. But retrieval alone is not sufficient. I have already indicated in the previous section the first kind of tools we need. We need databases that visualize and help understand the process of textual tradition, i.e. tools that give access to materials from the era of manuscripts, the era before the printing of books. Such tools connect the biblical text with Qumran fragments, Septuagint versions, New Testament quotations or interpretations from Jewish and Christian tradition. These instruments go beyond the work of the Scribe and the Librarian and they will grant the Scholar and the Reader access to understanding the hermeneutical processes of tradition and interpretation. Consider here the contribution on medieval illuminated manuscripts by Kate Lindemann. Her remarks on "seeing contemplatively" are another example of the hermeneutical process of appropriation. In the end also this process, though initially being a private experience, is part of a much broader tradition of "reading."

But we need to take a further step. We also need computerized tools that imitate the analytical instruments developed by biblical scholarship in the era of the book. Even the flexible text databases presenting materials from the era of manuscripts will be of no use in answering the question of, for example, which translation to choose for a particular Hebrew verse. To that end we need tools that can undertake linguistic analysis. Only if we knew more about lexical and syntactic patterns of the ancient Hebrew language, will we have better material to selecting or proposing specific translations. The real instruments required, therefore, would be computer programs that enable us to collect and compare linguistic data from the Hebrew texts and their various traditions. I am not suggesting a computer could prove for us which translating tradition would be the best one. Computers don't prove, but nevertheless, they could do more than just give access to and download texts: helping with analysis, according to the methods developed by critical scholarship in the era of the book. This means we need intelligent textual databases, capable of analyzing texts in proper linguistic categories at the level of syntax. Only then might scholars and other Web-users get the facilities required to collect the correct linguistic data they need to be able to argue about texts, traditions and translations. At the moment, however, we are just at the beginning of meeting these requirements (Tov, 1986). Text databases should present Hebrew, Greek, Latin texts or modern translations not only in words, in verses or half verses, but also consistently analyzed in categories of syntax, lexicon and textual structures. Only that type of database would allow for a linguistically high level of collecting and comparing data. (This is the main topic of my and my colleagues' current research in Amsterdam in close cooperation with Alan Groves in Philadelphia and Christof Hardmeier in Greifswald [see E. Talstra (1995), Doedens (1994), Syring (1998), and Talstra and Sikkel (2000)].) Only these instruments will in the future supply scholars and teachers with the evidence they need to reach conclusions about translations, interpretation and the hermeneutics of bible reading in our time. This is one reason why I have mixed feelings about enthusiastic talks on education in the electronic era. "Get beyond the traditional classroom using all the means afforded by the electronic culture," as Ben Witherington puts it in his contribution. Do we have 'all the means'? Besides making things easier, what can Powerpoint really do for you, if proper analytical tools for the humanities still have to be developed? When the new media only allow us easy processing of opinions about original texts, rather than giving us direct access to original texts allowing us to ask intelligent questions, what do we gain?

4. The task
To bridge the gap between retrieving and reading

To conclude, I will make some statements about tools and methods of biblical studies I believe are necessary to take with us into the new century.

The history of biblical studies demonstrates that the classical process of bible reading consists of two, sometimes conflicting procedures: analyzing and appropriation. This is visible within the Bible, its process of transmission and translation and also in the continuing Jewish and Christian traditions.

Historical-critical methods of biblical scholarship intend to select from the process of reading only the process of analysis and to avoid the process of appropriation. Its goal is to reconstruct the history and the historical reference of the texts. The process of appropriation is evaluated as being beyond scholarly standards.

Postmodern hermeneutics, expressing itself in rhetorical or critical types of reading, is more open to a reader's position and is fully aware of the impact of the process of appropriation. The continuing influence of historical-critical methods, however, is the loss of 'innocence.' Reading the Bible within the context of a particular theological tradition now needs to be a decision, it can no longer be presented as a matter of evidence.

Theologians representing 'critical thinking' or 'critical hermeneutics' usually present themselves as struggling with existing authority, ideology and tradition. However, in studying the hermeneutical processes that shaped biblical texts and religious traditions, they could feel free to experiment in line with their own needs for reading and appropriation of biblical texts. The real question is not how to get academic permission to become a feminist or another kind of critical exegete; rather the question is whether to be or not to be a creative continuation of the ancient communities of reading.

New electronic media operate on this changing hermeneutical field. The situation requires that the elementary processes of reading be being studied carefully. If we have techniques only for retrieving texts, we lose track of the process of reading and tradition. Therefore, some editors' habit of simply adding traditional commentaries or lexicons to the electronic texts as authorities of interpretation will not help. In that case only someone's hypertext will become our teacher.

The task is this: Combine the best from the era of the manuscripts and from the era of the book. Study the hermeneutical processes that shaped Jewish and Christian textual tradition and make them visible in electronic text corpora. Allow readers of these texts to have access to these communities, in terms of understanding their history and identity. As in Phil Mullins pointed out in response to our conference, "It is necessary to re-root in human responsibility and human communities." Create tools to analyze and compare a broad range of texts. It is not sufficient simply to create electronic copies of existing authorities. New tools for linguistic analysis and for the comparison of textual traditions are required to enable students of the Bible to perform reading and analysis in an independent way. In my view, the Bible Societies, in close cooperation with biblical scholars of various backgrounds, now have a full new century at their disposal to accomplish a tremendous task.

References

Bolter, J.D. 1984. *Turing's Man: Western Culture in the Computer Age*. Chapel Hill: University of North Carolina Press.

Doedens, C.J. 1994. *Text Databases. One Database Model and Several Retrieval Languages*. (Language and Computers, Studies in Practical Linguistics, 14) (Doctoral dissertation University of Utrecht). Amsterdam: Rodopi.

van der Kooij, A. 1998. *The Oracle of Tyre. The Septuagint of Isaiah XXIII as Version and Vision (Supplements to Vetus Testamentum 71)*. Leiden: Brill.

Midrash Leviticus Rabbah, edition Margaliot, Jerusalem, 1953-1960.

Pseudo Jonathan Targum Jonathan ben Uziel. 1974. D. Rieder (ed.). Jerusalem: ha-Akademyah ha-Amerikanit le-mada' e ha Yahadut.

Montgomery, J.A. 1976 (1951). *A Critical and Exegetical Commentary on the Books of Kings (ICC)*. Edinburgh: Clark.

Mülhaupt, W. (ed.). 1962. *D. Martin Luthers Psalmen-Auslegung. 2. Band Psalmen 26-90*. Göttingen: VandenHoeck & Ruprecht.

Mullins, P. 1996. "Sacred Text in the Sea of Texts" in Charles Ess, (ed.), *Philosophical Perspectives on Computer-mediated Communication*, 271-302. Albany, NY: State University of New York Press.

Rahlfs, A. (ed.). 1979 (1935). *Septuaginta. Id est Vetus Testamentum graece iuxta LXX interpretes*. Stuttgart: Württembergische Bibelanstalt.

Renz, J. and W. Röllig. 1995. *Handbuch der Althebräischen Epigraphik, Band I-III*. Darmstadt: Wissenschaftliche Buchgeselschaft.

Roach, E. and R. Schwarz (eds.). 1983. *Martin Luther Wolfenbüttler Psalter 1513-1515*. Frankfurt am Main: Insel Verlag.

Skehan, P.W. et al. 1992. *Qumran Cave 4. IV. Paleo-Hebrew and Greek Biblical Manuscripts (Discoveries in the Judean Desert IX)*. Oxford: Clarendon Press.

Steiner, G. 1997. *Errata: Een leven in onderzoek* [Dutch translation of: *Errata. An examined Life*]. Amsterdam: Meulenhoff.

Thiselton, A.C. 1992. *New Horizons in Hermeneutics, The Theory and Practice of Transforming Biblical Reading*. Grand Rapids: Zondervan.

Syring, W.-D. 1998. "QUEST 2 - Computergestützte Philologie und Exegese," *Zeitschrift für Althebraistik* 11: 85-89

Talstra, E. 1995. "Desk and Discipline. The Impact of Computers on the Study of the Bible." Opening Address of the 4th AIBI Conference, in: E. Talstra (ed.), *Proceedings of the Fourth International Colloquium Bible and*

Computer: Desk and Discipline, Amsterdam August 15-18 1994, 25-43. Paris/Geneva: Slatkine.

Talstra, E. and C. Sikkel. 2000. "Genese und Kategorienentwicklung der WIVU-Datenbank, oder: ein Versuch, dem Computer Hebräisch beizubringen" in Christof Hardmeier, Wolf-Dieter Syring, Jochen D. Range, Eep Talstra (eds.), *Ad Fontes! Quellen erfassen - lesen - deuten. Was ist Computerphilologie? [Applicatio 15]*, 33-68. Amsterdam: VU University Press.

Toulmin, S. 1990. *Cosmopolis. The Hidden Agenda of Modernity*. New York: The Free Press.

Tov, E. 1986. *A Computerized Data Base for Septuagint Studies. The Parallel Aligned Text of the Greek and Hebrew Bible.* (Computer Assisted Tools for Septuagint Studies 2 = JNWSL Suppl Series 1). Stellenbosch, South.Africa: Stellenbosch University Press.

Tov, E. 1992. *Textual Criticism of the Hebrew Bible.* Assen: Van Gorcum / Minneapolis: Fortress Press.

Weinfeld, M. 1991. Deuteronomy 1-11, in *The Anchor Bible*, vol. 5. New York: Doubleday.

14

Prayer and the Internet

Kate Lindemann

Introduction

The Internet has developed in two very different directions. The first form emphasizes the web page, its content and layout, as the entity for consideration. The second uses the Internet as a vehicle for downloading and playing audio, film or video clips. This second format, now in its infancy, may become the main direction in the future as film and video companies merge with Internet providers and as downloading technology becomes more widespread and uniform. Napster has served as an audio downloading portal but as yet, there are no official or unofficial downloading portals for commercial multi-media on the WWW. This second direction of the Internet is still in its infancy and web pages that offer it, such as the American Bible Society page at <http://www.newmediabible.org/>, do so within the format of the traditional web page. The article by Terry Lindvall in this volume address some of the issues raised by the multi-media delivery format for the Internet. This article is addresses the first form of Internet wherein layout and text establish the context and content of the online experience.

The article begins with a short review of the current use of web pages by Christian communities. It then moves to a discussion of reading and biblical text presentation. It describes a particular form of prayerful reading that developed during the Middle Ages and shows

311

how web pages could be used to re-centralize this prayerful reading of biblical texts. The final section offers some suggestions to those who might wish to explore or develop web pages that would enhance such prayerful reading of biblical texts.

Christian web sites

Christian scholars and Church communities make wide use of web pages. Christian sites include biblical texts, encyclopedias, pages about individual figures in the history of Christianity, and so forth. There are also sites for specific Christian denominations and individual Churches or Congregations. Most of these web sites are designed in the formats of printed books or publicity brochures.

Many scholarly Christian sites seem to use the Internet as an electronic library. Their sites offer search engines that function like library card catalogues and they design individual files and pages like printed articles or books. Some web sites offer electronic versions of printed texts, including a Bible available in twelve languages at <http://bible.gospelcom.net/> and the Catholic Encyclopedia at <http://www.newadvent.org/cathen/>. Other sites offer new materials, but they use the design of printed books with color and a few more illustrations added. The massive history of mysticism page at <http://www.clas.ufl.edu/users/gthursby/mys/whoswho.htm> fits this category. A few of sites, such as *Through the Bible Radio* at <http://www.ttb.org/> utilize the web's audio capability to include voice or music to accompany texts. These sites of on-line Christian texts form an as yet unlinked Christian library that continues the culture of the book but extends access to a wider audience. All these sites could be linked via a library portal that could serve as a meta-catalogue for online Christian texts.

Many Christian denominations, organizations and individual Church communities also have web sites. There are denominational sites such as the Church of Christ page at <http://www.church-of-christ.org/> and the Jehovah's Witness site at <http://www.watchtower.org/> . In addition there are thousands of individual Congregations with web sites such as St. Mary's in Huntsville, Alabama (<http://SMVparish.org/>), Prince of Peace Lutheran Church in Carrollton, Texas (<http://www.princeofpeace.org/pray_with_us.htm>), Broadway Methodist Church in Chicago (<http://www.brdwyumc.org/>), and All Saints Episcopal Church in Jackson, Mississippi (<http://members.aol.com/jxnsaints2/>).

Many of these pages were designed by public relations firms and they utilize the format of the public relations brochure. The sites are designed to encourage web surfers to explore the programs and services of the web site group. Some pages are simple; others include animated gifs, audio and/or a short video clips. What all of them have in common is that they are web extensions of print-based advertisements or brochures. Christian organizations wanting to hire professional web designers often go to printers or public relations firms who now offer web design among their services. Since the printed brochure is what the firm's designers know well, it is natural that they lay out web pages as they might do a brochure. Because the Web allows color and images to be used much less expensively than in paper printing, the Church group gets a "high end," brochure-like page at a very reasonable cost. Most of these web pages do not utilize the "new" communication forms inherent in the Web. They are laid out to inform and "sell" the services of the host group. In this their design differs little from that of e-commerce sites. Only the secure server for credit card transactions is missing from most of them.

There are a few Christian web sites that *do* include some of new possibilities inherent in web pages. Interactivity, for example, is a communications mode that is not possible with books or brochures, but is possible on Internet. The Evangelical Lutheran Church in America offers visitors an opportunity to send comments on specific topics under discussion and posts the responses for all to read at <http://www.elca.org/>. This gives asynchronous interactivity and encourages global communication among English-speaking web surfers. Other sites offer "real time" Christian chat rooms and there are an increasing number of Christian web portals such as Crosswalk.com (<http://www.christcom.net/>) with the latest news, chat rooms, e-mail lists and advertising. Such portals, unseen a few years ago in the Christian community, originate with technical web designers who understand that the Web offers new communication formats. However, the Christian portals seem to follow the direction set by secular web portals: sites such as the Evangelical web adviser at <http://www.briga-da.org/today/articles/web-evangelism2.html> embraces secular leadership in communication and design. The content is different but the same sales/entertainment format is used.

Besides interactivity and portal organization, the web can be used to encourage contemplative prayer. There are numerous non-Christian sites that offer web pages that engage the viewer in traditional prayer experiences. In Hindu religious traditions, discipleship and transmission of power from guru to the disciple are central practices. The web page <http://www.sahajayoga.org/ExperienceItNOW/textonly.html> engages the visitor in such a transmission. As well, there are Buddhist sites that teach meditation: they combine image and text to both teach the practice and to encourage the visitor to actually meditate. The Ven. Pannyavaro, for example, offers a page of walking meditation (<http://www.buddhanet.net/xmed7.htm>). The Wat Luang Phor Sod Dhammakayaram monastery gives both basic and advanced meditation instruction (<http://www.concentration.org/homepage.htm>). Beyond these, there are numerous other non-Christian pages that engage visitors in the contemplative practice of mandala gazing or sutra chanting.

By contrast, however, there are few Christian pages that attempt to engage the web visitor in actual prayer or religious practice on line. "Sacred Space" (<http://www.jesuit.ie/prayer/index.htm>), designed by the Irish Jesuits, is an exception. Using java script they have created a multi-lingual page whose whole purpose is for web visitors to pray the scriptures. This is one of the only Christian web pages that both utilizes the Internet for prayerful activity and does not mimic secular designs. I believe that web pages could become prime vehicles for biblical prayer. It is the aim of this paper to introduce some additional concept designs that could make prayer a central activity via the Internet.

Ways of reading

Most of us who have grown up in the world of the book engage in the modern way of reading texts. Reading is for us primarily a "left brained" activity. In the Western world, it is largely a left-to-right sequential activity. Practice in moving one's eyes from left to right is a central skill in "reading readiness" programs. Second, for moderns reading is primarily a reasoned and informational activity. If we have advanced education we engage in critical analysis of texts—but even without such education, information and logical sequencing remain central to the modern printed word. Finally, modern reading is primarily a silent activity. So surely have we been trained to read silently that we consider it a deficit to "move our lips" when we read, and many tend to judge those who do so as "less educated."

Reading was not always practiced this way. For the ancients and the medievals, reading was usually an oral and thus aural activity. First, much reading was communal, done in law courts and liturgical settings or during meals in the refectory [dining room] of the monastery.

Second, even private reading was done orally. The act of reading silently was so uncommon as to be remarked. For example, St. Augustine, a
bridge figure between classical and medieval thought, when telling the
story of his conversion in the *Confessions*, states that he took up the
book and he "sat under the tree and read silently" (XII, vii, 29). Today
we would not say we were reading silently; we would assume that all
reading is silent.

Further evidence of this oral/aural tradition is the voice rhythm in
ancient and medieval texts. It is natural to read these aloud; reading
them aloud aids the understanding. These texts were written to be read
aloud in a way that few modern texts for adults are. As one learns to
read ancient and medieval texts, one learns to "hear" the voice of the
writer. Length of line indicates length of breath; choices of vowels give
indication of pitch or tone. Ludwig Wittgenstein, a twentieth century
philosopher who retained the oral tradition in his later writings, says,
"Sometimes a sentence can be understood only if it is read at the *right
tempo*. My sentences must be read *slowly*" (1985, 57e).

In the modern world, children's books, at least those for youngest
children, still have texts with strong oral rhythms. Reading aloud a modern essay intended for adults, however, is often awkward. Even newspaper sentences are structured for silent rather than oral reading. Sometimes
the modern reader overlooks the oral nature of earlier reading; even much
of modern poetry is "visual" rather than aural. We forget that visual poetry is a relatively recent phenomenon. We also forget that oral rhythms in
prose were the norm in earlier times and that such oral rhythms continued
for some time after the advent of the printing press and modern book.
Now, however, our prose does not lend itself to recitation unless it is
specifically written for recitation, e.g., sermons or speeches.

For ancient and medieval persons, however, "Hearing the Word of
God" was part of reading the Word of God, not just in the church or
monastic chapel or refectory but also in the solitude of one's cell.

One *said* the Psalms and the New Testament texts. There is some
carryover of this form of reading in the practice of Roman Catholic clergy who say the Office or Breviary aloud or at least by "moving their
lips." They say the Divine Office each day as they read it and it is an
obligation to *say* it as they read. For the ancient and medieval, a separate injunction to *say* the office when reading it was not necessary, since
reading involved "saying."

Another major difference between modern reading and earlier
reading is the speed of reading. The 20th century has produced so many

documents that "speed reading courses," none of which allow oral reading, are taught and all reading tests in the schools are timed tests. This
was not so in earlier times when texts were read slowly, pondered, envisioned. Karl Jaspers, a 20th century existential philosopher, reminds us
that Nietzsche is a "teacher of slow reading"—a form of reading that
Nietzsche learned especially as a student and then as a professor of
philology. Philology, Nietzsche wrote, "teaches people to read well,
that is, slowly, profoundly, looking forward and backward, with mental
reservations, with doors left ajar, and with tender fingers and eyes."
((Nietzsche, Preface to *Daybreak*, section 5, quoted in Jaspers, 1965, 8).
Such reading, Nietzsche insists, is essential to understanding him—and,
we can add, to understanding philosophy as such. The slow reading
associated with oral reading, however, is completely foreign to most
20th century university students.

In summary, in earlier times reading was a slow, multi-sensory
experience. It was oral, aural. Often it was imaginative. It was "right
brained" as much as "left brained."

Medieval illuminated manuscripts

Printing images is expensive. This has been true since the beginnings of mechanical printing. The first printed books kept some aspects
of the medieval manuscript's illumination, such as the use of illuminated letters or words to indicate new sections. But as the printed book
developed, it created non-imagistic means for indicating new chapters,
new sections and their endings.

The illuminated manuscript was different. Copying was always a
labor-intensive activity from the preparation of the skins, the blocking
of texts on through to the final illuminations . No one aimed to keep
expenses down: the copyist was devoting his/her life to the task and so
time and expense were not a question. The scribe's work, like all
monastic work, was a form of prayer, a labor of love. Copy work had its
own penance, its own "way of the cross"—from the cold, from cramped
muscles, poor lighting and careful exactitude. Since the whole work
was "expensive," the limitation on images and color were more determined by available pigments and theological imagination than by business budgets (*Medieval Manuscripts*). Thus, the creator of an illuminated manuscript could use images as freely as contemporary web page
designers can. This lack of concern about expense in incorporating
imagery is but one of several similarities between illuminated manuscripts and contemporary web pages.

There are many libraries that offer pages of illuminated manuscripts online so anyone with Internet access can study them. The aspect of these texts that I find significant is the relationship between text and image. A study of some samples reveals three basic relationships between text and image:

1. *The text is dominant* and the image is used to highlight some aspect of the text. See, for example, <http://www.byu.edu/~hurlbut/ dscriptorium/spalding/spald001.html> where image is used to frame the text to mark its importance, or <http://www.byu.edu/ ~hurlbut/dscriptorium/ukentucky/ky3/ky3-003.html> where illumination is used to make certain words dominant. The illumination makes it clear that "Bendedicite" (Bless) is the word to emphasize in the reading of this Psalm. No other reading, no other interpretation of the text is possible given the illumination. Such use of image to illuminate texts could easily be accomplished in web designs.

2. *Text and image are of equal importance* and the eye is forced to move back and forth between them. See, for example, <http:// www.kb.nl/kb/100hoogte/hh-en/hh006-en.html>. When reading these pages, it is not possible to see text without the image calling for attention at the same time. Modern web pages in this mode can be found at sites such as   <http://www.nelson-atkins.org/sculpture/eastgarden/shapir1.htm >. Image vies with text for attention in a way that makes us hold both in attention as we read.

3. *Image dominates the text* such as in <http://www.bodley.ox.ac.uk/ dept/scwmss/wmss/medieval/jpegs/lat/bib/e/007/500/00700633 .jpg> or <http://www.kb.nl/kb/100hoogte/hh-en/hh013-en.html>. Note how the image dominates your mind when reading the text. The eye is called to the image and only secondarily to the words, but the image illuminates, throws light on the text and so it helps the reading of the text.

How does this use of image-text affect reading? In the first case, the illumination is used to indicate importance. It is not possible to read the Psalm in the illuminated manuscript above in a tone such as "Bless the **Lord** all ye stars" or even as, "Bless the Lord, oh **MY SOUL**" The illumination makes it clear that **Bless** is the dominant word through the text. The alternate readings, both of which I have heard from those reading the Psalm out of printed books, are almost impossible in reading the illuminated text as depicted. The illuminator has used image not to illustrate but to illuminate or shape the acceptable meaning for the text.

For the import of the second and third form of image-text relationship, we need to review some early forms of prayerful reading.

Prayerful reading of texts

Christianity, like Judaism, is a religion of the word. There has always been a centrality of text, especially biblical texts, in its spiritual traditions. The European medieval monastic tradition from the 7th century onward utilized a number of different text-based prayer forms. These included the communal chanting of the Psalms, the reading from a holy book during meals in the refectory and the private practice of *lectio divina* or "divine reading." This last practice, with its origins in the Benedictine tradition, is most relevant to this article. *Lectio divina* is a multi-sensory approach to texts, usually the Bible. Its purpose is to contemplate the texts until one is transformed by them <http://www.osb.org/lectio/about.html>. *Lectio divina* is not based on mere intellectual understanding of the text; rather, its contemplative form opens one's whole being, one's soul to the text, and the text "entering in" shapes the soul/psyche.

This form of reading has not been common for the past three hundred years. When Francis Bacon published the *Novum Organum* in 1620, he centralized observation as the mode of seeing and the empirical sciences as the mode of thinking. Observation and empirical thinking are the foundations of the modern Euro-American ways of scientific thinking and as such are central to our culture. *Lectio divina* uses a different form of seeing and thinking: it uses contemplative seeing and imagistic thinking—it allows the sound of the Word to enter the psyche.

Seeing

Observation is objective; it is distancing. One holds the object of observation at a distance; one goes out and takes in data about it, and one names its parts or aspects. I look at a tree outside my office window. When I observe it, it is as though my energy moves out through my eyes and takes in the characteristics of the tree: its V-shaped trunk, the almost parallel direction of the limbs to each other and to the earth, the solid green of its needles, the few rust color tips. I take all these separate bits and use them to identify the tree and apply theory or come to some conclusions about this tree's relative health, economic worth, etc. Health care workers are trained to observe their patients in this way—to look and take in various aspects of skin color, moistness or dryness, hair texture, body position and movement, voice tone, etc. These observations, coupled with theory, lead to hypotheses about patient. Then the health care worker can conclude whether intervention is needed.

Contemplative seeing is different from observation. Instead of distancing ourselves, sending out energy, and taking in characteristics of the object of observation—contemplative seeing involves letting down our barriers so the object is free to impress itself upon us, to enter into us, to enter our souls. I contemplate that tree by sitting here in my office and looking at it with soft eyes, dropping the barriers to my heart and mind and allowing the tree to reveal itself, to enter into me. I gaze upon the tree wordlessly for the same amount of time as I gave to observing it. When I am finished contemplating, I do not have a list of characteristics of this tree but a sense of the tree itself. It is as though the very essence of the tree has revealed itself. Sometimes I find myself at a loss for words to express my knowledge but there is a kinship: I **know** the tree.

I can contemplate a child at play or a patient in bed. I gaze with soft eyes. I allow my word-chattering mind to become still; I let down my barriers and become open to what this person reveals in her being. I have a sense of this person, knowing who they are right now in a very deep and profound way. I may feel their melancholy or denial or weariness, their joy or sense of adventure. I sense them as a whole and not as individual separate aspects . . . and what is interesting is that I feel a deep respect, a respect that I know, from experience, that would turn to love if I continued to contemplate them. What we contemplate we grow to love; what we contemplate we become. This is the psychological truth behind mandala or icon gazing. It is also the truth behind *lectio divina*.

Gazing in contemplation is akin to Martin Buber's I-THOU relationship. When as a child Buber communed with the horse, he knew the horse because he contemplated it: he stood before it in a non-observational way. (1965, 11, cited in Buber 1967, 10)

Image, text and the WWW

Web pages are absorbing. There is something about the luminosity of the computer screen that, in itself, engages the contemplative faculty. This faculty is the aspect of the consciousness that, unlike the analytic faculty that steps back from its object to do its work, becomes fully absorbed in its object and thus contemplation leads to a loss of sense of time. How many go online for "just a few minutes"—only to find that an hour is passed before they realize it? It is this characteristic of the Web that can be utilized by the religious web page designer to create pages that the secular page designer could not anticipate.

A web page is a "layout" of text and image in relation. It is an exercise in design and the text appeals to the language-processing left brain, but the luminosity, the images, the color, and the layout engage the contemplative and passionate right brain. One can lose the sense of time and present space on the Web in the same way that one can get lost in a well-written novel. However, on the Web it is not my personal imagination that constructs fictive images: the images and text are laid out right in front of me. The layout seems to replicate the form we know through the printed brochure. But there is something about the Web that is absorbing in a way that no brochure can replicate. It is this absorbing quality, this engagement, that offers possibilities for prayer enhancing pages.

Web pages could be designed so that equal attention is given by the mind to both the image and the text or so that the image surrounds the written word in ways that engage the mind in contemplative reading. Imagistic seeing moves us to contemplation because imagery is non-sequential: the eye alternates between holistic and detail orientation. Moreover, it is important to note that imagery affects *action* in a way that words do not. Ignatius Loyola knew this and he taught his followers to imagine themselves living the Christian life and imagine themselves turning away from temptation (Loyola). Contemporary sport coaches and diet gurus use the transformative power of imagery in their use of visualization meditations.

There is much in Christian tradition that includes visual elements in prayer. Both the use of icons for contemplative prayer in Eastern Christianity and the form of biblical prayer called *lectio divina* would be most suitable for web-based prayer practice. The latter, so common during the Middle Ages, is a prayer form that fell into disuse with advent of the printing press in part, perhaps, because of the expense of including pictures in printed texts. The Web, with its inexpensive visual-text format, allows a return to this earlier prayer form and it allows any Congregation to provide prayer space and prayer content on the Web much as the many Buddhist and Hindu communities have done through their "virtual temples".

Religious groups could begin to design web pages that included a section for prayer if they could illuminate texts, i.e., use images to shed light on the text rather than just illustrate the text. One of the easiest web-based prayer forms would be to illuminate a Psalm. To image words or letters to show what should be emphasized, as in the University of Kentucky page above.

Perhaps the community would add an audio file so the web visitor would be encouraged to see and hear the text. It would be good to include several audio files, different voices from the community all reading the text slowly, and with the emphasis shown in the illumination. Most audio files that are on the Web are spoken in "white, middle class" tones. The Bible is meant for all. If Church communities began adding the voices of their members to the reading of the Psalms and if their illuminations were done by Church members who have pondered and studied the Psalms, a whole new dimension would be added to the Web just as the *communidad de base* ("base communities") in Latin America added new dimensions to reading the Gospel as depicted in *The Gospel of Solentiname.* Slow multi-sensory reading, repeated slow multi-sensory reading of the Psalm, this is transformative prayer; this is *lectio divina.*

Another text-image format that could be developed is the third image-text relationship, where *image dominates the text.* The drawings of children who have pondered a biblical text during several Bible classes or the drawings of adults who have prayed a text could be used to surround a few lines of the text. A person who has gazed on the image in the illuminated manuscript of Mary holding her dead Son with the words "He was taken down" embedded in the image, never forgets that interpretation of the text and the text is often called to mind as the image floats up to consciousness. Such use of the Web, such adaptation of the medieval prayer forms to contemporary persons, is something that individual Congregations could offer on their web sites. The presence of such web pages that use the Web to encourage contemplative prayer could transform the web surfing experience.

Further research.

The encouragement of *lectio divina* is not just for individual Congregations or Churches. Much of the Bible, Psalms, wisdom literature, and the prophets is not easily adapted to the film genre in the way that history texts or parables are. There could be a giant publishing venture in doing such texts in illuminated versions either on the Web or on CDs. In addition, just as individual medieval monasteries became centers for exploration and research, there needs to be research into the effect of specific colors and the effect of different rhythms and tones on human consciousness. The Institute of Suggestology in Sophia, Bulgaria, has, for example, done much research on the effect of 4-4 rhythms of speech—silence on learning (Osttrader). Academics interested in developing the use of the web page for transformative prayer need to understand these studies and to expand them with other studies on the use of rhythm and tone on the human psyche. Such work would enhance the work of those seeking to make Internet I a medium for Christian prayer.

References

All Saints Episcopal Church. February 14, 1998. Available online: <http://members.aol.com/jxnsaints2/>. (Consulted March, 2001).

Augustine, Saint. 1952 *Confessions.* Trans. Edward Bouverie Pusey. In *Augustine.* Vol. 18. Ed. Robert Maynard Hutchins. *Great Books of the Western World,* 1-128. Chicago: Encyclopaedia Britannica.

Bacon, Francis. 1955. *Advancement of learning. Novum Organum. New Atlantis.* Chicago: Encyclopedia Britannica.

The Bible Gateway. Available online: <http://bible.gospelcom.net/>. (Consulted March, 26, 2001.)

Book of Hours of Simon de Varie. Koninklijke Bibliotheek. National Library of Netherlands. Available online: <http://www.kb.nl/kb/100hoogte/hh-en/hh006-en.html>. (Consulted March, 2001.)

Broadway Methodist Church. Available online: <http://www.brdwyumc.org/>. (Consulted March, 2001.)

Buber, Martin. 1965. *Between Man and Man.* Introd. by Maurice Friedman, Ronald Gregor Smith, trans. New York: Macmillan.

_____. 1967. *The Philosophy of Martin Buber,* Paul Arthur Schilpp and Maurice Friedman (eds). La Salle: Open Court.

The Catholic Encyclopedia. Available online: < http://www.newadvent.org/cathen/>. (Consulted March 26, 2001.)

Church of Christ. Available online: < http://www.chruch-of-christ.org/>. (Consulted March, 2001.)

Crosswalk.com. 1998-2001. Available online: <http://www.christcom.net/>. (Consulted March, 2001.)

Dammakaya Buddhist Meditation Institute, Thailand. Available online: <http://www.concentration.org/plain.htm>. (Consulted March, 2001.)

Evangelical Lutheran Church In America. Available online: <http:www.elca.org/>. (Consulted March 29, 2001.)

Experience Now. Sahaja Yoga International. Available online: <http://www.sahajayoga.org/ExperienceItNOW/textonly.html>. (Consulted March, 2001.)

Insight Meditation Online. Available online: < http://www.buddhanet.net/ xmed7.htm>. (Consulted March 2001).

Jaspers, Karl. 1965. *Nietzsche: An Introduction to the Understanding of His Philosophical Activity.* Charles F. Wallraff and Frederick J. Schmitz, trans. Tucson: University of Arizona Press.

van Maerlant, Jacob. *Der Naturen Bloeme.* Koninklijke Bibliotheek. National Library of Netherlands. Available online: <http://www.kb.nl/kb/ 100hoogte/hh-en/hh006-en.html>. (Consulted March, 2001.)

Loyola, Ignatius. *The Spiritual Exercises of St. Ignatius of Loyola.* Trans. Father Elder Mullan, S.J. July, 1999. Available online: < http://www.ccel.org/ i/ignatius/exercises/exercises.html>. (Consulted March, 2001.)

Medieval manuscripts. (Videorecording). Princeton, NJ: Films for the Humanities & Sciences, c1993.

Miniature of Moses. In Jerome's Prologue. Ms.Lat. bib. E.7. Bodleian Library. University Oxford. Available online: <http://www.bodley.ox.ac.uk/ dept/scwmss/wmss/medieval/mss/lat/bib/e/007.htm>. (Consulted March, 30, 2001.)

OSB. *Lectio Divina.* About Lectio Divina. Available online: <http://www.osb.org/lectio/about.html>. (Consulted March 26, 2001).

Ostrader, Sheila and Lynn Schroeder. 1979. *Superlearning.* Delacourt: New York.

Prince of Peace Lutheran Church and Christian School. Available online: <http://www.princeofpeace.org/pray_with_us.htm>. (Consulted March 27, 2001).

Sacred Space. Produced at the Jesuit Communication Centre, 36 Lower Leeson St, Dublin 2, Ireland. Available online: <http://www.jesuit.ie/prayer/ index.htm>. (Consulted March, 2001.)

Shapiro, Joel. *Untitled.* The Nelson-Atkins Museum of Art Sculpture Park -East Garden. Available online: <http://www.nelson-atkins.org/sculpture/east-garden/shapir1.htm>. (Consulted March, 2001.)

Spaulding University Book of Hours. Available online: <http://www.byu.edu/ ~hurlbut/dscriptorium/spalding/spald001.html>. (Consulted March, 2001.)

St. Mary of the Visitation Parish. Available online: < http://SMVparish.org/>. (Consulted March, 2001.)

Through the Bible Radio. [1997-1999] Available online: <http://www.ttb.org/>. (Consulted March, 2001.)

University of Kentucky Special Collections Kentuckiensis III - fols. 22v-23. Available online: <http://www.byu.edu/~hurlbut/dscriptorium/uken-tucky/ky3/ky3-003.html>. (Consulted March 28, 2000).

Watchtower: The Official Web Site of Jehovah's Witnesses. Watch Tower Bible
    and Tract Society of Pennsylvania. Available online: <http://www
    .watchtower.org/>. (Consulted March, 2001.)
Web Evangelism Exciting New Tool for the Millennium. January, 2001.
    Available online: <http://www.brigada.org/today/articles/web-evangel-
    ism2.html>. (Consulted March, 2001.)
Who's Who in the History of Mysticism. Text © 1997-2001 by Bruce B. Janz.
    Web pages © 1996-2001 by Gene R. Thursby. Available online:
    <http://www.clas.ufl.edu/users/gthursby/mys/whoswho.htm>.
    (Consulted March, 2001.)
Wittgenstein, Ludwig. 1985. *Culture and Value.* Trans. Peter Winch. Chicago:
    University of Chicago Press.

Contributors

Susan and James Bachman have collaborated on a variety of projects over many years. They research critical thinking from different directions but share a common perspective. Susan has studied argumentation and reasoning in the context of rhetoric and the teaching of composition. James studies argumentation and reasoning in the context of theories of decision making in health ethics and the teaching of philosophical logic. Susan was educated at Valparaiso University, Indiana (BA German and English), the University of Florida (MA German language and literature), and earned her Ph.D. in rhetoric at Florida State University in Tallahassee. James was educated at Valparaiso University, Indiana (BS mathematics and philosophy), Cambridge University, England (MA theology), Concordia Seminary, St. Louis (MDiv), and earned his Ph.D. in philosophy at Florida State University in Tallahassee. Both James and Susan hold appointments at Concordia University in Irvine, California. Susan is appointed as Associate Professor of rhetoric and James as Professor of philosophy and ethics. Both have been visiting professors at Concordia Seminary in St. Louis and have taught at a variety of colleges and universities. They worked together for a decade in parish ministry, and have collaborated in campus ministry for many years. Susan is currently overseeing the critical thinking program at Concordia University. James continues to do research and teaching in the intersection between Christian faith and religious and philosophical ethics. James and Susan have three adult children and one granddaughter, Beth.

Donald Colhour worked at ABC Television for twenty years and owned his own company for five years before receiving a grant to do research in Theology and Ethics of Communication at New College, University of Edinburgh. While there he received his MTh, and went on to earn his MPhil in 1997. He was ordained in 1998 and presently serves as Senior Minister at Wilshire Christian Church in Los Angeles, California. His particular academic interests center around the topic of his MPhil. thesis, which dealt with the relevance of the electronic communication context to religion. It centers on his critique of Marshall McLuhan's unpublished Ph.D. dissertation at Cambridge in 1943 on the origin of electronic communication contexts in patristic theology. It involves the time line and evolution of critical thinking from the ancients' *rations* of revealed truth as practiced by the grammarians before the advancement of New Logic with the moderns through the return of Old Logic and the rule of the trivium by the grammarians in the electronic context. His thesis was the first interactive thesis accepted by the University of Edinburgh. It has 80,000 words, 250 minutes of video and 90 minutes of audio, plus artistic illustrations, which all center around the process of grammar and the trivium in Marshall McLuhan's Laws of Media.

Charles Ess is Professor of Philosophy and Religion and Distinguished Research Professor, Interdisciplinary Studies, Drury University (Springfield, Missouri). His B.A. (Philosophy and German) is from Texas Christian University; his M.A. and Ph.D. (Philosophy) are from Penn State. For his dissertation (on Kant's use of analogical predication) he received a research stipend at the University of Zürich (1976-78). Ess teaches history of philosophy, ethics, logic, world religions, philosophy of religion, philosophy of science, and interdisciplinary courses. He has published articles, reviews, and special journal issues in ethics, history of philosophy, feminist biblical studies, contemporary Continental philosophy, computer resources for humanists, and computer-mediated communication. His book, *Philosophical Perspectives on Computer-Mediated Communication* (SUNY Press, 1996) is used nationally and abroad as a textbook. Ess has received awards for teaching excellence, as well as an EDUCOM award for his work in hypermedia. Beginning in 1998, Ess has co-chaired with Fay Sudweeks CATaC, a biannual international conference devoted to interdisciplinary exploration of "Cultural Attitudes towards Technology and Communication." A collection of articles based on CATaC'98 is also published by SUNY Press, *Culture, Technology, Communication: Towards an Intercultural Global Village* (2001). Ess has served on the

Board of Directors of ASIANetwork, a consortium of liberal arts colleges supporting Asian studies. Holding dual membership in the United Church of Christ and Christian Church/Disciples of Christ, Ess has preached and served the local and regional church in every capacity from van driver and Sunday School teacher to Stewardship Chair, Board Chair, and President of the Elders. Conni, his spouse, is a MDiv. student at Phillips Seminary (Tulsa, Oklahoma) and regional coordinator of Christian Women's Fellowship for the Mid-America Region of the Christian Church/Disciples of Christ. With their children—now young adults—Joshua and Kathleen, they enjoy travel, camping, canoing, and making music.

Byron Eubanks is Department Chair and Associate Professor of Philosophy and Ethics at Ouachita Baptist University, Arkadelphia, Arkansas, where he has taught since 1987. Eubanks received his BA in 1980 from Ouachita with majors in religion and philosophy, an MDiv in 1985 from The Southern Baptist Theological Seminary in Louisville, Kentucky, and an MA and Ph.D. in 1997 in philosophy from the University of Arkansas. His dissertation was an analysis and critique of "perfect being" theology, and philosophical theology continues to be one research interest. His regular teaching duties include courses in ethics, logic, history of philosophy, and death and dying. Byron is currently working on two projects: critical thinking for ordinary believers and ethics in local government. He is a member of the Society of Christian Philosophers, the Association of Practical and Professional Ethics, the American Association of Philosophy Teachers, and the Baptist Association of Philosophy Teachers. In addition to teaching, he has worked as a hospital chaplain and as a pastor. His wife, Amy, and he are parents of two daughters: Hannah, age thirteen, and Ellen, age ten. Away from the office he enjoys racquetball, basketball, canoeing, and whitewater kayaking.

Peter Facione is Provost, Loyola University, Chicago. He earned his Ph.D. in 1971 from Michigan State University. Peter has served as Chair of Philosophy at Bowling Green State University 1972-77, Director of General Studies at Bowling Green, 1977-79, and Dean of the School of Human Development and Community Service at California State University Fullerton 1979-1986. In 1990 he joined Santa Clara University, where he was a Scholar of the Markkula Center for Applied Ethics, and Dean of the College of Arts and Sciences and

Dean of the Division of Counseling Psychology and Education until 2002. Peter is frequently invited to give keynote addresses and present workshops at national conferences of education leaders. He is nationally and internationally known for his work on the definition and measurement of those skills and habits of mind that are at the core of human decision making and professional judgment, what academics often call "critical thinking." Peter and his research colleagues have authored several critical thinking assessment tools, the California Critical Thinking Skills Test and the California Critical Thinking Disposition Inventory (both of which are used in English, Chinese, Spanish, Hebrew, and other languages around the world) being the two most widely known. In 1998 the Faciones, with Dr. Carol Giancarlo, a psychologist of education, co-authored the California Measure of Mental Motivation. Two new tools currently being introduced with accompanying validity and reliability information are designed for use in business and professional settings and with the general population: The Test of Everyday Reasoning, and The California Reasoning Appraisal.

Elizabeth Dodson Gray is a feminist theologian and author. She has been the Coordinator of the Theological Opportunities Program at Harvard Divinity School since 1978. She has taught at Massachusetts Institute of Technology's Sloan School of Management, Williams College, Antioch/New England Graduate School, and for nine years at Boston College in the Catholic Schools Leadership Program. In the early and mid-1990s she was the only woman on the Editorial Board of Macmillan's *Encyclopedia of the Future* (1996). Her first book *Green Paradise Lost* (1979) had a pioneering role in the development of eco-feminism. She is also the author of *Patriarchy as a Conceptual Trap* (1982), a serious book with 59 cartoons, and editor of *Sacred Dimensions of Women s Experience* (1988) Her most recent book, *Sunday School Manifesto: In the Image of her?* (1994), is a call for the gender reformation of Christianity. In 1989 the National Film Board of Canada released a 19-minute film entitled "Adam's World" about her work.

Christof Hardmeier was born in 1942 at Zürich. He began studies at the University of Zürich in 1961 in theology, philosophy, psychology and aesthetics. He studied New Testament with Ernst Kaesemann, hermeneutics with Gerhard Ebeling, and philosophy with Ernst Bloch at the University of Tübingen. He later studied Hebrew Bible with Hans-Walter Wolff at the University of Mainz. In 1967, he returned to Zürich to study hermeneutics and systematic theology under Eberhard Mangel. He received a degree in theology at Zürich in 1968. That same year, he married Ursula Hardmeier and moved to Heidelberg where their son, Martin, was born. He held a doctoral scholarship from DAAD from 1972 to 1974, and undertook postgraduate studies in linguistics and literary studies (theories of text and communication). Christof and Ursula celebrated the birth of their daughter, Ruth, in 1973. Christof served as an assistant lecturer of Old Testament studies from 1974 to 1977, while earning his doctorate in 1975 in the areas of text theory and biblical exegesis. His thesis was entitled "The Rhetorical Function of Mourning Imagery in Prophecy." Christof earned his Ph.D. from the University of Bielefeld in 1988 under the direction of Elisabeth Guelich in the areas of linguistics and narratology. His dissertation was entitled "Prophecy in Dispute before the Downfall of Judah." From 1985 to 1988, along with Eep Talstra, he created and developed an interactive computer-based concordance. He was appointed to the University of Greifswald as a professor of Old Testament studies, and founded the Center of Computer Philology in 1997. Presently, he is working on diverse studies of macrostructures and the literary history of the book of Jeremiah, the deuteronomistic history and the Book of Deuteronomy.

Kate Lindemann is Professor of Philosophy at Mount Saint Mary College in Newburgh, New York, where she has taught a theory and practice course in the philosophical and religious traditions of meditation for the last ten years. Kate's interest in the World Wide Web is sparked by her interest in contemplative gazing; she believes that the luminosity of the web makes images of mandalas, icons and illuminated manuscripts more akin to the originals than those found in paper reproductions. Kate is a member of the American Philosophical Association, the American Catholic Philosophical Association, the Society for Philosophy in the Contemporary World, the Association for Philosophy of Liberation and the Association for Religion in the Intellectual Life. She is on the editorial board of Philosophy in the Contemporary World and founder of the Elizabeth Goudge archives. Kate recently returned from research at the Bodleian Library on medieval manuscripts and archives at the University of London. She has publications on both ethics and philosophy teaching in various academic journals. Currently she is working on a web-based History of Women Philosophers and a CD about eight basic meditation forms.

Terry Lindvall is Professor of Film at Regent University. He did his undergraduate work at Southern California College. He earned his MDiv in 1973 from Fuller Theological Seminary and was awarded his Ph.D. by the University of Southern California in 1981. Terry's most recent publications include "Apocalyptic Imagination in Popular Culture" in Christianity and the Arts (November 1999) and "The Gift of Taboo Humor", also in Christianity and the Arts (August 1999). His book, *The Silents of God: Silent American Film and Religion,* will be published by the University of South Carolina Press in 2000. Terry has been the executive producer of over fifty films and media projects including two National Student Academy Award Winners (Bird in a Cage, 1987 and Turtle Races, 1989), and films exhibited on PBS, HBO, CineMax, Showtime, and Fox Network. He served as the critical consultant on Prince of Egypt, with Jeffrey Katzenberg, at DreamWorks and has been a Staley Lecture Speaker at several colleges and universities.

Phil Mullins teaches in an interdisciplinary humanities program at Missouri Western State College in St. Joseph, Missouri, bringing together topics in philosophy, religious studies, and cultural history. He earned his Ph.D. at the Graduate Theological Union, Berkeley, with a dissertation treating the thought of Michael Polanyi. Recent professional papers and articles have focused on topics in philosophy and on cultural changes brought by the computer. Since 1991, he has edited *Tradition and Discovery,* the journal of the Polanyi Society. He is active in the American Academy of Religion and the Polanyi Society and has been the recipient of numerous grants from the National Endowment for the Humanities.

Isaac Mwase is an Associate Professor of Philosophy and Ethics at Ouachita Baptist University, Arkadelphia, Arkansas. A native of Zimbabwe, Isaac has a BTh (1983) from the Baptist Theological Seminary of Zimbabwe. He was the first to ever receive this degree. Upon graduation he assumed responsibilities as associate pastor at the Bulawayo Baptist Church. Nagging hermeneutical and philosophical questions led him to seek further training, first at Gardner-Webb College in Boiling Springs, North Carolina. He graduated from there in 1987 with a BS in Management Information Systems. He has graduate degrees from Dallas Baptist University were he received an MBA (1990) and from Southwestern Baptist Seminary, Fort Worth, Texas, were he earned an MDiv (1990) and a Ph.D. (1993) in Philosophy of

Religion. His dissertation was a critical analysis of J. N. K. Mugambi's philosophical theology. Isaac has taught a variety of courses including surveys of the Bible, introduction to philosophy, world religion, philosophy of religion, and courses in the history of philosophy and ethics. In addition to his professorial duties Isaac is in his third year of service as pastor of the New Bethel Baptist Church, Arkadelphia, Arkansas. He has memberships in the American Academy of Religion, the Association of Practical and Professional Ethics, and the Baptist Association of Philosophy Teachers. Isaac and his wife, Ruth-Anne Nziramasanga, are parents of fourteen year-old Rebecca. The whole family is heavily involved with soccer. Running marathons has been one of Isaac's other major interest; he ran the 1999 Boston Marathon!

Michael Palmer is Professor of Philosophy and Chair of the Department of Biblical Studies and Philosophy at Evangel University in Springfield, Missouri, where he regularly teaches courses in the history of philosophy, ethics, logic, and critical reasoning. A native of western Montana, Michael is a third generation Pentecostal and an active member of the Assemblies of God. His educational preparation includes BA and MA degrees in philosophy from the University of Montana and a Ph.D. in philosophy from Marquette University (1984). Although his doctoral studies and early scholarly work centered primarily on ancient philosophy (Plato), he now conducts research mainly in the area of moral theory. He is the author of two books and numerous professional articles and scholarly reviews. His most recent book, *Elements of a Christian Worldview* (1998), attempts to develop a Christian philosophical frame of reference for responding to several notable perennial and contemporary issues in the arts, sciences, and popular culture. Michael is currently writing a book on ethics entitled *Conduct and Character, An Introduction to Moral Theory.*

Eep Talstra received his MA in Theology and Semitic Languages in 1975 from the Vrije Universiteit in Amsterdam. His studies included courses in Old Testament and Semitic languages at the University of Manchester in England in 1973. From 1978 to 1986 he supervised the Old Testament section of the Netherlands Bible Society translations project called "Bijbel in eenvoudig Nederlands" ("Bible in easy-to-read Dutch"). In 1987 he received a Ph.D. from the University of Leiden in Old Testament Theology. Currently he is director of the "Werkgroep Informatica" (a research group of Bible and Computer), founded in

1977 by the Faculty of Theology. Since 1991 he has also held a special professorship in Theology on "Biblical Studies and Computer." In 1992, in cooperation with Christoph Hardmeier (Greifswald, Germany), Alan Groves (Westminster Theological Seminary, Philadelphia) and the Netherlands Bible Society, he published a Hebrew Bible computer project: Quest, Hebrew Database and retrieval software. The continued project, supported by the German Bible Society released a CD-ROM with an Hebrew syntactic database, translations and retrieval software in 2000. Eep teaches classes in Biblical Hebrew discourse, Methods of Old Testament exegesis, translation of the Hebrew Bible and the use of computers, and Old Testament Theology. He is a guest professor of Westminster Theological Seminary in Philadelphia.

James Voelz is Professor of Exegetical Theology and Dean of the Graduate School at Concordia Seminary, St. Louis, Missouri. He has impacted pastoral formation in the Lutheran Church Missouri Synod for 24 years through the classroom, conference presentations, and writings. His hermeneutics text, *What Does This Mean?* (1995) is now used at many institutions, as is his elementary Greek textbook, *Fundamental Greek Grammar* (1993). James has been active in scholarly societies both in the United States and around the world. As a member of Studiorum Novi Testamenti Societas (SNTS), he is co-chair of the organization's "Hermeneutics and the Biblical Text" seminar. As part of the Society of Biblical Literature, he has presented papers and has participated regularly in sections as diverse as "Bible Translation," "Biblical Greek Language and Linguistics," "Literary Aspects of the Gospels and Acts," "Semiotics and Exegesis," and "Bible in Ancient and Modern Media." James has also served for four years as assistant pastor at Zion Lutheran Church in Fort Wayne, Indiana, and is currently on his church's Commission on Theology and Church Relations. Married with one teenage son, James is a native of Milwaukee, Wisconsin, and has wide-ranging extra-curricular interests, including soccer, golf, basketball, wine, bridge, and professional wrestling.

Ben Witherington III is Professor of New Testament at Asbury Theological Seminary in Wilmore, Kentucky. Ben joined the Asbury Seminary faculty in 1995 after teaching at Ashland Theological Seminary for more than a decade. He has also taught at High Point College, Duke Divinity School and Gordon-Conwell Theological Seminary. A prolific author, he has written a dozen books, including

The Christology of Jesus (Augsburg-Fortress Press, (1990), *Jesus the Sage: the Pilgrimage of Wisdom* (Ausburg-Fortress/T&T Clark, 1994) and *John's Wisdom* (Westminster, 1995), a commentary on the fourth gospel. One of his most recent works, *The Jesus Quest: The Third Search for the Jew of Nazareth* (Intervarsity Press, 1995), was selected as the top biblical studies book of 1995 by Christianity Today and the Academy of Parish Clergy. In *The Jesus Quest,* Ben surveys the contemporary christological landscape in New Testament scholarship, offering a helpful perspective on one of the most significant and controversial religious debates of the past decade. Ben is known for bringing the text to life through incisive historical and cultural analysis. He is a John Wesley Fellow for Life, a research fellow at Cambridge University and a member of numerous professional organizations, including the Society of Biblical Literature, Society for the Study of the New Testament and the Institute for Biblical Research. In his leisure time, Ben appreciates both music and sports. It is hard to say which sound he prefers: the sophisticated sonance of jazz sensation Pat Metheny or the incessant tomahawk chant of the Atlanta Braves faithful. He and his wife, Ann, have two children: Christy Ann and David Benjamin.

Index

A

Abrahamic religions, 40
affirming the consequent (fallacy), 125
ambiguity, as intrinsic to critical thinking, 248
American Bible Society
mediated products study, 227
a-millennialism, 139
analogy, 81, 91, 124
in "fear-critical thinking," 85
in performative theology, 81, 83
analogy, in Christian scriptures, 106
anonymity, 261, 262
Anselm, 65
anti-evolution, as example of uncritical dogmatism, 141
anti-realism, 29, 39
Apollo, 13 63
Aquinas, Thomas, 37, 38
argument (see also evidence), 78, 101
in Paul, 98, 99
in Torah, 78
Jesus' use of, 101
Peter's use of, 100
Aristotle, 23, 29, 41, 59, 120, 122, 128

Augustine, 33, 65, 216, 219, 231, 288, 315
conception of the Fall, 33
Averroes, 37

B

Bachman, Susan & James, 279, 296
Bacon, Francis, 318
Barbour, Ian, ftn. 16, 147
Barlow, John Perry, 33, 201
Becker, Barbara, 33, 34
belief-thinking (Paul), as practical critical thinking, 83
Benedictine, 318
Bible software, 242, 296
as echo of traditional scholarship, 296
as improving Bible study, 244
as simple extension of print, 247
deficiencies of, 242
Bible study, 240, 270
and literalism, 273
conservative approaches, 273
Constantinian paradigm, 272
cultivate critical thinking disposition, 283-285
devotional/confessional, 238-240
historical-critical approaches, 270-273